Rus. Bus   Dec. 19
Rus for   Dec 19
Rus Pol.   Dec 20

LOCAL POWER AND POST-SOVIET POLITICS

EDITED BY

Theodore H. Friedgut
Jeffrey W. Hahn

LOCAL POWER AND POST-SOVIET POLITICS

Contemporary Soviet/Post-Soviet Politics

LOCAL POWER AND POST-SOVIET POLITICS

EDITED BY

Theodore H. Friedgut
Jeffrey W. Hahn

M.E. Sharpe

Armonk, New York   London, England

Library of Congress Cataloging-in-Publication Data

Local power and post-Soviet politics / edited by Theodore H. Friedgut and Jeffrey W. Hahn.
      p.   cm.—(Contemporary Soviet/post-Soviet politics)
      Includes bibliographical references and index.
      ISBN 1-56324-403-9.—ISBN 1-56324-404-7
      1. Local government—Russia (Federation)
    2. Local government—Russia (Federation)—Case studies.
    3. Russia (Federation)—Politics and government—1991– .
          I. Friedgut, Theodore H.
          II. Hahn, Jeffrey W., 1944–
          III. Series.
         JS6117.3.A8L63   1994
          320.8′0947—dc20
            94-10151
             CIP

Printed in the United States of America

The paper used in this publication meets the minimum requirements
of American National Standard for Information Sciences—
Permanence of Paper for Printed Library Materials,
ANSI Z39.48-1984.

BM (c)   10   9   8   7   6   5   4   3   2   1
BM (p)   10   9   8   7   6   5   4   3   2   1

This Volume is Dedicated
with Respect and Affection

TO THE MEMORY OF

GEORGII VASIL´EVICH BARABASHEV

TEACHER, COLLEAGUE, FRIEND

Contents

List of Tables and Figures

Figures

Tables

About the Editors and the Contributors

THEODORE H. FRIEDGUT is Professor of Russian and Slavic Studies at the Hebrew University of Jerusalem. He is the author of *Political Participation in the USSR*, the two-volume study *Iuzovka and Revolution*, and, with Lewis H. Siegelbaum, *The Soviet Miners' Strike, July 1984: Perestroika From Below*.

JEFFREY W. HAHN is Professor of Political Science at Villanova University, where he specializes in Russian politics. He is the author of *Soviet Grassroots: Citizen Participation in Local Soviet Government* and many articles on politics and political culture. He is currently studying the development of legislative institutions in Russia since 1990. Professor Hahn served two four-year terms on the board of commissioners in Radnor Township, Pennsylvania.

JO ANDREWS is a doctoral candidate in the Department of Government at Harvard University and a Graduate Fellow at the Russian Research Center. She is writing a dissertation on the former Russian parliament.

DANIEL BERKOWITZ is Assistant Professor of Economics at the University of Pittsburgh. In addition to the economics of the Russian Federation, he is interested in comparative economic systems, public finance, and microeconomics. He has published scholarly articles in a number of economics journals.

VLADIMIR GEL'MAN is deputy director of the Institute for the Humanities and Political Studies in Moscow, and a researcher at the Institute of Sociology of the Russian Academy of Sciences in St. Petersburg. He has published numerous articles on contemporary Russian politics. He heads the research program "Political Monitoring of the Russian Regions" for the Institute of Humanities and Political Studies.

MARY MCAULEY is a Fellow and Tutor in Politics at St. Hilda's College of Oxford University. She is also British Academy Research Reader at the Institute of Sociology of the Russian Academy of Sciences in St. Petersburg. Her most recent publication is *Soviet Politics, 1917–1991*. Her current research deals with post-Soviet Russian politics.

BETH MITCHNECK is Assistant Professor of Geography and Regional Development at the University of Arizona. Her research interests lie in the fields of population geography and economic geography. Her current research deals with urban and regional development and local government in the Russian Federation.

JOEL C. MOSES is Professor of Political Science at Iowa State University. He is coauthor of the forthcoming ninth edition of *Major European Governments*. His current research is on the politics of the regions and republics of the Russian Federation.

DARRELL SLIDER is Associate Professor of Government and International Affairs at the University of South Florida. He is coauthor of *The Politics of Transition: Shaping a Post-Soviet Future*.

ALEXANDRA VACROUX is a doctoral candidate in the Department of Government at Harvard University and a Graduate Fellow at the Russian Research Center. She is writing a dissertation on privatization in Russia. She currently resides in Moscow.

JOHN F. YOUNG is a doctoral candidate in the Department of Political Science at the University of Toronto. He has been a lecturer in political science at the University of Alberta and joined the faculty at the University of Northern British Columbia in the fall of 1994.

In Memoriam

Georgii Vasil′evich Barabashev (1929–1993)

In June 1984, when I began a study of local government in what was then the Soviet Union, I was able, thanks to a short-term grant from the Kennan Institute for Advanced Russian Studies, to spend a month at the Library of Congress, developing a complete bibliography of Western and Soviet source material on the subject of my research in preparation for field work to be conducted that autumn. It did not take me long to realize from the available Russian-language references on soviets that, even by sheer number of publications alone, the leading academic specialist on this subject was one G.V. Barabashev.

Further encouraged by a warm recommendation from my colleague, Ted Friedgut, whose research advisor Georgii Vasil′evich had been several years earlier, I listed Professor Barabashev first among those with whom I wished to work when I got to Moscow. Shortly before my arrival, I learned that he had, indeed, been assigned as my *nauchnyi rukovoditel′*, or scientific advisor.

Following a cordial, but correct, initial meeting, he invited me back the next day to continue our conversation. This time he pulled out a bottle of Georgian cognac and some nuts from his bottom drawer. The nuts he cracked using a small bust of Lenin, which he kept at hand for that purpose. Then he began to probe, more informally, as to what I really wanted to study and why it was of interest. After I mentioned that I had spent eight years as a city councilman, our conversation continued for some time, ending over a bowl of soup at the Barabashevs' apartment on Lomonosovskii Prospekt. At the time, such an invitation seemed to me quite extraordinary. Only later did I come to realize that numerous foreign scholars had preceded me, including my coeditor, Ted Friedgut. Indeed, the Barabashev apartment was something of a salon for graduate students and foreign scholars studying Soviet politics. For me, the visit proved to be the beginning of a warm personal and professional relationship with the man who invited all of us to call him "George," a relationship that would last until his untimely death from cancer on March 23, 1993.

Georgii Vasil'evich was born on January 22, 1929, in the town of Darnitsa, a suburb of Kiev, the capital of Ukraine. Despite the vicissitudes of study during wartime, he performed exceptionally well in school. His grades were so high that he was admitted without examination to the school of mathematical sciences at Moscow State University (MGU) where he intended to take up the field of astronomy. After one year, however, he transferred to the juridical faculty, where he earned a gold medal for academic achievement and was awarded a "red diploma." After graduation, Georgii Vasil'evich joined the MGU juridical faculty where he spent the remainder of his professional life. His initial research and publications dealt with state and local government in the West, or what was referred to at the time as the "bourgeois countries." Much of his writing on local government in the United States drew upon time spent in Albany, New York, where he was one of the first Soviet scholars to take advantage of the exchange program established between MGU and the State University of New York. A revival of interest in the soviets in the 1960s led to the creation of a department within the juridical faculty at MGU called "Soviet Construction and State Law" of which Georgii Vasil'evich became the first chair. Most of his published work from that time on was devoted to the local soviets. A sentence related to me by Ted Friedgut might well stand as an epitaph, for it suggests the intellectual integrity that characterized Georgii Barabashev's scholarship. In the autumn of 1969, while showing Friedgut the section on local government in the law faculty library, and commenting on the importance and relevance of this or that author, Barabashev commented dryly: "In my own writings you will not find a single word of which I was later ashamed."

Georgii Vasil'evich's professional career was not limited to studying the local soviets. He was himself an active participant in both the Soviet and post-Soviet political process. He was elected to two terms as a deputy of the Moscow City Soviet where he chaired the committee on the work of the deputies. He was also a deputy for four terms to the Lenin Raion Soviet in the city of Moscow where he chaired the standing Committee on Socialist Legality and Public Order. Perestroika brought even more opportunities for Georgii Vasil'evich to participate in the reconstruction of Soviet politics. In addition to serving on the USSR Election Commission in 1989, he took an active part in drafting legislation affecting local government, a role he continued to play as a consultant to the Standing Committee on Questions Concerning Work of Deputies and Development of Self-Government in the Supreme Soviet of the Russian Federation. Much of the legislation that shaped the development of local government in Russia was written by, or reflects the contribution of, Georgii Vasil'evich Barabashev.

The chapter of this volume written by Georgii Vasil'evich was completed in November 1992 only a few months before his death. It is a comparatively short piece assessing the difficulties faced by local government in the first year after the fall of communism in Russia. Nevertheless, the chapter captures nicely many of the major themes of Georgii Vasil'evich's life work. First and foremost, there is his belief in the importance of local self-government (*mestnoe samoupravlenie*). It reflects his conviction that more local control over decision making and less by the center would result in better government. Closely related to that is his commitment to legislative power against that of the executive branch. He saw legislatures as the main link between the electorate and their government, and thus the main instrument of public accountability, a matter that he considers in his chapter to be one of "particular urgency." Finally, there is his abiding belief in the efficacy of law. Throughout his contribution, there are continued references to the need either to draft new legislation or to implement existing law more thoroughly. One may wonder after reading the other chapters in this book whether greater local power, more effective legislation, or even increased public accountability is the foremost need today in the former Soviet Union. However, one cannot doubt, I think, that these are worthy goals for a democratic polity nor question the sincerity of the man who spent a lifetime promoting them in a country where for many years they were not valued. He will be missed, not only by family, colleagues, and friends, but by the countrymen he tried so hard to serve.

Jeffrey W. Hahn

LOCAL POWER AND POST-SOVIET POLITICS

Introduction
Local Government Under the Old Regime

Theodore H. Friedgut

"All Power to the Soviets!" The cry rang out over the Russian Empire in 1917, penetrating to every corner of an over-administered but under-governed polity. Mass assemblies of citizens gathered to devise a new system of governance and to preserve some semblance of order in community life after the fall of Nicholas II's autocracy.[1] The early soviets were of many different configurations and of widely diverse outlooks, some radical in the extreme, others devoted to stability and the status quo. Some were from their inception authoritarian, while many others were models of participatory democracy. However, their history as independent bodies was too brief for the realization of all their governmental potential, for with the Bolshevik seizure of power and the civil war they were caught up in a turmoil that overwhelmed both local self-determination and political pluralism.

During the seventy-four years of Soviet rule, the soviets played a role far less than that envisaged for them in the spring of 1917. Despite a number of attempts to infuse them with greater powers and more effective oversight of local policy, they remained a clearly subordinate appendage of the state apparatus, administering services, but not governing their territories, despite the constitutional provisions for their local supremacy.[2] As the Soviet Union developed, the system of soviets grew, ultimately encompassing over 50,000 councils at various levels and more than 2 million elected deputies. With the breakup of the Soviet Union at the end of 1991, the configuration of the soviets changed.

In particular, there was change within the Russian Federation as the units previously designated autonomous republics and autonomous oblasts became constituent republics of the newly independent federated Russian polity. As can be seen in Table 1, however, this was not the only change. The

Table 1

Soviets of the Russian Federation, 1987 and 1992

Level of government	Number of soviets, January 1, 1987	Number of soviets, January 1, 1992
Republic	16	21
Autonomous oblast	5	1
Autonomous okrug	10	10
Krai (territory)	6	6
Oblast (region)	49	49
City or town	1,030	1,057
Urban raion (city district or borough)	396	343
Rural raion (rural district)	1,834	1,857
Poselok (industrial or other urban-type settlement)	2,178	2,164
Village	23,107	23,898

Sources: For 1987, Rolf H. Theen, "Russia at the Grassroots: Reform at the Local and Regional Levels," *In Depth,* vol. 3, no. 1 (winter 1993), p. 56. For 1992, *Narodnoe khoziaistvo Rossiiskoi federatsii. 1992.* (Moscow: Respublikanskii informatsionno-izdatel'skii tsentr, 1992), pp. 5–10.

Note: In 1987 the Russian Federation included sixteen autonomous republics in addition to the Russian Republic. The larger figure for 1992 distinguishes the Chechen and Ingush republics, although they had not yet formally separated at this date.

normal processes of development continued. New territorial-administrative units were formed, and local governments were created to administer their services. New villages, rural raions, and towns came into being, while urban districts were consolidated and the number of urban-type settlements declined.[3]

Structural Features of the Old Soviets

Our discussion of the structural features of the soviets emphasizes those aspects that appear to be persisting or reasserting themselves in the post-Soviet period. If, despite the purported changes in the political values and atmosphere of the country, these old institutions remain, it will be hard to look forward to positive developments in the popular authority and efficacy of local governments.

The soviets were a tightly organized hierarchical structure, very much in keeping with the theory of democratic centralism under which they operated. They were not, however, the only hierarchy in the USSR; rather, they were the least influential of three overlapping and interlocked pyramids of power. The Communist Party was the true locus of power, and beside it was the production hierarchy of ministerial branches controlling the factories and farms, with their ultimate supervisors ensconced in Moscow, whether in a ministry or in Gosplan, the State Planning Commission. This was not simply a Weberian bureaucracy of sharply defined subordinations, rights, and duties. In addition it contained a component of agenda-setting from above, particularly in all that concerned the rituals of political and social mobilization that were so much a feature of the Soviet regime.

The dismantling of the party's control and the introduction of a large measure of free-market competition with what had been ministerial monopolies did not mean the end of central government efforts to control local activities. Indeed, the central government simply absorbed many of the officials and functions that previously worked through the party or the economic ministries. In the localities discussed in this volume, questions regarding the powers and accountability of presidential representatives and heads of administration (*glava administratsii*) of the various localities loom large. As both John Young and Joel Moses observe in their chapters, these positions become the locus of contention among local forces as well as between the locality and the central authorities. One of the striking features of the new relations between center and locality is the ability of the localities today to exercise pressure on the center and to ignore the center's interests and orders. Indeed, through 1993 and into 1994 the growth of local economic separatism, involving nonpayment of taxes and produced revenues to the center, was seen as threatening the continued existence of the Russian Federation. Such leverage was totally absent under the old regime, when the Communist Party and the central ministries held both power and authority over local officials.

This did not mean that the soviets had no independent functions at the local level. In addition to being the transmission belts for central instructions and agendas, the oblast, city, and district (*raion*) soviets (both rural and urban) were charged with operating a great part of the consumer services in their territories. These included far more than the sanitation, education, public hygiene, and housing functions that almost everywhere are the province of local government and that were known in the Soviet administrative parlance as "the communal economy" (*kommunal'noe khoziaistvo*). The Soviet Union defined itself as a socialist state, and its particular definition of socialism (by no means the only possible definition) prescribed not only state ownership or control, but also state *operation* of the overwhelming majority of economic and social facilities. There was thus a broad potential field for local authorities' activities. Theaters, tearooms, dry cleaners, bakeries, grocery stores, appliance repairs, production of foodstuffs and construction materials for the local market—the entire local consumer economy (*bytovoe khoziaistvo*)—all these were the property and the operational responsibility of local government. What is more, throughout the Khrushchev and Brezhnev periods, as the Soviet authorities grappled with questions of governmental reform and as the consumer sector became progressively more important in Soviet life, there was an attempt to shift more of the actual administration of these service sectors out of the control of the industrial enterprises and into the soviets.

These distributive functions, however, were performed mainly by the executive arm of the local soviet, the executive committee (*ispolkom*) and the heads of its various departments. These full-time, salaried administrators generally served also as elected deputies, and thus created a nucleus for executive dominance of the representative body of elected deputies. There was a clear and ubiquitous tendency for the executives to turn the various standing committees and commissions of the soviet into ancillaries, preventing them from exercising the auditing functions that were a central part of their formal mandate, and emphasizing their possibilities as a mobilizing agency.[4] This was not some chance aberration, but a deliberate application of Lenin's precept, set forth in *The State and Revolution*, that there should be no separation of powers, but that elected representatives should at one and the same time function as all three branches of government: legislative, executive, and judicial. One of the most significant reforms instituted by Gorbachev was the attempt to bolster the parliamentary oversight powers of elected representatives over executives by instituting a formal separation of powers. This attempted reform played out differently in different locales; especially notable is the difference between Ukraine and the Russian Federation. By examining the sequence of changes in institutions and procedures in the various cities and regions presented in this volume, the reader will gain an appreciation for the varieties of political development that are occurring.

Another facet of adjustment of the local soviets was their response to the incipient market economy. Governmental monopolies over local production and distribution now had to contend with the beginnings of independent entrepreneurial provision of services. The differing political leanings of Omsk, Saratov, Volgograd, and Donetsk, among the cities represented here, each dictated a somewhat different course of development, particularly as regards the disposal of municipally owned housing. The chapters by Beth Mitchneck and Dan Berkowitz give particular food for thought on this question.

It is not mere chance that Georgii Barabashev, in his list of urgently needed reforms, puts the question of budgetary competence in first place. This had been recognized during Gorbachev's incumbency, and part of his political revolution was the promise of locally controlled budget sources for the soviets. First proposed among the resolutions of the Nineteenth Party Conference in July 1988, the measure, as Barabashev notes, was never signed into law.

The absence of any substantial sources of independent income has long been the Achilles' heel of local government. Even after the reforms of the 1970s, only some 10 percent of local budgets was generated from locally controlled sources. While this did not mean that local authorities were totally passive recipients of higher-ups' largesse, it did strip them of any power in their bargaining stance, limiting them to the role of petitioner.[5] We need dwell little on this point here, for Beth Mitchneck discusses it in some detail in her chapter and provides the interested reader with bibliographic references. To the extent that local governments are today obtaining control of resources, this is largely a matter of taking control of properties or levies that were formerly in the possession of higher levels of government, or in some current cases arbitrarily arrogating to themselves monies that were formally destined for the coffers of the central government. Such maneuvers are clearly both a constitutional and an administrative problem that must be resolved promptly if central government is not to decay. Control of budget is everywhere a key to political power, and is clearly used as such in the relations between city governments and their urban district governments, as well as between reform-minded municipalities and the more conservative regional governments. As Darrell Slider shows in the case of Iurii Goriachev of Ulianovsk Oblast, an incumbent could gain popularity by using budget control to maintain food subsidies. In the frictions that beset the relations between the Donetsk city government and the oblast soviet, this issue also figured prominently. Daniel Berkowitz provides the theoretical proof of why such a strategy of catering to a "consumption bias" is widely used by local officials.

Under the Soviet system, local governments' lack of independent resources, although debilitating, was supportable, for in keeping with the principles explained so graphically by William Taubman,[6] industrial enterprises took up much of the slack, providing the manpower and resources needed to keep the city functioning. When Communist Party discipline was removed, and economic pressures became the defining force in the work of industrial managers, this assistance to municipal governments shrank dramatically, as is shown particularly in the case of Donetsk.

Building New Local Institutions

The post-Soviet reconstruction of local government in the Russian Federation involves the creation or adaptation of essentially new sets of institutions. The local civil service must adapt from a role largely restricted to Lenin's "bookkeeping and accounting" concept, to that of initiating development and change. The separation of legislature and executive demands complete reconsideration of the political functions of these two arms, redrawing of boundaries between them, and a redistribution of authority. Rather than relying on the elected representatives to function as a mobilizing force in society, a richly articulated civil society must now be the matrix from which local representatives and government agendas come forth. Among other things this means the creation of stable local branches of political parties and civic movements, and ultimately the growth of that professional political class of local parliamentarians so sharply excoriated by Lenin, but so perfectly exemplified by the party apparat.

The soviets from their inception were mass assemblies. In the beginning they consciously followed the example of the Petrograd Soviet with its ever-changing mass of enthusiastic citizens. Later this became a convenient and effective form of assembly, considering that its primary functions were mobilization of the public and assistance to the executive arm in the distribution of services. Not only was the form of the soviet adapted to its function, but its personnel was carefully chosen to conform to mobilizational needs. The deputies were a mirror that was to reflect to the public its ideal image of devoted patriots, industrious producers, and devoted citizens, rather than civic fathers and articulators of local interests. Moreover, the elected deputies were not intended to become professional politicians. In all the local soviets the elected deputies continued in their prior employment, received paid leave to attend sessions of the soviet, and performed any public duties connected with being a deputy on their own free time. This quite naturally served to curb the interest of many rank-and-file citizens in holding office as deputies. At the same time, public election to the post of deputy served as legitimation for the status of party officials and party-appointed members of the *nomenklatura*. When, under the impact of perestroika, the party declined and then was disbanded, election to a local soviet became the last bastion of influence for the old elite. Politics then became real, as interests and values clashed both among groups of deputies in the soviets and between the legislative and executive branches. Speaking to an assembly of representatives of local soviets of the Russian Federation in the autumn of 1992, Anatolii Sobchak, the reformist mayor of St. Petersburg stated: "Today . . . we have the old system of Soviet power in the form of representative organs and a new system of executive democratic organs of power still in the process of creation. In my view the soviets have today in fact replaced the obkoms, raykoms, and the other party organs, which previously, without having the corresponding authority, were *de facto* the sole power."[7]

Although the root of this situation, as is shown vividly in the two chapters on Leningrad, lay in the fact that the elections took place in 1990, while the Communist Party was still in control, recent developments show the problem to be deeper. This is apparent from the strong showing of the Russian Communist Party and its alter ego, the Agrarian Party, which together won 112 seats in the December 1993 elections to the 450-seat Russian Duma, held under a new constitution and conditions of open competition. The situation became even clearer in the first of the regional elections, held in Penza Oblast at the start of February 1994, when persons classed as belonging to the "old oblast nomenklatura" won 40 of the 45 seats.[8] The problem would appear to be one part of the general question of creating appropriate institutions for the conduct of democratic and responsible politics.

Under the old system, the deputy was not expected to "live for politics," and was explicitly denied the possibility to "live from politics" unless he was part of the nomenklatura and/or the party or soviet apparat, the paid full-time executives and agents who were the modern metamorphosis of Lenin's professional revolutionaries. Professional politics is not only a skill, but a calling, demanding dedication and persistence. Professional politicians outside the nomenklatura were simply not allowed under the Soviet regime. Their development in an environment of turmoil, uncertainty, and enticing alternative opportunities must be a lengthy process.

The dropping-out of formerly enthusiastic deputies who were not prepared, whether emotionally or experientially, for the long haul of parliamentary reform will be noted by the reader as one of the problems affecting many of the urban and regional soviets surveyed in this volume. This dropping-out has taken its toll on the representative arm of the soviets and their executive as well. The political animus accompanying the change from communist rule made many administrators of the old executive committees unready to serve reform administrations. These veteran administrators were the ones who knew the ins and outs of all the localities, understood the budgeting and implementation processes, and had the local and central contacts that were needed for the successful management of their cities and regions. Their replacements, who enjoyed none of these advantages, often found themselves handicapped by their excessive enthusiasm for change and surrounded by a multitude of hostilities as local notables, numerous elected representatives, and superior authorities all frustrated their programs. The ethos of the professional and neutral civil servant was totally absent.

Compounding this difficulty is the lack of institutionalization of political parties, again an inheritance from the single-party rule of the CPSU. On the federal level, most parties were unstable alliances grouped around one or several leaders, and this was reflected at regional and municipal levels. Parties based on a well-defined interest, a stable power base, and a clearly articulated set of principles were lacking. This, too, was evident in the results of the Russian elections in December 1993. Not one of the eight parties that exceeded the cut-off level of 5 percent in the proportional voting was able to win the same percentage of constituencies. Vladimir Zhirinovsky's Liberal Democratic Party, for instance, received 59 of the 225 seats allotted by proportional representation, but won only five constituency seats. The party simply lacked local candidates with the drawing power of its leader. It seems that in the local constituencies the voters supported representatives of local interests rather than party people, for 129 of those elected were classed as independents.[9] Attempts to draw up and legislate a coherent set of projects thus often foundered on the Scylla of deputies' legislative inexperience and the Charybdis of unstable party support, both inherited from the Soviet past.

Just as in 1917 the citizens of the Russian Empire leaped into a new and participatory political era for which few were adequately prepared, so the demands of democratic local self-government seventy-five years later have caught the public by surprise. The new functions allotted to self-government demand new institutions, and these must be invented or adapted by a largely inexperienced political class that is itself only beginning to experience the democratic political process. This learning takes place not in some ivory tower but in conditions of pressure and instability exacerbated by economic hardships and ethnic tensions that threaten to tear apart both polity and society. Just as all regions were presented as alike in the "harmonious family of peoples that was the Soviet Union," so each is in some way unique in its post-Soviet travails. Although the localities discussed in these chapters all started from a common institutional base and face similar pressures and problems, each has its own outlook, political complexion, and proposed solutions. Only after we have analyzed the individual problem areas and cases will we be able to generalize, at the end of this volume, about "what is common, and what is not."

Notes

1. For a comprehensive history of the origins of the soviets, see Oskar Anweiler, *The Soviets* (New York: Pantheon, 1974). The concept of Russia as a territory administered, but not governed, and certainly not self-governed, is to be found in Rolf H.W. Theen, "Russia at the Grassroots: Reform at the Local and Regional Level," *In Depth*, vol. 3, no. 1 (winter 1993), p. 54.

2. For a brief discussion of these problems see Theodore H. Friedgut, *Political Participation in the USSR* (Princeton, NJ: Princeton University Press, 1979), pp. 41–59

and 156–62. For a detailed analysis of the limited status and powers of municipal government in the Soviet Union, see William Taubman, *Governing Soviet Cities: Bureaucratic Politics and Urban Development in the USSR* (New York: Praeger, 1973).

3. The growth in the number of villages may be attributed to a process of de-urbanization that appears to have developed in the Russian Federation, along with the stagnation of population growth there. Since the beginning of 1991 the urban population of the Russian Federation has declined by 900,000, while the rural population, which had been diminishing steadily for over thirty years, grew by 300,000 in 1991 and by an additional 800,000 in 1992. See *Narodnoe khoziaistvo, 1992* (Moscow: Republican Information and Publishing Centre, 1993), p. 81, and *The Russian Federation in Figures for 1992: Short Statistical Collection* (Moscow: Republican Information and Publishing Centre, 1993), p. 5. As a social phenomenon this is of some interest since it suggests a repetition of the historical pattern of retreat to the village, for example, in periods of upheaval during the industrialization drive at the end of the nineteenth century, and particularly during the civil war of 1918–21, when Soviet Russia's cities lost over a third of their population.

4. This tendency reached its apogee when Nikita Khrushchev attempted to realize Engels's vision of "the withering away of the state." For a discussion and statistics, see Jerry F. Hough, "Political Participation in the Soviet Union," *Soviet Studies,* vol. 28, no. 1 (January 1976), pp. 3–20.

5. The best description of the active, if powerless, role played by local authorities in the budget-making process is contained in B. Michael Frolic, "Decision-Making in Soviet Cities," *American Political Science Review,* vol. 66, no. 1 (March 1972), pp. 38–52.

6. Taubman, *Governing Soviet Cities.*

7. Quoted in Rolf Theen, "Russia at the Grassroots," p. 67.

8. *RFE/RL Daily Report,* 3 February 1994.

9. *The Economist* (London), January 8–14, 1994, p. 55. These results differ from an earlier report, supposedly the official final results, published in *RFE/RL Daily Report,* December 27, 1993, that lists only 30 independents, and gives Russia's Choice 96 seats rather than the 70 assigned it by *The Economist.*

I
Local Studies

1

The Politics of City Government
Leningrad/St. Petersburg, 1990–1992

Vladimir Gel'man and Mary McAuley

St. Petersburg, traditionally considered the most western of Russian cities, was founded by Peter the Great in 1703. Built at enormous cost in the marshes of the Finnish Gulf with its port linking it to Europe and its palaces and streets designed by western architects, the new imperial capital was intended to wrench Russia westward, away from the conservatism of old Russia that emanated from Moscow. Although lacking a natural resource base, the city became the country's leading industrial center and, by virtue of being the capital, the center of culture and science. In 1917 its citizens led the way, first in bringing down the tsar, and then in bringing the Bolsheviks to power. With the move of the capital to Moscow in 1918, St. Petersburg's preeminence was ended. Nevertheless, throughout the Soviet period and despite the devastating impact of the siege of Leningrad in World War II, the city retained its importance as Russia's "northern capital," an industrial and cultural magnet that drew people and resources from all over the Union. Because of its potential as a political rival, Leningrad's relationship with the central authorities has always been uneasy. The Brezhnev period witnessed the expansion of its huge industrial plants and network of research institutes, ever more closely tied to the defense sector (which employed, depending on definition, one-half to two-thirds of the labor force), but a shrinking of the central allocation of investment for the municipal economy. Leningrad politicians were not appointed to leading central posts, and as a result there was little turnover of the party and soviet elite. Meanwhile the cultural and educational institutions continued to replenish the ranks of the city's professional intelligentsia.

By the mid-1980s the consequences of damaging policies were becoming ever more apparent. The building of a dam, which had disastrous ecological consequences, contributed to the pollution of the water supply; the concentration of resources in the defense sector led to the deterioration of the physical and social infrastructure of the city (the transport network, roads, buildings, and educational and health facilities); the stifling of innovation, both technological and cultural, together with political repression, brought isolation and backwardness. By the late 1980s the population was over five million, but was aging and, in common with many areas of Russia, had a low and declining birthrate. While the city authorities could claim, with some justification, that responsibility for all key decisions lay with the central government, and not with them, and that Leningrad continually subsidized the central budget, there is little evidence of any effort on their part to alter the course.[1]

The population's discontent with the ever-worsening conditions of everyday life and the identification of the apparatus with privilege, corruption, and political repression laid the basis for the electoral defeat of the party apparatus in the 1989 and 1990 elections. Of crucial importance in producing the 1990 result, however, was the recognition by the city's professional and technical intelligentsia of the approaching crisis and the willingness of some of them to take the opportunity offered by *glasnost* to fight for access to the media, to organize, and to challenge the apparatus. The existence of a city party organization whose membership and apparatus produced both democrats and conservatives willing to do battle with each other was relevant too. The perestroika years, the electoral campaigns of 1989 and 1990, and their outcomes have, however, been described elsewhere.[2] Our concern is with the attempts that began in the spring of 1990 to construct a new form of city government, the problems that emerged, and the key issues and players that had come to dominate the agenda by the end of 1992.

The sheer importance of St. Petersburg—economically, culturally, and politically—distinguishes it from all other Russian cities (except Moscow) in two respects. First, it has always enjoyed a special status vis-à-vis the central government, and this remains so today. Second, its overshadowing of the surrounding region in terms of population and economic significance makes for an unusual city–region relationship. Although, until 1990 when *obkom* (oblast committee) and *gorkom* (city committee) were merged, the party structures followed the normal pattern with the obkom overseeing activities in region and city, the city soviet was not subordinate to the oblast soviet. Indeed it had the status of a regional soviet. Some institutions (for example, the police or Lentelradio) were under the jurisdiction of both soviets and the central authorities—an arrangement that caused no problems in a system in which the party took all decisions but that was inevitably to lead to conflict once the party lost control. As we shall see, the relationships with the oblast and with the center (and the added complication of the rivalry between the All-Union and Russian authorities) influenced and continue to influence politics within the city. We begin, however, with the critical event that changed the complexion of city politics forever: the election of a democratic city soviet in March 1990.

The Electoral Victory

Of the 400 seats in the Leningrad City Soviet, or Lensovet, 240 were won by candidates supported by the Democratic Bloc. The patriots, with 5 percent of the vote, picked up only two; OFT (the United Labor Front—a conservative pro-communist group) and "private entrepreneurs" won four seats each; the industrial lobby had its representatives (for example Georgii Khizha), as did the police and the military. The party apparatus was almost entirely absent (one obkom secretary, four *raikom*, or borough committee, secretaries, two party committee secretaries) although more than twenty of the deputies were members of the obkom or of raikoms. Sixty percent of the deputies, including some of the leading democrats, were party members, but only one-third of these could be counted on to support the official party line.[3] In April 1990, therefore, the city had a soviet in which a "democratic" majority, its legitimacy established by the ballot box, faced a demoralized "party" opposition and set out to remedy the city's ills.

Within a few months the soviet was struggling, both to retain its popularity and to exercise any effective government of the city. Three main factors were responsible. First, there was the nature of "the democratic majority"; second, and perhaps the most important, all the administrative structures and state institutions in the city remained unchanged; and third, there was the inability of the city's democratic politicians, whose victory had given a powerful impetus to the democratic movement in Russia, to act until the ensuing battle between the Union and the republics, and between reformers and conservatives at the central level, was resolved. These three factors interacted throughout 1990–91 to produce particular patterns of behavior that militated against effective city government.

April 1990–August 1991: Institutional Wrangling

The Democratic Majority

We begin with the deputies themselves. The democrats, drawn heavily from the ranks of the professional and technical intelligentsia, shared only the vaguest of platforms: they were united by little more than opposition to apparatus rule, and by the conviction that a democratic city government should put the rights and welfare of its citizens at the top of the agenda. Membership in the Communist Party did not define political position. Very few of the noncommunists had any party affiliation, as would be expected in the still largely preparty days, and many were determinedly opposed to parties per se. The People's Front, the city-wide organization that had united the democratic opposition and from whose ranks many candidates had come, began to fade once the election had been won. As important, however, there were no mechanisms to bind a deputy to the Front, and no sense, on the part of the deputies, that they were or should be representatives of a party or organization, bound by its program and in turn able to draw upon party resources for support. Regardless of whether they had indeed been elected for their personal qualities, or because they were members of the democratic opposition, the democrats were convinced that they represented their electors and that the soviet had a historic role to play.[4] Not all their opponents, even in the soviet, were convinced that this was so. Some were far from enthusiastic at the thought of devoting time and energy to what they had envisaged as a largely honorific job, and began to absent themselves from the daily sessions; others took up cudgels to defend either ideological or specific interests in the novel and noisy environment. The opening session of the Lensovet, then, saw an "individualistic" democratic majority facing small "ideological" oppositions (orthodox communists and patriots) and an "interest-based" industrial lobby.

The failure of parties to take root in Leningrad, the city where ideological positions and group interests were more clearly defined than anywhere else in Russia, is a topic we can touch on only in passing: our concern here is with the consequences of their absence for city government.[5] By the early summer of 1990 after two months' wrangling, leading democrat Petr Filippov, was calling for a "party of reform" to take the lead in the soviet. This failed to materialize for the reasons given above. Political and ideological differences among the deputies, however, began to reflect themselves in factions (although not all deputies belonged to a faction), and the groupings changed as the political environment changed or as different issues came onto the agenda.[6] The existence of strong personalities was relevant, too. By June 1990 a radical, anticommunist, People's Front "platform" led by Marina Sal'e, which advocated confrontation with the still existing *nomenklatura* (for example, over the Leningrad TV station or Lenizdat, the publishing house appropriated by the obkom) had emerged.[7] In contrast there were those who favored a more gradualist approach and emphasized the importance of strict observance of the law. Among them, Filippov led a faction, Constructive Approach, that advocated free-market measures, and

Aleksei Kovalev organized an Anti-crisis group to support the candidacy first of Anatolii Sobchak as chairman of the soviet and then of Aleksandr Shchelkanov as chairman of the *ispolkom* (executive committee). Not surprisingly, both the Anti-crisis group and another, the Inter-Professionals, led by Ernst Perchik, also with no clear ideological orientation, had fallen apart by the end of the year. A conservative group, Rebirth of Leningrad, led by Viktor Sazonov, had a longer life. In February 1991 following the creation the previous autumn of Democratic Russia, a Democratic Russia bloc was formed in the soviet. It included deputies who belonged to no particular faction and a number of democratic factions: the People's Front Platform (74 deputies as of autumn 1991), the united Social-Democrats and Republicans (17 deputies), the Democratic Party of Russia (11), the Free Democratic Party (10), and the March faction (31 deputies), which was close to the People's Front faction but did not share its radicalism. During 1992 the lineup of the more active deputies on key questions changed little—approximately 150 democrats versus 60 communists.[8]

Municipal Structures and Administrative Practices: 1990–91

The position of the soviet within the wider institutional framework—and the city's dependence on the central government—precluded, however, any real action on the part of its democratic majority during the period 1990–91. Even had a united party of reform existed, it could not have introduced a set of reform policies. Hence, during this period a great deal of time and energy was spent on trying to establish new institutional arrangements. Differences in approach emerged, and rival political ambitions surfaced. As would be expected in an environment in which the participants were involved in struggles either to retain or gain control of institutional and financial resources, and of the means of communication, divisions ran deep. By the summer of 1991 a new set of institutional arrangements was more or less in place, but disputes over power and control were still very much in evidence.

Under the old system the Soviet met to approve policies worked out by the ispolkom under the guidance of the party bodies. The main policy guidelines, and the major part of the budget, were determined in Moscow. Key institutions such as the police, the KGB, and the prosecutor's office came under central government's jurisdiction, and much of Leningrad industry was controlled by All-Union ministries. Whole areas of decision making therefore lay outside the soviet's reach. This did not prevent the soviet from attempting to exert its authority. In November 1990 it voted to replace the incumbent police chief, an ex–party apparatchik named Gennadii Voshchinin, with a professional policeman, Arkadii Kramarev, and in this case succeeded—despite opposition from the All-Union MVD, the obkom, and Sobchak—but only because Vadim Bakatin, the previous minister of internal affairs, had delegated control over regional appointments to the Russian ministry.[9] Key questions of economic reform or control over the KGB had to await the victory of Yeltsin and the Russian government in August 1991. As far as relations between the soviet and the ispolkom were concerned, however, it was a different matter.

The chairman of the ispolkom, in this case Vladimir Khodyrev, was traditionally a key figure, controlling an administrative apparatus of two thousand city employees. As was customary he invited the newly elected deputies in March 1990 to a meeting to set up an organizing committee to plan the new soviet's agenda. It took a series of meetings before agreement was reached on an organizing committee of sixty-seven, and six working groups, to prepare the agenda.[10] The deputies' insistence on their right to control the ispolkom in tandem with their inability to agree on new mechanisms, to organize soviet affairs, or to regulate relationships with the ispolkom, were to prove very damaging. As far as soviet affairs were concerned, the choosing of a chairman proved difficult. After weeks of stalemate the deputies turned to Anatolii Sobchak, the popular All-Union deputy, who won a by-election and on May 23 was elected by a two-thirds majority. But Sobchak failed to establish good working relations with the deputies or to provide the policy lead that some had hoped for. The soviet had, in the meantime, opted for a presidium composed ex-officio of the chairman and deputy chairman of the soviet, and of the chairs and deputy chairs of the twenty-seven commissions that had been created. Some of these were concerned with traditional spheres of city administration—transport, education, health—others demonstrated the commitment to economic reform, glasnost, human rights. The commissions were composed of fifteen to twenty-five deputies (in 1990 individuals could belong to more than one commission), three or four of whom worked full-time, and could make recommendations to the presidium. Inevitably, given the structures and the lack of leadership, the presidium either simply accepted the recommendations or acted in a quite arbitrary fashion and, once it had been decided to hold shorter soviet sessions, became an important decision-making body. This led to a review of the procedures for its formation and, in the spring of 1991, to its being directly elected by the deputies.[11]

As far as the deputies' relations with the ispolkom were concerned, one factor was their deep distrust of Khodyrev and his staff of officials; another was the belief held by many, regardless of their political views, that the ispolkom, whoever staffed it, should simply execute soviet decisions. Such a view was shared by Sobchak, but in his case it meant that it should execute *his* decisions. Faced with this novel situation, the ispolkom, traditionally the body that prepared the policy decisions and administered the city, simply marked time. Khodyrev did nothing. By June, 20 percent of the officials (but less among the top administrators) had left; those who remained were no less hostile to what they considered to be politically undesirable and amateurish deputies most of whom, indeed, had very little knowledge of how the city was run or of how a city might be run. In the eyes of the deputies and of their chairman (for once in agreement), the officials not only threatened any possibility of change but were poor administrators. In mid-June the soviet elected Aleksandr Shchelkanov, another popular All-Union deputy, as chairman of the ispolkom and he began the slow process of recruiting a new team of top administrators, while the departments again began to prepare policy documents. Although the continuing conflict between the soviet and the ispolkom owed something to a personality clash between Sobchak and Shchelkanov, it had deeper roots. Sobchak revealed himself to be an advocate of interventionist "presidential" decision making, and at the same time impatient of any checks or attempts to control his actions. Shchelkanov, in contrast, was anxious to see rules of behavior established and observed. The deputies, while objecting to Sobchak's approach, in their turn wished to exercise control over an apparatus of officials who, they had every reason to fear, administered resources in their own interests. According to Shchelkanov, the deputies strove to make all decisions great and small, and to limit the ispolkom to the most unrewarding and menial tasks.[12] The deputies and Shchelkanov found themselves at odds, despite sharing much the same aim. The situation was further complicated by the inability of the members of the ispolkom, with their very different interests and concerns, to act together as a collegial organ. By the spring of 1991 Shchelkanov, convinced that existing arrangements were unworkable, put forward the first proposals for a new structure of city government that would include a mayor, separate from the soviet, and this was the solution adopted, not without conflict, in early summer.

In May 1991 Sobchak succeeded in obtaining a ruling from the presidium of the RSFSR Supreme Soviet that left the structure of the soviet unchanged and preserved its control over the budget, but gave a popularly elected mayor the right to appoint the heads of the city administration. Following Sobchak's election with 66 percent of the vote (Iurii Sevenard, his Communist Party opponent, received 26 percent), Shchelkanov left office. Meanwhile, Sobchak suggested a further reduction in the role of the soviet. The deputies responded by sending a delegation to the Supreme Soviet with a proposal that would have given the soviet the right to confirm appointments and administrative structures. The Supreme Soviet confirmed the original ruling in its essentials, including the soviet's right to determine its own structure, but suggested that revisions might be helpful.[13] The soviet had already voted to elect a smaller presidium on an individual basis; it now turned to the problem of a large and unwieldy soviet. In line with developments elsewhere, it resolved that the full soviet should meet briefly every three months to decide key issues and a "little soviet" (*malyi sovet*), elected from among the four hundred deputies, should work full time through its commissions, themselves reduced in number, while a presidium of thirteen should coordinate the work. At the beginning of July, Aleksandr Beliaev, a 37-year-old, middle-of-the road supporter of Democratic Russia, was elected as chairman.[14]

The District Soviets

When the soviet had met for its second session in September 1990, political analysts had identified four key areas of conflict: Sobchak versus the deputies, the Lensovet versus the ispolkom, the Lensovet versus the district soviets, and, finally, the relationship among the city, oblast, and republic levels of government.[15] As we have seen, more than one factor was responsible for the conflicts between individual politicians and city institutions. The same was true of those among institutions occupying different places in the territorial structure. Although in all cases the issue of who should control the property on a given territory was the underlying one, the problems it posed—and the possibility of its resolution—varied. City–oblast relations, which are discussed in a later section, were and continue to be more conflictual than intracity relations: here decisions taken in the summer of 1991 effectively curtailed the rights and authority of the district soviets. Briefly, events unfolded as follows. The city was divided into twenty-one districts (*raiony v gorode*), each with its soviet of more than a hundred deputies, its *raiispolkom* (district executive committee) and its budget determined from above. The election results here, where candidate affiliation was less well known, had been far less decisive than at the city level: the Communist Party retained control of ten, the democrats won in four, and the remaining seven were evenly balanced.[16] Regardless, however, of political composition, the district soviets and their administrations were anxious to lay claim to the property in their districts and to a tax and budget policy that would give them greater scope to handle their own affairs. The demands were no different from those being made by the Lensovet to the republic government and, in turn, from those being advanced by the Russian government to the federal authorities. If property was going to be redistributed, all wanted to be in a position to influence outcomes. If licenses to trade, to set up businesses, and to rent premises were going to be issued, someone was going to be the issuing authority—a powerful and lucrative position. If tax policy was going to be rethought, all were anxious to see changes that would increase their disposable income while maintaining subsidies from above to cover pressing needs. The centrifugal tendencies that were becoming ever stronger within the highly centralized system were reflected within the city itself, with a number of districts simply claiming ownership of all property on their territory.[17]

Although there were exceptions, the elections of 1990 had done little to undermine the power of district officialdom whose representatives dominated the soviets. The well-founded concern of the city soviet that property would be distributed quite unscrupulously (see below) strengthened their conviction that the city, rather than the districts, should retain the right of control and disposition of valuable land and property. Sobchak, too, did not hesitate to make it known that he considered the district soviets an unnecessary link in the city structure. A commission of the city soviet devoted itself to the question of self-government, another commission took up the issue of privatization, and the district soviets themselves created a coordinating council to try to devise a common strategy. Different proposals on structure, property rights, and taxation were canvassed but, in many ways, the often highly charged debate was academic because all recognized that until decisions were taken at RSFSR level on the rights of local authorities and rulings were given on the property question, the issues could not be resolved.[18] At the beginning of January 1991 the Lensovet took the initial step of claiming jurisdiction over land, housing, and nonresidential property, while leaving for the districts a share of the administration.[19] It was, however, summer before procedures for administering or leasing property were worked out and the city's control became effective. If this action curtailed the powers of the district administrations, the creation of the mayor's office and the appointment of the heads of district administration by the mayor meant that the district soviets were rendered largely redundant. They still adopted their own budgets, but this was essentially a formal affair. All that remained was the right of passing a vote of no confidence in the head of the district administration—but this did not oblige the mayor to make a replacement, and had the potential for becoming a source of conflict.[20]

Dependence Upon the Center and Its Consequences

In February 1991, faced with a critical food situation, ever-worsening city services, and plummeting popularity,[21] the Lensovet laid part of the blame on the ispolkom's failure to take preventive measures, and on its own preoccupation with long-term plans rather than with immediate problems. It noted, however, that "the crisis in the city's economy is the result, to a significant degree, of the general political and economic crisis in the USSR."[22] This was only too true. The city's finances were in a critical state but there was little either soviet or ispolkom could do to remedy this, just as little new could be done in the way of policy until the conflict between Russia and the All-Union authorities was resolved. Somehow the city limped through the year.

The proposal to create a Leningrad "free enterprise zone" (FEZ), which acquired currency during 1990–91, and the attempts to realize it in practice demonstrate the interplay of interests both at the city level and between city and central authorities. The proposal, pushed hard by Sobchak and supported by the soviet and by the ispolkom, gained a good deal of publicity. Its main elements included special arrangements for privatization, for foreign investors, for tax and hard-currency privileges, and for import–export licenses. Of crucial importance was the question of who would be responsible for striking the deals and issuing the privileges and licenses. Sobchak was adamant that he, either as chairman of the soviet or as mayor, should control the process. The soviet, incensed by a deal that Sobchak had negotiated with a French firm for the development of New Holland (part of the old port district) on terms very disadvantageous to the city, and increasingly concerned by the phenomenon of nomenklatura capital, was determined that it should be responsible. Sobchak looked to the All-Union authorities for support; the soviet, to the Russian government. Proposals went back and forth, finally bearing fruit in a ruling of June 11, 1991, from the Council of Ministers of the RSFSR, "On the Initial Measures to Develop a Leningrad (City) Free-Enterprise Zone." Even this, however, was cautious: apart from confirming tax-free credits for five years for certain specific projects, it spoke only of the intention to work out further measures.[23] The political motivation behind the Russian government's support, at a time when it was engaged in a struggle with the All-Union government, was only too obvious, as was its relative inability to influence the economic situation. The bulk of the city's industrial resources still came under the jurisdiction of All-Union ministries, and hence lay outside the control of the Russian government, let alone the Leningrad Soviet.[24] Not surprisingly, with the collapse of the center, the new Russian government became far less interested in supporting Leningrad's claims to special status, and the FEZ failed to materialize.

August 1991

By August 1991 two developments were clearly visible. First, as regards the structures of city government, there was the emergence of the mayor's office in control of the original administration and the transformation of the Lensovet into a "democratic" check upon the administration, rather than its development as a policymaker. Second, lobbies had entered the political arena (the directors of the defense industry plants, the new entrepreneurs, the democratic intelligentsia, the militia) as had institutional interests (district officials, housing administrations), but not political parties. This should not surprise us. Political parties accompany strong legislatures. Lobbies will develop in an environment in which decision making lies within an executive apparatus, and in this case the officials were particularly open to lobbying. The attempted putsch and its outcome did not substantially affect either the structures of government or the constellation of political forces within the city. Reactions to the declaration of the state of emergency did, however, shed light on the nature of that constellation, while the emergence of the Russian government as the one central authority finally put the process of privatization into gear.

The key features of the August days can be summarized briefly. First, both supporters and opponents of the so-called State Committee on the State of Emergency, or GKChP, were prepared to declare themselves: General Samsonov formed a local committee, as required by the GKChP, and appeared on television; the Lensovet, almost unanimously, declared its unqualified opposition and, with the return of Sobchak to the city, had a dynamic leader able to rally support within the city. Of crucial importance were the actions of those in charge of law and order and of the media. Tellingly, it was evening before the Lensovet, now led by Sobchak, managed to gain access to television or lift the censorship of the press: those most "reconstructed" institutions proved easily controllable. In contrast, police chief A. Kramarev refused to carry out Samsonov's orders on preventing street demonstrations, and sided openly with the Lensovet, while the KGB adopted a neutral position. The environment thus allowed individuals or institutions to take up positions, and reactions were revealing. Enterprise management proved able to counter any spontaneous protests from its labor force, and it was primarily management in the defense plants, under All-Union jurisdiction, who acted accordingly; the new entrepreneurs, in contrast, were among the most active in offering financial and other aid to the Lensovet. Boris Gidaspov, the obkom secretary, participated in the emergency committee but failed to give a clear lead to the Communist Party, which proved itself no longer capable of independent action. Although an opinion survey, as well as the demonstration on August 20, suggested overwhelming disapproval of the GKChP among the population, those prepared to take an active part in protests were limited to the original democratic activists, now joined by some youthful supporters. If one had to identify a single action as the most significant it would therefore be Kramarev's stance against the GKChP. It allowed the expression of protest (whether the small demonstrations of the nineteenth or the huge meeting of the twentieth) and thus undermined Samsonov's confidence that the situation could be controlled without bloodshed. From all accounts this factor weighed the most heavily with Samsonov. It resulted in his keeping the troops out of the city, and influenced his relationship with the leaders of the putsch. By the morning of August 21 the danger was over, and the democrats could celebrate.[25]

September 1991–December 1992:
City Politics and Policy Making

The two most immediate consequences of the putsch were the final discrediting of the Communist Party and the taking over of its property by the mayor's office and the soviet, and the renaming of the city as St. Petersburg.[26] Sobchak moved the mayor's office into the Smolny Institute, the party headquarters, and took over the party newspaper, *Leningradskaia pravda,* which became *Sankt-Peterburgskie vedomosti.* Far more important, however, were the consequences for the central government and center–city relationships. St. Petersburg politicians would henceforth be dealing with one central authority, the Russian government, a government that included among its leading members Petersburg activists committed to the introduction of economic reform and privatization. The economic reforms that the Russian government set in motion, beginning in the autumn of 1991, qualitatively affected both the character and the activities of the municipal authorities, and their ability to influence developments within the city. Whereas in the spring of 1991 the Lensovet was still best characterized as a nonparty assembly with a divided democratic majority whose members joined ranks in response to national crises or issues—the January 1991 crackdown in the Baltic states, the presidential elections in June 1991—the coming to power of the proreform Russian government meant that now, at long last, the democrats had some freedom of action as policy makers. This was to bring out the differences between them. At the same time the introduction of the office of mayor, with Sobchak in that post, led to an increase in conflict among the various municipal authorities.[27] The same was true of relations between the city and oblast, and between federal and local authorities. The year 1992 witnessed a growing crisis of governability, in the context of the rapid municipalization of the city's enterprises and increasing pressure upon the municipal authorities by various interest groups or lobbies. It saw, too, the destruction of the social infrastructure of the city, and a growing budget deficit.

The City Soviet

By the autumn of 1991 the St. Petersburg Soviet, as was true of soviets throughout Russia, was in deep crisis. A proposal to call new elections, put forward by some, was turned down by the Supreme Soviet. The ineffectiveness of the soviets did, however, persuade the federal authorities to pass a decision in favor of "little soviets," to be elected from among, and include up to a maximum of, 20 percent of the deputies, who would work full time on the soviet's affairs. In January 1992 the St. Petersburg Soviet, accordingly, elected a little soviet. The election ran into difficulties. After three rounds of balloting 38 deputies rather than the intended 80 had been elected from among 206 candidates and a halt was called.[28] Not a single candidate from either the procommunist Rebirth of Leningrad group nor from among Sobchak's supporters was elected. Nor, however, were many of those Democratic Russia activists who were known for their moderate views and willingness to compromise. It was the radical People's Front faction that succeeded in getting almost all its candidates elected and whose leader, Sergei Egorov, received the most votes and effectively became the majority leader in the little soviet.[29] This result can be explained first, by the stricter internal discipline of the People's Front and March factions and their ability to strike deals with one another, and secondly, by a change in political generations. There was now a second wave of activists who had cut their teeth as politicians in the soviet but were not particularly well known or popular outside its walls. Several well-known deputies had taken up full-time posts at the federal level (for example, Filippov, chair of the Supreme Soviet Subcommittee on Privatization, and Sergei Vasil'ev, head of the government's Center on Economic Reform) and did not run. Their absence also affected relationships within the soviet. The consequence was a definite strengthening of the anti-Sobchak opposition and a radicalization of the soviet.

In other ways, too, the soviet changed. The preparation of agenda items and the level of discussion clearly improved. It became a reasonably professional body both in terms of drawing up policy and in its control functions. However, the fact that, even with its increasing professionalization, it failed to function effectively draws our attention to the existence of factors that, inherent in the structure of the soviets, tended to undermine them as institutions. The St. Petersburg experience allows us, therefore, to identify the key elements in the systemic crisis gripping all the representative institutions. First, the presidium as before retained the right to make mandatory decisions, thus partly duplicating the little soviet. Meanwhile the relationship between the little soviet and the plenary soviet became in practice similar to that between the Supreme Soviet and the Congress of People's Deputies: a group of deputies, better informed (but at the same time more easily controlled by the leadership), acted de facto in place of the soviet. The group was not, however, representative of political opinion within the soviet, and still less of the electorate. In consequence, rather than becoming a properly representative institution, the soviet developed a five-tiered hierarchical structure consisting of, at the base, 359 deputies (as of September 1, 1992), 123 of whom worked full-time in the commissions, a little soviet of 38, a presidium of 15 (elected on an individual basis), and finally, the chairman.

Second, the chairman of the soviet, who had the right to issue instructions (*rasporiazheniia*), could in practice be likened to the director of an enterprise, in this case the soviet. He had the right to employ and dismiss its officials, to authorize *kommandirovki* (business trips), to award (or not to award) bonuses both to deputies and to officials, and so on. This inevitably led to a degree of patronage and political clientism, regardless of the intentions of the holder of the post. Third, and most important, the soviet was neither a representative institution expressing the interests of significant social groups, nor was it capable of effective policy making. With the exception of the People's Front faction, which produced policy proposals worked out by its leaders, all the factions limited their political activity to issues concerning individuals. In consequence it was the commissions that occupied themselves with policy making. It is hardly surprising that, in such circumstances, the pursuit and realization of a coherent policy agenda was impossible. A characteristic example of two decisions taken by the little soviet that contradicted each other, not in letter but in spirit, relates to economic reform. In April 1992 the little soviet adopted a proposal emanating from the commission on economic reform, which simplified the procedure for registering an enterprise, by abolishing, *inter alia,* the need for its having a license. In July, however, the little soviet adopted regulations for retail trade, worked out by the commission on trade and services, which were based on quite different fiscal principles, and included the licensing of trade by district administrations and a number of other restrictions.[30]

Two tendencies became ever more marked and influenced the character of the soviet's activities. On the one hand, there was a depoliticization. Straight "political" questions came on the agenda only when provoked by the action of an outside agency.[31] Without any doubt this resulted in the increasing professionalization of the corpus of deputies and worked to the soviet's advantage. On the other hand, the absence of effective, firmly grounded political organizations either within the soviet or in the wider society essentially turned the deputies into officials incapable of elaborating and implementing policies to meet the needs of the city. In addition, the soviet lacked the backing of a qualified civil service, and was unable to tap the intellectual expertise that existed within the city either for the working out of projects or for analyzing the situation in the city and the consequences of municipal policies. Decision making continued in an ad hoc fashion.

It needs to be stated clearly that these developments were not caused by bad faith on the part of either the deputies or the leaders of the soviet, but by a complex set of factors. To start, there was the poorly structured nature of Russian society and its ill-preparedness for autonomous political organization, as well as the catastrophic inability of society and its political institutions to organize an effective system of government. There were also, however, more directly relevant factors: the lack of a coherent policy on the part of the federal government, which forced the St. Petersburg Soviet to behave in a reactive fashion; and the extremely difficult relations between the soviet and the mayor, which meant that cooperation had to take place at the commission and the committee levels, rather than through political negotiation.

The Conflict Between the City Soviet and the Mayor's Office

The conflict between the majority in the soviet and Sobchak understandably continued once he became mayor. The soviet repeatedly annulled illegal instructions emanating from the mayor, while Sobchak continued to ignore the very existence of the soviet as a representative institution. This led the soviet, in the autumn of 1991, to prepare a draft law "Concerning the Status of St. Petersburg," which strengthened the soviet's control over the mayor. This draft was submitted to the Supreme Soviet.[32] The latter's unwillingness, however, to pass a law specifically for St. Petersburg, prompted the city soviet to change tack and concentrate on getting appropriate amendments included in the law "On the Krai and Oblast Soviet of People's Deputies and the Krai and Oblast Administration."[33] This law, passed in March 1992, placed the administration under the direct control of the representative organs (in a form similar to that of "the weak mayor" in the United States): the administration (in the case of St. Petersburg, the mayor) could disburse property and finances and within the limits and according to rules set by the soviet; the soviet acquired the right to ratify the structure of city administration, and the appointment of certain officers, including the chairs of the finance committee and the committee for the administration of property, and the police chief. Most important, the soviet received the right to pass a vote of no confidence in the head of the administration and to appeal for his removal both to the president and to the Constitutional Court.

The soviet was not slow to use its new rights. On March 30, with a vote of 148 in favor, the soviet voted "to consider it expedient to remove A. Sobchak from office. . . ."[34] Characteristically, both the overwhelming majority of Democratic Russia deputies and supporters of Fatherland and the OFT voted in favor, while support for Sobchak came primarily from officials in the administration and economic management. The lineup of the deputies was not, however, primarily prompted by a defense of their institutional interests (legislative versus executive) but rather was a consequence of the different ideological positions held by the mayor on the one hand and his opponents—both liberals and national-bolsheviks—on the other. The liberals were critical of Sobchak for his undemocratic behavior, and the national-bolsheviks objected to him as a democrat. Strictly speaking, the soviet vote had no legal significance (267 votes would have been necessary to achieve the required two-thirds majority), and even then the president is not obliged to remove the officeholder. Nevertheless, the action did have significant political repercussions in that it set a precedent, and the clause was then used to real effect in a number of other regions (Moscow, Krasnodar Krai, and Lipetsk).

Following the soviet's vote, confrontation between mayor and soviet took on a new character. In June 1992 the soviet received from the president's office the draft of an edict "On the Rights of the Organs of Administration of St. Petersburg During the Period of Radical Economic Reform." The essence of the proposal was that the mayor should be responsible for the territory of the city and the surrounding districts; he should form the government of the city, be responsible for the distribution of plots of land, for setting up and disbursing hard-currency and extra-budgetary funds, and for introducing local taxes—in other words—a mini-presidential system. The idea behind the proposal was clear enough: unable to achieve policy results under the existing arrangements, the mayor strove to lay the blame on his limited powers. The consequence was that the soviet, in its turn, appealed to the president to curtail Sobchak's voluntarist behavior, which was demonstrated by his attempt to obtain a presidential edict whose content would have contradicted the terms of the Federal Agreement. The draft passed from the president's office to the government, where (not without the help of the anti-Sobchak lobby) it disappeared forever. Sobchak's defeat should not, however, be attributed simply to the soviet's action but also to his own lack of resources. Accustomed to relying on personal connections and lacking a solid clientele, he was unable to obtain the "personal" rights he sought.[35]

The struggle between the soviet and the mayor's office reached a decisive stage at the beginning of 1993 when, in accordance with the decree of the Supreme Soviet "On the Procedure for Implementing the Law of the Russian Federation 'On the Krai and Oblast Soviet of People's Deputies and the Krai and Oblast Administration,' " the soviet began its first reading of the draft of the constitution (*Ustav*) of St. Petersburg in February, but it soon became clear that it was unlikely to be adopted before the autumn. The draft provided for stringent controls over the administration on the part of the soviet. Sobchak had almost no possibility of influencing the outcome because his amendments stood no chance of being accepted, and an attempt to blackmail deputies and electors with the threat of resignation gave him no leverage.

Faced with this, Sobchak, as far as one can tell, chose a different tactic, both original and characteristic. Toward the end of 1992 a draft proposal for the government of St. Petersburg was drawn up in the mayor's office. The essence of the project consisted of placing the city administration under a new "head of the city administration," appointed by the mayor and approved by the soviet; he in turn would propose the members of his government to the soviet for their approval. The government's activities would be controlled by the soviet while the mayor would carry out representative functions and stand above both soviet and administration, acting as adjudicator when necessary. Such a scheme could both work to Sobchak's advantage and appeal to the more moderate and pragmatically inclined deputies, led by Beliaev, who saw it as a lesser evil than a continuation of the existing conflict. It clearly had a chance of being accepted by the soviet.

Its realization would, however, surely bring a further decline in the governability of the city. It is likely that the membership of the government would change frequently, both from pressure by the soviet and at the mayor's initiative. If the soviet should demand from the city government speedy and effective cures to the city's problems (which, given the national crisis, it would hardly be able to find), Sobchak, ever ready to blame his own mistakes on others, would have sacrificial lambs to hand, and would bear no responsibility for their actions, whereas under the then-existing arrangements he at least bore responsibility for the choice of his team.

The Conflict Between City and Oblast

After·the signing of the Federation Treaty in March 1992, which gave city and oblast equal status as members of the federation, conflicts between the two became more difficult to resolve because the federal organs could no longer mediate between them but had to deal with each directly. Three issues proved to be the most contentious: those involving the allocation of land to city dwellers for dachas and allotments, the question of property, and tax collection.

Despite repeated attempts, it proved impossible to solve the land issue in 1992. The city soviet requested that the oblast soviet allocate 40,000 hectares of land within a radius of 50–100 km. from the city; the oblast soviet responded with an offer of 8,000 hectares, mainly outside the 100-km. radius. Subsequently, city dwellers received 6,400 hectares. The conflict was exacerbated by the absence of any normative regulation, and by the tough position adopted by both sides.[36] Property within the city became a highly contentious issue following a decree of the Russian government of September 10, 1992, which allocated to the oblast a number of properties standing on city territory, a decree that, furthermore, was passed without the agreement of the municipal authorities. This immediately produced a series of disputes, of which the following can serve as an example. In October 1992 the firm Lenkhlebprom, originally under the joint administration of city and oblast, became a shareholding company. The Oblast Committee for the Management of Property registered the company, which owned factories in the oblast, and whose administration, which operated the distribution network, was based in the city. In consequence the mayor's office lost control over the regular supply of bread products to the city. Sobchak declared that such decisions, taken without the agreement of the City Committee for the Management of Property, were invalid and, on November 18, he issued an instruction that the administration's building be removed from the jurisdiction of the company. The police were instructed to mount a guard and allow entry only with a permit. In reply the head of the oblast administration, A. Beliakov, issued a counterinstruction and ordered the police not to obey the mayor's order. Only when the dispute had degenerated to this level, with the possible consequence of paralyzing the food supply, did the two sides agree on temporary rules to govern the use of the disputed property and the joint use of the supply network.[37] Further disputes of this kind were only to be expected, given the absence of a proper legal procedure for dividing property between different federal subjects, and a situation such as existed in St. Petersburg and the oblast in which a large number of properties belonged to the one but were situated on the territory of the other.

The question of tax collection was an even more difficult issue. A large number of the huge St. Petersburg enterprises had subsidiaries in the oblast, whose taxes were either paid straight to the city or were received by the city indirectly, by way of federal allocations, while the enterprises and their employees benefited from oblast services, and the oblast had to provide finances for, for example, environmental protection. Understandably both the oblast soviet and its administration registered their objections. However, if earlier such problems were solved by a redistribution of funds from the All-Union budget, in 1992, when the budgets of the Russian Federation and its different subjects had not been clearly delineated, a solution could be sought only through discussions among St. Petersburg, Leningrad Oblast, and the Russian Federation.

The Privatization of Enterprises

Following the demise of the idea of the Free Enterprise Zone in the autumn of 1991, the mayor was faced with the task of devising an economic policy that would complement the government's policy of economic reform. In preparation for this the membership of the Committee for the Management of City Property (*KUGI*) was completely changed to include both branch and district administrative officials (by virtue of which different lobbies acquired their spokesmen) and individuals, not connected with the original elite and in favor of reform *à la* Gaidar.[38] On February 25 the little soviet approved a city program of privatization during 1992 drawn up by the *KUGI*. This proposed the privatization of 50–60 percent of the shops, services, food, light, and construction industries. The *KUGI* was to be responsible for decisions on the form privatization was to take and the procedures to be followed. The program stipulated that up to 40 percent of the enterprises should be privatized under a system of competitive tender that retained their existing profile, and that of the others the small enterprises should be auctioned off, while those with an issue capital of more than one million rubles should become shareholding companies.[39] Preferential terms were to be available to workers and employees who bought their own enterprise. Unfortunately, neither the *KUGI* specialists nor the city soviet considered the possible consequences of privatization for management–labor relations and a number of problems arose during the implementation of the program.[40] In particular, the auctioning off of a significant number of enterprises (which provided a welcome source of funds for the city budget) resulted, as a rule, in a change in their profile, particularly if the business location was good. At the first auction on May 13, for example, a hairdresser's on Nevskii Prospekt was bought by a furniture firm.[41] The offering of special terms to employees made little difference in this respect. They were unable to raise the substantial sums required out of their own pockets and, in consequence, a purchase by the labor collective was often the result of a deal done with wealthy entrepreneurs. Another hairdresser's on Nevskii was acquired, on a fifteen-year lease, by a company that included the employees and outside business interests; the em-

Institution Building
who gets to, who ought to have the power

ployees were then paid off (from 12,000 to 25,000 rubles depending on length of service) by the businessmen who intended to use the office space for a bank.[42]

There was, in consequence, some opposition to privatization and a number of conflicts arose. For example, in March 1992 a meeting of the labor collective of Dairy No. 3 opted for privatization and requested management to submit the appropriate application. Management, however, wished to ensure that the shareholding company should be formed, without "surplus" shareholders, in such a way that it would emerge as the owner of the substantial site in the center of the city. No application was submitted, and by October 1 the labor force had been cut from two hundred to twenty-eight. Machinery was dismantled and removed. In October some members of the independent trade union "Justice" visited the dairy, and seventy-four of those who had been fired formed a "Justice" branch organization. On November 9 a group called a conference of the (former) labor collective, which passed a vote of no confidence in the director and elected a new director proposed by the union. The workers who were present voted to begin a sit-in to prevent the further removal of machinery, while simultaneously the employees took a collective claim for reinstatement to the Dzerzhinskii District court. At the beginning of 1993 the court decision was anticipated, while the *KUGI* was to consider the labor collective's application for privatization with all due speed.[43]

Another problem was the effect on the retail-trade network in the central districts, for example, of the closing of bakeries. This made life even more difficult than it already was, particularly for pensioners, and naturally provoked a very negative reaction on the part of the population. Leading officials from the *KUGI* tended to justify their actions in ideological terms, such as "the need to create the infrastructure for the market," but one of the factors that encouraged such an approach to privatization was surely the clause in the program that linked bonuses for members of the *KUGI* and of the Property Fund to the money raised from property sales.

Auctions and competitive tendering became part of life. From a formal point of view, that is, in terms of numbers of enterprises involved, small-scale privatization proceeded very successfully in St. Petersburg—particularly in comparison with, for example, Saratov, where a Property Fund was set up only in June, or Pskov, which still had only one official working on such a fund in July. It was estimated that the 1992 program would be completed by the spring of 1993, and that by the end of the year the whole retail-trade network, catering, and services would be in private hands.[44] Privatization of the often huge enterprises in the state sector, which will have even more far-reaching consequences, was getting under way by the end of 1992;

531 enterprises had become shareholding companies by November. Here, too, the problem arose of workers and employees unable to afford to purchase a sufficient quantity of shares in order to retain control (perhaps six months' wages), in search of wealthy sponsors. Such sponsors, in turn, were less interested in the potential of the enterprise than in the land on which it stood. In the short run dividends from profits were unlikely to be high, given the fall in production, and the investors themselves lacked the funds to engage in long-term investment in the enterprise.

The failure or unwillingness of the *KUGI* to recognize that privatization would bring conflicts of interests and have social consequences caused problems. Very briefly, we should draw attention to three significant types of behavior that emerged: first, a concentration of energies on ensuring the survival of the work unit (the retail shop, the section within an enterprise, the existing or original labor collective), in other words the "artelization" of activity; second, the willingness of all parties involved to achieve their ends by illegal means; and third, in these conditions of "legal nihilism," the willingness of the *KUGI* to draw up privatization plans that benefited particular groups of "much needed" businessmen.

The Privatization of Housing

The privatization of apartments was featured in the election programs of the majority of the democratic candidates. Once in power, however, they were faced with the question of devising an appropriate policy. The age of the housing stock (more than a quarter of the housing was built before 1917 and had not been renovated), the huge number of communal apartments, and the difficulty of maintaining the existing stock while seeking finances for new construction all complicated the task of housing reform. In April 1991 the housing question began to be debated in the soviet and very quickly differences appeared within the democratic bloc. Some advocated that apartments be given to their present occupants at no charge; others favored the idea that apartments be purchased by their occupants in order to raise money to finance new housing. Compromise solutions were also put forward. It was clear that the deputies' views were influenced by their perception of the needs of different social groups. The Rebirth of Leningrad faction opposed the privatization of housing in any form, arguing that it would lead to the buying of property by dealers from the shadow economy.[45] No decision was taken. In July 1991, however, a ruling of the Supreme Soviet, which fixed the minimum living space to be allocated without charge in the course of privatization at 12 square meters for an individual, and at 18 for a family, allowed local authorities to raise these minima.[46] This reopened the debate in the soviet. The People's Front faction favored free privatization, but Sobchak, who at this time had become mayor, accused the deputies of adopting a socialist approach and argued for charging for any living space above the minima. This was the policy adopted. Both its complexity and the procedure for privatization devised by the mayor's office led to long queues, bureaucratic delays, and infringements. Only 14 percent of apartments had been privatized by November 1992. Under the amendment passed by the Supreme Soviet in that month, however, privatization of apartments became free, and this will undoubtedly speed up the process.[47]

The City Budget and the Standard of Living

At the end of September 1992 the soviet passed the budget for the second half of 1992. The budget envisaged an income of 34.5 trillion rubles and expenditure of 39.6 trillion rubles, that is, a deficit of more than 5 billion, of which a federal allocation would cover 4 billion.[48] The increase in the budget deficit was caused primarily by the rise in energy prices, which affected such major budget items as transport and municipal services. Property taxes, income from privatization, dividends from shares, and interest on credits were to provide new sources of income.[49] The scope for the municipal authorities to generate new income was, however, shrinking: it was estimated that in 1993 the city would be able to finance only 25 percent of its expenditure unless rents and fares were raised substantially. During 1992. the metro fare was increased from 10 kopecks to 3 rubles, telephone charges went up from 3 to 110 rubles a month and the population's standard of living had been maintained at something approaching an acceptable level only by keeping rents down. In 1992 they rose a scant 1.6 times.[50]

The claims by a number of politicians and in the press that the standard of living of the population in both city and oblast had fallen catastrophically were not so much exaggerated as in need of clarification. The per capita income required to maintain a daily energy intake of 2,391 calories was calculated in November 1992 at 4,438 rubles; the average wage at that time was 6,294 rubles; the minimum pension was 2,225 rubles.[51] The majority of people struggled to maintain a previous standard of living by cutting down on various types of expenditure and seeking extra sources of income. If during 1992, however, this enabled some to maintain and others to prevent a drastic fall in their living standards, a rapid deterioration in the near future seems all too probable, and may well be accompanied by a widespread refusal to pay rents and charges for municipal services. This, in turn, could produce all kinds of conflicts that neither the St. Petersburg nor the federal authorities have a strategy for solving.

The regions that are rich in natural resources—for example diamond-producing Yakutia or oil-rich Tiumen—can put pressure on the center by threatening to withhold supplies and thus get favorable allocations or terms from the federal budget. The proportion of the tax collected by the regional authorities that they retain for their own use thus varies significantly, and it is major industrial centers, such as St. Petersburg, with their substantial "tax producers," that did worst of all. In January 1993 Beliaev, the chairman of the soviet, and E. Krest'ianinov, the chairman of the Nizhnii Novgorod Oblast soviet, appealed to the Supreme Soviet to review the federation's draft budget for 1993 and adopt a uniform standard for regional taxation, but without success.[52] It remains for the St. Petersburg lobby in the government and the Supreme Soviet to do its best to procure as large a federal allocation for the city as possible, but even with that extra help it is extremely unlikely that the city will be able to avoid a severe financial crisis by the summer of 1993.

Conclusion

The character and direction of change in St. Petersburg is greatly influenced by developments in Russia as a whole, although it possesses its own specific characteristics. The experience of recent years suggests that economic and political developments in St. Petersburg are subsequently reproduced, albeit in softer contours, in other regions of the country and, for this reason, we should pay particular attention to the process and consequences of economic reform in the city. The social and economic consequences of the restructuring of the city's economy, and the accompanying unemployment, may be far greater than anyone can foresee. From 1991 onward the city experienced a sharper fall in its standard of living than elsewhere, a more rapid distribution of property, accompanied by corruption and protectionism, and a rise in crime against the background of slowly increasing unemployment. The result may be social upheavals of a kind for which neither the municipal nor the federal authorities are prepared.

The democratic elections of the new municipal organs—the city soviet and the mayor—the development of new political parties, the existence of independent means of communication, and the beginnings of the privatization of state and municipal enterprises created the preconditions for the city's overcoming the crisis facing it in the early eighties and embarking on economic development and a new political future. The changes that took place, however, did not transform society in any real sense. They represented little more than an unhealthy adaptation on the part of the existing socioeconomic and political structures to a changing situation. The adaptation was accompanied by a change in symbols, and by the replacement of an official ideology with the free exchange of a wide range of opinions. Political freedom became a reality. The original political institutions either disappeared (the Communist Party) or were transformed (the soviet), but none of this had any significant impact on the way the municipal economy was managed. In this sphere the way political power was exercised saw little change.

At the beginning of 1993 a significant number of politicians and observers saw new elections on a multiparty basis as a way out of the crisis. It is more realistic, however, to recognize that even if such elections do take place it will be some time before the legitimate authorities can overcome their weakness as policy makers and rulers. Even if a majority party should emerge as the victor, it is difficult to imagine its having the resources to carry out its program; furthermore, the city lacks (as does Russia in general) an effective civil service, operating on a bureaucratic and not a clientist basis. The struggle over the redistribution of resources is taking place in an environment in which both social organizations and municipal authorities are weak. This in turn encourages resorting to illegal and strong-arm methods to solve conflicts, and may produce a situation that the authorities will be unable to control. Political and economic democracy still remains a hope rather than a reality.

Notes

1. In 1991 the population included 1.7 million pensioners and invalids (*Nevskii kur'er*, 1991, no. 5, p. 6). For background on the city in the 1980s, see B. Ruble, *Governing Leningrad* (Berkeley: University of California Press, 1990); "Konseptsiia razvitiia Leningradskogo regiona v usloviakh radikal'noi reformy," Leningrad, FBT Leningradskaia, March 23, 1990 (unpublished working paper). The authors wish to thank both the British Academy and the Nuffield Foundation for funding a larger project in which political developments in St. Petersburg play a part, and colleagues at the Institute of Sociology, RAN, St. Petersburg, including in particular A. Alekseev, the director of the St. Petersburg Archival Collection, Sector of Social Movements, for help with documentation.

2. The best account is still "Obshchestvennye dvizheniia i stanovlenie novoi vlasti v Leningrade (1986–1991). Predvaritel'nye materialy," (unpublished working paper), Sector of the Sociology of Social Movements, Institute of Sociology, Academy of Sciences, St. Petersburg, 1991. See also N. Kornev, "The Leningrad People's Front," *Russia and the World*, 1991, no. 19, pp. 26–29; Mary McAuley, "Politics, Economics, and Elite Realignment in Russia: A Regional Perspective," *Soviet Economy*, vol. 8 (1992), no. 1, pp. 46–88; P. Duncan, "The return of St. Petersburg," in G. Hosking, J. Ayes, P. Duncan, eds., *The Road to Post-Communism*, Pinter, 1992; Robert W. Ortturg, "St. Petersburg: Economic Reform and Democratic Institutions," *RFE/RL Research Reports*, vol. 1, no. 16 (April 17, 1992); Jo Andrews and Alexandra Vacroux, "Political Change in Leningrad: The Elections of 1990," in this volume.

3. Of the 33 seats for the Russian parliament, 25 were won by the democrats. Gidaspov, the obkom secretary, requested a meeting of the Communist Party faction but was rebuffed. See McAuley, "Politics, Economics." Of the 250 deputies elected to the oblast soviet, only about 20 were supported by the democratic movement. As in other regions the oblast soviet was a more conservative body than the city soviet, but as noted in this chapter political differences were not responsible for the conflicts between the two bodies.

4. For the manifesto of the People's Front, *Nevskii kur'er,* 1990, no. 2, p. 7; on discussion of the Front's future after April, *Nevskii kur'er,* 1990, no. 8, p. 1; see also no. 9, pp. 1–3, for Filippov on views among the deputies that any person holding a post in the soviet should be nonparty, and that individuals were elected personally to fight the apparatus.

5. We do not deal with the emergence of a variety of minor parties in the city since during 1990–92 they did not influence political developments within the city.

6. Housing, as we have shown, was an issue that produced new divisions among political allies.

7. The struggle over control of the TV station became a *cause célèbre* in April 1990 when Petrov, director of the station, blocked an interview with Ivanov, the well-known prosecutor and All-Union deputy, and a group of deputies advocated direct action to gain control of the station. See *Smena,* April 6, 1991, p. 1; April 7, p. 1; April 9, p. 1; *Leningradskaia pravda,* April 6, 1990, pp. 1, 3; April 7, p. 1. Ownership of Lenizdat, originally the Soviet publishing house but taken over by the party in 1947, became a highly contentious issue in June 1990, and remained so until August 1991.

8. Interviews with deputies, September 1990; *Nevskoe vremia,* November 7, 1991, p. 4.

9. Kramarev received 218 votes to Voshchinin's 100 at the Lensovet session; see *Vechernii Leningrad,* November 14, 1990, p. 1; November 15, p. 2; *Smena,* November 15, 1990, p. 2.

10. *Nevskii kur'er,* 1990, no. 6, pp. 1–2, and for a description of a preparatory meeting by a small group of deputies in the Writers' House.

11. *Smena,* May 24, 1990, p. 1, for Sobchak's appointment. For Sobchak more generally, see also: A. Sobchak, *Khozhdenie vo vlast',* Moscow, 1991. The deputies received 150 rubles a month while retaining their place of work and salary; the first session ran nearly full-time until the end of June. Thereafter it was agreed to hold short sessions of a few days each, initially bimonthly, and then monthly (see *Vestnik Lensoveta,* 1991 [1], pp. 6–13, for the sessions and decisions taken: April 1990–May 1991).

12. Shchelkanov interview, November 1992. For his election: *Smena,* June 19, 1990, p. 1; *Chas pik,* June 25, 1990, p. 1; for conflict between the two chairmen, see *Vechernii Leningrad,* September 19, 1990, p. 2; *Smena,* September 16, pp. 2–3; LenTV, September 17, 20, reported the conflict in interviews with deputies and with Sobchak.

13. *Vestnik Lensoveta,* 1991 (2), pp. 3–17 for the relevant rulings, election data, and Sobchak's acceptance speech. See also *Nevskoe vremia,* June 20, 1991, p. 1; June 27, p. 1.

14. *Nevskii kur'er,* 1991, no. 1, p. 1 for the different proposals for reorganization at the end of 1990; *Vestnik Lensoveta* 1991 (2), pp. 43–44, for the election of the presidium and of the chairman.

15. Paper by Alekseev, Gel'man, Beliak, et al., Institute of Sociology, RAN, St. Petersburg, summarized in *Smena,* September 16, 1990, pp. 2–3.

16. "Obshchestvennye dvizheniia," p. 29.

17. A satirical TV report had Vasil'evskii Island declaring independence, setting up customs, raising its flag, and so forth.

18. Interviews with M. Gornyi (Lensovet), O. Zdasiuk (Kuibyshev District [raion] Soviet); *Vechernii Leningrad,* August 1, 1990, p. 1; August 30, p. 2; September 20, p. 2; *Moskovskie zastava,* 1990, no. 7, p. 4, for an appeal to the Lensovet from the presidium of the raisoviet for a delineation of power; no. 10, p. 3, for a speech by its chairman, V. Malyshev, at the Lensovet objecting to its usurpation of power.

19. For the Lensovet decision "O razgranichenii polnomochii mezhdu Lensovetom i raionnymi sovetami" of January 4, 1991, *Vestnik Lensoveta,* 1991 (1), p. 37.

20. The Vasil'evskii Island District Soviet, for example, passed a vote of no confidence in the head of the district administration and requested that Sobchak replace him; Sobchak, in turn, proposed that the district soviet elect a new chair, and the conflict lasted for more than a year. See *Sankt-Peterburgskie vedomosti,* December 2, 1992, p. 1; *Vechernii Peterburg,* January 22, 1993, p. 2.

21. Only 23 percent of the respondents to a telephone survey, conducted in February 1991, expressed any confidence in the soviet (*Leningradskaia pravda,* February 20, 1991, p. 2), but no more than 20 percent were in favor of its resignation (*Smena,* February 19, 1991, p. 2).

22. "O prognoze i vazhneishikh pokazateliakh plana kompleksnogo ekonomicheskogo i sotsial'nogo razvitiia Leningrada na 1991 goda . . . ," Reshenie Leningradskogo gorodskogo soveta, no. 2 (February 26, 1991), *Vestnik Lensoveta,* 1991 (1), pp. 14–15.

23. *Leningradskaia zona svobodnogo predprinimatel'stva, dokumenty i materialy,* Leningrad, 1991; *Leningradskaia zona svobodnogo predprinimatel'stva, osnovnye kontseptsii,* Leningrad, 1991. See also: *Vechernii Leningrad,* August 1, 1990, p. 1, for the Lensovet commission under Beliaev; *Nevskoe vremia,* February 7, 1991, p. 2, for a comment by A. Chubais; *Vestnik Lensoveta,* 1991 (3), pp. 55–60, for the Russian government's decision.

24. A report in *Nevskoe vremia,* March 14, 1991, p. 2, suggested 80 percent.

25. A. Veretin, N. Miloserdova, G. Petrov, eds., *Protivostoianie,* St. Petersburg, 1992, for the most complete documentary account; see also Sobchak, *Khozhdenie vo vlast',* 2d ed.

26. Although the referendum in June had gone in favor, by a small majority, of returning to "St. Petersburg," this had no legal force. After the failed putsch, the Presidium of the RSFSR Supreme Soviet, September 6, 1991, ratified the name change.

27. The structure and functioning of the mayor's office requires a treatment in its own right. Limitations of space preclude an analysis of both soviet and mayor's office in any detail; we concentrate primarily on the soviet in this chapter because it existed throughout the period and because its fortunes are more revealing of different aspects of the changing political situation. In September 1991, following the creation of the post of presidential representative at the regional level, Iurii Iarov, chairman of the oblast soviet and deputy to the Russian parliament, was appointed to the post in St. Petersburg. In November 1991, however, he was elected as deputy chairman of the Supreme Soviet, and his replacement, Sergei Tsyplaev, a physicist and former USSR deputy, was appointed only in September 1992. During the period with which we are concerned the office was largely vacant.

28. For the members of the *malyi sovet,* see *Vechernii Peterburg,* January 25, 1992, p. 1; on the election, *Vechernii Peterburg,* January 16, 1992, p. 1; *Smena,* January 15, 1992, p. 1; M. Dmitriev, V. Ludin, in *Reiting,* 1992, no. 5, p. 6.

29. Ten members of the People's Front and March factions, four from the Free Democratic Party, two from the combined Social Democratic and Republican parties, and twelve who did not belong to any faction were elected. See *Reiting,* 1992, no. 5, p. 6.

30. "O poriadke gosudarstvennoi registratsii predpriiatii i fizicheskikh lits, zanimaiushchikhsia predprinimatel'skoi deiatel'nost'iu," Decision of the Little Soviet, no. 102, April 23, 1992, (*Vestnik Sankt-Peterburgskogo gorodskogo soveta,* 1992, no. 8, pp. 51–57); "O dopolnitel'nykh merakh po organizatsii ulichnoi melkoroznichnoi torgovli," Decision of the Little Soviet, no. 214 (July 3, 1992), (*Vestnik Sankt-Peterburgskogo gorodskogo soveta,* 1992, no. 10, pp. 46–54).

31. In autumn 1992, for example, when Colonel Viktor Cherkesov, who had been involved in investigations of dissidents in the 1980s, was appointed as head of administration of the Ministry of State Security (KGB), the soviet registered a protest and appealed to the president to revoke the appointment (*Smena,* November 21, 1992, p. 1; *Nevskoe vremia,* November 21, p. 1).

32. The draft law proposed a series of restrictions on the powers of the mayor (making the post similar to that of "the weak mayor" in the American system). It reached the Supreme Soviet but was not discussed. For the text: *Vestnik Lensoveta,* 1991 (6), pp. 19–29; see also *Vechernii Peterburg,* October 2, 1991, p. 1; October 3, p. 1; October 15, p. 1; *Smena,* October 2, p. 1; October 3, p. 1.

33. *Rossiiskaia gazeta,* March 20, 1992, pp. 4–6.

34. *Vechernii Peterburg,* March 31, 1992, p. 1; *Smena,* March 30, 1992, p. 1; March 31, 1992, p. 1; *Nevskoe vremia,* March 31, 1992, p. 1.

35. The conflict between Sobchak and the soviet also reached the courts which, of itself, can be considered a positive development. In March, to give but one example, the soviet had annulled an instruction from the mayor that the administration of justice be included within the structure of the legal committee of the mayor's office. The mayor appealed to the court but on July 4, 1992, the city court rejected the claim. V. Gel'man, "Politicheskii protsess v Sankt-Peterburge (Iiul' 1992)," in "Politicheskii monitoring," 1992, no. 6, pp. 139–48 (Institut gumanitarno-politicheskikh issledovanii, Moscow).

36. V. Gel'man, "Politicheskii protsess . . . Ianvar'–fevral' 1992," in "Politicheskii monitoring," demonstration issue, 1992. See also *Sankt-Peterburgskie vedomosti,* November 18, 1992, p. 5; *Smena,* November 18, p. 1.

37. As a consequence of the privatization of the bakery industry, the supplying of bread to the city came into private hands but the retail network remained under the municipal authorities. They could no longer ensure that bread reached the shops, and the supply system was disrupted. See Gel'man, "Politicheskii monitoring," 1992, no. 10; *Nevskoe vremia,* November 24, 1992, p. 1; *Sankt-Peterburgskie vedomosti,* November 20, p. 1; November 26, p. 3; December 31, p. 2; *Vechernii Peterburg,* November 19, p. 1; *Smena,* December 30, p. 1.

38. In accordance with the law "On the Privatization of State and Municipal Enterprises . . ." (*Rossiiskaia gazeta,* July 17, 1991, pp. 2–3), committees for the management of property have jurisdiction over the property of state and municipal enterprises, organize the preparatory stages of privatization, and the procedures to be followed; committees exist at both central and regional level as part of the state administrative structure. The sale of enterprises, being privatized, is carried out by the Property Funds—agencies set up by, and subordinate to, the soviets.

39. Gel'man, "Politicheskii monitoring," 1992, no. 5; *Vechernii Peterburg,* May 14, 1992, p. 1.

40. Interview with A. Kokh, deputy chairman of the *KUGI,* in *Chas Pik,* 1992, no. 42, p. 7.

41. "O programme privatizatsii gosudarstvennykh i munitsipal'nykh predpriiatii v Sankt-Peterburge na 1992 god," Decision of the Malyi Soviet, no. 40, February 25, 1991, in *Vestnik Sankt-Peterburgskogo gorodskogo soveta narodnykh deputatov,* 1992, no. 5–6, pp. 3–153.

42. Gel'man, "Politicheskii monitoring," 1992, no. 5; *Sankt-Peterburgskie vedomosti,* July 3, 1992, p. 1.

43. *Vechernii Peterburg,* December 1, 1992, p. 1; January 16, 1993.

44. Interviews with G. Tomchin (State Institute for the Problems of Privatization), and A. Shvedov (*KUGI*); see also interview with A. Fishkov, deputy director, St. Petersburg Property Fund, in *Nevskoe vremia,* August 25, 1992, p. 2.

45. *Smena,* April 17, 18, 1991, p. 1; *Leningradskaia pravda,* April 17, 18, 19, pp. 1, 3; *Nevskoe vremia,* April 18, 20, p. 1.

46. *Smena,* November 28, 1991, p. 1; *Vechernii Peterburg,* November 28, 1991, p. 1.

47. The amendments were published in *Rossiiskaia gazeta,* January 10, 1993, p. 5.

48. In 1990 the soviet had faced a budget deficit of 6 billion rubles, if the federal contribution was discounted; the budget for 1991 was passed only at the end of February, once the federal tax regulations were known (*Vestnik Lensoveta,* 1991 [1], pp. 26–31). For the budget for the second half of 1992: *Smena,* October 8, 1992, p. 1.

49. *Vechernii Peterburg,* October 28, 1992, p. 1; December 8, 1992, p. 2; *Nevskoe vremia,* December 8, 1992, p. 2; December 10, p. 2.

50. "Sotsial'no-ekonomicheskoe razvitie Sankt-Peterburga i Leningradskoi oblasti v ianvare–noiabre 1992 goda," St. Petersburg Committee for Statistics, St. Petersburg, 1992.

51. For state employees in the nonindustrial sector salaries ranged from 3,882 rubles in culture, education, and health to 11,154 rubles in credit and insurance institutions; in industry wages were generally higher. A family budget survey carried out during January–September 1992 suggested that family incomes had risen 6.6 times in the city and 8 times in the oblast; expenditure had risen accordingly. The structure of expenditure has changed. Outlays for food increased 9.3 times, children's preschool care 8.2 times, while expenditure on durable consumer goods increased only 4.5 times. The average St. Petersburg family was spending 54 percent of its income on food, 24 percent on other consumer goods, 8 percent on services, 8 percent on taxes, and 6 percent on other items. Ibid.

52. Beliaev in *Vechernii Peterburg,* January 13, 1993, p. 1; on the differential budget policy toward regions, see also *Izvestiia,* January 5, 1993, pp. 1–2.

2

Political Change in Leningrad
The Elections of 1990

Jo Andrews and Alexandra Vacroux

Introduction

In this chapter we analyze the results of the March 1990 elections to the Lensovet, the Leningrad city council. Given the lack of demographic information about the electorate, we cannot ask why individual voters voted the way they did, so we ask instead why some candidates fared better than others. The use of regression analysis allows us to weigh the influence of various characteristics of the candidates—their age, gender, occupation, and, most interestingly, their affiliation with a reformist political group—and thereby investigate the relative importance of these factors to voters in Leningrad.

Ours is an exploratory study, based on the results of a single local election. Nevertheless, our empirical findings are striking and highlight some interesting puzzles for further study. We show conclusively that candidates who were backed by democratic political groups, even if they also belonged to the Communist Party, received overwhelmingly more votes than other candidates.[1] We also find that candidates who were employed by the Communist Party—that is, candidates who were members of the apparatus—were neither hurt nor helped by this fact. These findings raise several questions. Given the success of reform-oriented candidates in Leningrad, it is hard to understand how voters could remain indifferent to the Communist candidates. Our finding that members of the Communist Party apparatus did neither better nor worse on average than other candidates appears even more striking in light of our findings regarding members of other institutions of state power. Voters responded positively to candidates from both the KGB and the executive branch (*ispolkom*) of the local soviets. How could voters indifferent to Communist Party candidates support organizations that were either under the control of the Communist Party (as were the executive committees)[2] or had played a historic role in supporting the Communist regime (as had the KGB)?

We have organized our paper into several sections. In the next section, we describe the Leningrad city election and review the work of scholars who have analyzed other elections in the former Soviet Union. We briefly outline the rules that governed the election and nomination processes in the then Russian Republic (RSFSR). In the background section, we provide details of the political situation in March 1990 and discuss the political positions of the various pre-electoral political groups that came into existence at the time of the election. Next, we discuss the data on which our analysis is based, and outline the methodology employed in our analysis. We have separate sections to discuss the dependent variable as well as our two key categories of explanatory variables: political affiliation and personal characteristics. Lastly, we discuss the results of the regression analysis and highlight our findings in the concluding section.

General Description of the 1990
Local Elections in Leningrad

The election of 400 deputies to the city soviet was one of four elections in which Leningrad residents participated in the spring of 1990; voters were also asked to elect deputies to the RSFSR Congress of People's Deputies, the Leningrad regional (*oblast*) soviet, and the urban district (*raion*) soviets.

These elections were competitive in that most electoral districts for the first time offered choices among candidates. In addition, in certain of the local elections, voters had access to information about the different political positions of some or all of the candidates.

Several Russian cities, including Leningrad, saw the rise of political associations even before the 1990 elections. Finding a haven in the new era of *perestroika,* groups organized around specific issues such as the environment, Stalinist repression, and nationalism. While few of these groups in 1989 played any real role in the pseudocompetitive[3] elections for the USSR Congress of People's Deputies, Michael Urban identified at least one political organization, Elections '89, that united several political groupings in Leningrad to promote democratically inclined candidates.[4] Despite the fact that Article 6 of the USSR Constitution in effect outlawed political parties other than the Communist Party, these groups, especially those dedicated to achieving political change, continued to multiply up to the 1990 elections.

Such groups influenced the elections to the RSFSR Congress of People's Deputies and to the city councils in many large cities, most notably in Moscow, Leningrad, and Sverdlovsk.

Research on elections held in a number of Russian cities and regions suggests that there was great variation in how much influence reform-oriented groups had on the 1990 elections. In his study of the 1990 elections to the Moscow City Soviet, Timothy Colton discovered that reform-oriented political groups adapted quickly to the new political environment and were better organized than either the Communists or right-wing groups.[5] Putting aside their differences, reformers joined forces under the umbrella of Democratic Russia which, in Colton's words, acted as a "quasi-party" for the purposes of the election, and even published a list of endorsed candidates. This strategy was successful, and candidates supported by Democratic Russia won a majority of the 498 seats in the city legislature. In Leningrad, democratically oriented candidates came together under the banner of Democratic Elections '90 and were, as in Moscow, successful in garnering a majority of the seats on the city soviet.

In a few other cities and regions voters were able to identify reform-oriented candidates, and in a few cases sizable minorities were elected; this was true in the Yaroslavl city and oblast soviets,[6] and in the Volgograd Oblast Soviet.[7] In many cities and regions no political groups or associations existed other than the Communist Party; in others, such as Kostroma,[8] or Arkhangelsk and Perm,[9] the existence of such groups had no effect on the elections, perhaps because candidates did not associate themselves either with or against reforms. Apart from studies of a handful of cities, we know very little about most of the elections to the regional and city soviets. While we believe that our findings are relevant to broader studies of Russian political reform, without similar analyses of elections in other Russian cities and regions we can only speculate on the comparability of our findings with the results of elections across Russia.

Political scientists analyze election results to understand better the electorate of a city, region, or country. Examining the political and personal characteristics of successful and unsuccessful candidates enables a researcher to draw conclusions about voters' political values and preferences. Ideally, researchers also have access to exit polls and demographic data that can provide additional clues to explain why voters chose certain candidates and not others. To our knowledge, exit polls of Russian voters were not conducted in the 1990 elections, nor is a sufficiently detailed level of demographic information on the electorate available. Therefore, our analysis of the Leningrad election relies on information available through newspapers and in interviews with a small sample of voters conducted over the course of three years after the 1990 elections.

The absence of formal political parties presents an additional complication in this study. In an established party system, voters depend primarily on candidates' party affiliations to decide for whom they will or will not vote; political scientists interpreting election results can thus safely assume that a key determinant of candidate success will be his or her political affiliation. In 1990, however, candidates were not allowed to belong to political groups other than the Communist Party. Instead, candidates endorsed or were endorsed by the political groups that were active in pre-election campaigning. Was candidate affiliation with a political group a key determinant of candidate success? The answer to this question will enable us to determine whether the Leningrad groups acted as political parties in the last Soviet elections, despite constitutional prohibitions against pluralist politics.

In other statistical studies of recent Soviet elections, researchers have concluded that a candidate's political and professional profile affects how he or she fared in an election. Kiernan and Aistrup[10] offer evidence that, at least in Moscow, supporting Yeltsin may have increased a candidate's chances of winning either the first or second round of the 1989 election to the USSR Congress of People's Deputies. Colton[11] discovered that certain personal and professional characteristics affected how a candidate fared in the 1990 city soviet elections in Moscow. However, neither of these studies assesses how an individual candidate's alignment with the new democratic groups affected his or her performance in the election.[12] Our analysis of the first competitive elections in Leningrad since 1917 focuses on this very issue.[13]

Rules of the Election

It is important to keep in mind that in all elections the rules that govern how candidates are nominated have an impact on the results. The 1989 elections to the USSR Congress of People's Deputies were controlled mostly by the Communist Party and related organizations. At that time, according to the laws governing the nomination of candidates, "public organizations"— the Communist Party, official trade unions, the Komsomol, and conservative organizations such as the National Academy of Sciences—were allotted a certain number of seats. In many such cases, only a single candidate or at best two similar candidates were nominated for the seat. The only way that these candidates could be defeated was if a majority of voters crossed the name(s) off the ballot so that no candidate received 50 percent of the votes cast. After a great deal of public outcry, especially in Moscow, some independent organizations were granted the right to nominate candidates, although the number of these seats was small. The practice of setting aside seats for public organizations was viewed by the public, and even by many of the deputies elected to the USSR Congress of People's Deputies, as unfair.

Prior to the 1990 Russian elections, the law pertaining to the nomination of candidates was changed by the outgoing RSFSR Supreme Soviet.[14] According to articles 10 and 34 of the new law on elections, nominations could come from three sources: the workplace, social organizations, and convocations of voters within a district. In addition, the practice of setting aside seats for "social organizations" was abolished. Even so, given that most nominations came from the workplace, and given the ubiquitous presence of Communist Party apparatchiki in the upper echelons of enterprise management, there were plenty of opportunities for the Communist Party to attempt to influence the nomination of candidates.

In all elections held in Russia in 1990, as in all elections held in the Soviet Union since 1936, voters cast their ballot by crossing off those candidates they did not want. Thus, to vote *for* a candidate, a voter had to cross off the names of all other candidates. In the past, voters had the option of crossing off the single name on the ballot or letting it stand. Due to the complete lack of privacy accorded to voters under the old system, most voters chose to put the ballot, unmarked, directly into the ballot box, thereby "voting" for the single candidate listed on the ballot. In the new competitive elections, voters had the choice of crossing off either all candidates on the list, thereby voting for "none of the above," or all but one. Curtained voting booths or some other private areas were provided, and apparently used. Any ballot having two or more candidates unmarked was considered invalid. According to the RSFSR Law on Elections,[15] a winning candidate had to receive over half of the votes cast in his or her district, and at least 50 percent of a district's registered voters had to have turned out for the election round. In the (frequent) event that no candidate received the requisite proportion of positive votes, first and second place finishers advanced to a second round held along the same principles, except that a candidate now had to receive only a plurality of votes cast in order to win. If voter turnout in any round of the election did not reach 50 percent of the registered voters, or when one candidate ran but did not receive at least 50 percent of the votes cast, or when two candidates ran and neither received 50 percent of the votes, the election results, along with the candidates, were scrapped and an entirely new election was held. (In every district, "none of the above" received a substantial proportion of the votes, even winning in some cases.)

Background: Setting the Political Scene

St. Petersburg, Petrograd, Leningrad—the city founded by Peter the Great —has always been a haven for intellectuals and radical thinkers. Even during the Soviet period, as Blair Ruble describes,[16] the high-tech and defense industries that formed the base of Leningrad's economy attracted a good number of the Soviet Union's best technical people. The presence of Leningrad State University, second only to Moscow State University in national reputation, and many other renowned institutes of higher learning have ensured that a large number of academic professionals reside in Leningrad. People engaged in the work of these institutions—academics and technical specialists—formed the backbone of democratic political groups and the candidates they put forth in Leningrad.[17]

The weeks leading up to the 1990 elections were a time of learning for all political groups in Leningrad. Having witnessed the surprising and highly publicized defeats of the Leningrad Communist Party first secretary and five of his senior officials in the 1989 elections to the USSR Congress of People's Deputies,[18] the regional Communist Party committee (or *obkom*) understood the danger of competitive elections. Despite this realization, the local party leadership remained divided and unable to present a unified political position or program in the 1990 elections. According to Mary McAuley, "All the *obkom* could do was try to salvage something from the forthcoming elections ... by dividing the opposition and hampering and discrediting its opponents."[19] In the face of unified democratic opposition, this strategy was unsuccessful. No longer granted a certain number of seats by law or by custom, and unable to rely on control of the press, the party apparatus had even less control over the electoral process than it had in the 1989 elections to the USSR Congress of People's Deputies.[20] Revealing its inexperience in the arena of competitive public politics, the Communist Party was outperformed by the democrats.

How did voters get information about candidates? Interviews with Leningrad voters indicated that residents learned about the elections from several sources. As in Moscow,[21] Leningrad was littered with posters, and more energetic candidates stood in metro stations or on street corners in the early morning, late afternoon, and on weekends giving speeches.[22] Along with such direct appeals from candidates, most residents would have observed some of the candidates' televised debates that were shown several times a week before the elections, though a voter would have to have made a special effort to find and watch the debate for his or her electoral district. Candidates who were aligned with a particular political platform mentioned this affiliation during the televised debates, and all candidates answered questions from the audience. But despite obvious differences among candidates, in the spotlight of the television cameras almost all candidates said that they were for freedom and a market economy and against the privileges of the *nomenklatura*. Consequently, people probably learned little about the true political positions of the candidates from these sessions, even if viewer interest was high.

In February 1990 the local Komsomol newspaper *Smena* published information on several informal groups that represented a range of political views. These political positions were called "pre-election platforms," suggesting the idea of political parties, though these groups were not parties in the formal sense of the word—at best, they were active organizations of like-minded individuals seeking to influence the March elections. (No candidate, once elected, owed allegiance to any of these groups, even if he or she had been endorsed by one of them. After the elections, many of the pre-election political groups played no role or only a short-lived role within the city soviet.) Later in February, *Smena* published a list of all candidates who were supported by or who themselves supported any of these pre-electoral platforms. At that time, *Smena* was one of the most popular official daily newspapers in Leningrad, and the platforms and lists of candidates endorsed by each platform were most likely seen by many of Leningrad's five million residents.[23]

Nineteen pre-election political platforms were published in the February 9, 1990, issue of *Smena*. The most important of these was "*DemVybory '90*" or "Democratic Elections '90" (DE '90) an association of democratic forces in Leningrad. Dozens of organizations and groups participated in this association and lent it their support, including the Leningrad People's Front, the Union of Leningrad Voters (SIL) and Club of Voters, the Memorial and Survivors of the Leningrad Blockade societies, the Democratic platform of the CPSU, workers' clubs, creative unions, a union of scholars, the Perestroika club, the independent trade unions Unity and Justice, social-democratic groups, Leningrad Tribune, the Union of Greens, and other ecological groups, the Group of Salvation, World Watch, medical associations, and ethnic-cultural and Christian societies. These groups joined forces to try to ensure that candidates committed to reform would be elected in the March elections. The alliance's main political goals were as follows: to bring union and republican legislation into full conformity with the Universal Declaration of Human Rights; to abolish Article 6 of the USSR and RSFSR constitutions, which stipulated the Communist Party of the Soviet Union's leading role in organizing society; to guarantee the freedom to form social associations, including political parties and free trade unions; to guarantee freedom of speech and freedom of the press; to establish the national and economic sovereignty of the RSFSR; to guarantee "equality of rights" to various forms of property by demonopolizing the economy; to grant the right to own land; to give high priority to ecology; and to carry out democratization of the local and republic soviets.

The platforms of several other political groups that supported democratic reforms and a market economy appeared in *Smena*, which joined in overall support for DE '90. Thus, although the platform of the Leningrad People's Front was printed separately in *Smena*, this group also joined the DE '90 coalition.

The platforms of other democratically oriented groups were essentially the same as those espoused by DE '90. If a group supported DE '90, or if it espoused its basic goals, we considered it to be a democratic group; all others were treated as non–democratically oriented groups. Although the Democratic Platform of the Communist Party did not submit a written summary of its political platform, it did appear in the lists of groups supported by individual candidates. Based on articles in the national press and on published pamphlets available from the organization itself, we treated the CPSU Democratic Platform as democratically oriented.

Non–democratically oriented groups included the United Front of Leningrad Workers and the Fatherland patriotic society, both of which espoused a nationalist version of communism. Neither the Leningrad Komsomol nor the Communist Party provided a statement of their political positions, probably assuming that voters were already familiar with the official annual programs that had been published in earlier editions of *Smena* and other local and national newspapers.

In the same issue that carried the pre-election political platforms, *Smena* called on pre-election groups and individual candidates to come forward and indicate to the newspaper which candidates they endorsed (in the case of groups) or which groups they supported (in the case of candidates).[24] In explaining their reasons for printing the pre-electoral platforms, the editors of *Smena* stated that they wished to inform the electorate and to provide candidates and groups with an opportunity to associate themselves publicly with one another. According to residents interviewed by us, the lists of candidates affiliated with the different political platforms (published in the March 2, 1990, issue of *Smena*) were widely used by interested voters as guidelines for deciding whom to support.

The Data

In addition to the information published in *Smena*, much of the data on which this paper is based—the personal characteristics for all candidates and the election results for each district—were published in the newspaper *Vechernii Leningrad*. Pre-election listings of candidates (by district) included their name, gender,[25] year of birth, occupation, employer, city of residence, and whether they were a member of the Communist Party, Komsomol, or unaffiliated with either (*bespartiinyi*). In the early months of 1990, this latter category was synonymous with non-membership in the Communist Party.

Results of each round of the elections provided the number of registered voters and voter turnout for each electoral district. Each candidate's performance was broken down into the number and percentage of "yes" (*za*) votes received.

In this paper, we concentrate on the results of the first round of the elections. It was in this round that the largest number and variety of candidates competed, and therefore variation in the percentage of votes received was also at its greatest.[26] In all, 2,503 candidates participated in the first round of the Leningrad elections, 2,502 of whom were used in this analysis.[27] The large number of candidates affected the election by reducing the likelihood that many candidates would win the first round of the election, and indeed, only 31 did so. The number of candidates running in each district ranged from 1 to 17, the average being 6.3 candidates per district (see Figure 2.1). For each additional candidate running in a district, every candidate in that district could expect to receive about 1.6 percent fewer votes.[28] Candidates running against two other competitors (for a total of 3 candidates) received about 5 percent fewer votes than if they had run unopposed; candidates running against 6 competitors received about 12 percent fewer votes; and candidates running against 10 others received about 18 percent fewer votes than they would have, had they run unopposed.

We can suppose that so many candidates entered the race as a result of several factors, including high public interest, the nomination process, and perhaps most significantly, the absence of political parties. If political parties had participated in these elections, not only would candidates have supported coherent party programs, but parties would have approached the election strategically, placing no more than one of their ranks in each district, and ensuring that at least one representative competed in every district. Although Democratic Elections '90 endorsed 542 of the 2,502 candidates who competed in the elections, there were 18 districts in which no DE '90 candidate ran, 103 districts in which two of their candidates competed against each other, and 32 in which more than two competed. The leaders of DE '90 could not have known in advance that support for their candidates would be so high. By endorsing so many candidates, they may have been hedging their bets, hoping that at least one DE '90 candidate in each district

Figure 2.1. **Distribution of Candidates per District**

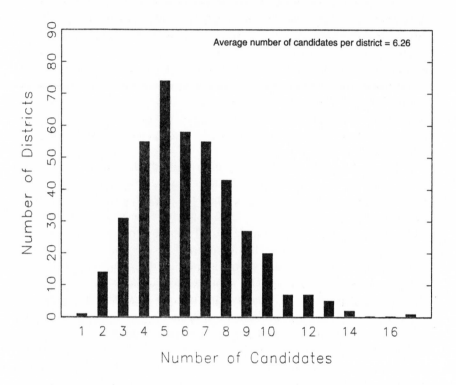

Source: January and February 1990 issues of *Vechernii Leningrad*.

would appeal to a plurality of voters. It is also important to remember that DE '90 was a political platform, not a political party, and its organizational resources were limited.

The Communist Party apparatus also failed to place its candidates strategically. One hundred nineteen members of the Communist Party competed in 107 districts. Even though in only ten districts did two Communist Party candidates compete against each other, and in only one district did more than two candidates (three) run against each other, there were nevertheless 293 districts in which no member of the party apparatus competed. The Communist Party seems to have been unprepared for competitive elections and deeply ignorant as to the extent of voter discontent with the economic and political goals of communism. Perhaps they believed that no matter how many reform-oriented candidates ran, a sufficient number of conservative communists would win, as they had in the 1989 elections to the USSR Congress of People's Deputies. Recall, however, that in the 1989 elections the Communist Party was provided a certain number of seats by law. Thus, due to lack of experience in truly competitive contests, and due to their lack of connection with the voters, the Communist Party, in effect, gave up the election without a fight.

A breakdown of personal characteristics for all candidates, for candidates endorsed by DE '90, and for winning candidates is presented in the three columns of Table 2.1. Interestingly, of the 2,502 candidates who ran, only 22 percent were endorsed by Democratic Elections '90; these candidates were among the most successful, however, and candidates endorsed by DE '90 made up 61 percent of the eventual winners. Of the original candidates, 1,732 (69 percent) were members of the Communist Party, as were 56 percent of the eventual election winners. About 12 percent (213) of the 1,732 Communists who ran were also endorsed by DE '90; these individuals were most likely members of the Democratic Platform of the CPSU.[29]

Given the nature of Communist Party–dominated Soviet society, separating a candidate's political affiliation from his or her occupation can be difficult. A candidate who works in the party apparatus, for example, automatically holds both a job and a specific political status. In addition, almost everyone holding a position equal to or higher than assistant director or engineer (in production), manager of a laboratory or department (in science), or dean (in academics) had to be a party member to attain that position. We chose to segregate occupational information from political information by using two different variables; a candidate who held an important position and was a member of the Communist Party was automatically registered as such in any regression analysis that took both occupational and political variables into account.

A large number of the candidates who went on to win either the first or second round of the election were engineers or scientific workers. Of the original 2,502 candidates, 19 percent (496) were engineers, technicians, and scientific workers in the combined industrial and scientific sectors. In contrast, of the 376 eventual winners of the first or second round of the elections, 117 (or 31 percent) were members of these occupations. The reason that engineers and technical specialists were so successful in these elections was that so many were endorsed by DE '90. Nearly 40 percent of the candidates endorsed by DE '90 were engineers, technicians, or scientific workers. Our regression analysis shows that it was endorsement by DE '90 that had the greatest influence on how many votes a candidate received in the first round of the election—not the fact that he or she was a member of these technically oriented professions. Exactly why so many of the reform-

Table 2.1

Characteristics of the Candidates

	All candidates entered		Candidates supported by DE '90		Winners of 1st or 2nd round	
	No.	(%)	No.	(%)	No.	(%)
Total candidates	2,502		542		376	
Age						
60 and over	122	(4.88)	15	(2.76)	4	(1.07)
50 – 59	784	(31.33)	161	(29.72)	102	(27.13)
40 – 49	864	(34.53)	164	(30.25)	134	(35.65)
30 – 39	606	(24.22)	160	(29.52)	117	(31.12)
Under 30	126	(5.04)	42	(7.75)	19	(5.05)
Gender						
Men	2,199	(87.89)	480	(88.56)	351	(93.35)
Women	303	(12.11)	62	(11.44)	25	(6.65)
Affiliation with Communist Party						
Member of CPSU	1,732	(69.22)	213	(39.30)	210	(55.85)
Member of Komsomol	37	(1.48)	13	(2.40)	6	(1.60)
No party affiliation	732	(29.26)	316	(58.30)	160	(42.55)
Association with Democratic Left						
Endorsed by Democratic Elections '90	542	(21.66)	N.A.		228	(60.64)
Endorsed democratic platform(s)[a]	483	(19.30)	323	(59.59)	159	(42.29)
Endorsed by Leningrad Komsomol	47	(1.88)	0		3	(.80)
Occupational Group						
Industrial/production sector						
Director	181	(7.23)	6	(1.11)	9	(2.39)
Assistant director, chief engineer	110	(4.40)	11	(2.03)	6	(1.60)
Head of shop or department	168	(6.71)	27	(4.98)	14	(3.72)
Engineer, technician, master craftsman	184	(7.35)	53	(9.78)	36	(9.57)
Worker	258	(10.31)	49	(9.04)	33	(8.78)
Total industrial sector	900	(35.96)				
Scientific sector						
Director	28	(1.12)	2	(.37)	4	(1.06)
Assistant director	22	(.88)	3	(.55)	2	(.53)
Manager of a laboratory, sector, or department	131	(5.24)	35	(6.46)	23	(6.12)
Scientific worker, engineer	310	(12.39)	159	(29.34)	80	(21.28)
Laboratory assistant						
Total scientific sector	499	(19.95)				

	No.	(%)	No.	(%)	No.	(%)
Education						
Rector of an institute	21	(.84)	0		1	(.27)
Dean, manager of faculty	33	(1.32)	7	(1.29)	6	(1.60)
Instructor, lecturer	127	(5.08)	38	(7.01)	33	(8.78)
Director of a school	33	(1.32)	3	(.55)	5	(1.33)
School teacher	29	(1.16)	10	(1.85)	5	(1.33)
Student	12	(.48)	4	(.74)	3	(.80)
Total education	252	(10.08)				
Medicine						
Director of a medical institute, hospital	47	(1.88)	2	(.37)	7	(1.86)
Doctor	19	(.76)	6	(1.11)	5	(1.33)
Total medicine	77	(3.08)				
Law enforcement						
Military						
Career military	61	(2.44)	10	(1.85)	14	(3.72)
Military (enlisted)	40	(1.60)	12	(2.21)	9	(2.39)
Militia (MVD)	55	(2.20)	3	(.55)	17	(4.52)
KGB	5	(.20)	0		2	(.53)
Judge, prosecutor	15	(.60)	5	(.92)	4	(1.06)
Total law enforcement	176	(7.04)				
Politics						
Apparatus of CPSU	119	(4.76)	3	(.55)	7	(1.86)
Apparatus of trade unions	47	(1.88)	2	(.37)	1	(.27)
Apparatus of Komsomol	20	(.80)	5	(.92)	3	(.80)
Organs of the soviets	103	(4.12)	5	(.92)	16	(4.26)
Total politics	289	(11.56)				
Culture						
Culture, general category including artists, actors, museum directors, etc.	72	(2.88)	23	(4.24)	2	(.53)
Press	40	(1.60)	16	(2.95)	7	(1.86)
Radio, television	12	(.48)	3	(.55)	3	(.80)
Private sector						
Directors, employees of cooperative or small enterprises	32	(1.28)	5	(.92)	2	(.53)
Service employees	33	(1.32)	0		1	(.27)
Pensioners	49	(1.96)	10	(1.85)	3	(.80)
Unemployed	22	(.88)	9	(1.66)	3	(.80)
Employees of social organizations or foundations	47	(1.88)	12	(2.21)	5	(1.33)
Miscellaneous (difficult to categorize)	7	(.28)	0		0	
Unknown	2	(.08)	0		1	(.27)

[a] Because many candidates were both endorsed by DE '90 and themselves endorsed either DE '90 or some other democratic platform, the totals for this subsection are greater than 100%.

minded candidates were members of technical professions is unclear, but makes an interesting contrast with Western democracies in which the lion's share of politicians are lawyers, business leaders, or bureaucrats. It may be that engineers and technical specialists, and even academics in scientific fields were less susceptible to Communist dogma and judged more on the merits of their work than on their adherence to Marxist-Leninist dogma. Perhaps such professional freedom bred a certain freedom of thought as well.

While one can draw general conclusions on the basis of summary data from Table 2.1, regression analysis is helpful in that it allows one to distinguish the relative importance of these many characteristics. The second half of this paper uses regression analysis to identify the personal or political characteristics that made candidates more or less attractive to voters. The results of the analysis allow us, in turn, to draw conclusions about voters' political attitudes in early 1990.

Methodology

In order to determine the relative importance of the characteristics summarized in Table 1, we employ ordinary least squares (OLS) regression analysis.[30] Regression analysis enables the researcher to account for the variation in a dependent variable (here, candidates' shares of the "yes" votes), controlling for several explanatory variables simultaneously. Least squares regression techniques allowed us to weigh the various factors that contributed to a candidate's success or failure in the electoral contest. The factors, or explanatory variables, were those candidate characteristics that voters knew, namely, the traits discussed above.

The Dependent Variable

Our goal is to identify the characteristics that contributed most to the aspiring deputies' success or failure. A natural choice for a measure of how a candidate fared in the election is the percentage of votes that he or she received in the first round. Values for this variable range from 0.28 percent to 82.6 percent, with a mean of 13.22 percent. Using this measure of performance as our dependent variable poses some problems. Because a given candidate's share of the vote depends on the share of the vote received by candidates in the same district against whom he or she is running, the percentage of votes a candidate receives cannot be considered independent of the percentage that another candidate in his or her same district receives. For example, if a candidate in District 1 received 50 percent of the "yes" votes cast, no other candidate in that district could receive more than 50 percent of the vote. This is a problem, since one of the assumptions of ordinary least squares regression analysis is that all values of the dependent variable are independent of one another. After testing, we found that adding a variable that captured the number of candidates running in each district was the most effective solution to this problem.[31]

Political Variables

The five political variables in our study cover whether or not a candidate was a member of the Communist Party or Komsomol, in addition to his or her unofficial affiliation with the informal groups that achieved prominence at the time of the elections.

The lists that identified candidates with pre-election platforms distinguished between candidates that were endorsed by particular groups and those that themselves supported groups. Of the nineteen pre-electoral platforms, only DE '90, the Union of Leningrad Voters (SIL), and one of the Green groups submitted to *Smena* lists of endorsed candidates, for a total of 557 candidates who were supported by at least one of these political platforms. Of these, 542 were supported by DE '90. Although SIL and the Green group espoused democratic goals, only the message of DE '90 can be assessed unambiguously. For this reason, as well as for the fact that only about 3 percent of those endorsed were endorsed by one of the other two groups, we concentrated on support by DE '90, rather than on support by a "democratic" platform. Our variable is thus called "endorsed by DE '90" in this analysis. Candidates themselves, however, supported a wide variety of platforms, the majority of which espoused democratic goals. Therefore, we also consider whether or not a candidate supported *any* democratic platform. This variable is referred to as "endorsed democratic platforms." Under this scheme, 483 candidates are classified as having endorsed a democratic platform.

We hypothesized that an endorsement from a given group would be more important to voters than the fact that a candidate personally supported a particular platform, the former being a more objective assessment of the political position of a given candidate. In addition, given that nearly all candidates were anxious to appear progressive and that they all said more or less the same things during televised pre-electoral meetings, it is logical that voters would look to endorsement by a third party for information about political views. To test this hypothesis, we treated these two forms of endorsement separately. A candidate's personal affiliation or lack thereof with a democratically oriented platform, and whether or not the platform supported the candidate, is captured through the use of two dummy variables.[32] A candidate's official affiliation with the Communist Party or Komsomol is summarized by four dummy variables, the first of which indicates whether the candidate was a member of the Communist Party, the second whether the candidate was a member of the Komsomol, and the third whether the candidate was unaffiliated with either the Communist Party or the Komsomol (i.e., the candidate was listed as *bespartiinyi*). The *bespartiinyi* variable was left out of the equation for purposes of estimation.[33] The fourth variable indicates whether a candidate was supported by the Komsomol. Before the election, *Vechernii Leningrad* published separately a list of candidates supported by the Leningrad Komsomol.

In assessing the impact of official membership in the Communist Party on how candidates fared in the election, it is important to keep in mind that in most cases, membership in the Communist Party was a prerequisite to obtaining a job above a certain level. Thus, to assess voters' attitudes toward the Communist Party, one would like to know how candidates who openly supported or were supported by the official Communist Party platform would have fared in the election. Unfortunately, the Communist Party did not publish a list of supported candidates, nor were many candidates in Leningrad willing to align themselves openly with the Communist Party official political platform. Voters' reactions to those candidates endorsed by the Komsomol may provide some insight into voters' attitudes toward the Communist Party. In our analysis, probably the best way to understand voters' attitudes toward the Communist Party is by examining how members of the Communist Party apparatus fared in the election. This question is discussed in the next section.

Personal Variables

There is less information available about the candidates in the Leningrad election than for any candidate in a Western election. While this is inconvenient from the perspective of Western political science, it is not a problem for our analysis of election results. When combined with the political information described above, the facts we have about a candidate's gender, residency, age, and employment represent the full range of information that was easily accessible to the average Leningrad voter.[34]

A candidate's gender was included as a dummy variable. A candidate's age was indicated in the newspaper by a reference to his or her year of birth. We recoded this variable into age by subtracting the year of birth from 1990, the year in which the elections were held.

Both the official job title and place of employment were listed for each candidate, providing a reasonably complete summary of occupation and employment status. Although it would be interesting to measure the varying effects of different types of occupations on voters' perceptions of candidates, the results of our analysis suggest that except for a few striking exceptions, a candidate's job played little or no role in determining whether voters chose him or her. Colton's study, in which he initially grouped the Moscow candidates into forty precise occupational categories, produced similar results. In his regression analysis, he found that while some occupations enhanced or detracted from the percentage of votes received by the Democratic Russia slate, the results of estimating the occupational variable clearly revealed the "messiness of voters' perceptions and of the resultant relationship between occupation and electability."[35]

Using the categories devised by Colton as a starting point, we came up with a series of broader occupational groupings. We then gave our coded variable to an advanced sociology student at Moscow State University and asked her to refine the categories in accordance with accepted Russian norms. She began by dividing occupations into spheres commonly used in Russian sociology—the industrial/production sector, sciences, education, medicine, law enforcement, and so on (see Table 2.1). Within these spheres, she classified respondents by professional hierarchy, a relatively simple task for anyone familiar with the Russian educational system, since more prestigious jobs usually require higher, specialized education. Where there were disagreements between our categories and her coding, we tended to adopt her interpretation, since we were trying to approximate Russian perceptions, not our own. Once we had defined the occupational categories, we treated each profession as a dummy variable with a value of one or zero.

Results of the Regression Analysis

The results of our regression analysis are presented in Table 2.2. When interpreting the results of regression analyses, one is interested mainly in the coefficient for a given variable. This coefficient is an estimate of how much, on the average—and controlling for the other explanatory variables —a unit increase in a particular variable affects the dependent variable. For instance, in equation (2), the coefficient for the variable "endorsed by DE '90" is 11.8, and we interpret this to mean that if a candidate was endorsed by DE '90, the percentage of votes he or she received was 11.8 percent higher on average than the candidate who was not endorsed by DE '90, controlling for the effects of all other explanatory variables. (Since "endorsed by DE '90" is a dummy variable, a unit increase from zero to one means that the candidate takes on the qualitative characteristic.) It is also important to look at the standard error of the coefficient (the number in parentheses). The standard error provides information about the precision of the estimated coefficient. The smaller the standard error, the more certain

Table 2.2

Results of Four Linear Regression Equations

	(1)		(2)		(3)		(4)[a]	
Intercept	33.24	(1.18)	25.26	(1.11)	23.07	(1.29)	22.96	(1.06)
Number of candidates in district [b]	−1.83	(−0.08)	−1.66	(0.07)	−1.64	(0.07)	−1.64	(0.06)
Age	−0.09	(−0.02)	−0.06	(0.02)	−0.05	(0.02)	−.05	(0.02)
Gender	−2.73	(0.62)	−2.07	(0.55)	−2.98	(0.54)	−2.98	(0.53)
Member CPSU	−3.50	(0.45)	0.41	(0.42)	−0.24	(0.44)		
Member Komsomol	−2.62	(1.75)	−0.67	(1.56)	−0.81	(1.54)		
Endorsed by DE '90			11.72	(0.53)	11.65	(0.52)	11.69	(0.50)
Endorses democratic platform(s)			1.16	(0.54)	0.97	(0.52)	.96	(0.51)
Endorsed by Leningrad Komsomol			−2.33	(1.38)	−2.26	(1.40)		
Occupational Group								
Production sector								
Director, asst. director, or chief engineer					−0.11	(0.76)		
Head of department					−0.35	(0.86)		
Engineer, technician, master craftsman					1.20	(0.84)	*1.18*	*(0.68)*
Worker					1.42	(0.77)	*1.41*	*(0.59)*
Scientific sector								
Director or asst. director					0.94	(1.32)		
Manager of laboratory or department					1.75	(0.92)	*1.73*	*(0.79)*
Scientific worker or engineer					1.49	(0.75)	*1.52*	*(0.58)*
Education								
Rector of institute					1.83	(1.93)		
Dean, head of faculty					4.71	*(1.57)*	*4.64*	*(1.50)*
Instructor, lecturer					4.35	*(0.93)*	*4.32*	*(0.80)*
Director of a school					7.64	*(1.57)*	*7.59*	*(1.50)*
School teacher					7.47	*(1.67)*	*7.48*	*(1.60)*
Student					4.43	(2.62)	4.06	(2.50)
Medicine								
Director of medical institute, hospital					6.26	(1.36)	6.19	(1.27)
Doctor, nurse					8.04	(2.02)	8.12	(1.96)
Military								
Career military					7.99	(1.22)	7.91	(1.11)
Military serviceman					4.51	(1.45)	4.43	(1.36)
Law enforcement								
Militia (MVD)					11.68	(1.28)	11.60	(1.17)
KGB					14.30	(3.82)	14.19	(3.78)
Judge, prosecutor					6.61	(2.25)	6.50	(2.20)
Politics								
Apparatus of CPSU					0.92	(0.98)		
Apparatus of trade unions					−0.94	(1.35)		

	(1)	(2)	(3)		(4)	
Apparatus of						
Komsomol			1.12	(2.11)		
Organs of the soviets			*5.67*	(1.01)	5.59	(0.87)
Culture						
Press			5.56	(1.44)	5.49	(1.37)
Radio, television			12.30	(2.51)	12.32	(2.47)
Private sector						
Directors, employees of cooperative or small enterprises			−0.94	(1.59)		
Miscellaneous (miscellaneous personnel in cultural and service sectors, employees of social organizations or foundations, the unemployed, pensioners, and two unknowns)			(Neutral category of dummy variables left out for purpose of estimation)			
Corrected R^b for this regression	0.22	0.39	0.45		0.45	
Standard error of regression	10.05	8.85	8.44		8.42	
N = 2502						

[a] We assumed that voters used all available information in making their choices among candidates, and that all political, personal, and professional variables ought to be included in the model. The full model is depicted in Equation (3). Regression Equation (4) was estimated by including all variables that appear in Equation (3), except those for which the standard errors of the estimated coefficients did not meet an arbitrarily relaxed standard of significance (.80). The purpose of this determination was to estimate an equation which included as many of the variables as possible, which we hypothesized ought to be included in our model but at the same time to exclude those occupation variables that were contributing only "noise" to the regression. In the case of many variables used in the social sciences, it is often unreasonable to hold one's results to rigid standards of significance. Doing so may imply more precision than one's data can support. It is mainly for this reason that we include four regressions in our presentation. Our criteria for elimination of variables were useful in that once very imprecisely estimated variables were excluded (such as "Director" in the production section, or "Apparatus" in either the CPSU, Komsomol, or trade unions), several interesting variables, such as "engineer" and "scientific worker," could be more precisely estimated.

[b] *Italics* denotes significance at the .95 level, i.e., there is at least a .95 probability that the coefficient does *not* equal zero.

we can be that the estimated value of the coefficient is close to the true value of the coefficient.

In the course of estimating a statistical model, one generally runs many regression equations, each a variation on the initial hypothesis. One can never be sure of the best configuration and weight of explanatory variables. In most cases researchers present the model that best fits their data, regardless of any previously held theory or knowledge of the best model for the data. In our analysis, we have chosen to present four versions of the regression equations, to account better for our uncertainty of how to specify our model correctly. In addition to "age," "gender," and "number of candidates in a district," equations (1) and (2) include only political variables, and highlight the effect of the pre-election platforms on the election. The full model—that is, the model that includes all the variables from equation (2) as well as all occupation dummy variables—is presented in equation (3); a refined version of this model is presented in equation (4). By comparing the four equations, one can see which coefficients remain approximately the same across all permutations of the model (e.g., "endorsed by DE '90," "age," "gender," and some of the occupation variables: dean of a faculty, instructor, doctor, KGB employee, etc.) and which coefficients change when the specification of the model changes (e.g., "member of CPSU," "endorses democratic platform(s)," and all occupation variables that do not appear in equation (4)). A researcher has more confidence in estimates that are stable than in those that are sensitive to permutations of the model.

Interpretation: Why Did Some Candidates Do Well and Not Others?

How Did Political Affiliation Affect Candidate Success?

Of the political variables included in our analysis, only a candidate's affiliation with DE '90 had a significant effect on the percentage of votes he or she received [36] (see equations (1) and (2) in Table 2.2). In the first regression, only the characteristics of age, gender, and a candidate's membership or non-membership in the Communist Party or the Komsomol were considered in order to check the effect of Communist Party membership. If we looked only at this incomplete model (equation (1) in Table 2.2), we would conclude that being a member of the Communist Party decreased a candidate's percentage of votes by 3.5 percent. However, once one controls for a candidate's affiliation with the democratic left (equation (2) in Table 2.2), the effect of being a party member becomes statistically indistinguishable from zero. Thus, we conclude that membership in the Communist Party did not affect Leningrad voters one way or another.

Although in some ways surprising, this finding supports the view long held by some analysts[37] that in the late Soviet period, membership in the Communist Party had little political or ideological meaning, but only facilitated entry into the type of upper-level career held by many of the successful candidates in this election. It would be of interest to know whether being a party member had a significant effect on candidate performance in cities where voters knew little else about a candidate's political views.

The estimated coefficient for the "endorsed by DE '90" variable is remarkably stable. Across the many permutations of explanatory variables—three of which are described in equations (2), (3), and (4) in Table 2.2—the coefficient and standard errors for this variable remained almost identical. The results of regression equations (2), (3), and (4) indicate endorsement by DE '90 greatly affected how a candidate did in the first round of the election, increasing the percentage of votes received by over 11 percent.

Much less striking was the effect of a candidate's own endorsement of any democratic platform. Except in equation (2), we cannot conclude that this endorsement had a significant effect on the percentage of votes he or she received in the election. We can thus reasonably conclude that our hypothesis was correct: voters were less likely to believe the candidate's claim that he or she supported a given political platform than they were to believe the political group that endorsed the candidate, in this case DE '90. In an environment without political parties to nominate candidates, the role of the democratic platforms in informing voters of favored candidates was particularly important.

How Did Personal Characteristics Affect Candidate Success?

The effect of personal characteristics on candidate success or failure can also be measured, albeit with difficulty in the case of occupational variables. The impact of age and gender was consistently estimated across our equations; for every year older a candidate was, he or she received slightly fewer votes. Adding ten years to a candidate's age translated into receiving about 5 percent fewer votes. The effect of being a female candidate was such that women received about 3 percent fewer votes than men.

Depending on how many occupational variables are included in the regression—whether or not all occupation variables are included, or whether only "significant" variables are included—the estimates and standard errors of the coefficients for the occupational variables tend to vary. In Table 2.3, we have reported the 95 percent confidence intervals for those occupational variables included in regression equation (4) whose estimated effects differ significantly from zero.

We expected to find that being an academic or technical specialist increased the number of votes received by a candidate. The results of our regression, however, demonstrate that being an engineer or scientific worker did little to increase one's share.[38] Much more important to the success of candidates in these professions was the fact that a large percentage of them were endorsed by DE '90. Being an academic, on the other hand, had a positive

Table 2.3

Confidence Intervals for Coefficients of Occupation Variables[a]

Occupation interval	.95 confidence
Scientific and technical specialists	
Engineer, technician, master craftsman	0.0 to 2.8
Manager of laboratory or department	0.2 to 3.4
Scientific worker or engineer	0.4 to 2.8
Academic professions	
Dean, head of faculty	1.7 to 7.7
Instructor, lecturer	2.8 to 6.0
Director of a school	5.4 to 11.5
School teacher	4.6 to 11.4
Military	4.7 to 8.3
Law enforcement	
Militia (MVD)	9.4 to 14.1
KGB	6.4 to 21.5
Judge, prosecutor	2.3 to 11.1
Organs of the soviets	4.0 to 7.5
Health care	
Director of medical institute, hospital	3.7 to 9.1
Doctor, nurse	3.0 to 8.8
Press	2.9 to 8.4
Radio, television	7.4 to 17.3
Worker	0.2 to 2.7

[a] A .95 confidence interval is interpreted in the following way: Based on the results of our regression analysis, there is .95 probability that the *true effect* of an explanatory variable falls within the specified interval. The smaller the standard error for any given estimated coefficient, the smaller the confidence interval, and the more precise one can be about stated effects.

effect on the number of votes received, even when controlling for endorsement by DE '90.[39]

One of our most interesting findings was the effect of being in the military or law enforcement professions. Members of the military, the militia, and the KGB received many more votes than average, even when controlling for support by DE '90. One might hypothesize that these groups, especially the KGB, did well because they managed to manipulate the nomination and election process in their respective districts. However, in no district in which a KGB candidate ran did he oppose fewer than four other candidates. In one of the two districts in which the KGB candidate eventually won, he did not oppose a candidate endorsed by DE '90; but, in the other district in which the KGB candidate won, he opposed two candidates supported by DE '90. Moreover, a significant number of military and law enforcement candidates did not fail to run against candidates supported by DE '90. Therefore, we conclude that voters responded more positively than average to candidates in the military or in law enforcement. This conclusion supports the findings of various opinion polls conducted before the collapse of the Soviet Union.[40]

Although we hypothesized that members of the Communist Party apparatus (individuals who worked for the party, as opposed to party members) would have done more poorly than average in competitive elections, the results of our regression analysis show that candidates who were employed by the Communist Party neither benefited nor suffered as a result of their profession, at least in terms of the percentage of votes they received in the first round of the election. In an election in which most candidates faced 6 or 7 opponents, the unimportance of a party job was in itself important. Having a job to which voters were indifferent meant that the apparatus candidates had little chance of being one of the top two vote getters and thus advancing to the second round. Indeed, only 7 of the 119 members of the party apparatus eventually went on to win in their district.

Being employed in some capacity by local government (that is, in the organs of the legislative soviets) increased a candidate's share of the vote by around 6 percent, taking us somewhat by surprise. These relatively successful candidates were for the most part employees or leaders in the executive-administrative apparatus, that is, in the Communist Party–dominated *ispolkom*.[41] Most likely voters perceived that members of this body, responsible for implementing the functions of the local soviet, were familiar with the responsibilities of soviets and therefore well qualified to fulfill them.

Taking into account the effect of employment in either law enforcement or politics and controlling for the effect of endorsement by DE '90, it would seem that voters did not perceive all centers of power in the same way. Candidates from organizations such as the military, the KGB, and other institutions of state power such as the local soviets seem to have been evaluated positively by Leningrad voters in 1990. Candidates from Communist Party–based institutions, however, did not receive the same automatic advantage accorded to those in other powerful institutions. While some voters may have blamed the Communist Party elite for the ills of the country, most voters were indifferent to a candidate's membership in the Communist Party apparatus. This result is intriguing because it suggests that despite the overlap between Communist Party and state institutions, voters appear to have discriminated between candidates employed in "state" bodies and those engaged in "party" organizations.

Conclusions

By far the most important candidate characteristic was his or her endorsement by Democratic Elections '90. Other characteristics played important

Table 2.4

Some Profiles of Representative Candidates[a]

| | | | Percentage of yes votes received by candidates who were: | |
| | | | Endorsed by DE '90 (%) | Not endorsed by DE '90 (%) |
Age	Gender	Occupation		
45	male	Scientific worker/Engineer	22.3	10.5
45	male	MVD	32.4	20.7
45	male	KGB	34.6	22.9
45	male	Organs of soviets	26.4	14.7
45	male	University instructor	29.9	17.2
45	male	School director	29.1	17.4
45	male	Doctor	26.6	14.8
45	male	Press	26.3	14.6
45	male	Radio/Television	33.1	21.3

[a] It should be remembered that whether a candidate was a member of the CPSU had no significant effect on the dependent variable in our regression analysis. Therefore, while of theoretical interest, that characteristic had no discernible effect on the values reported here and is not included in the table.

roles in how a candidate fared in the election, but none was as precisely or consistently estimated in our analysis. Consider the effect that being endorsed by DE '90 had on a typical candidate. According to the results of regression equation (4), a 45-year-old male engineer who was endorsed by DE '90 would receive 22 percent of the vote in his district; the same candidate would receive only 10.5 percent without the endorsement. In Table 2.4 we list several profiles of typical candidates, showing the predicted percentage of the vote that such candidates would receive if they were or were not endorsed by DE '90. This table also demonstrates the differences in predicted votes for candidates in different professions. In addition, subtracting about 3 percentage points from each value in the table yields the predicted percentage of votes a typical female candidate would get, and thereby highlights the pronounced disadvantage that women faced in the election.

Also significant are the effects that we did not find. We wanted to test the hypothesis that being a member of the Communist Party affected the percentage of votes a candidate received. We also wanted to see if working for the Communist Party apparatus, the Komsomol, or official trade unions had any significant influence on the percentage of votes a candidate received in the election. By using regression analysis, we were able to show that once a candidate's endorsement by DE '90 was taken into account, the impact of affiliation with the Communist Party in any capacity did not on average have any effect on the percentage of votes he or she received in the first round of the election.

It is clear from our study that voters responded positively to candidates supported by democratic platforms, though it is difficult to discern whether they did so out of support for democratic ideas or out of a desire to reject the old system. Had it not been for our finding that being a member of the Communist Party apparatus had no significant effect on how a candidate fared, we would have been tempted to conclude that the victory of democratically oriented candidates was little more than a strong negative reaction to the Communist Party. The unimportance of Communist Party connections to voters, however, lends support to the notion that there was an important positive component to voters' support for the democratic candidates. Our analysis also highlights the dramatic role that a coherent political organization played in making up voters' minds. McAuley found in her comparative study of four Russian cities that it was much harder for democratic groups to organize in Perm and Arkhangelsk than in Leningrad, and that what democratic forces there were in these two cities had no impact on the outcome of the local elections.[42] This would seem to be the decisive factor distinguishing the elections in Leningrad and in Moscow from those held in other Russian cities. We have found that in Leningrad the most important factor contributing to the success of candidates who supported democratic reforms appears to have been the presence of political groups and the general availability of information regarding the affiliation of candidates with these groups.

Although we plan to carry out a comparative analysis of election results in a sample of Russian cities in order to better assess the role of political groups in the 1990 local elections, we can draw some tentative conclusions regarding the influence of political groups in other city elections based on the work of other scholars. In his discussion of the 1990 local elections in Yaroslavl, Jeffrey Hahn points out that there was no formal organization whereby voters could be informed of the political positions of the candidates.[43] We know from Hahn's research that reform-oriented candidates ran in the 1990 elections in Yaroslavl and that a sizable minority were elected to the city and oblast soviets. However, since political parties could not register and thereby identify their candidates, and since lists of candidates supported by the reform-oriented Yaroslavl People's Front were not published in the newspapers, we cannot know whom voters would have chosen if the political views of candidates had been as widely available as they were in Leningrad. We thus cannot decide if Leningrad was a unique case, or if the presence of organized democratic political groups anywhere in Russia would have significantly affected the outcome of elections to local soviets. We do know, however, that in many areas where conservative candidates fared well in the 1990 local elections, voters later overwhelmingly supported Yeltsin against more conservative candidates in the 1991 Russian presidential election.[44] Yeltsin's campaign was orchestrated by Democratic Russia, the same group that helped ensure the victory of democratically oriented candidates in Moscow's 1990 elections to the city soviet.[45] Having had time to further enlarge its organizational base, Democratic Russia strongly influenced national debate and helped ensure that voters all over Russia were well informed on the candidates' positions.

We must bear in mind that support for democratic ideas in principle may not be synonymous with support for genuine reform and movement toward pluralist, parliamentary democracy. While many deputies may have been relatively democratic at the time of the elections, the majority could never have anticipated that a coup in August 1991 would thrust them into a period of radical democratization and economic reform. The Supreme Soviet of the RSFSR may have been radical when compared to the USSR Supreme Soviet, but it has proven to be far less committed to reform than the executive branch of government in the Russian Federation. Indeed, in late 1992 and 1993, it has become clear that many legislative soviets—from the Russian Federation Congress of People's Deputies and its Supreme Soviet on down —have become the main source of organized opposition to economic reforms such as privatization.

Regardless of its true attractiveness to the electorate, Democratic Elections '90 acted much like a political party and managed to sweep the 1990 elections in Leningrad. Like Democratic Russia in Moscow and in the national elections to the RSFSR Congress of People's Deputies, DE '90 brought about the election of a majority of reform-minded deputies and initiated the process of the formation of political parties and pluralism in Russia.

Above all, the results of the 1990 elections in Leningrad suggest the important role that political parties could play in future competitive elections in Russia. When new elections for local and national legislative and executive positions are held in Russia, competing political parties (legalized since March 14, 1990)[46] will participate, and voters will be offered a wide range of choices among contending political agendas, many of which are already being actively developed by all parties, from Democratic Russia to the Socialists to the nationalist parties. Only after these upcoming elections will we have a clear sense of how Russian voters feel about the critical issues facing their country. Until then, we hope that this study and others like it can serve as a baseline with which we can produce fruitful conclusions about the pace and nature of political change in post-Communist Russia.

Notes

1. Other factors beyond the scope of this paper may have contributed to candidates' success. Michael Urban in *More Power to the Soviets* (Brookfield, VT: Edward Elgar, 1990) discusses how the Communist Party controlled the nomination of candidates in the 1989 elections to the USSR Congress of People's Deputies. Gavin Helf and Jeffrey Hahn ("Old Dogs and New Tricks: Party Elites in the Russian Regional Elections of 1990," *Slavic Review*, vol. 51, no. 3 [1992], pp. 511–30) investigate the possible effects of gerrymandering on the local elections in Yaroslavl.

2. Theodore Friedgut, *Political Participation in the USSR* (Princeton, NJ: Princeton University Press, 1979), pp. 163–64.

3. The 1989 elections to the USSR Congress of People's Deputies were "pseudo-competitive" for several reasons. In the first place, not all seats were open to all candidates. One-third of the seats were set aside for candidates from "social organizations," such as the CPSU, the Komsomol, and official trade unions. In the second place, in most electoral districts, one or at most two candidates ran for the contested seat. See Urban, *More Power*, for a complete discussion of this election.

4. Urban, *More Power*, p. 112.

5. Timothy J. Colton, "The Politics of Democratization: The Moscow Election of 1990," *Soviet Economy*, vol. 6, no. 4 (1990), pp. 285–344.

6. Jeffrey Hahn, "Local Politics and Political Power in Russia: The Case of Yaroslavl'," *Soviet Economy*, vol. 7, no. 4 (1991), pp. 322–41. See especially the discussion on p. 327.

7. Joel Moses, "Soviet Provincial Politics in an Era of Transition and Revolution, 1989–91," *Soviet Economy*, vol. 44, no. 3 (1992), pp. 479–509. Also see Darrell Slider, "The CIS: Republican Leaders Confront Local Opposition," *RFE/RL*, vol. 1, no. 10 (1992), pp. 7–11.

8. This conclusion is based on research by Andrews, carried out in the winter of 1991.

9. Mary McAuley, "Politics, Economics, and Elite Realignment in Russia: A Regional Perspective," *Soviet Economy*, vol. 8, no. 1 (1992), pp. 46–88.

10. Brendon Kiernan and Joseph Aistrup, "The 1989 Elections to the Congress of People's Deputies in Moscow," *Soviet Studies*, vol. 43, no. 6 (1991), pp. 1,049–64. See especially p. 1,056.

11. Colton, "Politics of Democratization."

12. Colton chose to study the success or failure of the left slate in each electoral district in Moscow, which he defined as those candidates within a particular electoral district who had been endorsed by the political association Democratic Russia. (These correspond to our "reform-oriented" candidates.) In most districts more than one left candidate competed. As his dependent variable, Colton used the combined percentage of "yes" votes received by the left slate. In order to see how particular personal and professional characteristics—such as gender, age, and occupation—affected how this slate fared in each district, Colton averaged the characteristics for all left candidates in each district. For example, in a given district the left slate might have included three candidates with a combined "yes" vote total of 56 percent (the dependent variable) and

characterized as 33 percent female (one woman), 66 percent engineers (two engineers), 66 percent CPSU members, and so forth (the explanatory variables). Because his unit of analysis was the district and he looked only at how the left slate performed, his results cannot differentiate among the performances of individual candidates and among different political groups. In our study the unit of analysis is the candidate, his or her political affiliation can be included among the explanatory variables in our regression analysis, and its affect on the candidate's success can be estimated.

13. For a discussion of the first Russian national elections held in 1917 see Oliver Radkey, *Russia Goes to the Polls: The Elections to the All-Russian Constituent Assembly, 1917* (Ithaca: Cornell University Press, 1989), and Terence Emmons, *The Formation of Political Parties and the First National Elections in Russia* (Cambridge, MA: Harvard University Press, 1983).

14. "Law of the RSFSR on Elections of Peoples' Deputies to Local Soviets," October 27, 1989.

15. Ibid.

16. Blair Ruble, *Leningrad: Shaping a City* (Berkeley, CA: University of California Press, 1990).

17. Grigory A. Tomchin, a Leningrad resident active in democratic political groups in 1990 and now cochairman of the St. Petersburg Democratic Russia Party, noted in an interview that engineers and other specialists, particularly those employed in the military-industrial complex, were active supporters of the democratic movement because they were the most "marginal" in the communist system. Their intellectual capabilities outstripped their professional opportunities, and their career tracks were unlikely to bring significant financial rewards (May 5, 1993).

18. As noted earlier, the 1989 elections were "pseudocompetitive." In the first round a single candidate was listed on the ballot, but as usual, voters were given the opportunity to cross out the single name and vote "none of the above." In the case of the first secretary and his officials, a majority of the electorate chose not to vote for the unchallenged candidates. In the second round, alternative candidates were permitted and some thirty-four candidates were nominated.

19. McAuley, "Politics, Economics, and Elite Realignment," p. 60.

20. Urban, *More Power.*

21. Colton, "Politics of Democratization."

22. As transport hubs in neighborhoods, subway stations were apparently viewed by candidates as a prime means to reach voters. At peak times three or four candidates could be found in each station, each usually standing before a big board with posters and information. One individual who was active in the campaign stated that voters went deliberately to the stations to pick up information on competing candidates.

23. In 1990 *Smena* had a circulation of 140,000. Approximately 110,000 copies of each issue went to subscribers, and 30,000 were sold through kiosks and other vendors. Tomchin pointed out that while circulation figures may seem small given the large population of Leningrad, they are not indicative of the newspaper's actual readership. Many subscribers brought their papers to work and shared them with coworkers, and many residents read the newspapers posted in public locations. In addition, the newspaper's circulation doubled in 1991, suggesting that it was indeed popular. (Source: telephone interview with Galina Leont'eva, chief editor of *Smena* in 1989–90, April 19, 1993.)

24. This was done by personally visiting the newspaper's offices, or by sending an authorized person in one's stead. Special dates were designated for each raion.

25. Gender was deduced from the first name, patronymic, and last name listed in the newspaper.

26. For the sake of comparison, we analyzed the results of the second round, using the same dependent variable—the percentage of "yes" votes received. The results of the regression were similar, but a few caveats are in order. First, the effect of all explanatory variables was dampened. This was to be expected, given that the variation among competitors was much smaller; fewer candidates meant that the range in the percentage of "yes" votes was reduced, and all second-round nominees had already been favored once by voters. The support of DE '90 continued to have a significant effect on a candidate's success. As in the first round, occupation rarely affected the candidate's performance. Only the professions of engineer, scientific worker, or instructor in an institute of higher learning, or employment in the militia or as a judge or lawyer had significant positive effects on a candidate's success. Interestingly, employment as an engineer or a scientific worker increased a candidate's share of "yes" votes by about 6 percent, and instructors received about 11 percent more "yes" votes than average. It appears that these two types of candidates did much better in the second round of the election than in the first.

27. One candidate was eliminated from our analysis because the only information published about him was his name.

28. This figure was obtained through the regression analysis discussed below and is summarized in Table 2.2.

29. This conclusion is based on an interview with Grigory A. Tomchin, May 5, 1993.

30. Although our dependent variable is not, technically speaking, normally distributed —it is bounded by 0 below and 100 above—we were limited in our options, given the necessity of estimating an equation with over 400 dummy variables (our test of the effect of including dummy variables for each district; see discussion of the dependent variable).

31. Technically, the best way to circumvent this problem is to include a separate dummy variable for each electoral district, thereby controlling for all differences among the districts, including the number of candidates. (This solution is similar to that used in time-series analysis—another situation in which the dependent variable is not independently generated. In time-series regressions, a lagged value of the dependent variable is included in the regression as an explanatory variable.) We ran our regressions, including 399 district dummy variables, and found that our results were almost identical to those achieved when we included a single variable that controlled for the number of candidates in each district. To be exact, estimates of coefficients as well as their standard errors were within 1 to 5 percent of each other for those variables whose coefficients were precisely estimated. For those variables whose coefficients were imprecisely estimated, the range of differences between the estimates was greater. Thus, the number of candidates running in each district serves as an excellent proxy for including a separate dummy variable for each district, allowing us to run our regressions with far fewer explanatory variables, and thereby increasing the precision of our estimates.

32. Dummy variables are variables that capture the presence or absence of a qualitative characteristic. Thus, the variable can take on one of two values, usually coded "0" or "1," with zero corresponding to the absence of the characteristic and one corresponding to its presence. Typical dummy variables include gender, race, or a candidate's support for a particular political idea or party. For a good discussion of dummy variables, see Eric A. Hanushek and John E. Jackson, *Statistical Methods for Social Scientists* (Orlando: Academic Press, Inc., 1977), pp. 101–6.

33. If a series of dummy variables is created by recoding a categorical variable, such as political affiliation, one of the resulting dummy variables must be left out of the regression equation for purposes of estimation.

34. The emphasis here is on "easily." We know that people could have obtained additional information on a candidate with some effort. The assumption that this infor-

mation is sufficient is not so different from the assumption that a political scientist studying an American election might make: some information is readily accessible to all voters, but more information can be had by voters willing to make an effort to examine the candidate.

35. Colton, "Politics of Democratization," p. 336.

36. All references to statistical significance refer to a .95 probability that the coefficient is not zero. By this criterion, a significant coefficient is one in which the standard error (in parentheses) is about twice as small as the coefficient.

37. This point is made by Jerry Hough in *The Soviet Union and Social Science Theory* (Cambridge, MA: Harvard University Press, 1977), chapter 5.

38. We concluded that being a member of these professions did not increase vote share in the first round of the elections because of the proximity to zero of the lower bound of the confidence intervals for engineers and scientific workers (see Table 2.4). Recall that the coefficients for these professions were significant (and positive) in Round 2 (see note 26.)

39. "Controlling for endorsement by DE '90" implies that we included both the variable of interest (e.g., the occupation of technical worker) and the variable "endorsed by DE '90" in the regression. The advantage of regression analysis is that it allows us to isolate the effect of a specific variable (e.g., endorsed by DE '90) on the dependent variable (in our case, votes received) from the effects of other explanatory variables included in the regression (e.g., profession, gender, age, and so forth).

40. The All-Russian Center for the Study of Public Opinion (VTsIOM) found that trust (*doverie*) in the KGB was expressed by 40 percent of the 1,152 Russians surveyed in late 1989. In March 1990 this figure was slightly lower (38 percent of 1,192 respondents believed the KGB was deserving of trust), but still significant, especially if one considers that another 30 percent of respondents answered that the KGB was partially, but not completely, deserving of trust. Only 13 percent said that the KGB was completely untrustworthy. Eighteen percent of respondents said it was "difficult to answer." When asked about their trust in the militia, 22 percent of those questioned thought that this institution deserved complete trust, while 21 percent said it was completely undeserving of trust. The army fared much better, receiving the equivalent of a full endorsement from 42 percent of respondents, partial endorsement from 30 percent, and rejection by 12 percent. Interestingly, the least trusted organizations were the courts and prosecutor's office, which garnered the full trust of 21 percent of respondents, the partial trust of 39 percent, and the mistrust of 21 percent.

41. Candidates did not indicate whether they had been deputies to past city soviets.

42. McAuley, "Politics, Economics, and Elite Realignment," pp. 62–66.

43. Hahn, "Local Politics and Political Power," p. 327.

44. McAuley, "Politics, Economics, and Elite Realignment," and Hahn, "Local Politics and Political Power."

45. Michael E. Urban, "Boris Yeltsin, Democratic Russia and the Campaign for the Russian Presidency," *Soviet Studies,* vol. 44, no. 2 (1992), pp. 187–207.

46. "On Establishment of the Position of President of the USSR and Introduction of Changes and Additions to the Constitution (Basic Law) of the USSR." March 14, 1990.

3

The Changing Role of the Local Budget in Russian Cities

The Case of Yaroslavl

Beth Mitchneck

Local public finance provides the backdrop for political and economic change on the subnational level. Tracking the evolution of an independent local fiscal system measures the institutional response to change in the Russian economy. City budgets fund most expenditures on quality of life and social welfare. They reflect simultaneously central government requirements and local priorities. In Russia, local budgetary composition received serious attention within the scope of reforms beginning in the mid-1980s. Until recently, however, information was not available to measure the impact of central reforms at the city level. Using recently available detailed city budgetary data, this chapter traces fiscal decentralization and the development of independent expenditure policies and priorities at the local level in one Russian city, Yaroslavl.[1]

Field work in Yaroslavl and analysis of budgetary data from Yaroslavl and from other localities in Russia show that local governments still have little *formal* control over the formation of their budgets and the composition of budgetary expenditures. Yet in reality there is substantial evidence of fiscal decentralization, growing independence in the spheres of local tax and expenditure policies, and mounting initiative by local government. Local government has gained incentive to tax and to collect tax and non-tax revenues in order to pursue independent policies, particularly through the use of off-budgetary means. This scenario shows a local government beginning to form its own priorities for urban development and local economic activity.

The chapter provides an overview of Soviet (i.e., pre-1992) and current budgetary systems at the city level. The information from the case study of Yaroslavl documents and interprets the formal and informal changes during the restructuring period following the breakup of the Soviet Union. The purpose is to demonstrate the evolution of local government from an administrative arm of the center to a semiautonomous, policy-making body. It is argued that a local government uses the fiscal system to carve out a new economic role in order to implement its own priorities, sometimes in conflict with central priorities. The evolution occurs at the same time as the concept of territorial jurisdiction changes within Russia, and evolution is possible because of a new meaning of territorial jurisdiction. In the new institutional environment, territory becomes a place over which local authority may be extended, rather than a place subject to central jurisdiction only.

During the restructuring (*perestroika*) period, cities and districts best illustrate the local government level in Russia. The municipal or city level of government, rather than the oblast, represents the non–central government apparatus and thus the non–central government. The oblast has become part of the central government, in that previously republic-level property devolved to the oblast level and, perhaps most importantly, city-level officials refer to the oblast officials as part of the central or federal apparatus. In addition to the above reasons, the majority of Russians live in cities and form opinions and beliefs in part according to their perception of the urban environment. The consequences of the restructuring period, therefore, are experienced at the urban level. Accordingly, Russian cities will be the focus of our analysis of restructuring.

Prior to the breakup of the Soviet Union, few studied public finance in the centrally planned economy. Some notable exceptions provide a foundation on which we can begin the analysis of the restructuring period (e.g., Friedgut 1983; Lewis 1976 and 1983; Raimondo and Stuart 1984 and 1986). Continual examination allows us to trace the evolution of fiscal decentralization (Berkowitz and Mitchneck 1992); but only case studies can document the actual process. Analyses of Russian cities during the restructuring period provide a rare opportunity to observe the attempt to create a market-type system. In addition to empirical evidence that we can collect, the Russian city is a laboratory in which we may trace the evolution of the empowerment of local government and the governing of territory.

The next section reviews what we know about the role of city government and the local budgetary system as it functioned in the past and as it appears to function during restructuring. The following sections discuss some theoretical issues inherent in the analysis of the Russian city and the data and methodology used to construct the case study. The final section is the case study itself.

The Russian City Government and Budgetary Policy

In the Soviet case, the local political system included the local Communist Party and government institutions and the central economic bureaucracy, such as the local office of the State Planning Committee (Gosplan), in addition to the local executive (the city hall or mayor's office) and the legislative branches of government (the local soviet or the council of people's deputies). The current city-level legislative branch is divided into the council of people's deputies (city soviet) and the small soviet (*malyi sovet*), which is a subgroup of the larger city soviet. In the formal political system of the Soviet Union, the local state apparatus was structurally part of the central apparatus. By the principle of dual subordination, the local executive branch, although formally accountable to the city soviet that elected it, was in fact primarily responsible to central government ministries for policies dealing with personnel, regional development, and finance. Studies focusing on the informal system, however, have noted local influence over economic decisions made by the central apparatus through the intervention of local Communist Party and government organizations (see Hough 1969; Bahry 1987; Ruble 1990). These studies and others (e.g., Moses 1982; Breslauer 1986) on the role of the local government in the Soviet Union also suggest that the local government did not act only as the administrative apparatus of higher levels of government, but also acted in its own interest, particularly while demanding attention to regional issues at central forums.

Structural changes have occurred since the late 1980s and more so since 1992 that set the legal framework for new authority at the city level through a substantial redistribution of fiscal powers (Berkowitz and Mitchneck 1992). This fiscal decentralization allows for local public-policy formation and the increased participation of local government in the economy. The central government, for instance, passed new legislation on taxation and local government that broadened local power and authority, and Russian Republic laws from 1991 and 1992 give broader fiscal rights to administrative units below the republic level.[2]

Despite new legislation, the formal political and economic responsibilities of the local government remain firmly in the area of supporting and maintaining the social and economic infrastructure. The economic responsibility of city and oblast governments in the 1980s was limited to the areas of public utilities, housing, mass transit, education, culture, health, and the retail system (otherwise known as the communal economy and the nonproductive sectors of the economy). The formal areas of authority were carried over into the Russian structure of local government as evidenced by the distribution of state property during 1992. The city retains property and enterprises involved in the communal economy and the retail system while the oblast—the immediate higher level of government—received property belonging to the productive sector of the economy.

Although the city soviet was responsible for making expenditures related to urban development and the local economy, it did not have the independent decision-making authority to determine its own budgetary priorities or influence the direction of the local economy. The limitation of local authority and decision making was significant because external decisions, made by bodies that were not responsible for local infrastructure, influenced demand for local services. Local responsibility did not include planning for economic growth. The current formal sphere of influence of city government remains in those areas that influence the development and maintenance of social overhead capital, with only limited responsibility for economic overhead capital and the industrial sector (i.e., local economic growth). As is shown below, the case study of Yaroslavl indicates that city government, however, has been able to push the formal boundaries of authority and responsibility into other, non-traditional areas, due mainly to manipulation of the formal budgetary system.

Budgetary and Off-Budgetary Revenues

Under the previous system, the city government had limited sources of its own income (i.e., tax revenues that flowed directly into the local budget). Therefore, much of the revenue generated on a specific territory flowed directly into either the Russian Republic or the central (All-Union) budget in the form of turnover taxes or profit taxes. City governments had three sources of budgetary revenue—own income, regulated income, and transfers from higher-level budgets. Own income consisted of profit taxes on local enterprises and cooperatives (in the case of the city, local enterprises consisted of the state-run retail system), the bachelor tax, and local duties. These revenues amounted to a relatively small proportion of the amounts needed to fulfill planned expenditures (see Berkowitz and Mitchneck 1992). Local officials negotiated yearly with higher-level officials for payments out of regulated sources like the turnover tax and profits tax on enterprises under the jurisdiction of the republic or the All-Union (central) level (Lewis 1983; Berkowitz and Mitchneck 1992). A large portion of revenues from Yaroslavl went to higher-level budgets. For example, in 1988, 83 percent of budgetary revenues produced in Yaroslavl Oblast were sent to the republic and All-Union budgets (Goskomstat RSFSR 1990). Oblast and city officials then negotiated for the return of these revenues through the system of regulated income and transfers. Also under the previous system, the city officials had little control over the use of carryover funds (the surplus from planned revenues or carryover funds from a previous fiscal year). Higher-level officials could command the local branch of the central bank to transfer these funds directly from the local-government accounts to higher-level accounts. These latter two aspects have changed—deductions into the city budget, in theory, come from all enterprises located in the city and the city government has the legal right to use its carryover funds, including surplus revenues.

The surplus revenues, however, cannot be freely directed into additional areas of unplanned expenditures. These revenues are accumulated above the planned revenues. Interviews indicate that, as of 1992, a portion must be used to pay for the planned deficit with the remainder financing additional budgetary expenditures at the discretion of the local government. The incentive for city government lies in maximizing carryover and off-budgetary revenues, over which the central government has no legal control. This means that we should not see tremendous changes in the planned budgets of cities during restructuring; the changes to indicate the presence of independent fiscal policy and local priorities should be found in the use of off-budgetary resources and the use of local legislative means to create sources of income outside the formal budget.

Under the previous system, few sources of off-budgetary revenues existed for the city government. Off-budgetary revenues are formed from the surplus of the revenue plan and from extra-budgetary sources. Extra-budgetary revenues are formed by law from specific sources other than those that go into the formal budget. For example, in 1991, the city of Yaroslavl had off-budgetary revenues from two sources: carryover and a portion of the price of vodka sold in the city. A separate, extra-budgetary account contains these revenues. In the past, the city government needed to rely on off-budgetary expenditures from enterprises and ministries functioning in the city but not necessarily under its jurisdiction (see Shomina 1992). In the informal system, city officials would routinely approach enterprise and ministry officials conducting economic activity in the city to make expenditures, such as road construction or other capital construction. Thus, the off-budgetary expenditures of enterprises not under local jurisdiction were an integral part of urban development for which the local government was responsible.

Currently, off-budgetary revenues are still formed from two sources: carryover (surplus) and formalized extra-budgetary revenues. Extra-budgetary revenues legally are formed mainly from penalties (fines) levied against enterprises and individuals within the jurisdiction (e.g., traffic fines, economic sanctions, and fines for late payment of taxes), vodka sales, privatization of city property, and fees for registering local businesses. Both the executive branch of the city and of districts[3] within cities (raions) can legally form extra-budgetary funds. The size of a city's and a district's extra-budgetary fund differs greatly by place, thereby spatially differentiating a locality's ability independently to determine expenditure policies and priorities.[4]

Budgetary and Off-Budgetary Expenditures

Municipal officials of Yaroslavl, and those in smaller towns, such as Pushkin and Petrodvorets (under the jurisdiction of St. Petersburg) stress that city budgets form the mainstay of "social protection" for the population. Indeed, the traditional role of the city budget is to fund, at centrally determined, minimum normatives, portions of the local economy related to collective and individual consumption—such as services for the population and the maintenance of infrastructure. As noted above, budgetary expenditure items traditionally include the maintenance of housing, heating, local transportation, education, culture, health, sports, city planning, and the provision of social security. The city budget also funds the upkeep of militia and all facets of local administration. Additions to 1991 city budgetary expenditures included subsidies for the provision of a social safety net, for example, subsidies on the prices of meat and milk products, and wage compensation for price increases. Due to recent central legislation, cities have much greater financial responsibility to finance these expenditures. The obligation to provide a large portion of the social safety net at the local level places tremendous stress on local resources to cover the social services without dramatically increasing the budget deficit (Mitchneck 1992).

Despite the planned nature of city budgetary expenditures, cities have the greatest amount of discretion over expenditures from extra-budgetary funds and carryover funds. For example, Petrodvorets used a portion of its surplus to create a local police force. It had until 1992 relied upon St. Petersburg for its police protection. The creation of a local force is particularly important, since its members collect local fines that go into the extra-budgetary fund. Having its own police improves the likelihood of local fines' finding their way into the appropriate level of the extra-budgetary fund. The same locality also used extra-budgetary funds to subsidize food establishments over the winter. The composition of expenditures from carryover funds generally reflects traditional budgetary expenditures. Some notable exceptions and distinctions between the two types of off-budgetary expenditures, however, will be discussed in the case study of Yaroslavl.

Summary and Conceptualization of Current Changes

Cities and districts grew increasingly vocal and active during the 1980s with respect to the need for autonomy and the implementation of locally generated reform. Examples of such activity are found within the fiscal system and urban development planning. City and district governments are beginning to use independent expenditure policy to create a set of local priorities; such examples are enumerated below.

The changes in local public finance and the level and type of initiatives by local government in the urban economic development sphere are a local response to and a reflection of central restructuring. A new definition of the economic role of local government is evolving. Soviet local state institutions historically insured local consumption of both public and private goods and administered central directives; in other words, the local government reproduced the status quo. By the late 1980s, city and oblast governments began to call publicly for decentralization of economic and political decision making and to legislate spontaneously changes at the local level. The local response combined with central legislation brought about a redistribution of the loci of economic means, authority, responsibility, and information from higher government levels to the local level. In effect, a highly concentrated system of economic power and authority began to disperse and reconcentrate at the local level. The reconfiguration of economic power and authority has coincided with the reconfiguration of territorial jurisdiction.

The new territorial jurisdiction within the political system contributes to the increased economic role of local government. These changes occurred, in part, as a result of the delegitimization of the word Soviet. Soviet, as a national term, signified central authority throughout the territory, including central authority over cities. The Soviet central state viewed the entire territory as subject to its priorities first and foremost. As the concept of territory has contracted because of the delegitimization of the highly centralized system, a concomitant dispersal of control over resource allocation has occurred. This contraction contributed to the local level's obtaining new rights and power in the local economy. Local property rights, the right to use tax instruments, and the right to establish independent expenditure policies shifted to the local level meaningful territorial jurisdiction and, thereby, provided it with the means to change its economic role.

The local result of the reconfiguration of economic power and authority in Russia is the redefinition of the role of local government. The previous role of insuring the quality of life of residents and of meeting production targets by local enterprises has changed into a proactive and management role. Local government can now modify central normatives according to its own priorities and ability to make the expenditures. In the past, the local government had no legal or regulatory recourse to influence industrial location, but it can now actively pursue economic partnerships and approve and authorize the location of a firm within its jurisdiction. In the past, enterprises received subsidies from central state sources, but now the local government subsidizes production on its territory. These are examples of the new economic role of local government in the production process. The new local power has the potential to change dramatically the spatial pattern of industrial production, income distribution, and the location of economic activity within cities.

The processes of changing the meaning of territorial jurisdiction and the economic role of local government are not complete. Substantial continuity from the past system remains (Mitchneck and Berkowitz 1992). Nor have all local governments participated to the same degree in the redefinition of their economic role. One of the important questions to answer is in what specific ways does the local government push the boundaries of its formal economic role? From where does it draw the power and authority to change independently its economic behavior? How does city government influence industrial location? By answering these questions we can analyze the impact of fiscal decentralization and restructuring of cities in the Soviet and now Russian contexts. The case study of Yaroslavl begins to answer these questions.

Data and Methodology

Information was collected from several sources to construct the case study. The author held in-depth interviews with officials in the State Tax Inspection Office and Finance Departments of the *Meriia*[5] in Yaroslavl during June 1992 and again in January 1993. In addition, data were collected during interviews with other officials at the executive and soviet branches of government in the city of Yaroslavl and at the oblast level. The interviews focused on the following broad topics: traditional and new tax instruments, tax collection mechanisms, the structure of local expenditures, and any restrictions placed on them (see Mitchneck and Berkowitz 1992 for a complete discussion of June 1992 interviews).

These areas are important for the following reasons:

Tax Instruments

If Yaroslavl implements independent tax policies, then tax policy has become a matter of choice for the local government. We should also then see variation among localities. A manipulation of the system can substantively change the amount of budgetary and off-budgetary resources available to the local government that it can then apply toward creating an independent expenditure policy. The new forms should represent a direct response at the local level to new, central policies, a new role for local government, and an extension of local jurisdiction over territory.

Tax Collection

The government level and physical location of tax collection should influence the locus of decision-making power over the transfer of those revenues. The locus of collection defines the point to which other levels of government are beholden to obtain their revenues. If the local level can set and collect new taxes, this shows a tremendous amount of fiscal decentralization and some freedom over the use. If some changes have occurred in the collection process, they should signify a further extension of local authority over its jurisdiction.

Composition of Local Expenditures

Relevant issues for analyzing the composition of local expenditures include how formal budgetary expenditures have changed during the restructuring process and whether the nature of expenditures through the formal budget has changed. Answering these questions can determine the extent of changes to the fiscal system and the ability of the local government to actually use the fiscal system for its purposes. The composition of local expenditures also displays local government priorities.

Interviews and Data

The purpose of the interviews was to obtain budgetary data and information from practitioners in order to assess the evolving economic role of local government and its impact on the Russian economy. The initial results of the interviews reveal that substantial changes in the system of local public finance were not implemented until 1992 despite Soviet laws to the contrary. The results show continuity between prereform Soviet practices and current local public finance (Mitchneck and Berkowitz 1992).[6]

The main data sources are city government documents called *Protokoly*. Protocols are the collection of resolutions taken during meetings of the little soviet (*malyi sovet*) and are an important new data source. They give primary information regarding the financing of social and economic infrastructure and the development of local institutions relevant to market-type reforms. Resolutions document the formation of the budget and of off-budgetary expenditures. The Protocols provide evidence of the evolution of the economic role of local government by serving as a window into the local implementation of central reforms and by recording local legislative acts.

The Yaroslavl Case Study

Yaroslavl is an industrial city in the Central Economic Region of Russia. This group of oblasts has a long history of industrial activity dating to the sixteenth and seventeenth centuries when it was the Volga River port for Moscow. The surrounding oblast is relatively agricultural and tends to have more conservative political leanings than the city of Yaroslavl, which is viewed as having a reformist government (see Hahn 1991). According to the 1989 census, the population is 95 percent Russian. Yaroslavl, like other cities in the Central Economic Region, is considered an average Russian city. While the case study cannot claim to be representative of all Russian cities, the perception of its average Russian qualities and its industrial history do support its classification as typical.

Budgetary Revenues

The city government continues to rely heavily upon the collection of relatively few revenue sources to fund its budgetary expenditures, but a growing proportion of its budgetary revenues is coming from new sources. The total budgetary revenues of Yaroslavl increased about thirty-three times between 1991 and 1992 as compared to doubling between 1990 and 1991. The 1991 budgetary revenues were 312,287.7 thousand rubles (tr) compared to 10,372,960 tr in 1992. These figures, however, have little meaning by themselves, since they do not take into account inflation.[7] Three forms of taxes (i.e., profits tax, turnover tax, and income tax on the population) formed nearly 100 percent of the city's revenues in 1991, while they formed about 90 percent of the city's revenues in 1992 (see Table 3.1).[8]

The city began to use new tax instruments and levy new fees in 1992, but these sources remain a relatively small proportion of the total revenues (approximately 9 percent). The city did avail itself of the ability to use twenty-one new taxes and fees as allowed by law (see Table 3.1). In 1992

Table 3.1

Percentage Share of Yaroslavl City Budgetary Revenues, 1992
(in thousands of rubles)

Source	Percentage
Profit tax on enterprises and organizations	58.4
Value-added tax	14.3
Excise fees	0.9
Income tax on population	17.5
Property tax	1.7
Income from privatization	1.2
Water fees	0.1
Gosposhlina (state excise)	0.2
Fees and other non-tax income	1.0
Land tax	2.3
Carryover for unpaid expenses	0.8
Other	0.0
Oblast budget for shared expenses	1.6
Total revenues	100.0

Source: Informatsionnyi material k XII sessii gorodskogo soveta narodnykh deputatov 21 sozyva [Yaroslavl city documents].

the city received budgetary revenues from privatization, bonds, a tax on property, a land tax, fees and payments such as those due on water use, fees on dog ownership, fees for parking, fees on vehicles, and registration and license fees. The new revenue source in 1992—the carryover of budgetary funds from the previous year—appears only in quarterly budgets.

Off-Budgetary Revenues

Yaroslavl appears to be in an advantageous position with respect to forming surplus revenues, funding its planned deficit, and forming extra-budgetary revenues. A substantial change in the composition of off-budgetary revenues and the number of sources of extra-budgetary revenues occurred between 1991 and 1992 in Yaroslavl. In 1991, the city had 29.5 million rubles of surplus and 21.4 million rubles to spend from extra-budgetary funds. According to city accounting sheets, vodka sales accounted for all of Yaroslavl's extra-budgetary revenues in 1991. By 1992, the city accounting office no longer included extra-budgetary revenues as a single line item in its revenue and expenditure accounting, but produced a separate accounting sheet for extra-budgetary revenues and expenditures.

In 1992, the city had total surplus revenues of 4.7 billion rubles, of which approximately 2 billion rubles financed the budget deficit and 15.4 million

---

Table 3.2

Sources of Extra-Budgetary Revenues: Yaroslavl, 1992

Fines
 Traffic fines
 Public transportation fines on passengers
 Fines related to use and protection of land
 Fines against employers for violating Law on Employment of Population in Russia
  (re: firing of workers)
 Fines for the violation of state discipline of prices
 Fines for presenting fraudulent documents to Office of Finance and Prices
 Fines for overstating prices
Other
 Privatization of municipal property
 Liquor and vodka sales mark-up of 25 percent on commercial prices
 Fees for forming private motor-transport establishment
 Allocation of land

 Source: Yaroslavl City little soviet resolutions from 1992.

---

rubles were used in 1992 to finance expenditures from the 1991 budget. The remainder was used in 1992 for wage compensation and other social safety net expenditures. The ability to accumulate surplus funds substantially increases a city government's ability to conduct independent expenditure policy.

Total extra-budgetary revenues increased more than eight times between 1991 and 1992 to 182.2 million rubles. Revenues from vodka sales declined dramatically in both absolute and relative terms. Due to increased sources of extra-budgetary revenues, revenues from vodka sales dropped to about 7 percent of the total from nearly 100 percent the previous year. Table 3.2 displays most sources of extra-budgetary revenues in Yaroslavl in 1992. Since fines are a major source of extra-budgetary revenues, local government has great incentive to collect the fines and enforce compliance with these laws. The collection of fines and the concomitant increase in extra-budgetary revenues enhance the city's ability to conduct independent expenditure policy.

Tax Collection

Formal tax collection mechanisms for the city are still under the jurisdiction of the federal government level. As under the previous system, the tax inspection office, physically located in city hall, is still responsible for collecting tax revenues due to all levels of government. Interviews indicate that the workers in the office view their jobs as implementing federal government laws on taxation and as insuring that the law is followed at the local and individual levels. The city government appears to have little or no control over tax collection of federally levied taxes or over tax revenues that they share with higher levels of government.

The Yaroslavl city government has experimented with new forms of collecting local taxes and accomplished an innovation in the sphere of tax collection and distribution within the city's districts. This experiment consists of "traders" purchasing coupons (*talony*) at kiosks in the districts to pay their profits taxes. The innovation, initiated by the city-level Office of Finances and Prices, established "a unified budget" for the city. Under the previous system, the city had a unified budget with the oblast. Also under the previous system, districts within the city had bank accounts into which their own tax revenues (e.g., income tax on the population) would flow. Now there is only one city bank account for each revenue source. Under the previous system, the practice of distribution of taxes on the income of the population did not equitably account for the distribution of population within the city. The tax remained in the district of employment rather than of residence. Soviet urban planning created an urban spatial structure in which the industrial districts did not coincide with residential ones. The creation of a unified budget for the city consolidates the budgetary revenues and expenditures at the city level. This means that rather than having seven budgets for the city of Yaroslavl, one for the city and one for each of six districts, there is one unified budget. Not only has this simplified the budgetary system, but it also allows the city government to redistribute tax revenues, theoretically, in a more equitable manner. The city has in effect taken over lower-level revenues allowing it to conduct a more integrated, city-wide expenditure policy. According to the head of the Prices and Administration in Yaroslavl, two other cities in Russia (Krasnodar and Kaliningrad) have considered adopting the same system after consulting with the Yaroslavl city government.

The unified budget for the city clearly defines its jurisdictional authority and power throughout the territory of the city. In a reformist city like Yaroslavl, the city government can then carry out its decisions by minimizing interference from district governments. The city, however, has not left districts completely powerless. District governments still have extra-budgetary revenues and make independent expenditures using those revenues. The size of extra-budgetary revenues varies according to district-level initiative to form them by using sources such as the registration of private firms and cooperatives located on their territories.

Budgetary Expenditures

During restructuring, the city government has increased the level of its budgetary expenditures. The ruble value of budgetary expenditures increased about 36 times between 1991 and 1992 (from 246,925.7 tr to 9,016,678 tr respectively) as opposed to 1.6 times between 1990 and 1991. These figures reflect both inflation and actual increased expenditures on the part of the municipality. The composition of the formal budget for the city is still largely controlled by higher government levels. For example, in 1992 the Yaroslavl Oblast government instructed the Yaroslavl city government to increase its 1993 planned budget by 50 percent. It was thought that this increase would account for inflation and additional expenditures. This will, of course, change during 1993 as the plan is adjusted at least quarterly.

The formal budget continues to fund mainly quality of life expenditures as it did under the previous system (Table 3.3), but the proportion of expenditures on the economy has increased over time. In the 1980s, local government spent about one-third of its total budgetary expenditures on the national economy (Lewis 1983); but in Yaroslavl in 1992 nearly 60 percent of total budgetary expenditures were made in the area of the national economy. The housing and the communal-economy category in the national economy alone received the largest proportion of expenditures (45.6 percent). The next largest expenditures were in the sociocultural category—education and physical education and sports. These are traditional areas of responsibility, but still retain particular priority for the city. The city also spends a large proportion of its surplus and extra-budgetary funds on physical education and sports. The fourth largest expenditure category, within the national economy, was on automotive transportation. This category includes the municipal public transportation system. The city government did add expenditures categories in 1992 for sociocultural measures that reflect increased involvement in the urban economy and in the social safety net. The examples of new categories of expenditures indicate that the city has taken on a larger role in the urban economy by making expenditures that were previously in the central government's domain. Loans through the city budget are an important addition to the composition of budgetary expenditures in the formal system, particularly because they show clearly the increased importance of the city government in the urban economy. Loans to enterprises located in the city were the fifth largest expenditure in 1992 (5.8 percent of total expenditures).

Beginning with the 1991 budget, a new line item appears for wage compensation for families with children. Social assistance and improvement of welfare appear institutionalized in the city budget by 1992. The city would

Table 3.3

Percentage Share of Yaroslavl City Budgetary Expenditures, 1992
(in thousands of rubles)

Item	Percentage
National Economy	
Fuel industry	0.2
Construction	0.0
Agriculture	0.1
Public health in productive sphere	0.6
Housing-communal economy	45.6
Telephone communications	0.5
Automotive transportation	7.9
River transportation	0.2
Other sectors of national economy	1.3
Trade	1.9
Sociocultural Expenditures	
Education	16.1
Culture	0.2
Health	12.9
Physical culture and sports	0.2
Social assistance	1.0
Youth policy	0.1
Upkeep of law and order organizations	0.5
Upkeep of organs of state authority	0.0
Upkeep of organs of state management	1.3
Other	0.7
Chernobyl nuclear accident victims	0.0
Elections and referendums	0.0
Improvement of welfare	3.0
Loans	5.8
Total Expenditures	100.0

Source: Informatsionnyi material k XII sessii gorodskogo soveta narodnykh deputatov 21 sozyva [Yaroslavl city documents].

pay to the oblast amounts to be added onto workers' wages in the city. The oblast would then pass on to enterprises social welfare payments from the city, oblast, and federal levels. Depending on the economic situation of the city, it passed resolutions allocating additional funds during the year for wage compensation. The city-level funding of the social safety net did not occur significantly until 1992.

The city also paid for compensation to workers from enterprises that were involved in the clean-up of the Chernobyl nuclear accident. The city budget provided health benefits, wage compensation, and extra leave for these workers. The city also paid for run-off elections for people's deputies for the Russian parliament from two districts. (The money for run-off elections originally came from the oblast budget.)

The 1992 quarterly budgets had a new line item—development budget—signifying an increased role for local government in the city's economy.[9] The development budget funds capital construction of city property, consisting of social and economic infrastructure. This fund is formed through the combination of revenue sources from surplus revenues, extra-budgetary funds, and a very small amount from the oblast budget. In 1991, the development budget appeared as a line item in the accounting of off-budgetary expenditures. In the past, these expenditures were made in the city only through informal or higher-level means. The inclusion of a development budget in the city budget marks a significant change in the formal, economic responsibility and authority of the city government.

Also included only in the quarterly expenditure budgets is a reserve fund. This institutionalizes a practice used by state enterprises to carry over funds for investment purposes. The practice began in Yaroslavl as the city government was unable to spend the planned amount but needed to allocate the funds within the budget. The city now sets aside up to 10 percent of planned expenditures for the reserve fund. In the second and third quarters of 1992, this fund paid for additional compensation to pensioners and the city's poor, school lunches, and the construction of cooperative housing and mini-markets. Yaroslavl city officials called this their way of being able to put out fires. Other cities also reportedly created reserve funds.

Off-Budgetary Expenditures

Off-budgetary expenditures have changed significantly since the late 1980s. Under the previous system, the city made few such expenditures since it did not have a legal right to form off-budgetary revenues as discussed above. The composition of off-budgetary expenditures varies according to revenue source. Certain revenue sources can be used only to make specific categories of expenditures and, furthermore, the right to use carryover funds or extra-budgetary funds varies within city government between the legislative and executive branches. It is important to note, however, that despite the significance of off-budgetary expenditures, they still form a relatively small proportion of the total expenditures made by the city government (roughly 11 percent).

Table 3.4 displays representative items that were financed by surplus revenues in Yaroslavl during 1992. Many of these categories of expenditures are funded by the formal budget as well. The exceptions, however, indicate that the federal level has decentralized expenditures to the city level

Table 3.4

Yaroslavl City Expenditure Categories and Selected Detailed Items from 1992 Carryover Funds

Communal Economy
Purchase loading equipment for road administration
Acquisition of technology
Additional Expenditures on City Economy
Sister cities
Compensation for lunches
Committee on Land Reform
Reimburse cafeteria No. 13 for expenses
Ambulance for city health administration
Reimburse enterprises for credit to schools and grants to poor
District elections (1991 paid by republic)
Automobiles for municipal militia
Repair facade of historic military hospital
Repair Philharmonic Society concert hall
Repair store for the needy
Organization of city electric and automobile transportation
Social assistance to workers of the city health administration and decontamination
    station
Seasonal procurement of potatoes and vegetables from 1992 harvest
Ten city buses
Newspaper *Gorodskie novosti* (subsidize subscriptions for the needy)
IBM-386 computer for Department of Theoretical and Experimental Physics
    at Yaroslavl State Pedagogical Institute
Supplemental financing for housing in fourth quarter
Bureau of Technical Information (assessment of buildings owned by individuals)
Salary increases for workers of budget administration
Construction of municipal fire station
Construction of automatic telephone exchange (in Zavolzhskii Raion)
Social assistance to students of city schools
Finance television broadcasts
Implement land use policy
Education
Equipment for Department of Education
Bonuses and stipends to pedagogical workers of schools, preschools, and vocational
    training schools
Finance preschool system
Presentations of medals to graduates of city schools
Health
Replenishment of cash-on-hand of Supply Department in Medical Institute
Creation of Pharmacy Section in Health Care Administration
Sports
Professional hockey club "Torpedo"
Participation in Russian-Canadian tournament "Sports for All"

Source: Yaroslavl City little soviet resolutions from 1992.

through informal means. Activities of federal importance, like the Committee on Land Reform, must now obtain local funding in addition to federal funding. The implementation of land-use policy is also now funded locally; in the past, the central government controlled urban land-use policies. The city government has even helped to finance television broadcasts, previously under strict control of the central government. Social security and social protection also became a significant local responsibility and priority (e.g., compensation for lunches and grants to the poor). Given that the city perceives federal normatives as inadequate, a city's ability to overfulfill the planned revenues and then to direct funds into maintaining local infrastructure and quality of life takes on paramount importance to the city government.

Expenditures from the carryover revenues are much greater in ruble value than expenditures from extra-budgetary funds (approximately 956,593,000 rubles versus approximately 132,527,000 respectively for 1992). The expenditures from carryover mainly target quality of life issues and are constrained by the formal budget. Extra-budgetary expenditures are geared more toward nontraditional, local responsibilities, such as maintaining the physical infrastructure of the city, supporting the morale of the inhabitants, and advertising the city of Yaroslavl on the national and international levels. Table 3.5 displays extra-budgetary expenditures in Yaroslavl during 1992.

Despite few significant departures from traditional municipal expenditures, several items merit further discussion. First, the city makes expenditures aimed at advertising the city and at creating (if not supporting) place-related consciousness.[10] Expenditures such as financial support of sports clubs, support of cultural activities in Yaroslavl, restoration of a historical landmark (Vlas'evskaia tower), commemoration of veterans from Yaroslavl, and a contest and prize for a Yaroslavl city emblem clearly point toward increasing public morale and Yaroslavl name recognition in the national and international arenas. Second, the city makes expenditures that clearly support local enterprises. For example, the city government subsidized a municipal newspaper in order to compensate for the increased market price of newsprint. Soviet enterprises have always been subsidized, but this is clear evidence that the city government is taking on a role of protecting enterprises from the vagaries of the market.

Data on extra-budgetary expenditures by the city in December 1992 indicate that toward the end of the year, the city substantially subsidized local enterprises through direct grants and credits. It also shows a wide variety of expenditures from one million rubles on the Soviet-German Society to 150,000 rubles to the oblast executive branch. These kinds of expen-

Table 3.5

Yaroslavl City Expenditure Categories and Selected Items from 1992 Extra-Budgetary Funds

Capital Investment
Construction
Education
 Construction of annex to schools
 Construction of workers' areas at educational enterprise
Health
 Construction of annex to hospital
Communal Construction
 Water supply
 Roads
 Engineering network
 Equipment for main pumping station
Social Assistance
Other
 Restoration of Vlas'evskaia tower
 Small-scale wholesale base (Dzerzhinskii Raion)
 Road construction on Oktiabr'skaia Ulitsa (automated traffic management)
Health and Welfare
 Material assistance
 Community Red Cross (charity services)
 Oblast Soviet International League of Sobriety and Health
 New Year's gifts and party for 570 foster children
 Organization of city medical insurance fund
 Health care
 Charity
Education
Municipal Militia
Sports and Culture
Sports club travel
Tournament for technical sports and for the participation of Yaroslavl in Russian tournaments
Participation of basketball team "Spartak" (Kirovskii Raion) in the championship of Russia
Firing ranges at youth sports-technical schools
Subsidy to enterprise for sports
Baseball equipment for Yaroslavl children
Annual prize for track and field teams at local newspaper
Reception of sports delegation of school children from sister city (Germany)
V.A. Sokova Memorial International Checkers Tournament in Yaroslavl
Subsidies to Enterprises
 Subsidy to newspaper
Other
 Transportation
 Contest and prize for Yaroslavl city emblem
 Philanthropic contribution to Tolgsky Monastery of the Holy Presentation
 Concert by Yaroslavl Oblast Philharmonic for international mission
 Seminar conducted by Association of Oblasts and Cities of Central Russia
 Equipment for the Tax Inspection Office
 Annual dues to the Union of Russian Cities
 Publication of *Book of Memories*, about soldiers from Yaroslavl killed in Afghanistan
 Organization of exhibits in honor of the historian N.V. Kuznetsova
Administration upkeep
 Return of loans made by city
 Town planning, public services, and amenities
 Needs of the city (e.g., computers, subsidies, capital construction)

Source: Yaroslavl City little soviet resolutions from 1992.

ditures on foreign relations, enterprise subsidies, morale, and entertainment, indicate both the priorities and the substantial new authority of local government. Under the previous system only the central government or enterprises would make such expenditures. The subsidization of firms will inhibit the process of privatization by supporting enterprises that do not make a profit and by preserving irrational economic structures. But subsidization serves several other purposes. The city can help maintain a veneer of economic activity resembling the past and keep the local economy functioning. It can also secure the provision of certain goods and services that the government deems necessary that may not be possible under "market" conditions.[11] By subsidizing enterprises in the city, the city government has clearly turned its attention toward supporting and developing economic activity within its boundaries.[12] Despite legal constraints that define the retail and service sector as municipal property, the city gives financial assistance to enterprises of any type located on their territory.

The increasing importance of extra-budgetary expenditures, noted above, highlights an additional political factor of the budgetary system in Russia. Only the executive branch—the mayor's office—may expend the extra-budgetary revenues. The legislative branch—the city soviet and little soviet —monitors these expenditures but can independently expend funds only from the carryover funds. Since only the executive can expend the extra-budgetary funds, these expenditures do not necessarily reflect legislated policy.

If we view off-budgetary expenditures as evidence of independent expenditure policy, then we can identify particular economic priorities of the Yaroslavl local government (see Tables 3.4 and 3.5). Independent expenditure priorities are social assistance, improvement of local and interregional communications (both telecommunications and road transportation), place-related consciousness-building, and infrastructure in general. These priorities straddle traditional responsibilities of insuring quality of life and new responsibilities, such as preparing the city to enter the world economy by improving infrastructure and by advertising the city. Despite potential negative consequences of city-level credit and subsidization from the point of view of market economics, these practices keep the urban economy functioning during restructuring, albeit inefficiently.

Summary and Conclusion

The case study of Yaroslavl leads to the conclusion that while a new fiscal system appears to function in Russia, elements of continuity with the previous system still exist. These limit, but do not preclude, the city's ability to conduct independent fiscal policy. Despite Soviet laws to initiate fiscal decentralization, major changes in the formation of local budgetary revenues and the composition of local budgetary expenditures did not occur until the breakup of the Soviet Union. Elements of independent fiscal policy are evident in an examination of the city budget in Yaroslavl. These indicate that the economic role of local government has grown and that the local government itself, not the central government, is pushing the boundaries of political and economic influence over territorial-administrative jurisdictions. The increasing importance of off-budgetary revenues and expenditures, the creation of a unified budget for the city of Yaroslavl, and the city-level subsidies to both the population for the social safety net and to enterprises for propping up the local economy represent significant changes in the economic role of local government during restructuring.

The city of Yaroslavl redefined both its economic role vis-à-vis central authority and its territorial power by independently forming revenues and by creating new areas of fiscal responsibility with its budgetary and off-budgetary expenditures. The city moved from using budgetary revenues for the financing of limited elements of social infrastructure to providing the industrial sector of the economy with subsidies, credits, and loans. The city also took on the role of financing the social safety net above and beyond the criteria set by the central government. The city extended its fiscal authority and political jurisdiction throughout the districts of the city by forming a unified budget that reduced district-level fiscal means. The case study of Yaroslavl shows a vital city government attempting to produce a new system, rather than reproduce the old system.

Notes

The research leading to this chapter was supported from funds provided by the National Council for Soviet and East European Research and the University of Arizona, who are not responsible, however, for the contents or findings of the chapter. The author gratefully acknowledges the assistance of Jeffrey Hahn and the Joint Russian-American Study of Legislative Systems sponsored by a grant from the Carnegie Corporation of New York for organizing the field work that lead to the Yaroslavl case study. The author would also like to thank the other members of the project—Timothy Colton, Jerry Hough, and Blair Ruble—for their assistance, James Metzger, reader of a previous version of the chapter, for his helpful comments, and Tim Brown for tireless research assistance.

1. Yaroslavl is an industrial city about 175 miles northeast of Moscow along the Volga River in the Central Economic Region. The city is the capital of Yaroslavl Oblast and has a population of about 640,000.

2. See *Sovetskaia Rossiia,* December 30, 1990; *FBIS-SOV–91–003,* January 7, 1991; and *Ekonomicheskaia gazeta,* 1992, no. 11 (March), for laws on increased tax powers at the local level; and Zakon "Ob obshchikh nachalakh mestnogo samoupravleniia i

mestnogo khoziaistva v SSSR" [USSR law "On basic principles of local self-management and local economic activity"], *Izvestiia,* February 16, 1991, p. 2 for additional rights granted to the local level.

3. Districts (*raiony*) are either subdivisions of cities (*raiony v gorode*) or rural areas, the latter usually under the jurisdiction of oblast governments.

4. This chapter views the availability and use of extra-budgetary and off-budgetary funds as a potential benefit for local governments, because under the current system this is the only way that a local government can independently deal with local issues within the existing legal framework. The use and existence of extra-budgetary funds by local governments are also considered inefficient for macroeconomic stability and budgetary management (see Wallich 1992). For example, the overuse of extra-budgetary funds in China is partially blamed for increased deficit spending at the local level (see Kojima 1992). However, the use of off-budgetary funds is quite rational from the point of view of the local government and local conditions. Local governments operate under great uncertainty, particularly with respect to central assistance from the legal and financial points of view.

5. The *Meriia* is currently the executive branch of the city government. It handles day-to-day operations and implements policy. It was formerly called the city executive committee (gorispolkom). The head of the Meriia is the mayor, an official who is currently appointed by the legislative branch and approved by the central government. These arrangements are, however, temporary; mayors are to be directly elected by the public in the future.

6. A report from Kemerovo in West Siberia confirms interview evidence supporting continuity through 1991, rather than change during late perestroika (see Rechko 1992).

7. Yet if we view inflation as a tax, with the state budget at all levels receiving higher levels of revenues, then inflation becomes an important "new" budgetary source of revenue.

8. The 1992 figures include the value-added tax rather than the turnover tax.

9. This line item does not appear in the city's budget summary for 1992. The expenditures, however, do appear as part of housing-communal economy and several other categories under the national economy heading.

10. Local governments in the United States often commit local funds or issue bonds in order to support amateur and professional sports as a means of advertisement (see Johnson 1993).

11. For example, the city subsidized an enterprise that provided laundry services to local hospitals when the hospitals decided to decline their services due to lack of funds. In the interest of insuring a supply of clean laundry to hospitals, the city granted the enterprise credit for a limited period of time.

12. This, too, is evident in the Chinese case in the 1980s after fiscal decentralization was instituted (Kojima 1992). Local governments in China have also gained new authority and responsibility in the sphere of local economic development. One reform model to stimulate local economic growth in China has the local government as the active participant and "owner" of the means of production (Fureng 1992).

References

Bahry, Donna. (1987). *Outside Moscow: Power, Politics, and Budgetary Policy in the Soviet Republics.* New York: Columbia University Press.

Berkowitz, Daniel, and Mitchneck, Beth. (1992). "Fiscal Decentralization in the Soviet Economy." *Comparative Economic Studies,* summer: 1–18.

Breslauer, George W. (1986). "Provincial Party Leaders Demand Articulation and the Nature of Center-Periphery Relations in the USSR." *Slavic Review,* vol. 45 (winter): 650–72.

Friedgut, Theodore H. (1983). "A Local Soviet at Work: the 1970 Budget and Budget Discussion of the Oktyabr Borough Soviet of Moscow." In Everett M. Jacobs, ed., *Soviet Local Politics and Government.* London: George Allen & Unwin, pp. 157–71.

Fureng, Dong. (1992). *Industrialization and China's Rural Modernization.* New York: St. Martin's Press.

Goskomstat RSFSR. (1990). *Statisticheskii Press-Biulleten',* no. 8.

Hahn, Jeffrey D. (1991). "Local Politics and Political Power in Russia: The Case of Yaroslavl." *Soviet Economy,* vol. 7, no. 4 (October–December): 322–41.

Hough, Jerry. (1969). *The Soviet Prefects: The Role of Local Party Organs in Industrial Decision-Making.* Cambridge, MA: Harvard University Press.

Johnson, Arthur T. (1993). *Minor League Baseball and Local Economic Development.* Urbana: University of Illinois Press.

Kojima, Reeitsu. (1992). "The Growing Fiscal Authority or Provincial-Level Governments in China." *The Developing Economies,* vol. 30, no. 4: 315–46.

Lewis, Carol W. (1976). "The Budgetary Process in Soviet Cities." Center for Government Studies: Graduate School of Business, Columbia University.

———. (1983). "The Economic Functions of Local Soviets." In Everett M. Jacobs, ed., *Soviet Local Politics and Government.* London: George Allen & Unwin, pp. 48–66.

Mitchneck, Beth. (1992). "The Soviet Locality in Transition or is it Transformed?" Paper presented at the Annual Meeting of the Association of American Geographers, San Diego, California, April.

Mitchneck, Beth, and Daniel Berkowitz. (1992). "Local Public Finance in Russia: Continuity and Change." Photocopied manuscript.

Moses, Joel C. (1985). "Regionalism in Soviet Politics: Continuity as a Source of Change, 1953–1982." *Soviet Studies,* vol. 37 (April): 184–211.

Rechko, Galina N. (1992). "Increasing the Role of Financial Resources of the Region in Social-Economic Development (in Kuzbass case)." Kemerovo, Russia. (Typewritten.)

Romaindo, Henry J., and Stuart, Robert C. (1984). "Financing Soviet Cities." In Henry W. Morton and Robert C. Stuart, eds., *The Contemporary Soviet City.* Armonk, NY: M.E. Sharpe, pp. 45–64.

———. (1986). "Variations in Soviet City Finances." *Growth and Change,* vol. 17, no. 2 (April): 56–67.

Ruble, Blair A. (1990). *Leningrad: Shaping a Soviet City.* Berkeley: University of California Press.

Shomina, E.S. (1992). "Enterprises and the Urban Environment in the USSR." *International Journal of Urban and Regional Research,* vol. 16, no. 2: 222–33.

Wallich, Christine I. (1992). *Fiscal Decentralization, Intergovernmental Relations in Russia.* Washington, DC: The International Bank for Reconstruction and Development/The World Bank.

4

Saratov and Volgograd, 1990–1992

A Tale of Two Russian Provinces

Joel C. Moses

The provinces of Saratov and Volgograd so epitomize the diversities of the Russian Federation that existed in 1993 that they could very nearly be termed a Russian political version of a *Tale of Two Cities*. They represent polar opposites in the "Second Russian Revolution" taking place since the abortive coup of August 1991. In Saratov, former Communist Party and state officials and economic managers remained firmly in control of the post-Soviet and post-communist provincial government and economy in 1993; little seemed to have changed in the three years since the March 1990 local and republic elections. In Volgograd by 1993, a new post-communist elite governed, a number of political parties and movements contested policies and competed for power, and local entrepreneurs provided the support for the rapid privatization of agriculture, commerce, and industry. Saratov would be considered one of the most conservative local strongholds in Russia, opposed to the economic and political reforms of President Yeltsin. Volgograd by reputation would be ranked along with Nizhnii Novgorod (formerly Gorky) and the city governments of Moscow and St. Petersburg as one of the most economically liberal and politically democratic areas in Russia.

The anomaly is that it would have been difficult before 1990 to have found two other oblasts and their capitals so geographically similar, so closely linked over the previous three hundred years of Russian history, and so similar in their problems. This chapter attempts to explain the anomaly of how and why these two otherwise identical neighbors came to differ so much politically.

Saratov and Volgograd: Overview

Bordering each other on the lower Volga River, Saratov and Volgograd almost mirrored each other in the 1989 Soviet census.[1] The 2.69 million people of Saratov Oblast and the 2.59 million people of Volgograd Oblast lived in territories each approximately 100,000 square kilometers and each geographically equivalent to the size of an entire central European country such as Czechoslovakia. By 1989 Saratov and Volgograd typified the Russian Federation demographically. Seventy-four percent of the federation's 150 million people lived in areas classified as urban. In 1989, 74 percent of Saratov's predominantly Russian ethnic population, and 76 percent of Volgograd's, were urban. Both oblasts had even grown exactly the same 5 percent during the ten years since the 1979 census.

Their capitals—approximately 400 kilometers apart and connected by a republic highway winding along the right bank of the Volga River—were as much alike as the two oblasts. The cities Saratov and Volgograd with populations of 905,000 and 999,000 respectively in 1989 had even grown by an equivalent 6 and 8 percent during the previous ten years. Outside their capitals, accounting for 34 and 39 percent of their entire oblast populations, large cities of up to 200,000 residents had formed along their common waterway of the Volga River. In Saratov, the heavily industrialized Volga River cities of Balakovo and Engels with populations of 100,000–200,000 each in 1989 were matched by their almost exact counterpart river cities of Kamyshin and Volzhskii on the banks of the Volga in Volgograd, with similar-sized populations.

History

By 1990 the striking parallels between the two oblasts and their capitals take on additional significance, because Saratov in the north and Volgograd in the south had actually evolved together as a common regional area over most of the previous three hundred years of the Russian Empire and the Soviet era.[2] Both oblasts constituted a single jurisdiction in the Russian Empire and in the first decade after the 1917 Russian Revolution—at various times termed the Saratov *namestnichestvo* (administrative territory) or the Saratov *guberniia* (province). Situated on the steppe between the Don and Volga rivers, the Saratov–Astrakhan region with its elevated bluff extending along the right bank of the Volga had been the last stronghold of the Tatars defeated by Ivan IV in the sixteenth century as Muscovy extended its political control over the former Tatar empire. Indeed, the very name

Saratov is derived from the Volga Tatar language and means literally "yellow mountain."

By the seventeenth century, the Saratov region had already emerged as a booming commercial and trading center at the eastern end of what was then the Russian frontier, or "wild steppe" (*dikoe pole*). On the left bank of the Saratov region was the frontier extending through modern-day Kazakhstan, from which non-Russian nomadic ethnic groups, freebooters, Volga pirates, Cossacks, and others periodically arose and threatened the "civilized" area of the Russian Empire on the right bank of the Volga with its elevated bluff. Saratov was the very first city conquered by the Don Cossack brigand Sten´ka Razin in the 1670s and the very last city conquered by the "Cossack tsar" Emelian Pugachev 100 years later in the 1770s.

From the time of Saratov's emergence as a booming frontier town and trading center, the region had become a natural magnet for political dissidents, radical populists and socialists, liberal gentry, rebellious peasants, Cossacks, and ethnic minorities—all of whom contributed to the highly cosmopolitan and politically charged culture reflected in the Saratov city *duma* and the Saratov regional *zemstvo* from 1878 through 1917.[3] One of Saratov's most famous pre-revolutionary officials had been Petr Stolypin, the governor-general of Saratov in 1903–7 immediately prior to his becoming Russian prime minister. His vigorous advocacy of private-land ownership for peasants when he became prime minister very likely was shaped by his experiences in attempting to deal with the contentious liberal, radical, and reactionary political forces in Saratov during these five years—particularly during the 1905 Revolution.

The rich and fertile black-earth soil on the right bank of the Volga-Don steppe also accounted for the region's development as a major grain-producing and agricultural center of Russia—one rivaled in the Russian imperial and Soviet eras only by the fertile Volga–Don delta region and the northern Caucasus between the Caspian and Black seas and by the southern grain-growing provinces of Ukraine. During the Soviet era, agricultural industry developed in the broad regional area. It was best symbolized by the Tractor Plant in the city of Volgograd, which employed tens of thousands and became the prototype of the behemoth Stalinist industrial enterprises for the Five-Year Plans of the 1920s and 1930s. Even at the end of the Soviet era in 1991 the plant produced over half of the tractors used for ploughing in Russia.

At the time of the Russian Revolution, the city of Volgograd at the border of Saratov with Astrakhan was named Tsaritsyn, the most southern port city of the Saratov guberniia along the Volga River. With rail lines connecting it to the western industrial centers of the Russian Empire and with its population of 90,000 at the beginning of the twentieth century, Tsaritsyn was the industrial boomtown of the Saratov region. Saratov, the capital of the region, had already grown to 250,000 by the beginning of World War I. In 1925 Tsaritsyn was renamed Stalingrad to commemorate the newly built Tractor Plant in the city.

In 1928–34, Saratov and Stalingrad constituted the Southern Volga *Krai* (territory) with its capital transferred to Stalingrad in 1932–34. In January 1934, the Southern Volga Krai was divided into the two administrative subdivisions of the Saratov and Stalingrad krais, later renamed *oblasts* (provinces) in 1936.

The two provinces of Saratov and Volgograd retained their territories and borders from 1936 through the collapse of the Soviet Union and the formation of the independent nation–state of the Russian Federation in 1991–92. In the new Russian state, as in the former Russian Republic, the oblasts of Tambov, Penza, Ulianovsk, and Kuibyshev border Saratov from west to east in the north; the oblasts of Rostov and Astrakhan and the Kalmyk Republic border Volgograd (the name Stalingrad was dropped in 1961) from west to east in the south. East of the common border of Volgograd and Saratov on the left bank of the Volga River are the far western provinces of the Republic of Kazakhstan.

Political Economy

Agriculture defined the distinctive economic profile of the two oblasts throughout the Soviet era. This was particularly true of Volgograd. Volgograd remained one of the largest grain-producing regions of the Soviet Union, and many of Volgograd's provincial communist leaders over the decades since the early 1950s had been commonly recruited from those with extensive careers and backgrounds overseeing local agricultural production.[4] In the last few decades before 1990, however, both oblasts had evolved into major energy and heavy industrial centers of the Russian Federation. Oil and gas production and refineries and petrochemical plants became major economic sectors in both oblasts, along with the development of hydroelectric and nuclear power plants along the Volga River.

Their diversification economically was not without a major price for the populations in both oblasts. The oil and gas refineries and petrochemical plants dotting both sides of the Volga River spewed toxic pollutants into their common air and water basins, making the southern Volga region among the most highly contaminated and environmentally unhealthy areas in the Soviet Union. With large unregulated petrochemical plants discharging dangerous carcinogens such as formaldehyde into the atmosphere, the city of Saratov by 1990 alone had a cancer ratio of 340 contractions per 100,000 residents and had the dubious distinction of ranking third among all cities in the Soviet Union in total number of those with lung cancer. In 1992 Saratov still ranked as one of the twenty most polluted cities in the Russian Federation, based on air quality samples.[5]

During the first six months of 1990, the Saratov oblast hydrometeorological center had issued 28 different pollution warnings to the Saratov city government and health department, with little effect. The center had also encountered no success in obtaining municipal cooperation in having seventeen petrochemical enterprises in the city cut back operations to reduce the level of dangerous pollutants spreading throughout the region of the lower Volga. The problem of atmospheric pollution in Saratov had been raised first by local citizen–activists in the early 1980s, yet nothing changed because of the close interdependency of the oblast party–state establishment and the management of the large petrochemical industries.

By 1990 a new controversy pitting the public in the southern Volga region against big industry was the Balakovo nuclear power plant. Located on the shore of the Volga in northern Saratov, the Balakovo nuclear power station was the same model that had partially melted down at Chernobyl in 1986. By 1989–90, the Balakovo station had become notorious for its poor safety record and technical failures requiring frequent shut-downs and repairs, and citizens' groups arose, alarmed by the incidence of diseases affecting children in the immediate area of the station. The plan to add a fifth and sixth energy block to the Balakovo station aroused public protests in 1989–90, with human chains blocking the entrance to the station in fears that the same human and technical failures of a Chernobyl, should they occur at Balakovo, would produce an ecological catastrophe far surpassing even that of 1986 for the entire southern Volga region.[6]

As Stalingrad, Volgograd was the site of the famous battle and turning point of World War II with the defeat of the German army in December 1942. Volgograd's subsequent recognition as a national hero–city of the Soviet Union had profound local economic and political consequences for both oblasts. After 1945, the military-defense sector became a major employer and dominant political influence on both Saratov and Volgograd, as well as on the life of the entire region. That economic impact and the political influence accompanying it were particularly evident in Saratov. The Saratov Aviation Plant was the largest single employer in the province, and several local party–state leaders since the 1950s were recruited from prior positions managing either the aviation plant or related petrochemical and military enterprises in Saratov.[7]

With its defense industry, testing ranges for weapons, secret disposal sites for biological and chemical weapons, and military academies, Saratov was until 1991–92 officially designated for security reasons as a "closed" province that all Westerners were forbidden even to visit. As was true throughout the Soviet Union, the defense-related enterprises and testing ranges in Saratov were virtually excluded from any environmental supervision by local governmental authorities or health commissions. Thus, the enterprises, ranges, and dump-sites only compounded the problem of pollution in the overall region. In 1990, the military-defense complex in Saratov was characterized in an independent oblast newspaper as one of the two industrial sectors that through the communist establishment controlled all aspects of leadership and policy making in the province.[8]

The other sector that allegedly ran Saratov was water resources construction, with its irrigation–drainage projects along the Volga River. Its political influence derived locally from employment of 34,000 people and from the billions in rubles that it funneled into the local economy directly from Moscow as the local administrative trust for land reclamation and irrigation construction of the All-Union Ministry of Land Reclamation and Water Resources. In Saratov, these projects had been headed since the early 1970s by Ivan Kuznetsov, a former party secretary of the city of Marx in Saratov. Over these two decades in Saratov, Kuznetsov's influence was attributed to three factors: (1) his long-term ties with the Saratov establishment, spanning the tenures of four different provincial Communist first secretaries; (2) his willingness to divert millions in slush funds out of his construction budget to local party and state officials; and (3) the ability of these grateful officials to control the Saratov police, prosecutors, and judges and to protect Kuznetsov from investigations into his embezzlement and misuse of funds.[9]

Political Establishment

The unofficial political "godfather" of Saratov through his control over irrigation construction, Kuznetsov was so powerful in the province that in August 1989 he allegedly arranged the election of Konstantin Murenin as the new *obkom* (oblast committee) Communist Party first secretary.[10] In 1972–76, Murenin had been the deputy chair for construction in the *oblispolkom* (the oblast government executive committee) and from 1976 until August 1989, the obkom party secretary for industry and construction.[11] It seems likely that his ties with Kuznetsov were formed there.

A native of a rural district in Saratov and a graduate of the Saratov Polytechnical Institute, Murenin typified the underlying continuity of the

Saratov establishment over several decades prior to the March 1990 elections. The chair of the oblispolkom, Nikolai Aleksandrov, had held this position since 1971 and was not replaced until just prior to the March 1990 elections by Nikolai Grishin, the obkom second secretary since 1988.[12] Grishin in turn was replaced by internal rotation within the Saratov establishment as second secretary by Kim Ponamarev, the first deputy chair of the oblispolkom since at least 1987 under Aleksandrov.[13] Even Nikolai Shabanov, the editor of the oblast party newspaper at the beginning of 1990, had run the publication continuously since at least 1976.[14]

Murenin was only the fourth person since 1959 to have been Saratov oblast first party secretary, and in the late 1960s he was personal assistant to obkom first secretary Aleksandr Shibaev. Shibaev ruled the province for seventeen years—from 1959 until he was promoted to chair of the All-Union Council of Trade Unions in 1976. He was succeeded by his provincial second secretary, Viktor Gusev, who ruled Saratov until he was promoted to deputy chair of the Russian Council of Ministers a month after Gorbachev became General Secretary in April 1985.[15]

In the capital of Saratov, only two different persons had ruled city government since 1974 as the *gorkom* (city committee) first secretary. Iurii Kochetkov, a former long-term foreman, Komsomol, and party official at the Saratov Aviation Plant, had been the Saratov gorkom first secretary continuously from 1974 until late 1984, when he was appointed inspector of the All-Union Central Committee and then second secretary of the Armenian Communist Party in April 1985 coincidental with Gusev's promotion to deputy chair in the Russian government.[16] Kochetkov was succeeded in 1985 as head of the Saratov gorkom by Vladimir Golovachev. As we shall see, Golovachev came to dominate the course of political events in both the city and oblast of Saratov in 1990–91.

If continuity describes politics in Saratov prior to the 1990 elections, instability best characterizes Volgograd.[17] Twice within the previous six years, the Volgograd political establishment had been displaced, almost *en masse*. The first time was an intentional purge of the entire Volgograd establishment, orchestrated through Vladimir Kalashnikov, a political protégé who had worked under Gorbachev in Stavropol in the 1970s. In January 1984, Kalashnikov was sent from Moscow to replace Leonid Kulichenko as the Volgograd obkom first secretary. Kulichenko was retired after twenty continuous years in this position and, prior to that, more than three decades as a high-ranking party or state official in Volgograd. Kalashnikov had been dispatched to Volgograd with a mandate both to eliminate the corruption and incompetence of a leadership firmly entrenched after two decades of Kulichenko's rule, and to increase the province's agricultural output.

Kalashnikov accomplished the first task, removing all of Kulichenko's cohorts from the previous two decades. The entire oblast party secretariat, averaging ten to fifteen years in their same positions in 1984, were all replaced by 1986. In filling these positions, Kalashnikov recruited his new secretaries from the powerful agricultural-machinery sector, identified with the Volgograd Tractor Plant.[18] Yet the leadership changes by Kalashnikov extended beyond the provincial secretariat.[19]

Kalashnikov faltered in his second task of boosting agricultural output. He had been the chief of irrigation projects in Stavropol in the 1970s, and most recently in 1983–84 had been head of the Russian Federation Ministry of Land Reclamation and Water Resources. Drawing on his past, Kalashnikov wrongly presumed that the key to improving agricultural output in Volgograd was to adopt the large-scale irrigation and drainage projects that had been instituted in neighboring Saratov since the 1970s under Ivan Kuznetsov. The results in Volgograd in 1984–89 were not unlike those over the previous two decades in Saratov under Kuznetsov—the destruction of thousands of hectares of previously fertile farmlands and a drop in agricultural output. Extremely sensitive, Kalashnikov rejected any criticism regarding his program of irrigation projects and by 1989 had alienated even some of those whom he had just recently promoted to major party–state positions in the province.

By 1989 Kalashnikov was undone politically when he failed to gain confirmation by the All-Union Supreme Soviet for the position of first deputy chair of the Council of Ministers. Following his rejection, Kalashnikov was portrayed through an article and interview in *Ogonek* as prototypical of the very worst kind of overbearing and corrupt party apparatchik (in what may have been a premeditated attempt to discredit Gorbachev through one of his political protégés). He came across in *Ogonek* as someone who presumed a right to special privileges for himself and his entourage in the provincial party bureau and blithely ignored the declining standard of living experienced by Volgograders since 1985. His mismanagement of agriculture and responsibility for the environmental damage caused by his irrigation projects were now disclosed nationally. This national exposure forced Kalashnikov to submit his resignation and retire in disgrace as head of the Volgograd party organization in mid-January 1990, but the political fallout did not end with his retirement.

In the subsequent two weeks, almost the entire provincial party bureau—several of whom had themselves held their positions only since 1988–89, but all of whom were tainted by association with Kalashnikov—were removed by a vote of no confidence by the oblast party committee. The committee itself was forced to act under political siege by the citizenry of Volgograd. In a reversion to the region's pre-1917 character as the "wild steppe" of Razin and Pugachev, an unprecedented wave of mass protests and public demonstrations demanding the ouster of the communist establishment had swept Volgograd throughout the week of January 24–29, 1990. Both rank-and-file party members and average Volgograders had been prominent in the protests and demonstrations against the establishment.

Political Issues

Three identical problems challenged the Communist Party–state establishment in both oblasts and capitals during the 1990 national and local elections. Health and safety were two overriding issues; repatriation of ethnic Germans was the third.

Environmental pollution from petrochemical and defense industries had already prompted public protests in both oblasts and forced health concerns to be addressed as a priority by the political leadership throughout 1990–91. Mounting grassroots opposition to the Balakovo nuclear power station in the northern Volga River border of Saratov, to the nuclear power station on the Don River in Rostov province just south of Volgograd, and to a second Don–Volga Canal in Volgograd sparked similar movements and polarized politics in both provinces.

The problem of AIDS cases among young children had become a highly emotional and visible health issue, especially in Volgograd. Reports in the local newspapers and at sessions of the city soviet in 1990–91 grimly revealed the consequences of the disease contracted through contaminated blood transfusions at local hospitals and clinics.[20] Families were impoverished, mothers forced to quit their jobs to care for their HIV-infected children. Those seriously ill had to be hospitalized in a converted civil-defense building and sent as far as St. Petersburg for treatment, because local health authorities had failed to appropriate funds and resources. As seen by critics in Volgograd, the inadequate response of local officials to AIDS only epitomized the generations of government indifference to public health and to the unregulated environmental pollution in the Volga basin accounting for even more widespread diseases, such as cancer.

The third major issue confronting the leaders of both oblasts was the repatriation of ethnic Volga Germans to their settlements overlapping both provinces along the Volga River. These were settlements first developed in the eighteenth century by German farmers invited by Catherine the Great to homestead the Volga River region. They were later reconstituted in 1921 by

Lenin as the Volga German Autonomous Republic. The same autonomous republic with its German ethnic settlements dating to 1763 was then abolished by Stalin in August 1941, when the entire Volga German nation was arrested and deported in boxcars to desolate areas of Central Asia for alleged collaboration with the invading German army.

Thirty to forty thousand ethnic Germans had returned to both oblasts by the late 1980s. Tension between the Russian and German communities in Saratov had already sparked sporadic conflicts between the two—especially in Marx (the former capital of the German Republic), Engels (right across the river), and Krasnoarmeisk (100 km. south of the capital). Local officials in the three cities had inflamed ethnic conflict by alleging that hundreds of thousands of ethnic Germans were about to return and reclaim their land and property. Leaders of the ethnic German community and journalists from liberal Russian newspapers contended that the local officials, in league with the Saratov oblast establishment, were deliberately and cynically inflaming anti-German fears to boost their own political popularity among the Russian ethnic majority of voters.

Actually, since the early 1970s, most ethnic Germans had chosen to emigrate to West Germany under its liberal policy of granting asylum and citizenship to those who could claim German ancestry. Anxious to slow down the wave of immigration, the German government by 1990–91 had already promised the Soviet government financial assistance in underwriting almost the entire cost of resettling the ethnic Germans in some form of their previous autonomous republic along the Volga. With the formal admission by the Soviet government in 1989 that the Volga Germans had been wronged by Stalin's action in 1941, the leadership of the Soviet Germans, through their political association "Revival" (*Vozrozhdenie*), now demanded autonomy and the full restoration of their political and economic rights in a reconstituted German republic within the territory of Saratov and Volgograd.

German repatriation confronted the leadership in Saratov and Volgograd with common challenges in 1990–91. How would this resettlement be reconciled with the changes in use and ownership of these same ethnic German lands over the past half-century? How would the potential conflict between ethnic Russians and Germans be averted? And would the political and economic benefits of repatriation and of reconciliation between the Russians and the Germans of the two provinces outweigh the potential costs? Ethnic German repatriation would mean not only economic assistance from the German government, but the return of a group renowned as farmers would be welcomed by any local leadership intending to carry out land reform and encourage private farming. In this sense, their overall response to the German issue in 1990–91 became something of a litmus test, revealing their real attitudes toward land reform, political pluralism, and ethnic tolerance in the democratic revolution unfolding in the late Soviet era.

Saratov, 1990–92 Provincial Government

The election to the capital and oblast soviets of Saratov in the early spring of 1990 seemed for all intents and purposes to have solidified the position of the Saratov party establishment and the general reputation of the province among democratic liberals in Russia as a political "swamp."[21] At least two-thirds of the 300 deputies elected to the oblast soviet were members of the regional *nomenklatura,* who fulfilled all expectations as an "obedient majority" in their voting behavior and provided automatic support for leadership proposals during 1990–91.[22] The democratic opposition in the oblast soviet could at best count on the support of fifteen to twenty deputies, who formed a Democratic Russia caucus with absolutely no ability to affect legislation or block the rubber-stamping by the provincial executive branch completely under the control of the party establishment.

The nature of the 1990 election had produced an imbalance in the oblast soviet. Competitive elections in the rural districts to the oblast soviet had been the rare exception.[23] Even when competition for the oblast soviet seats did occur, the communist establishment skillfully managed its control over the rural electorate to ensure its candidates their seats. Local party and state officials had engaged in a blatant form of "city-bashing" to appeal to the rural voters. Rural voters were told that, unless they voted the party's candidates into the oblast soviet to protect their interests, an urban-dominated oblast soviet would discriminate against the countryside and agriculture to favor the cities and heavy industry.

Candidates from the party–state establishment swept the election, from the Saratov countryside to the oblast soviet, by promising rural voters political payoffs, such as gas and water lines and paved roads for their villages. In cities such as Marx and Engels, the principal settlement areas for ethnic Volga Germans before their forced deportation by Stalin, the party–state establishment won the seats to the oblast soviet by a blatant appeal to ethnic hatred and fear. The voters were encouraged to believe that hundreds of thousands of Volga Germans were about to return to these cities to reclaim all of their lands and property in their autonomous republic—unless the candidates nominated by the party–state establishment were elected to protect the interests of the ethnic Russians.

According to an investigative journalist from the national weekly *Literaturnaia gazeta* and a former KGB officer responsible for arranging the resettlement of ethnic Germans but who was fired for his disclosure of widespread official corruption in Saratov, the anti-German campaign inaugurated in the fall of 1989 had been orchestrated personally by Ivan Kuznetsov, Saratov's political "godfather."[24] Basing their charges on personal investigations in Saratov, as well as on local informants, the journalist and the former KGB officer contended that Kuznetsov had deliberately inflamed anti-German hysteria through his local television and radio interviews, speeches at anti-German rallies, and secret financing and organizing of allegedly spontaneous protests and demonstrations against the return of the Volga Germans. Kuznetsov's motive for preventing the return of the Germans to their former farms in Marx, Engels, and other areas along the Volga was obvious to local sources and informants. The resettlement of Germans would have disclosed his criminal syndicate that, over the past two decades, had embezzled funds and bribed local party–state officials, and his personal culpability in authorizing many irrigation projects that had senselessly swamped and salinated much of the former fertile farmlands along the Volga.

As much as Kuznetsov denied any charges of conspiratorial or criminal wrongdoing on his part, he was undeniably aided and abetted in his openly anti-German statements of 1990–91 by a former Saratov official from the same ethnic German homeland area, Vladimir Gusev. Gusev, who had been the Saratov obkom first secretary from 1976 through 1985, had spent most of his career prior to 1976 as an industrial executive of a major chemical enterprise in the city of Engels. By 1989–90, Gusev was the deputy chair of the All-Union Council of Ministers under Nikolai Ryzhkov—a position from which he also chaired the special council's commission established to determine policy for resettling Germans to their original homeland in the lower Volga region. In 1990–91 Gusev was the one individual held most responsible by the leaders of the Volga German association "Revival" for obstructing their return to some form of autonomous jurisdiction.[25]

The members of the presidium of the Saratov oblast soviet, comprised of the oblast soviet commission chairs, were almost exclusively local party–state officials or prominent economic managers of the Saratov establishment.[26] The presidium in turn could be expected to follow and obey the presidium chair, Konstantin Murenin—someone who had been allegedly hand-picked by Ivan Kuznetsov in 1989 to become obkom first secretary and who was very soon sarcastically labeled the Saratov *batiushka*—the affectionate term of reference for the tsar by Russian serfs—by the minority of the fifteen to twenty Democratic Russia deputies on the oblast soviet. In 1990–91 Murenin imperially defied a Russian Congress resolution passed at the behest of Chairman Boris Yeltsin in December 1990 prohibiting any elected local chief executives in Russia from simultaneously holding an elected paid position in any political party. With at most twenty deputies even likely to question his authority, Murenin remained obkom first secretary and chair of the oblast soviet right up until the abortive August 1991 putsch. This pattern was duplicated at local levels of government throughout Saratov, where the chairs of the city and urban district soviets in almost all instances were still the local first secretaries or chairs of the executive committees right until the August putsch.[27]

Given the overlap between the composition of the Saratov obkom and the oblast soviet, the sessions of the provincial soviet in 1990–91 until the abortive August putsch were transformed almost into de facto plenums of the Saratov obkom, and the sessions of the presidium under Murenin into de facto meetings of the Saratov obkom bureau.[28] The same automatic majorities guaranteed Murenin support for his policies and personnel appointments to head departments in the Saratov government from the interchangeable communist functionaries on the provincial soviet and presidium. Not coincidentally, most of the newly appointed heads of executive departments approved by the soviet were former Communist Party first secretaries of urban and rural districts in Saratov.

The small Democratic Russia opposition on the oblast soviet was not alone in being powerless to resist Murenin and the nomenklatura. Grigorii Akhtyrko, an outspoken and popular local radio journalist, had been pressured by the oblast KGB to act as an informer on his fellow deputies and the Saratov democratic community since 1989, until he quit the Communist Party and went public with his disclosure in late 1990.[29] The opposition's very ability to "publicly contest" local policies in Saratov was limited to a very few nonparty and independent Saratov newspapers, registered by the more moderate and pluralistic Saratov city government but themselves intimidated in their ability to publish by the provincial authorities under Murenin's control.

Dominated by the traditional nomenklatura of Saratov, the soviet sessions chaired by Murenin turned into democratic charades. For example, new democratic procedures instituted in 1990 required all local judges and assessors in Russia to be elected by the oblast soviet for ten-year terms, rather than as in the past being periodically elected directly by the voters from a single slate of judges and assessors screened by the Communist Party. The change was intended to induce greater impartiality and adherence to the rule of law among more qualified judges and assessors who, with their ten-year terms, would be insulated from the all-pervasive intimidation and control of the local judiciary by party–state officials.

The intent sharply diverged from the reality in Saratov.[30] At the soviet session convened to elect the judges for the province and the people's assessors for the courts, 96 of 104 candidates for judgeships nominated by Murenin were members of the Communist Party. Several of those judges and the assessors approved by the provincial soviet lacked any formal judicial training or background, and some of those appointed for ten-year terms to the bench were already well past 65 years of age. None of the judges elected to the circuits for the cities of Marx and Engels were queried as to their judicial temperament for impartiality by asking them about their prejudices toward ethnic Germans, and at least one judge appointed to head a borough court in the city of Saratov was most noted for having jailed the organizers of the first demonstration of "informals" in Saratov in February 1989. After a pro forma vote on the candidates for judges, the people's assessors were approved by voice vote as an entire list.

City Soviet

Less dominated by the party–state establishment, the city soviet and government of Saratov seemed much more democratic in the first ten months of 1990 than its oblast counterpart.[31] A little more than one-third of the almost 200 deputies elected to the Saratov City Soviet in 1990 identified themselves as the liberal-radical minority, openly opposed to the party–state establishment. At the first session of the city soviet following the 1990 election, the liberal-radical minority formed their own organizational committee and caucus, "For Progress and Democracy in Saratov," and succeeded in forcing the rest of the city soviet to surrender one-third of the commission chairs in the soviet.

Composed of intellectuals, teachers, workers, and military officers, the liberal-radical minority contrasted with the majority of the city soviet deputies, who were still drawn from the nomenklatura of party, state, and economic officials in the city. The liberal-radical minority had gained a political foothold in the city soviet, despite clear attempts to harass and intimidate them during the campaign for the city soviet in March 1990. They also persisted in attempting to get economic and political reforms adopted by the city government, despite the absence of any real alternative political parties in Saratov to mobilize public support until after the abortive August putsch of 1991.[32]

If nothing else, the difference between a moderately pluralistic Saratov city soviet and an oblast soviet almost completely dominated by the provincial establishment under Murenin could be seen in their different approaches toward the local media. By the late fall of 1990, the Saratov City

Soviet funded and cofounded with the editorial board a nonparty city newspaper called *Saratov,* and registered two entirely independent liberal newspapers, the weekly *Mestnoe vremia* and the monthly *Saratovskii listok.* *(Saratovskie vesti,* an independent oblast newspaper, was neither registered by the provincial soviet nor published until after the abortive August putsch. *Kommunist*, the daily provincial newspaper, continued through the summer of 1991 as a joint organ of the provincial soviet and Communist Party and was issued by the Communist Publishing House, which owned the only printing presses for newspapers in the province—including the independents licensed by the Saratov City Soviet.

A media war in the province in 1990–91 pitted *Kommunist* as the organ of the oblast soviet and government against the nonparty newspapers registered by the city soviet of Saratov. Both sides published articles denouncing the political bias of the other relative to the party establishment and powerful local interests.[33] At times the nonparty media were unable to publish because of an alleged shortage of either newsprint or printing presses at the Communist Publishing House. After publishing its first two issues, *Saratov* was effectively shut down for the first six weeks of 1991 by the refusal of the Communist Publishing House to print it, and the editors finally were able to restart publication only by using a press in the city of Volgograd, 400 kilometers away.[34]

The nonparty newspapers were further hampered by the city soviet's Commission on the Media that oversaw and funded them. It was chaired in 1990–91 by Nikolai Zorin, the very same newly elected editor of the provincial Communist newspaper *Kommunist,* who remained chair of the commission until the August putsch. In an article published by *Kommunist* right before the putsch, the deputy chair of the same oblast soviet Commission on the Media blasted the official city soviet newspaper *Saratov* for its allegedly biased reporting.[35] Under Zorin, *Kommunist* maintained an unflagging hard-line Party perspective on Saratov issues and conflicts right until its dissolution after August 1991 for having supported the Emergency Committee during the putsch.

City Government

If the Saratov City Soviet elected in 1990 was more pluralistic, its election of Vladimir Golovachev to chair the presidium at its first session after the 1990 election appeared at the time to be a major political concession to the Saratov establishment. His election was generally seen as extending the establishment's control over city government, a control already evident in their complete domination of every other administrative jurisdiction in the province. Not only had Golovachev been the first secretary of the Saratov City Communist Party since 1985, but, following the precedent of Murenin on the provincial level, Golovachev remained capital gorkom first secretary of the party until early October 1990.[36]

Even discounting his previous six years as the head of the Communist Party in the city of Saratov, Golovachev's ties with the provincial establishment headed by Murenin and with the powerful petrochemical and construction industries seemed indisputable in early 1990.[37] After graduating from a local Saratov institute, Golovachev had worked his first thirteen years overseeing construction sites for the local oil refinery and petrochemical industries. First secretary of a Saratov urban district in the mid-1970s, by 1980 Golovachev was promoted to head the construction department of the oblast Communist Party.

He remained in this position until 1985 under Konstantin Murenin's tenure as obkom party secretary for industry and construction in 1976–89. In August 1989, A.A. Khomiakov, the Saratov CPSU provincial first secretary, was promoted to deputy chair of the Russian Council of Ministers in Moscow. At the plenary session to replace Khomkiakov, Golovachev—who had represented the Saratov Communist Party as a delegate to the Twenty-seventh Party Congress in 1986 and to the Nineteenth Party Conference in 1988—was apparently considered politically safe enough to be nominated as one of the three candidates for first secretary.[38] Golovachev lost, but he was defeated by his erstwhile political mentor, Konstantin Murenin—the very person who had overseen Golovachev in the secretariat in 1980–85 and who had almost certainly recommended Golovachev as gorkom first secretary of Saratov in 1985.

Nor were there any signs through the spring and summer of 1990 following his election to chair the Saratov City Soviet that Golovachev had suddenly become liberal and antiestablishment in his convictions and outlook. Golovachev was conspicuously present among the Saratov CPSU delegates at the founding conference of the Russian Communist Party in June 1990. Indeed, an article critical of the conference had singled out Golovachev's speech as prototypical of the right-wing conservative views prevalent among the delegates.[39] Until he resigned as head of the city party organization, Golovachev also rejected constant opposition by the liberal-radical minority on the city soviet to his remaining the full-time paid first secretary of the gorkom.[40] In essence, when Golovachev had been elected to chair the presidium of the city soviet, he had promised to comply with an amendment passed by the majority that obligated anyone elected to the position to resign all other outside paid positions in order to devote himself completely to the responsibilities of presidium chair. The minority complained that

Golovachev was violating both the letter and the spirit of the amendment by his retention of the paid office of gorkom first secretary and by his frequent absences from Saratov on party business.

Golovachev had been elected chair of the city soviet by a margin roughly parallel to the political division of deputies on the council between the two-thirds identified with the establishment and the one-third aligned with the liberal-radical caucus. Golovachev won by a margin of 118 votes against 80 for his sole opponent. The conventional political wisdom at the time attributed his election to the nomenklatura in the city of Saratov, who had lobbied their supporters among the majority of the city soviet deputies to vote for Golovachev.[41] Confirming this impression, Golovachev's first action following his own election was to nominate Aleksandr Ezhov to be his deputy chair of the city soviet presidium. Ezhov at the time was the chair of the Frunze *raiispolkom* (urban district executive committee) in Saratov and, in accordance with Golovachev's request, was subsequently elected deputy chair by the same majority that had just elected Golovachev himself.

At least ten of the nineteen members of the city soviet presidium were assumed to be under the control of the Saratov party establishment, an assumption based on their voting records, their stated positions, and endorsement by the same Saratov obkom party officials in 1990–91.[42] Throughout 1990 and the first half of 1991 the city Communist Party leadership under Golovachev's successor was conspicuously hostile to any democratic pluralism in city government. At plenary sessions and meetings they were still insisting that they had the right to dictate the actions and votes of any Saratov soviet deputy who was a member of the Communist Party.[43]

RSFSR Deputies

Finally, the liberal-radical minority on the Saratov City Soviet could hardly hope to count on any political support from the Saratov delegation to the Russian Congress of People's Deputies in the same 1990 election. The factors that had determined the outcome of the election to the provincial soviet had equally influenced Saratov voters in choosing their republic deputies. The Saratov delegation to the Russian Congress, made up of the traditional political and economic establishment of the province, could not have projected a more conservative image. The delegation to the Russian CDP was led by Konstantin Murenin. It included the Saratov obkom party second secretary (Kim Ponomarev); the chair of the Saratov oblispolkom (Nikolai Grishin); and top management officials of the Saratov oil–gas

(Gennadii Luzianin and Vladimir Chirsko), chemical (Boris Koksharov and Nikolai Romanov), defense (Vadim Potapov), and agricultural (Iurii Belykh and Iurii Kitov) economic sectors.

There were two notable exceptions to this pattern. One was Iurii Vishnevskii, the chief inspector for work safety of the Atomic Power Ministry at the Balakovo nuclear station, who had publicly expressed empathy with the concerns for the safety of the station raised by protesters in 1990.[44] The Saratov delegation also provided one of Boris Yeltsin's first ministers to the government formed under Ivan Silaev right after Yeltsin had been elected chair of the Russian Supreme Soviet in 1990, albeit someone whose background closely tied him to the powerful oil–gas sector of the Saratov economy. Yeltsin chose Dmitrii Fedorov to be the chair of the Russian State Committee for Geology, Fuel, Energy Carriers, and Mineral Resources. A strong advocate of economic sovereignty for Russia and transformation of the USSR into a confederation under which Russia would be able to charge world prices for its oil exports to the other republics, Fedorov had won his run-off election as director of the Geology and Geophysics Institute at Saratov University.[45]

As a group, however, the Saratov delegation tended to act and vote so conservatively that they prompted at least two petitions from local democratic activists in Saratov, repudiating or seeking the recall of their entire delegation.[46] Led by Konstantin Murenin, the most conspicuous action by the Saratov delegation had been to push for the convening of a special session of the Russian Congress in March 1991 to impeach Boris Yeltsin as Supreme Soviet Chairman because of his denunciation of the Soviet military crackdown in the Baltic republics in January and his subsequent call for Gorbachev's resignation as Soviet President.

Establishment Divided

The Communist Party nationally was losing power with the defeat of its candidates in the 1990 republic and local elections, and irreconcilably dividing into factions evident in the bitter debates that raged at Central Committee plenums in 1990–91 and at the Twenty-eighth Party Congress in 1990. Nothing signaled the collapse of communist political authority and the polarization of Soviet society more than the splits and rivalries that emerged simultaneously within the presumably unified party and state establishments of the Russian Republic. Individuals seemingly tied by their past careers as *apparatchiki* were breaking openly from their local party and state establishments. They were emerging as populist antiestablishment leaders of city and oblast governments and aligning themselves with the bloc of antiparty democratic caucuses elected to their city and oblast soviets as a result of the March 1990 local elections. Their motivation at the time could easily be ascribed both to a sincere democratic conversion and to a calculating and opportunistic self-interest over their own political survival in the imminent, non-communist, Russia of the future. That was a future apparent to almost everyone except for the hard-line party conservatives and their sympathizers among extremist Russian nationalists, who combined forces in founding the Russian Communist Party in June 1990.

In Saratov by the time of the abortive August putsch, the person who came to symbolize the split in the establishment and the democratic conversion of a career apparatchik was none other than Vladimir Golovachev. Even before August 1991, Saratov politics had escalated into an open conflict between Golovachev, allied with the caucus of the liberal-radical opposition in the city soviet, and the Saratov establishment led by Murenin and supported by the majority of the oblast and city soviet deputies.

To Golovachev's credit, initial impressions about his true political loyalty may have been mistaken. He had remained head of the Saratov city Communist Party, partly because until the autumn, the city soviet had failed to appropriate money for his salary as the full-time chair of the soviet's presidium.[47] With his position now salaried, Golovachev finally conceded to the liberal-radical minority caucus that the position of city soviet chair was not to be held by someone on a "voluntary" basis and in early October 1990 resigned his position as Saratov gorkom first secretary. Murenin, unburdened by any restrictions of the oblast soviet and ignoring the Russian Republic resolution prohibiting chief executives from holding offices in political parties, remained presidium chair and obkom first secretary until the August putsch.

In the months that followed, it became evident that Golovachev's resignation was more than just a token gesture. It was a calculated political break from the Saratov establishment, to which policy differences and political conflicts in the first seven months of 1991 contributed. Golovachev supported elimination of Saratov's "closed" status and openly identified himself with the movement to attract firms from France and Germany to the city.[48] By February 1991, Golovachev had become a featured contributor to nonparty independent newspapers in the city.[49] He supported adoption of a new Russian constitution drafted by the Yeltsin government and denounced the distorted propaganda campaign that was being orchestrated by the Saratov obkom leadership against it.

The Party leadership under Murenin responded by attempting to smear Golovachev with charges of corruption, raising the issue of his personal use of an official automobile assigned to him as the city soviet chair.[50] An underlying political rivalry between Golovachev and Murenin and their respective factions in the Saratov establishment may only have exacerbated the split. It should be recalled that, despite Golovachev's junior status as a long-term political protégé of Murenin, he had run against Murenin for obkom first secretary in August 1989 and that Ivan Kuznetsov had allegedly interceded to influence obkom votes in Murenin's favor.

By the early spring of 1991, the Saratov establishment led by Murenin attempted to arrange for Golovachev's ouster as the head of the city government through their nominal majorities on the city soviet and the city soviet presidium.[51] Twelve of the nineteen members on the presidium passed a motion that Golovachev should resign, and attempted to have their motion introduced as a vote of no confidence before the entire city soviet. Their attempt fell short, receiving only ninety-six votes, when the bloc of liberals and democrats, by this time identifying with Golovachev as their nominal leader in the city government, boycotted the session. Lacking a quorum, and with 20 to 30 nomenklatura deputies on the city soviet absent, the move to oust Golovachev failed. The very attempt to remove him from office by the Saratov establishment led by Murenin only enhanced Golovachev's newly emergent democratic image among the liberal-radical minority bloc on the soviet. Golovachev finally broke openly with the establishment in June and resigned from the oblast party bureau, following a nationally published interview in which he accused the Communist leadership of sabotaging democratic and market-reform efforts and of fueling nationalistic hysteria against the restoration of the Volga German Republic.[52]

August 1991–1992

During the three days of August 19–21, the conflict pitting Murenin, the majority of the city–oblast soviets, the city–oblast presidiums, and the communist-oriented media on the one side, against Golovachev, the minority democratic opposition on the city soviet, and the liberal nonparty newspapers on the other, paralleled their reactions to the Emergency Committee and Boris Yeltsin.[53] Most of the print and electronic media in Saratov imposed a news blackout during the three days, essentially cutting off the public from Yeltsin's appeals and actions. The majority of the city presidium, which was tied to Murenin and the political establishment, refused to meet, and the city executive committee, beyond Golovachev's control, banned a rally of citizens in support of Yeltsin on August 20. Murenin conveniently isolated himself during the three days and refused to accept any news about Yeltsin and the resistance to the Emergency Committee from the democratic deputies on the oblast soviet.

The exception to the news blackout came predictably from one of the nonparty newspapers. The city soviet daily *Saratov* courageously published a special edition on August 20. On the front page it featured Yeltsin's decree denouncing the Emergency Committee and appealing to the Russian people, along with several articles on the political implications of the coup under the headline "August '91—Back to '64?" In the city soviet, Golovachev apparently learned from his indirect contacts that Yeltsin enjoyed support both in Moscow and in other Russian cities, and speaking to a visiting Spanish delegation, he characterized the actions of the Emergency Committee as a coup.[54] On August 20, Golovachev met with the democratic deputies on the city soviet to form a special staff to support Yeltsin.

Following the abortive putsch, the head of the oblast radio and television broadcasting department was fired; the communist provincial newspaper *Kommunist* was abolished; the independent newspaper *Saratovskie vesti* was registered and funded by the oblast soviet; and the editors of *Saratov* were rewarded by having the size of their newspaper more than doubled. At an emergency session of the oblast soviet, the overwhelming majority of conservatives voted to remove Murenin as the presidium chair, but in a way that avoided raising the issue of his silence and their own complicity during the coup. They formally voted Murenin out on the grounds that he had violated the Russian Congress of People's Deputies' resolution of 1990 prohibiting any Russian chief executives from simultaneously holding offices in any political party.[55] Murenin was replaced by Nikolai Makarevich, a jurist and one of the minority 15 to 20 democratic deputies on the soviet. Makarevich was praised by the chair of the Saratov branch of Democratic Russia as a long-time participant in the Saratov democratic movement.[56]

For not supporting the Emergency Committee and for warning Yeltsin in the weeks following August 21 that the conservative establishment still controlled Saratov despite the formal outlawing of the Communist Party, Golovachev was rewarded in early September with appointment as Yeltsin's presidential representative (*predstavitel'*), the equivalent of governor-general of Saratov. In this position—first created for all Russian oblasts and krais in late August 1991, and directly subordinate to the office of Russian President—Golovachev effectively assumed broad powers over all dimensions of policy making in Saratov previously controlled by Murenin in his dual positions as chair of the oblast soviet presidium and obkom first secretary. Golovachev's formal duty was to verify implementation of both letter and spirit of all reforms passed by the Russian Supreme Soviet or issued as presidential decrees by Yeltsin, as well as to serve as a general ombudsman and advocate for local democratic market reformers.

The presidential representative was invested with broad authority to participate in and influence all executive and legislative organs in the oblast and was directly empowered to recommend to Yeltsin the appointment and dismissal of the oblast head of administration (glava administratsii). The oblast head of administration was a new position created to supplant the former chief executive position in Russian provincial state government identified with the' oblispolkom chair. Oblast and krai administrative heads were supposed to have been elected directly by voters in each locale, but the position became an appointed office under Yeltsin until the Russian Congress in March 1993 reinstituted direct elections of the oblast-krai heads, revoking the president's right of appointment.

To demonstrate his commitment to the democratic community, Golovachev's first public appearances after his appointment found him addressing a rally against totalitarianism at a church in Engels, repudiating the anti-German hysteria by local city leaders in both Engels and Marx, and expressing confidence about the revival of an autonomous German republic sometime in the future.[57] Yet because Golovachev had been the Saratov gorkom first secretary from 1985 until October 1990, and a member of the obkom party bureau until only two months before the August putsch, not everyone in the Saratov democratic community was convinced of his conversion or of any real political change with his appointment. This was particularly true because Golovachev's major priority in his interviews and speeches after his appointment was to mobilize public support in Saratov for the dissolution of the oblast soviet and other local soviets in the province. Golovachev argued that because the election in 1990 had been rigged by the Communist Party, the majority of conservative deputies still on these councils and the majority of former party officials elected as their presidium chairs after August did not truly represent the Saratov public.[58]

The bitter irony for some in the Saratov democratic community was that the person who was now demanding that the executive authority be invested with more power, and that the legislative branch of government should be dissolved as undemocratic, was the same gorkom first secretary who had ruled the city of Saratov from 1985, heading a party committee that had subverted democratic reform throughout 1990–91.[59] As the unelected presidential representative, Golovachev now seemed to want to return all power to himself and to eliminate even the fledgling countervailing influence of the legislative branch in Saratov.

Local leaders of the Saratov branch of the Democratic Party of Russia were just as dismayed by the person whom President Yeltsin eventually appointed oblast head of administration in March 1992, presumably at the recommendation of Golovachev.[60] This was Iurii Belykh, who had been elected to the Russian Congress from Saratov in 1990 and who, by his votes and statements, had visibly aligned himself with the overwhelming nomenklatura majority in the province's delegation. As the director of the largest poultry factory in the province, Belykh had long-term ties to powerful economic interests in Saratov and dubious credentials as one who would implement the breakup of the state–collective farm system and other liberal economic reforms. In an interview two months after he was appointed, Belykh was still advocating "gradualism" in reforming the agricultural sector, questioning the adaptability of Saratov residents to the concept of private land ownership, and supporting the retention of collective farms.[61]

Clearly Yeltsin had been forced to concede to the majority of the oblast soviet in choosing Belykh as someone acceptable to them as chief executive. Although the oblast soviet could not legally block the individual selected as chief executive by Yeltsin, a majority of the soviet had essentially blackballed Yeltsin's first thirteen choices for the position by voting no confidence in them before finally approving Belykh. Filling the position was a particular urgency for Yeltsin by early 1992. The German government was threatening to reconsider its financial support for resettlement of ethnic Germans in their homeland along the Volga, and Yeltsin was attempting to fashion a policy mutually satisfactory to the ethnic Germans and to local residents. Emotions were running very high on this subject when Yeltsin visited Saratov in January 1992. Without a chief executive, the oblast soviet, to which several deputies had been elected in 1990 by inciting anti-German fears among voters, was threatening to consider a resolution declaring Saratov an independent republic to prevent the repatriation of ethnic Germans by the Russian government.

In the city of Saratov, a counterreformation successfully overcame pressures for democratic changes arising from the 1990 election. Even with the formal disappearance of Communism in the independent Russian Federation and with political parties, an independent press, and a reformist provincial chair like Makarevich, many of the same former party–state officials remained firmly entrenched in control of the provincial government and local cities into 1993. A conservative oblast soviet, and similarly conservative soviets in several municipalities, retained an effective veto over any reforms sponsored by the more pluralistic and liberal capital soviet. In Saratov, very little real political change occurred over 1990–92. Best typified by Vladimir Golovachev and Iurii Belykh as the new chief executives of the province and by Ivan Kuznetsov, who remained head of the state construction trust at the time of President Yeltsin's trip to Saratov in early

January 1992, the establishment seemed to have triumphed, even without the Communist Party and the Soviet Union.

Volgograd, 1990–92

In Volgograd the communist establishment had been overthrown by the end of January less than two months before the 1990 election to the provincial and city soviets. Public discontent across a range of problems in the province was blamed on a corrupt and unaccountable party establishment, forcing resignation of almost the entire party bureau. This successful populist movement, sardonically termed the "Volgograd disease" for inspiring similarly successful protests that forced the ouster of communist leaders in several other Russian provinces in early 1990, strongly influenced the campaign for the election of deputies to the Volgograd and capital soviets during the following six weeks. It was the catalyst for the political changes emanating from the outcome of the election in Volgograd that were to give the province its reputation over the next two years as one of the most liberal and antiestablishment locales in Russia.

The 1990 Elections

The January events in Volgograd had an immediate impact, if for no other reason than that they left the Volgograd Communist Party effectively leaderless, divided, and distracted for the critical six weeks leading up to the first round of the republic-local elections in mid-March. In neighboring Saratov, a unified party establishment was mobilizing its entire apparatus to get out the vote for their carefully selected candidates through an orchestrated campaign of city-bashing in the countryside and anti-German racism in the cities. In February and early March 1990, the Volgograd Communist Party could not mount any campaign. Leadership of the party had been assigned temporarily on a voluntary basis to two provincial Komsomol secretaries and to an interim first secretary, Iurii Nekrasov, formerly the director of the party's publishing house.[62]

These three lacked all political authority and experience to mobilize a party effort during the campaign. The January events had unleashed an open struggle for political power and an antiauthoritarian populist movement in the entire Volgograd Communist apparatus. The various local branches of the party were scrambling to disassociate themselves from the former provincial leadership and to position themselves to have their nominees elected to the new òbkom secretariat and bureau by the delegates at the party's forthcoming provincial conference, scheduled after the elections. Party activists, who until then had occupied second-tier positions of power in Volgograd as the first secretaries of district or city organizations, sought to take over leadership of the party. Thus their preoccupation with winning control of the apparat detracted from the time and effort devoted to the campaign for the local soviets and the Russian Congress of People's Deputies.

By default, the party's disarray and preoccupation with its own internal power struggle benefited the diverse nonparty informal interest groups and protoparties in Volgograd, who themselves had only been animated by the January events. On February 3, they were able to gain from the provincial government formal institutional recognition for the upcoming campaign. Discredited by the forced resignation of its own chair from the same party bureau, the oblispolkom leadership had been subjected to a raucous twelve-hour session of the oblast soviet, critical of its support for the projected second Volga–Don Canal and intolerant of its failure to address the real problems of health care and food shortages affecting average Volgograders.

The soviet session ended with a decision to form a public coordinating council to generate public involvement in changing policies and budgetary priorities, and to prevent the mistakes and abuses of power now associated equally with the former party bureau and with the oblispolkom.[63] The unintended consequence of this council's activities during the election campaign was to legitimate the more than thirty nonparty political organizations, their candidates, and their reformist agenda for the upcoming local election. Although nominally under the oblispolkom chair, members of the council were selected not only from among the oblast deputies, but from representatives of voters' clubs and other nonparty political organizations in the cities of Volgograd and Volzhskii.

Most of the candidates on the March ballot were still formally listed as members of the Communist Party. Yet since January and with the formation of the public council, party membership ceased to carry definitive significance. This was a campaign in which all candidates were defining themselves to the voters as radical, conservative, populist, or pragmatist—and not as Communists or nonparty. The January events and the antiestablishment movement had so splintered the Volgograd party as to make membership even less relevant in identifying a candidate's beliefs than in other Russian locales.

Indeed, after the four doctors elected from Volgograd to the Russian Congress of People's Deputies, the next largest subgroup by profession elected in the Volgograd delegation were party apparatchiki: Aleksandr Anipkin, Ivan Rybkin, and Mikhail Kharitonov.[64] All three were urban district secretaries in their forties who were also elected to head the entire Volgograd Communist Party as its top three provincial secretaries at the

March 22 conference. Their simultaneous victories against several opponents in both the party and state elections resulted from their well-publicized radical views, critical of the former autocratic party leadership under Kalashnikov, and from their populist youthful image as representatives of the so-called "new wave" generation of Communist leaders—pro-environment, pro-reform, pro-Russian sovereignty, and pro-Volgograd.[65]

Oblast and City Soviets

Given the highly politicized nature of the campaign, nothing precluded the forming of majority coalitions among ideologically diverse, albeit nominally communist, deputies to support radical political-economic reforms and leaders in the post-election local soviets. Although 204 of the 250 deputies elected to the Volgograd Oblast Soviet were Communist Party members and even as late as June 1991 only 6 were openly affiliated with other political parties, the voting in the soviet during 1990–91 produced shifting majorities and a very fluid balance of power between establishment and antiestablishment deputies. Rather than the 204 party members against the 46 nonparty members, the 250 deputies on the Volgograd Oblast Soviet tended to cluster and vote in support of economic-political reforms relative to three distinctive blocs.[66]

Approximately 65 of the deputies identified themselves as the informal "democratic wing," and throughout 1990–91 voted together fairly consistently in support of liberal economic and political reforms. Approximately 100 of the deputies constituted a bloc derisively labeled by the democratic wing as the "partocrats." These, just as consistently, could be counted upon to vote against the same reforms. Holding the swing votes on the provincial soviet was the third bloc—the so-called "swamp." These 85 deputies, with no definable political convictions, tended to vote with either of the first two blocs, depending on the personal advantage for themselves or the significance of the reform under consideration. Leaders of the democratic wing in the oblast soviet contended that relatively the same political alignments and balance of power between advocates and opponents of reforms after the 1990 election could be found among the approximately 150 deputies elected to the Volgograd City Soviet and among several of the 33 newly elected district soviets throughout the province.

Even within these blocs, clear differences emerged by 1991 in both the oblast and capital soviets. After the founding of the Russian Communist Party, 33 of the 100 "partocrats" elected in 1990 as full-time party functionaries formed a right-wing "Communists of Russia" caucus within the oblast soviet.[67] The caucus appeared in the spring of 1991 coincidental with a clear abandonment of their former "new wave" populist image by the provincial communist leadership of Anipkin, Rybkin, and Kharitonov. Through the party's two daily Volgograd newspapers, these leaders orchestrated a systematic campaign to discredit market reforms as well as the democratic tendencies of deputies and chairs in several local Volgograd soviets.

This caucus attempted to pressure the other 171 party members of the oblast soviet to oppose land reform and to undermine general public confidence in the newly elected soviets throughout the province, even though the chairs in twenty-six of the thirty-three district soviets were former local party or state officials, all confirmed by their corresponding district party bureaus for these positions after the 1990 election.

On the other side, philosophical differences arose within the "democratic wing" of both the Volgograd oblast and city soviets. By the summer of 1991 these differences divided between those who saw themselves as "liberals" and "populists" on the right of the reform movement and those identifying as "social democrats" and "pragmatists" on the left.[68] Liberals favored rapid and comprehensive privatization and free-market capitalism; populists opposed as immoral any compromise with or tolerance toward party functionaries. Social democrats advocated a mixed economy and more gradual implementation of capitalist reforms to lessen the immediate impact of unemployment and inflation; pragmatists endorsed bargaining with Communist functionaries on the oblast and city soviets and even ruling coalitions with the "nomenklatura liberals" who had evinced a willingness to work with the antiestablishment reform movement.

The lack of a cohesive majority among reform-minded deputies on the Volgograd oblast and capital soviets had both negative and positive consequences during 1990–91. On the one hand, political pluralism at times meant legislative gridlock. For the last six months of 1991, the majority of deputies in the oblast soviet who had approved on first reading a bill to privatize state housing found it impossible to produce the 126 votes needed to pass any of several alternative versions of the bill, providing for different-sized apartments to be given free or sold to Volgograd residents.[69] On the other hand, the deputies were able to overcome their differences at critical junctures, forming temporary majorities to elect and support antiestablishment leaders of their respective soviets. None better came to personify this potential reformist majority than Valerii Makharadze, who defeated two other candidates in his election as chair of the oblast soviet presidium in April 1990, and profoundly influenced Volgograd politics in a liberal democratic direction over the next seventeen months preceding the abortive August putsch.

Oblast Government

By his very origins and background, Makharadze was an unconventional choice to lead the oblast soviet, but a very clear repudiation of the past Volgograd establishment, which had been led for decades almost exclusively by ethnic Russian natives of the province.[70] The son of a Russian mother and Georgian father, Makharadze was born in 1940 and raised in the Caspian port city of Makhachkala in the Dagestan Autonomous Republic, where he worked in a shipbuilding plant in the 1960s and early 1970s. His somewhat eclectic career in Dagestan, Kamchatka, and Udmurtia found him as a Komsomol secretary in a plant, the manager of construction-materials plants, and even for four years in Dagestan as a local television journalist. Assigned to Volgograd for the first time in 1981, he was the manager of the Kamyshin Forging and Foundry Plant when he was first elected deputy to the All-Union Congress of People's Deputies in May 1989 and later deputy to both the Russian Congress of People's Deputies and the Volgograd Oblast Soviet in March of 1990.

The mustachioed Makharadze very soon proved himself to be a political iconoclast in both appearance and action. Immediately after his election as chair of the oblast soviet, he gave out his personal telephone number and encouraged Volgograders to call him with their complaints and suggestions.[71] Although retaining his own membership in the Communist Party, he quickly challenged traditional notions about the presumed right of the Volgograd Communist Party to control the region's government.

That control had always been manifested by the automatic inclusion of all leading government officials in the party's provincial bureau, thus obligating them to follow party policy and enforce party priorities in their capacity as government officials. Two months after he was elected chair, the "new wave" communist leadership in Volgograd decided to elect Makharadze to the party's obkom bureau. Makharadze not only turned down his election to the bureau, but openly denounced it in the press as an attempt by the party to control him and to subvert the independence of the oblast soviet, presumably elected on a competitive basis in March 1990.[72]

As chair, Makharadze continued to set his own course against the Volgograd establishment. He continually defied attempts by the Volgograd Communist officials to dictate personnel changes among those appointed by the oblast soviet serving under him, and he used interviews in the national liberal press of *Izvestiia* and *Rossiiskaia gazeta* to rouse the public against the conspiratorial intrigues of a resurgent Volgograd establishment.[73] His popularity and overwhelming support by a majority of the oblast soviet proved sufficient to abort an attempt by the "Communists of Russia" faction in the soviet to have him voted out as chair and replaced by one of their own in December 1990.[74]

Because the principal publishing house in Volgograd was owned by the provincial government, Makharadze was able to create a climate for diversity and independence for newspapers published throughout Volgograd in 1990–91. Of thirty newspapers in Volgograd, only *Vechernii Volgograd* and *Volgogradskaia pravda* continued to be registered and published as organs of the Communist Party. In contrast, *Nasha gazeta* was founded and funded by the oblast soviet as an independent daily. An independent weekly of the Volgograd City Soviet, *Gorodskie vesti,* was funded and published already in June 1990. Numerous other city and Komsomol newspapers independent of the Communist Party appeared throughout 1990–91.

A fervent advocate of market economics, Makharadze launched the equivalent of an open political assault on the grassroots level of Volgograd against the entrenched farm system of collective and state farms and their officialdom through his active direct sponsorship and successful implementation of private land ownership. By July 1991, under the December 1990 Russian Republic law allowing private farms, more than a thousand individual private farms had been created in Volgograd. Makharadze's national reputation as a reformer led to his selection by Boris Yeltsin in April 1991 to the President's republic-level consultative council.[75]

As early as September 1990, Makharadze had already instituted a somewhat similar body in Volgograd called the Political Consultative Council within the presidium of the oblast soviet.[76] Composed of the leaders of the most prominent political parties and movements in the oblast and capital and chaired by Makharadze as the head of the oblast government, the council was intended both to generate public consensus over legislation pending in the oblast and capital soviets, and to integrate parties and movements of Volgograd into the decision-making process. Council members participated in sessions of the provincial soviet presidium and cast advisory votes during the sessions.

The council, potentially the most significant political reform of Makharadze's brief tenure, has continued to function under his successor.[77] Co-chaired by both the chair of the oblast soviet presidium and by the oblast administrator, the council includes the heads of the regional Democratic Party of Russia, the Republican Party, the Social Democratic Party, the Christian-Democratic Union, the Democratic Russia Movement, the Democratic Workers' Movement, the Movement for Democratic Reforms, the Free Russian People's Party, the Socialist Workers' Party, the Don Cossacks, the Volga Germans' Revival Association, the Association for Victims of Unlawful Political Repressions, and the leaders of the capital Voters' Committee and Civic Action. As a locus of power and decision making in Volgograd, the council was called upon to recommend procedures and potential nominees for the little soviet of thirty deputies elected by the 250 oblast soviet deputies in December 1991. Reflecting a wide spectrum of political views and interests, the council has served as a public sounding board for the presidium and commissions of the oblast soviet over legislation such as housing privatization.

As small in actual membership as the political parties and movements represented on it, the council in certain ways evolved by 1991–92 into a democratic pluralistic alternative to the former provincial bureau of the Volgograd Communist Party. The contrast with Saratov on one issue is sufficient to illustrate the difference. In the Saratov cities of Marx and Krasnoarmeisk, still ruled by their former communist officials in October 1991, the local leaders were urging the dynamiting of bridges across the Volga and the mining of the region's roads if the Russian government forced a German autonomous republic on them. Boris Yeltsin feared that he would be pelted by rotten eggs during his trip to Saratov in January 1992 if he said anything too favorable about Volga Germans; the Saratov Oblast Soviet passed a resolution in December 1992, protesting even a gradual restoration of ethnic German statehood in the lower Volga as set forth in the protocol signed by the Russian and German governments.[78] In Volgograd by December of 1991, the leaders of parties and movements in the Volgograd Council were being asked to advise the presidium on steps to avert ethnic conflicts and to facilitate the return of some form of territorial autonomy for both Germans and Cossacks in the province.

August 1991–1992

Makharadze was brought to Moscow in early August by Yeltsin to serve as his administrator of all Russian provinces, overseeing the appointment of presidential representatives. Later in 1992 he was appointed deputy prime minister in the cabinet of Yegor Gaidar. Yet his absence was hardly noticed in the response of Volgograders to the Emergency Committee on August 19–21 and in the political aftermath during the subsequent year.

In a replay of the January 1990 movement, tens of thousands of Volgograders rallied at the capital's Central Embankment on the evening of August 19 to protest the seizure of power by the Emergency Committee.[79] Marching to the building of the provincial soviet, they were greeted by Makharadze's hand-picked successors, who reported that the just-concluded session of the oblast presidium and oblispolkom had decided that the Volgograd city and oblast authorities would obey and be guided in their actions solely by the decisions of the Russian president. Similar rallies drawing an equivalent number and supported by Volgograd leaders were staged on August 20 and 21.

Because so much had already changed politically in Volgograd before August 1991 and because all the officials had unanimously spoken out against the putsch during those three days, there was much less need after August 21 for an ostentatious repudiation of the immediate past in Volgograd than there had been in Saratov. The only noticeable difference was that the former daily oblast communist newspaper, *Volgogradskaia pravda,* was suspended for two months with the outlawing of the party and the seizure of its assets. Yet it resumed publication beginning in October, and has continued through 1992 as a fairly balanced independent daily under the ownership of a revamped editorial board.

The reason that little had to change after August 21 in Volgograd was clear. Even before August 19, a new reformist elite had already emerged during the brief tenure of Makharadze. In Volgograd, the new reformist elite was characterized as the "professors" and the "nomenklatura liberals." As a group, they allied Volgograd intellectuals—especially those affiliated with scientific-research institutes or local institutions of higher education—with party–state officials who split in 1990 from the provincial establishment.

As an outgrowth of public activism generated by the populist movement against the party bureau in January 1990, a few of the "professors" formed political parties and civic groups and gained local visibility as members of the Political Consultative Council. Some became known as policy advocates and chairs of commissions on the Volgograd oblast or capital soviets. Others achieved recognition as reformers among the Volgograd deputies elected in 1989 or 1990 to the All-Union and Russian Congresses. Yet all of them had emerged as an influential group in Volgograd under the political tutelage of Makharadze. After August 1991, they became the leaders elected locally by their soviets, or appointed by Yeltsin, to head the executive branch of both the oblast and capital governments. Anatolii Iushchenko, Vladimir Kudriavtsev, Aleksandr Morozov, Valerian Sobolev, Pavel Ivanov, and Evgenii Kuznetsov typify this academic wing of the new reformist elite.

The 54-year-old Anatolii Iushchenko is a native of the capital of Volgograd who has spent his entire career in the city.[80] An assistant professor of the Volgograd Pedagogical Institute, Iushchenko became active in public political life in 1985–90, first forming a democratic group within his Communist Party cell, and later the Volgograd branch of the Democratic Platform, attempting to reform the Communist Party from within. As a declared reformist, Iushchenko failed to win a seat to either the Nineteenth Party Conference in 1988 or the Twenty-eighth Congress in 1990.

In the 1990 elections he participated in the Volgograd Voters' Association and was elected to the oblast soviet as a liberal Communist. By 1991 he had joined other local liberal Communists in reconstituting themselves as the Saratov branch of the Republican Party of Russia. Iushchenko had been one of the two original candidates nominated in October 1991 to succeed Makharadze as the chair of the oblast soviet presidium. Unsuccessful in his bid to become the head of the provincial government but endorsed by the bloc of Volgograd parties of a democratic orientation on the city council, Iushchenko was then appointed the first deputy mayor of the capital in April 1992. Iushchenko's counterpart, the elected first deputy chair of the Volgograd City Soviet, is Vladimir Kudriavtsev, a former chair of the city soviet's Mandate Commission and director of the Department of State and Administrative Law at the Higher School of the USSR Ministry of Internal Affairs.[81]

The individual who was eventually elected by the oblast soviet to succeed Makharadze in October 1991 was Aleksandr Morozov.[82] A graduate of Novosibirsk State University and the Institute of Catalytics of the Siberian Academy of Sciences with a candidate's degree from the Institute of Space Exploration of the USSR Academy of Sciences and a doctorate in astrophysics from Leningrad State University, Morozov had first come to Volgograd in August 1980 at the age of 35. Over the subsequent decade he had advanced from senior instructor to professor, head of the faculty of theoretical physics, and prorector of Volgograd State University. His first identifiable involvement in public life was winning a seat to the oblast soviet in 1990, but his local political reputation derived equally from widespread concern over environmental pollution in the region and his development of a mathematical model for ecological systems. The computer program based on his model has been employed in Volgograd to monitor the level of toxic pollutants and acid rain produced by local Volgograd enterprises and to establish thresholds of environmental pollution particularly dangerous to vulnerable groups such as pregnant women and nursing mothers in the immediate area of the enterprises.

By June 1992, the official responsible for investment policy in the province was Valerian Sobolev, the first deputy head of the oblast administration.[83] Like Morozov, Sobolev was a professor at the Volgograd Polytechnic Institute elected to the All-Union Congress in 1989, but his real claim to fame was as a scientist-entrepreneur. In 1990, he had founded the first Russian international joint-stock company formed out of defense industries, and prior to assuming his position in the provincial government had been director of the Titan Construction-Design Bureau, converting defense plants to civilian production and locally renowned for producing washing machines. Appointed along with Sobolev as the deputy head of the oblast administration was Pavel Ivanov, a doctor at the Volgograd Veterans' Hospital who had been elected to the Russian Congress in 1990.[84]

Yeltsin's choice as presidential representative for Volgograd Oblast was Evgenii Kuznetsov.[85] Kuznetsov, was a leader of the Republican Party in Volgograd who had been elected to the Russian Congress in 1990, and served as the head of the construction department in the design bureau of the same defense production association at which Sobolev had worked until 1990. A political ally of Makharadze, Kuznetsov actually had been with Makharadze in the Russian White House on August 19–21, and was one of the very first persons appointed as Yeltsin's provincial representative by the Russian republic administration headed by Makharadze.

In 1991–92, the most typical representatives of the liberal nomenklatura wing of the new Volgograd elite were those appointed by Yeltsin to head the oblast and capital administrations, Ivan Shabunin and Iurii Chekhov. As Makharadze's right-hand man in 1990–91, Shabunin alternatively was chair or first deputy chair of the oblispolkom when at various times in 1990–91 Makharadze felt obliged to assume direct control over the administrative departments in the provincial government, acting temporarily as chair of both the oblast presidium and oblispolkom. Shabunin had been associated with agriculture in Volgograd during the preceding two decades in various positions, ranging from director of the Volgograd Association of State Farms in the 1970s to first deputy chair of the oblispolkom and the head of the province's agro-industrial association in the 1980s.[86] Because Shabunin did not hold a very high a position in January 1990, he escaped the fate of those very top Volgograd party–state officials ousted from the bureau and their posts in January and February.

Shabunin's familiarity with agriculture in Volgograd most likely influenced the decision by Makharadze—an industrial specialist who had been in Volgograd only since 1981—to keep Shabunin as his administrator of the provincial government. Shabunin's willingness at least to endorse private farms by January 1991 also represented a clear ideological break from the provincial Communist Party leaders, who were still adamantly defending the collective–state farm system.[87] By December 1991 under Shabunin's administration, almost 1,500 private farms with 144,000 hectares had formed in Volgograd.[88] Shabunin's reformist image was only enhanced during the August putsch, when he addressed the evening rally of August 19 and informed its participants that the presidium and executive committee of the soviet endorsed their support of Boris Yeltsin.

Iurii Chekhov was the chair of the Volgograd capital soviet in 1990–91, paralleling Makharadze's tenure as provincial soviet chair. An early advocate of privatizing the housing stock in the city of Volgograd, Chekhov had stood by Makharadze on the issue of election to the provincial party bureau, repudiating it along with Makharadze as an attempt of the party leadership to control him.[89] Chekhov was rewarded by Yeltsin, presumably at Makhardze's suggestion, by being appointed head of the city administration, the equivalent of mayor of Volgograd. Preceding his appointment in November 1991, the Volgograd City Soviet by a vote of 148 to 2 had endorsed Chekhov as the preferred choice to run the city.[90] Following his appointment, Chekhov's liberal political inclinations were evident in his appointment in January 1992 of two women, Svetlana Kosenkova and Valentina Lapina, as his deputy mayors responsible for overseeing trade and public catering and environmental reforms.[91]

Conclusion

Two generalizations emerge from our case study. The first is that the differences between Saratov and Volgograd in 1993 still reflect the distinct political context of each oblast crystallized four years earlier in the run-up to the March 1990 election. The context of 1989–90 was the equivalent of a political "big bang," but in each oblast it had a distinctively different effect, and in each the echoes and waves continue to reverberate through 1993, shaping quite different political constellations. Given the stalemate between President Yeltsin and the Russian parliament and the inability of the central Russian government to implement changes systematically throughout the country since independence, the political contexts of 1989–90 may be the single most important factor accounting for differences in all the constituent units of the Russian Federation even four years later.

In Saratov, the Communist Party–state establishment entered 1990 relatively unified and almost unchallenged in its authority and control of the election from any antiestablishment movements or parties in the province. The Saratov establishment could even project itself to the electorate as a different communist leadership that had significantly renewed itself, thus earning trust and support for the party's designated candidates. After all, Konstantin Murenin had become obkom first secretary only in August 1989, and he had been only one of several new officials promoted to the top party–state leadership positions immediately prior to March 1990. In this context, the establishment and its candidates set the tone and determined the agenda for the campaign, appealing to material insecurity and self-interest among rural voters and to fear of Germans among all ethnic Russian voters.

In Volgograd, the communist establishment contesting the March 1990 election was also quite different in composition than it had been a year before, but its renewal had been forced in late January 1990 by a spontaneous grassroots populist movement. That movement accounted for both the outcome of the Volgograd election in March 1990 and for all of the subsequent differences marking Volgograd's anti-establishment political evolution through 1992. The ouster of Kalashnikov and the entire communist bureau left the Volgograd Communist establishment effectively leaderless, divided, and distracted for the critical weeks before the first round of the March election. It legitimated the right of various interest groups, voters' clubs, and political parties to mobilize during the electoral campaign, and brought their reformist agenda to the forefront both during and after the election. The events in late January had made the corruption of the communist establishment the central issue of the campaign, leading to the election of a large bloc of anti-establishment deputies to the Volgograd oblast and capital soviets. Had Kalashnikov never been appointed to head the party in 1984, or had he been removed even as late as 1989, the sequence of events and the political outcome in Volgograd might have been exactly like that in Saratov.

The second generalization is that the nature of the governing elites in Saratov and Volgograd since 1990 were paramount in influencing their own different courses of political development. Throughout Russia, political parties and the independent media are weak, as is the authority and administrative effectiveness of the new governing institutions that have replaced the Communist Party. The nature of the governing elite in 1991–93 would therefore seem to be the most important single determinant of political development in many other Russian locales as well.[92]

In Saratov, a Golovachev or a Belykh may have come from the more reformist wing of the Saratov establishment, but they were still tied by their previous backgrounds and associations to the political-economic elite that has ruled Saratov for so many decades. This is particularly true of Golovachev, who, given his position as the head of the Communist Party in the city of Volgograd from 1985 until October 1990, would have been a prime candidate to become the obkom first secretary under the old communist system. Golovachev had actually been one of three candidates nominated to become obkom first secretary as late as August 1989. Appointed oblast presidential representative by Yeltsin, Golovachev has been invested with a position of executive authority insulated from any direct accountability to the Saratov public, exactly like his former position as obkom first secretary.

In Volgograd, there was a real realignment or transformation of leadership in 1990–91 under Makharadze's tenure as chair of the Volgograd Oblast Soviet presidium. By-products of the civic activism directed against the communist establishment in 1990, the new Volgograd governing elites are academics and liberal officials with few ties to the former Volgograd establishment. The astrophysicist Morozov typifies the emergence of a post-Soviet and post-Communist Volgograd; the career apparatchik Golovachev personifies the ambiguity surrounding any real political change in Saratov since 1990.

In post-Soviet Volgograd, democratic pluralism is evolving out of the give-and-take between the executive and legislative branches and among various factions and caucuses in the local soviets. Even the 65 democratic deputies in the oblast soviet reconstituted themselves as a loyal opposition to the Volgograd government because they felt betrayed by Shabunin's willingness to retain the three-fourths of the former communist officials serving in the local executive officials.[93] The Volgograd governing elite have been similarly challenged and checked by the minority bloc of conservatives in the oblast soviet, led by Aleksandr Anipkin and Mikhail Kharitonov, the former "new wave" antiestablishment communist leaders from 1990–91. In May 1993, the conservative minority was able to get a majority of the oblast deputies to vote for Anipkin's resolution on a forthcoming draft Russian constitution, opposing the draft of President Yeltsin and essentially obligating Shabunin and Morozov as Volgograd's two representatives in the June 1993 Constituent Assembly to support the version advocated by Yeltsin's opponents.[94]

Yet democratic pluralism has not led to political gridlock in Volgograd. The Volgograd governing elite effectively oversaw a successful auctioning of municipal property by July 1992, establishing a foundation for 336 private trade and commercial outlets by June 1993.[95] With almost 2,000 private farms in Volgograd, its liberal reputation as a pacesetter of market reform was only confirmed in February 1993, when the Russian government selected Volgograd to be the very first province to auction its medium and large industrial enterprises for private vouchers.[96] Fifty medium and large enterprises had already been sold by June 1993, including the Tractor Plant, which, with its origins in 1925 and its 26,000 employees, epitomizes the former era of the communist command economy.

The contrast is Saratov, where the former establishment remains influential enough to delay or subvert any such reform proposals and is relatively unchallenged by local political rivals. By the summer of 1992, the Saratov government, like Volgograd, had begun privatizing sectors of its own local economy. One highly visible sector privatized was construction, with the former state construction trust and construction materials plants reconstituted as a joint-stock company. At the same time, the privatization of construction more than anything symbolizes how very little Saratov has changed since 1990 in terms of leadership and political power, especially when compared to Volgograd. The official chairing the newly founded joint-stock company in Saratov is none other than Ivan Kuznetsov, the notorious political "godfather" of the province.[97]

Notes

I am indebted to the staff of the Radio Free Europe/Radio Liberty Institute in Munich, Germany, for allowing me access to their extensive collection of current local newspapers from Saratov and Volgograd in April–May 1991 and July–August 1992.

1. "Po predvaritel'nym itogam 1989 vsesoiuznoi narodnoi perepisi," *Izvestiia,* April 28, 1989, pp. 1–3.

2. Rex A. Wade and Scott J. Seregny, eds., *Politics and Society in Provincial Russia: Saratov, 1590–1917* (Columbus, Ohio: Ohio State University Press, 1989); Philip D. Stewart, *Political Power in the Soviet Union: A Study of Decision-Making in Stalingrad* (Indianapolis and New York: The Bobbs-Merrill Company, Inc., 1968); and I. Pugin, "Rodoslovnaia kraia," *Saratovskii listok,* 8 (August–September 1990), p. 2.

3. See the related chapters on the period 1878–1917 in "Saratov" by Michael Melancon, Scott Seregny, Thomas Fallows, and Donald Raleigh in Wade and Seregny, eds., *Politics and Society.*

4. Stewart, *Political Power,* and Joel C. Moses, "Regionalism in Soviet Politics: Continuity as a Source of Change, 1953–1982," *Soviet Studies,* 37, 2 (April 1985), pp. 196–98.

5. N. Markevich, "Desiatiletniaia bol'," *Saratovskii listok,* 6 (June–July 1990), p. 3; Andrew R. Bond, "Environmental Disruption During Economic Downturn: 'White Book' Report," *Post-Soviet Geography,* 34, 1 (January 1993), p. 76.

6. "Gorod Balakovo Saratovskoi oblasti, AES, lager' protesta obshchestvennosti," "Osoboe mnenie," and "Lager' protesta," *Saratovskii listok,* 2 (June 1990), p. 1; A. Vorotnikov, "Shadow of Chernobyl Over the Volga," *Pravda,* May 18, 1990, p. 2 [translated in *Foreign Broadcast Information Service: Daily Report–Soviet Union,* hereafter *FBIS*], May 31, 1990, p. 89; and "Vremia," 1700 GMT, June 2, 1990, *FBIS,* June 12, 1990, p. 109.

7. Aleksandr Shibaev, director of the Saratov Aviation Plant (1950–55) and first secretary of the Saratov Oblast Communist Party (1959–76); Iurii Kochetkov, Komsomol–Party leader of Saratov Aviation Plant (1954–70) and first secretary of the Saratov City Communist Party (1974–84); Vladimir Gusev, chief engineer–director of Engels Chemical Combine (1963–75) and first secretary of the Saratov Oblast Communist Party (1976–85); and Nikolai Aleksandrov, head of the oblast Communist Party's department for the petrochemical and gas industries (1968–70) and chair of the oblast executive committee (1971–90).

8. I. Sergeev, "Vy ch'i, ptentsy?—Razmyshleniia rassuditel'nogo gorozhanina o mudrykh nachal'nikakh," *Saratovskii listok,* 2 (June 1990), p. 2.

9. N. Gamaiunov, "Kommandant 'Brestskikh krepostei,' " and A. Kichikhin, "Anatomiia shovinizma," *Saratovskii listok,* 7 (July 1990), p. 3. By February 1991, the commission on legality of the Saratov City Soviet had voted to discuss urgently the issue of Kuznetsov and his activities as director of the Saratov land reclamation and irrigation–construction projects: "Iz zhizni Saratova," *Saratovskii listok,* 17 (February 1991), p. 1.

10. A. Kichikhin, "Anatomiia shovinizma," p. 3.

11. *Izvestiia TsK KPSS,* 11 (November 1990). Also, see articles by Murenin on repairing rural roads torn up by tractors during spring sowing (*Izvestiia,* August 18, 1974) and on construction (*Partiinaia zhizn',* 21, 1982, pp. 39–44).

12. On references spanning Aleksandrov's tenure as chair, see first citation as chair in *Pravda*, June 4, 1971, and last citation as chair as a member of a standing committee in the Russian Supreme Soviet (*Vedomosti Verkhovnogo soveta RSFSR*, 51, 1988, p. 1,070). Grishin attended the Nineteenth Party Conference in June 1988 as the Saratov second secretary, but was elected to the Russian Congress of People's Deputies in March 1990 as the chair of the executive committee (*Sovetskaia Rossiia*, March 14, 1990, p. 3).

13. *Izvestiia TsK KPSS*, 3 (March 1990). As first deputy chair of the executive committee, see TASS, June 15, 1987 (Soviet delegation accompanying the USSR Minister of Agriculture to Canada).

14. On Shabanov's career as editor of the Saratov oblast newspaper *Kommunist*, see notice of his appointment in 1976–77 (*Zhurnalist*, April 1977, p. 31), references to him as editor in 1983 (*Partiinaia zhizn'*, 16, p. 22), 1986 (*Pravda*, August 6), and January 1990 (back page of Saratov *Kommunist*).

15. See Gusev's biography in the appendix to the 1981 *Ezhegodnik Bol'shoi Sovetskoi Entsiklopedii*. On his promotion, *Pravda*, April 12, 1985.

16. See Kochetkov's biography at the time of his election as Armenian second secretary in *Kommunist* (Armenia), April 13, 1985, p. 1, in the appendix to the 1987 *Ezhegodnik Bol'shoi Sovetskoi Entsiklopedii*, and in *Izvestiia TsK KPSS*, 6 (June 1989), p. 36.

17. Dawn Mann, "Authority of Regional Party Leaders Crumbling," *Report on the USSR*, 2, 8 (February 23, 1990), pp. 1–6.

18. Vladimir Balandin, the newly elected oblast second secretary in 1986, had been in succession party secretary (1975–79), chief engineer (1980–82), and general director (1983–85) of the Volgograd Tractor Plant. Elected oblast agriculture secretary in 1989, Valerii Khvatov had succeeded Balandin as party secretary of the Tractor Plant (1980–84) before a short stint as first secretary of the Volzhskii City Party.

19. Implicated in at least two scandals involving local official corruption, Iurii Lomakin, chair of the oblast state executive committee since 1973, was reassigned to a ministerial position in the Russian government in 1985 and replaced by Al'bert Orlov. Georgii Boiko, chair of the regional trade-union council since 1969, was replaced in 1986 by a non-Russian woman, Khelvi Lattu. Valentin Karpov, who had run the city of Volgograd as the first party secretary since 1967, actually was forced out in 1983 before Kalashnikov; but under Kalashnikov the position was held in succession for three years by Viktor Kochetov and Aleksandr Anipkin.

20. "Spid ne spit, a vlasti dremliut," *Gorodskie vesti* (Saratov), November 29–December 5, 1991, p. 4. On the outbreak of AIDS among children in Volgograd, see Andrei Baiduzhy, "Medicine: AIDS in Russia Has a Child's Face—Everything Is Ready for the Beginning of an Epidemic in the Country," *Nezavisimaia gazeta*, December 5, 1992, p. 6 [trans. in *The Current Digest of the Post-Soviet Press*, 44, 49 (January 6, 1993), p. 31].

21. I. Maliakin, "Rossiia vspriala?" *Mestnoe vremia* (Saratov), 3 (November 1990), p. 6. The characterization of Saratov as a political "swamp" was made by M.K. Tolstoi, a leader of the Democratic Party of Russia from Moscow, during its organizational meeting for the local branch in Saratov.

22. Grigorii Akhtyrko, "Parlament bez reglamenta (delo bylo v Saratove, na sessii oblsoveta no. 2)," *Mestnoe vremia* (Saratov), 3 (November 1990), p. 2.; and S. Nikolaev, "Tribuna—deputatu: Ia protiv kompromissov s sobstvennoi sovest'iu," *Saratovskie vesti*, October 16, 1991, p. 2.

23. I. Sergeev, "Vy ch'i," p. 2. Reports by the national media in March 1990 reinforced the impression that in rural areas the election was heavily controlled and manip-

ulated by the rural party elite: Valentina Nikolaeva, "First Secretary Became Angry," *Izvestiia,* March 20, 1990, p. 2 [trans. in *FBIS,* April 5, 1990, pp. 109–10].

24. A. Kichikhin, p. 3; Liubov' Sharshavova, "State Committee for State of Emergency Against German Autonomy," *Rossiiskaia gazeta,* October 17, 1991, p. 7 [trans. in *FBIS,* October 17, 1991, pp. 54–55]; and Elena Martynova, "Summary: Yeltsin Prepares for Trip to Volga Region. Province Bosses Prepare 'Public Indignation,' " *Megapolis-Express,* 2 (January 9, 1992) [trans. in *The Current Digest of the Post-Soviet Press,* 44, 1 (February 5, 1992), p. 32].

25. See Genrikh Grout (Cochair of the Soviet German Revival Association), "Segodnia i zavtra: natsional'no-osvoboditel'nogo dvizheniia rossiiskikh nemtsev," *Mestnoe vremia* (Saratov), 31 (August 1991), pp. 2–3; and Elena Nikol'skaia (interview with Grout), "Soviet Germans: To Go or Not to Go?" *Moscow News,* 28 (July 14–21, 1991), p. 7.

26. G. Akhtyrko, "Parlament bez reglamenta," p. 2.

27. Typifying the interlocking nature of government and the Communist Party in Saratov maintained by Murenin right until the abortive August putsch of 1991 were two brief articles that appeared on the front page of *Kommunist,* the Saratov oblast Communist newspaper, as late as July 23, 1991. In the first article, Murenin in his position of oblast first secretary oversaw and spoke at a plenum of the Rovenskii District at which the first secretary Dukhovnov resigned relative to his transfer to other work. In the second article, Murenin in his other position of oblast soviet chair spoke on the economic and political situation in the province at a soviet session of the same Rovenskii District, during which the same Dukhovnov resigned as the chair of the district soviet presidium.

28. G. Akhtyrko, "Parlament bez reglamenta," p. 2.

29. Igor Gamaiunov, "Former KGB Agent: 'I Gave Information about Events, Very Rarely about People,' " *Literaturnaia gazeta,* 43 (October 24, 1990), p. 13 [trans. in *FBIS,* October 31, 1990, pp. 39–42].

30. G. Akhtyrko, "Parlament bez reglamenta," p. 2.

31. "Sessiia gorsoveta: kartinki s natury," *Saratovskii listok,* 1 (May 1990), pp. 1–2; "Pervaia sessiia gorsoveta: delo bylo v Saratove," *Saratovskii listok,* 2 (June 1990), p. 2.

32. On intimidation of the Saratov Voters' Club during the 1990 election, see Valentina Nikolaeva, "Don't Assemble on the Square," *Izvestiia,* February 11, 1990, p. 2 [trans. in *FBIS,* February 15, 1990, pp. 106–7]. That political parties were suppressed until after the abortive August putsch was most clearly indicated by the inability to form a local branch of Democratic Russia with its founding conference until October 1991.

33. V. Golovachev, "Ne v boi 'stremit'sia'—nado zhit'—O proekte Konstitutsii RSFSR i sobytiiakh vokrug nee," *Saratov,* February 23, 1991, p. 3; and S. Makarov, "Na gazetnye temy: Sovety nepostoronnego, ili chto 'Saratov' dlia Saratova," *Kommunist* (Saratov), July 20, 1991, p. 3.

34. Editorial Board, "Chitatel' dolzhen znat'—Ukroshchenie 'Saratova'?" *Saratov,* February 23, 1991, p. 2. *Saratov* was not the only Saratov independent unable to publish during the first two months in 1991: Editorial Board, "Son demokratii rozhdaet chudovishch," *Mestnoe vremia* (Saratov), 6 (February 1991), p. 1.

35. S. Makarov, "Na gazetnye temy," p. 3.

36. Valentina Nikolaeva, "Est' li v gorsovete predsedatel'?" *Izvestiia,* June 30, 1990, p. 2.

37. On Golovachev's origins, see the interview with him by Oleg Zlobin, "Vperedi bol'shaia rabota," *Volzhskie novosti* (Volgograd), 41 (November 1991), p. 6. For individual confirmations of his previous positions in Saratov, see articles by or references to

Golovachev: *Pravda,* June 5, 1975, p. 2; *Pravda,* May 22, 1980, p. 2; *Pravda,* September 9, 1985, p. 2.

38. "Plenary Sessions of Party Committees," *Pravda,* August 11, 1989, p. 2 [trans. in *FBIS,* September 5, 1989, pp. 26–27].

39. Pavel Gutentov, "Conference Becomes Constituent Congress," *Izvestiia,* June 21, 1990, pp. 1–2 [trans. in *FBIS,* July 2, 1990, pp. 92–93].

40. Valentina Nikolaeva, "One Seat Too Many," *Izvestiia,* October 7, 1990, p. 1 [trans. in *FBIS,* October 10, 1990, p. 116]. "Sessiia gorsoveta"; and V. Nikolaeva, "Strasti vokrug predsedatelia," *Izvestiia,* July 9, 1991, p. 3.

42. Aleksandr Dzhashitov, "Bezvlastie sovetov: komu ono vygodno?" *Saratov,* February 23, 1991, pp. 1–2; and Vladimir Iuzhakov, "Gorkom delaet politiku?" *Saratov,* July 23, 1991, p. 1.

43. Iuzhakov, "Gorkom delaet politiku?"

44. A. Vorotnikov, "Shadow of Chernobyl," p. 2.

45. Unattributed, "The Yeltsin Team: Russia's Parliament Appoints the Federation's First Ministers," *New Times,* 31 (July 31–August 6, 1990), pp. 44–45.

46. "Pochta," *Ogonek,* 33 (July 1990), and "Boris, ty—prav!" *Saratov,* March 2, 1991, p. 1.

47. "Pervaia sessiia," p. 2; and V. Nikolaeva, "One Seat Too Many," p. 1.

48. Valentina Nikolaeva, "Saratov Will Become Open City," *Izvestiia,* October 31, 1990, p. 2 [trans. in *FBIS,* November 1, 1990, p. 85].

49. Golovachev, "Ne v boi," p. 3.

50. "Ob"edinennyi plenum obkoma KPSS i kontrol'noi komissii oblastnoi organizatsii KPSS," *Po Leninskomu puti* (Voskresenskii district, Saratov), February 15, 1991, p. 1.

51. Valentina Nikolaeva, "Strasti," p. 3; and A. Praskov'in, "Kriziz nazrel? Vchera v Saratove nachala rabotu VI ocherednaia sessiia gorodskogo soveta," *Saratovskie vesti,* October 16, 1991, p. 1.

52. Oleg Zlobin, "Why Does One Leave the Oblast Committee Bureau," *Rossiiskaia gazeta,* June 20, 1991, p. 1 [trans. in FBIS, July 2, 1991, p. 58].

53. Valentina Nikolaeva, "Coup Failure Changes Political Situation Locally. *Izvestiia* Correspondent's Report: Saratov," *Izvestiia,* August 24, 1991, p. 4 [trans. in *FBIS,* August 29, 1991, p. 108].

54. Tat'iana Artemova, "Oni popytaiutsia vziat' revansh" (Interview with Vladimir Golovachev), *Saratov,* October 29, 1991, p. 3.

55. Untitled, *Rossiiskaia gazeta,* September 3, 1991, p. 1 [trans. in *FBIS,* September 24, 1991, p. 57].

56. S. Nikolaev, "Tribuna deputatu," p. 2.

57. Valentina Nikolaeva, "Sorrowful Anniversary for Soviet Germans," *Izvestiia,* September 2, 1991, p. 1 [trans. in *FBIS,* September 4, 1991, p. 96]; L. Sharshavova, "State Committee," p. 7.

58. Oleg Zlobin, "Vperedi," p. 6.; T. Artemova, "Oni popitaiutsia," p. 3; and Il'fov i Petr, "Posledniaia osen' Demrossii? Korol' umer, da zdravstvuet korol'?" *Mestnoe vremia* (Saratov), 38 (October 18–24, 1991), p. 3.

59. Il'fov i Petr, "Posledniaia osen'?", p. 3.

60. Oleg Zlobin, "Saratov People Have Failed to Secede—Yeltsin Has Appointed Governor," *Rossiiskaia gazeta,* March 5, 1992, p. 5 [trans. in *FBIS,* March 11, 1992, p. 46]; Radio Rossii, 7:00 P.M., March 19, 1992.

61. Oleg Zlobin, "We Must Help the Government Overcome Its Mistakes," *Rossiiskaia gazeta,* May 7, 1992, p. 1 [trans. in *FBIS,* May 20, 1992, pp. 53–54].

62. Dmitrii Shevarov, "Paralich krepkoi ruki—o tekushchem momente," *Komsomol'skaia pravda,* February 15, 1990, p. 1; and V. Cherkasov, "Notes from the

Volgograd Oblast Party Conference: Recovering from Illness," *Sovetskaia Rossiia,* March 22, 1990, p. 1 [trans. in *FBIS,* April 6, 1990, pp. 94–96].

63. V. Kornev, "Public Council Founded," *Izvestiia,* February 5, 1990, p. 1 [trans. in *FBIS,* February 7, 1990, pp. 120–21].

64. TASS, March 20, 1991 [trans. in *FBIS,* March 21, 1990, p. 101]; V. Cherkasov, "Notes from Volgograd," p. 1.

65. On Anipkin's projected image as a Russian populist representative of the "new wave" generation of party leaders, see the transcript of his maiden speech as a deputy to the Russian Congress, "Vystuplenie A.M. Anipkina," *Volgogradskaia pravda,* May 24, 1990, p. 1, and Aleksandr Anipkin, "Krizis soznaniia ili osoznanie krizisa?" *Kommunist,* 15 (October 1990), pp. 1–12. On Rybkin's populist image with his frequent plane trips from Moscow to Volgograd to confer with his constituents, see TASS, June 17, 1990.

66. N. Selezneva, "Predstavliaem kandidata v predsedateli oblsoveta A. Iushchenko 'Konsolidirovat' vsekh dolzhna ekonomika,' " (Interview with Anatolii Iushchenko), *Volgogradskaia pravda,* October 19, 1991, pp. 1–2.

67. V. Kornev, "When the Party Rules Hold Sway in the Soviet" (Interview with Valerii Makharadze), *Izvestiia,* June 17, 1991, p. 3 [trans. in *FBIS,* July 30, 1991, pp. 62–66]; Vitalii Cherkasov, "Whose Power in the Soviets?" (Roundtable discussion with V. Makharadze, P. Ivanov, and E. Kuznetsov), *Rossiiskaia gazeta,* June 19, 1991, p. 3 [trans. in *FBIS,* July 12, 1991, pp. 80–83].

68. N. Selezneva, "Predstavliaem kandidata," pp. 1–2; N. Selezneva, "Predstavliaem pretendentov v mery Volgograda—'U menia net lichnogo interes k vysokoi dolzhnosti' " (Interview with Igor' Lukashev), *Volgogradskaia pravda,* October 1, 1991, pp. 1–2; N. Marchenko, " 'Nam nuzhna terpimost' ' "—schitaet odin iz liderov Volgogradskikh respublikantsev Vladimir Bush" (Interview with Vladimir Bush), *Volgogradskaia pravda,* January 30, 1992, p. 5.

69. "Otvety dast sessiia," *Volgogradskaia pravda,* December 14, 1991, p. 1; V. Bush, "Obsuzhdaetsia na sessii oblsoveta—Privatizatsiia zhil'ia: tseli i prioritety," *Volgogradskaia pravda,* December 26, 1991, p. 2.

70. Aleksandr Tikhonov, "Bor'ba za vlast'. S kem?" (Interview with Valerii Makharadze), *Volzhskie novosti* (Volgograd), 3 (July 1990), p. 3; Leonid Petrov, "Right to Obtain Satisfaction" (Interview with Valerii Makharadze), *Rossiiskaia gazeta,* October 2, 1991, pp. 1–2 [trans. in *FBIS,* October 4, 1991, pp. 52–54].

71. V. Kornev, "Rabochaia komanda oblsoveta," *Izvestiia,* April 11, 1990, p. 3.

72. V. Kornev, "He Refused to Join the Bureau," *Izvestiia,* May 27, 1990, p. 2 [trans. in *FBIS,* June 13, 1990, pp. 123–24]; and A. Tikhonov, "Bor'ba za vlast'," p. 3.

73. V. Kornev, "When the Party Rules," p. 3; and V. Cherkasov, "Whose Power?" p. 3.

74. Irina Chernova, "V oblastnom sovete," *Volzhskie novosti* (Volgograd), 15 (December 1990), p. 7.

75. Elizabeth Teague, "Boris Yeltsin Introduces His Brain Trust," *Report on the USSR,* 3 (April 12, 1991), p. 15.

76. V. Kornev, "Agreement on Joint Actions Signed," *Izvestiia,* September 17, 1990, p. 1 [trans. in *FBIS,* September 19, 1990, p. 76].

77. "Ob''ediniaia usiliia i otvetsvennost'—polozhenie o politicheskom konsul'tativnom sovete (PKS)," *Volgogradskaia pravda,* November 27, 1991, p. 1; and "Trebuiutsia reshitel'nost' i professionalizm," and A.V. Petrov, "Samoizoliatsiia opasnyi kurs," *Volgogradskaia pravda,* December 25, 1991, p. 2.

78. L. Sharshavova, "State Committee," p. 7; E. Martynova, "Summary: Yeltsin Prepares for Trip," p. 32; A. Vorotnikov, "And Who Asked 'Our' Germans?" *Pravda,* December 23, 1992, p. 1 [trans. in *FBIS,* January 8, 1993, p. 58].

79. Vladimir Mikliukov, "Volgograd 19–21 August," *Khristiianskaia demokratiia,* 14 (July–August 1991), pp. 20–22.

80. N. Selezneva, "Konsolidirovat' vsekh," pp. 1–2; *Volgogradskaia pravda,* January 22, 1992, p. 3.

81. *Volgogradskaia pravda,* February 27, 1991, p. 1, and January 22, 1992, p. 2.

82. *Volgogradskaia pravda,* October 25, 1991, p. 1; and Andrei Filippov, "Who Has More Money Has Great Responsibility: Leaving the World of Stars and Galaxies, Theoretical Physicist Ends Up in the Chair of the Speaker of the Regional Parliament," *Literaturnaia gazeta,* 40 (September 30, 1992), p. 12 [trans. in *FBIS,* October 9, 1992, pp. 49–50].

83. T. Davydova, "With An Adjustment for the Degree of Risk," *Volgogradskaia pravda,* June 4, 1992, p. 1 [trans. in *FBIS,* August 28, 1992, pp. 28–29].

84. N. Selezneva, "Novyi chelovek v koridorakh vlasti: 'Ispol'zovat' pre-imushchestva; a ne vypiachivat' nedostatki,'" (Interview with Valerian Sobolev) *Volgogradskaia pravda,* December 13, 1991, p. 2.

85. V. Kornev, "Representatives of Russian President See Their Duty in Ensuring that Local Administrations Are Effective" (Interview with Valerii Makharadze), *Izvestiia,* September 13, 1991, p. 3 [trans. in *FBIS,* September 13, 1991, pp. 74–75].

86. *Pravda,* September 12, 1974, p. 2; *Pravda,* March 11, 1983, p. 1; and "Rabochaia komanda," loc. cit.

87. N. Selezneva, "Vybiraite varianty" (Interview with Ivan Shabunin) *Volgogradskaia pravda,* February 2, 1991, p. 2; and M.M. Kharitonov (oblast party agriculture secretary), "Selo: vremia aktivnykh deistvii," *Volgogradskaia pravda,* February 12, 1991, pp. 1–2.

88. A.V. Vorob'ev, "Zemel'naia reforma: 'V etom dele mozhno tol'ko pozdat''" *Volgogradskaia pravda,* December 24, 1991, p. 2.

89. V. Kornev, "He Refused to Join the Bureau," p. 2.

90. *Gorodskie vesti* (Volgograd), 47 (November 22–28, 1991), p. 1.

91. *Volgogradskaia pravda,* January 22, 1992, p. 3, and March 24, 1992, p. 1.

92. Elizabeth Teague and Philip Hanson, "Nikolai Travkin Attempts Painless Economic Reform," *RFE/RL Research Report,* 1, 38 (September 25, 1992), pp. 39–44; and Kathryn Brown, "Nizhnii Novgorod: A Regional Solution to National Problems?" *RFE/RL Research Report,* 2, 5 (January 29, 1993), pp. 17–23.

93. Valerii Kornev, "The Democrats Have Gone Over to Opposition in Order to Defend the Reforms of the Government," *Izvestiia,* April 1, 1992, p. 2 [trans. in *FBIS,* April 17, 1992, pp. 25–26].

94. Valerii Kornev, "V oppozitsii k reformam prodolzhaiut ostavat'sia volgogradskie vlasti," *Izvestiia,* May 22, 1993, p. 4. Ivan Rybkin, the third leader of the former "new wave" Communist antiestablishment in Volgoglad from 1990, gained national prominence in 1994 with his election as speaker of the Russian State Duma, the lower chamber of the newly formed Russian Federal Assembly (parliament) in Moscow.

95. Valerii Kornev, "Volgograd Gets 140 Million Rubles From Privatization in Just One Day," *Izvestiia,* July 3, 1992, p. 1 [trans. in *FBIS,* August 7, 1992, p. 61]; and Edward Balls and Gillian Tett, "Mass Privatisation in Practice," *Financial Times,* May 27, 1993, Section III, p. 5.

96. Igor Karpenko and Valerii Kornev, "A Tractor Plant for Vouchers; Mass Check Auctions Have Begun in Volgograd," *Izvestiia,* February 10, 1993, pp. 1–2 [trans. in *FBIS,* February 26, 1993, pp. 40–41]; and Balls and Tett, "Mass Privatisation," p. 5.

97. Igor Gamaiunov, "A Duel With the President," *Literaturnaia gazeta,* 44 (October 28, 1992), p. 10 [trans. in *FBIS,* November 11, 1992, pp. 28–30].

5

Institutions, Elites, and Local Politics in Russia

The Case of Omsk

John F. Young

This chapter is a study of reform and political change in Omsk from the failed August coup through 1992. In Omsk, local politics is animated by a variety of factors. The most dominant of these is the activity of elites, both old and new, in positions of influence.[1] There are, however, other factors at work, not the least of which are the weak and confused state of essentially new oblast, city, and lower administrative and governmental organs. The interplay of elites and institutions in Omsk helps explain why Yeltsin's reforms have bogged down, and reflects the current dynamics of local politics in Russia.

Omsk is a sedate city of some 1.2 million inhabitants situated along the Irtysh River in southwestern Siberia, some 2,500 kilometers east of Moscow. It is the capital of Omsk Oblast, which covers 140,000 square kilometers and has 2.2 million inhabitants (68 percent urban). From its early role as a transportation center for western Siberia, Omsk emerged during the Soviet period as a strong industrial center, ranking fourth among Russian cities in gross volume of production behind Moscow, St. Petersburg, and Ekaterinburg. But in spite of a strong and diverse industrial base, there is much more than distance that separates Omsk from Moscow or St. Petersburg. Because of the strategic importance of much of its production, Omsk was closed to foreigners until 1991.[2] There is a palpable difference in character and temperament among the city's inhabitants that reflects not only a pronounced detachment from the nation's capital, but also a certain disdain for anything connected to Moscow. Omsk possesses a small town feel that exudes strong civic pride and yet, paradoxically, also possesses a certain inferiority complex about how it measures up to other cities in Russia or the West. In the current economic and political climate, *Omichi,* the residents, are quick to admit that things are undoubtedly bad, but even quicker to point out that life in Omsk is certainly better than most anywhere else in the country.

It would be difficult for the average resident to suggest otherwise. While economic production declined sharply and some of the large enterprises worked at less than half capacity, Omsk displayed none of the disparities in wealth evidenced in Moscow. Through 1992 the ruble remained the currency of use, if only because an alternative choice was nonexistent (the circulation of the German mark or American dollar in Omsk was virtually nil). Foreign currency bars and restaurants remained foreign to Omsk. New crowds packed churches and markets, but the old crowds were still found in state stores and public transit. For the layperson, in spite of rampant inflation and the shift to marketization, Omsk maintained more in common with its Soviet past than with the post-Soviet future. In this regard, Omsk is part of the *"glukhoman',"* the "boonies" or backwoods of Russia, often characterized as places where Yeltsin's reforms have bogged down.

Local Institutions and Local Power

The nature of political power at the local level has been the subject of many noteworthy studies in political science.[3] The fault line for much of this literature is the debate between "pluralists" and "elitists." The former suggest that resources necessary for political power are distributed throughout a local community, and that the distribution differs depending on the realm and scope of a particular issue.[4] The elitist approach, in contrast, argues that power is connected to an identifiable elitist, in possession of a preponderance of resources that allow them to dominate community politics.[5] The elitist argument has been advanced by at least two groups: those suggesting that a social class dominates within a community by possessing an abundance of social, economic, and political power (instrumentalist); and by those suggesting that government is distinct from, but subordinate to, economic elites (structuralist).

Rooted in the elitist paradigm, Clarence Stone has advanced the concept of "systemic" power at the local level. Stone takes as a given that resources are hierarchically arranged, and suggests that local officials thus form their alliances, make their decisions, and plan their futures within the context of this stratification. Since capital is mobile, and local economic elites wield a disproportionate amount of power, local officials are predisposed to favor "elite" interests above those of the general public.[6] Bryan Jones and Lynn

Bachelor have contested Stone's approach, and claim that local economic elites, rather than exercising what elitists might refer to as a "controlling" hand over local politics, possess instead a "sustaining" hand. Jones's and Bachelor's research in one-company towns in Michigan shows that local officials are not actively guided by economic elites, but are constrained by an awareness of their economic interests.[7]

What does all this have to do with the institutions of local government? Margaret Levi has noted that in order to understand institutions, we must recognize that they "represent concessions of power by one group of actors to at least one other individual in order to resolve potentially major conflicts among strategic actors."[8] Later, she points out that some institutions serve the interests of the many while others serve the interests of the few. "But all facilitate and regulate the resources of power."[9] A functional political system is thus one in which a workable power-sharing arrangement has been achieved, and at least marginally institutionalized.

At issue here is the involvement of elites in community politics and their relations with the organs of local government. Such a theme is particularly relevant to the study of Russian politics, because Russian governments, both federal and local, are currently in a formative stage. The genesis of new government institutions at the local level in Russia and their vulnerability to elite interests may help explain a good part of the problems currently experienced in the Russian provinces.

The Breakdown of Local Administration in the Soviet Union

Prior to August 1991, Soviet reform had led to the breakdown of local government and administration in Omsk.[10] The effects of the Law on the State Enterprise, for example, curbed the levers of party-state control over economic production, and granted more authority to factory directors. Local elections, which aimed at increasing political input and administrative control from below, essentially removed the remaining "glue" of the Communist Party that had held the Soviet administrative system together. Such changes led to a ruptured system of political representation and chaos concerning executive authority and accountability. Attempts by the Soviet government to establish a "new" administrative order in the face of local economic and political chaos were half-hearted and passed responsibility for the separation of powers to the various republics.[11] The Union government gave inadequate attention to both the separation of executive and legislative branches of government, and to the problems of blurred and overlapping jurisdictions. Until republican law was passed more than a year later, these two issues were primary factors in the decline of local government and administration.

In spite of campaign slogans of "All power to the Soviets!" the local soviets that were elected in the spring of 1990 soon found that they were little more than loud debating chambers, with few independent revenues, little authority, and virtually no political power. Amidst the resultant administrative chaos, experienced members of the party–state apparatus and factory directors strengthened their positions as powerful and identifiable interests in the local political arena. With a relative preponderance of economic and political resources, such groups continued to exist as local elites in spite of the numerous changes in local government.

In contrast to Soviet reform, the Russian government experienced at least modest success in establishing a more ordered and functional system of local government. The Russian Federation Supreme Soviet passed a Law on Local Self-Government in July 1991, and followed that with a corresponding Law on Oblast and Krai Soviets and Administrations in March 1992, which attempted to resolve the fundamental problems of local government and administration noted above.[12] New laws provided for a separation of powers between executive and legislative bodies, and also divided authority along a vertical axis, among federal, oblast/krai, municipal, and rural governments. But numerous obstacles still remain to a functional state system of government and administration. This essay will also shed some light on the nature of some of these obstacles.

Introducing the New Administrations in Omsk

The Oblast

After the failed coup, as the Soviet Union vanished from the political map, politics in Omsk were marked by increased activity directed toward establishing political and administrative order. The first move came when Yeltsin appointed Aleksandr Minzhurenko as presidential representative to Omsk in September 1991. Minzhurenko was then a deputy in the soon to be abolished USSR Congress of People's Deputies. He had worked previously as an instructor at the Omsk Pedagogical Institute, and had risen to local prominence during the election campaign of 1989. During the August coup, Minzhurenko had led small public street meetings, and had formed the Committee for the Defense of Legal Organs of Power. Minzhurenko's new duties were to function as the president's "eyes and ears" in the oblast, informing Yeltsin on the fulfillment of central laws and decrees, and assisting the federal executive in establishing political power and authority throughout the oblast.

The most significant move in establishing such executive power was the president's decision to delay elections for local executives—initially for one year, and then later until 1995—and instead appoint the heads of oblast administration by presidential *ukaz*. The oblast-level executives would then appoint lower-level executives in agreement with the corresponding soviets, and allow these executives to appoint subordinate executives in turn.[13] Defending this decision, Minzhurenko stated that he himself "was a democrat through and through," but that he had become convinced that direct appointment was the only real solution to the current dilemma of executive power. Elections, simply put, were too risky. They would lead to conservative local executives that would cause a fractured executive along the vertical axis. He pointed out that almost all rural areas in the oblast were staunchly conservative, and that a third of the city would also support a conservative candidate. The democrats in the oblast would thus have poor chances of winning a general election. Direct appointments, on the other hand, would establish a stronger system of executive power throughout the country, and would place local executives on a "short leash," which would compel local administrators to support and implement presidential decrees. Given the need for radical economic and political reform, Minzhurenko suggested that no other alternative was available.[14]

Minzhurenko had asked the local democratic movement to advance a candidate for *glava administratsii* of the oblast, but none was forthcoming. The name of Vladimir Ispravnikov had been raised, but the Russian deputy representing Omsk in the Russian parliament had already agreed to join Khasbulatov's parliamentary team. Yeltsin wanted to make the appointment quickly, and Minzhurenko was pressured to come up with a recommendation. He felt that he had two choices: either the chair of the oblast soviet, Anatolii Leont'ev, or the chair of the *oblispolkom* (oblast executive committee), Leonid Polezhaev. He justified his decision by claiming that "one does not change horses midstream," and that some professional experience was mandatory. While Leont'ev had served as chairman of the oblast executive committee for many years prior to his election to the soviet in 1990, his connections to the discredited Communist Party (he had also served as obkom first secretary) and the old guard ruled him out as a credible candidate for the position.

That left only Polezhaev, a 51-year-old native of Omsk, who had spent much of his adult life in Kazakhstan supervising canal construction. He had worked as deputy chair of the Karaganda oblispolkom until conflict with local officials convinced him to quit and return home. Within two years, he became an assistant to Leont'ev in the oblast executive committee, and then succeeded him as chair of the ispolkom in 1990, after Leont'ev became chair of the oblast soviet. Polezhaev had a credible reputation as an effective administrator, but had been defeated in elections to the Russian Congress.[15] During the coup, Polezhaev had been the most vocal supporter of legality and the Russian government at a joint meeting of the oblast soviet presidium and ispolkom, although the general tenor of the meeting was one of waiting out central intrigues and encouraging life in Omsk to continue as before.[16] Polezhaev appeared on local television on the evening of August 20, the second day of the coup, but his appeal was for public calm in the face of political uncertainty. In the end, however, Polezhaev was instrumental in encouraging the oblast leadership to ignore calls for emergency measures from the State Commission on the State of Emergency, or the GKChP. His rationale was that the local situation in Omsk was stable and that such measures were not needed.[17] After the failed coup, Polezhaev claimed to support strong executive power, suggesting that responsibility for reforms without an effective structure with which to implement them was impossible.[18]

The oblast ispolkom suspended its existence on November 11, 1991, and Polezhaev was officially appointed head of administration, or *gubernator,* of Omsk Oblast. In accordance with presidential decree, Polezhaev quickly began to select his administrative team. His appointments were a mix of former *apparatchiki* and supposedly fresh faces (though established administrators) from local institutes and enterprises, with an emphasis on qualifications of expertise and experience. Chairman of the economic committee, for example, was V.V. Malykhin, who had functioned in that capacity since Polezhaev had become chairman of the ispolkom in 1990. N.D. Lykhenko, the director of a large collective farm, was appointed as new head of agriculture, while an instructor with administrative experience from the local pedagogical institute was given responsibility over education. Defending his choices, Polezhaev stated that new demands required new faces, but the public could not entrust the fate of the economy and society to the hands of novices. There was also a need for experienced organizers of production.[19] On relations with the oblast soviet (*obsovet*), Polezhaev was optimistic. He expressed his belief that a common language, or mutual understanding, would be found, and pointed out that there were no objective reasons for conflict with the soviet. The obsovet, he suggested, should concentrate its attention on deputies' affairs and legislation, and should not bother to interfere in the managerial affairs of the administration. Although he acknowledged that the obsovet presidium had often interfered in oblispolkom work in the past, he was confident that the oblast administration would be allowed to take responsibility for its managerial activity, and would answer to the people and the president.[20]

Almost immediately after Polezhaev's appointment, Minzhurenko began to express second thoughts over his recommendation. He stated publicly that he thought Polezhaev was inconsistent, and that he had hoped the new gubernator would be more progressive, particularly concerning his appointments.[21] Polezhaev himself felt that the oblast was caught in the middle of reform—between a public worried about the realities of daily life and a Russian government that continued to promulgate laws and decrees that pushed radical change. The task, as he perceived it, was to try to fit such decrees and laws into local conditions, or to "smooth the sharp corners of reform so that they would be less difficult for the people."[22] Later, he emphasized his recognition that reform was necessary, but conceded his opposition to the techniques and principles of acting Prime Minister Gaidar's radical policies—on the grounds that they were not in the best interests of residents of Omsk.[23] And in response to criticism that Omsk Oblast lagged behind Novosibirsk in agricultural reform, Polezhaev responded, "What of it? This is not a race." [24]

In the obsovet, Leont'ev and his staff were also attempting to come to grips with the new realities of local power. Leont'ev had staffed the leadership with many of his old assistants from the party and the executive committee. And among this crowd there was not much love or respect for Minzhurenko, who was viewed as an unelected and inexperienced puppet without any real authority. The legislative body remained relatively immune to Yeltsin's decrees, and organized a *malyi sovet,* or small soviet, by the new year, to strengthen legislative authority through a smaller, more effective chamber.[25] The small soviet of Omsk Oblast was comprised of 34 deputies, including Leont'ev, a few of his assistants, one representative from each of the fourteen standing committees, and a number of oblast deputies elected to full-time positions in the small soviet.[26] The fourteen soviet committees paralleled the committees, departments, and administrations of the oblast executive, and were geared toward drafting legislation and supervising the implementation of obsovet legislation. The small soviet soon came under criticism from reformist deputies in the obsovet for aggrandizing legislative power. Of particular concern, many urban deputies in the oblast soviet opposed the perceived "rural bias" of Leont'ev's leadership.[27]

Initially, the relationship between obsovet and administration had been amiable, a function of the personal relationship between Leont'ev and Polezhaev, who was generally willing to defer to his former boss. After Polezhaev's appointment as gubernator, however, executive–legislative relations began to show cracks as Polezhaev bore increased responsibility for implementation of central decrees. As the relationship declined, Polezhaev suggested that for all their good, soviets really only complicated matters of administration.[28] An early source of conflict between the two concerned a rivalry between the property committees of each branch of government. In early 1992, the obsovet demanded that the administration implement specific decisions regarding the allocation of property, including office space for legislative committees. The administration, however, ignored much of the soviet's demands, and allocated only 40 percent of the requested office space. To clear up any confusion surrounding authority over state property, Polezhaev issued an executive decree, which granted to the administration's property committee sole authority over the creation, reorganization, and liquidation of government enterprises belonging to the oblast, as well as sole right to make any contracts with enterprise directors (including the rental and use of oblast property).[29]

Conflict also emerged over planned expenditures in the first quarter budget of 1992. The oblast administration pushed for capital investment in construction and industrial conversion. But while the administration pointed out the 78 percent shortfall in funding for buildings already under construction (many already abandoned), the oblast soviet countered by pointing out fiscal responsibilities that had been transferred from lower-level soviets to the oblast: health clinics, schools, and kindergartens. Debate over what constituency should get how big a slice from the shrinking budget pie raged along urban–rural, industry–agriculture, and capital investment–social services axes.[30] Further conflict developed when obsovet deputies began to pressure Polezhaev to withhold money due for transfer to the federal budget. They wanted to express opposition to acting Prime Minister Gaidar's economic reforms. While pointing out his own reservations regarding these reforms, Polezhaev refused to accede to their demands and delivered a strong speech to the soviet that linked the fall of the Soviet Union to republics withholding their required contributions to the Union budget. Questioning the position adopted by conservative deputies, he asked them if they now wanted Russia to break apart as well. He requested deputy support in making the required payments, and received the necessary number of votes.[31]

At the roots of conflict between oblast soviet and administration in Omsk were two dominant factors: first, that Polezhaev was accountable to both the federal executive and the oblast soviet; and second, that there was a natural conflict between the constituencies represented by the two institutions. Yeltsin's "short leash" over local executives obliged Polezhaev to walk a fine line between local and central interests. That the oblast soviet represented a constituency different from that of President Yeltsin, and possessed different, even rival, perspectives and goals, made this walk a difficult task for the oblast gubernator. Through the second half of 1992, Polezhaev was forced to compromise on issues of conflict between obsovet and executive. These compromises caused cracks within his administration.

In September 1992 for example, the oblast small soviet passed a decision that infringed on the authority of the administration and increased the wholesale price of milk and meat by more than 30 percent.[32] Polezhaev responded by declaring that the whole reform process would be impossible if the administration did not have control over prices. He pointed out that such increases would create too big a difference between retail and whole-sale prices, that increased subsidies were beyond the capacity of the oblast budget, and that the new prices were beyond what the public could afford. He blamed the small soviet for bowing to a strong agricultural lobby, and for allowing political factors to transcend economic reality. Within his ad-ministration, however, Lykhenko (head of agriculture) endorsed the price hikes, while Malykhin (economic committee) vociferously denounced the decision at a meeting of the oblast small soviet. When the Union of Agricul-tural Workers threatened to strike over the issue, Polezhaev worked out a compromise that allowed a 15 percent increase in wholesale prices.[33] Malykhin made a public display of opposition.[34]

For Polezhaev, the issue remained one of tailoring central policy to local interests. Price regulation and subsidies were defended as crucial to main-taining a balance between purchase and retail prices. Opponents, he claimed, either did not understand the dangers of ending such regulation, or desired to bring social concerns in Omsk to a boil.[35] While he worked to implement central policy, Polezhaev remained sensitive to local interests. He publicly advocated increased input from local administrations in federal government policy, and also for more clearly defined powers between both executive and legislative branches, and central and local organs.[36] Contin-ual conflict over which organ had authority over pricing, property, or in-vestment policy served neither the cause of reform nor the goals of effective government.

Perhaps the most telling aspect of Polezhaev's political position requires that we examine his perception of local interests. The gubernator was an open advocate on behalf of the large industrial enterprises in Omsk. In a speech to the oblast soviet in February 1992, Polezhaev pointed out that industrial production accounted for more than half of the oblast income, and that it had fallen in virtually every sector. Gross agricultural production, on the other hand, accounted for about one-quarter of oblast economic output, and procurement prices had risen almost 90 percent since 1990. Less atten-tion, he suggested, should be given to agricultural problems, and more effort and attention given to industrial questions: subsidies, investment, conversion, interregional trade, and the coordination of supplies.[37]

The gubernator's inclination toward large industry was not the result of any sudden change in perception. Since April 1991, Polezhaev had been a founding member of a conglomerate of large industries and commercial enterprises in the oblast known as *Omskii Torgovyi Dom* (OTD). OTD functions as a large insiders' club, local trade cartel, and lobby group, and had been buying up profitable local industries. Polezhaev had served as OTD's first president, but the position was soon given to Iurii Glebov, former chair of the city executive committee.[38] For his part, Polezhaev saw nothing out of the ordinary in his connections to OTD. The problems of the oblast economy were directly connected to industrial production, and therefore of concern to all residents. What was good for industrial production and OTD was good for Omsk.

The City

In municipal politics, the executive committee and its chairman, G. Pavlov, faced a scandal in late October 1991, when it became known that the ispolkom had transferred title of two municipal buildings to OTD. Compounding the scandal, the ispolkom had invested some 500,000 rubles in OTD, led by Pavlov's predecessor in the ispolkom, Glebov.[39] Pavlov's credibility was damaged further when he tried to appoint a number of members of the previous executive to his administration. The city soviet pushed for open nominations, and thirteen candidates vied for two posts in the ispolkom. An emboldened soviet then began to push its own candidates for appointment by Polezhaev to head the city administration. The oblast head of administration was invited to attend a meeting of the city small soviet to discuss the appointment of a mayor. Given the prodemocracy euphoria of late 1991, city deputies put Polezhaev on the spot by suggesting he nominate the candidate put forward by a vote in the city small soviet. A prominent local businessman, Iurii Shoikhet, won a plurality of the votes, and his name was immediately advanced for the position. By all accounts, Polezhaev was visibly flustered by the unforeseen circumstance, but agreed to appoint Shoikhet, a man with no government experience, as mayor.[40] The new head of the city administration had received support from local enterprises and cooperatives, from the presidential representative Minzhurenko, and from various social organizations.

Shoikhet was somewhat of a local hero among the emergent small business class. Born in 1950 in Perm, he was a former fighter pilot in the Soviet air force who had been stationed in Omsk in the 1970s. Retiring at age thirty-five (fighter pilots received double time for service), he started a small fishing enterprise in 1986, and then began a cooperative that employed pensioners and invalids in the manufacturing of fishing tackle. He was instrumental in the emergence of the Omsk Oblast Union of Cooperatives, and in early 1991 established AO Omsk, a shareholder's company that enjoyed immediate success in food services and other sectors of the local economy.[41]

Shoikhet's well-intentioned point of departure was that the new statutes and structures of administration possessed clearly defined authority and a separation of executive and legislative power. His understanding of the responsibility of the city administration was to prepare normative acts and introduce them to the soviet, which would then pass municipal statutes and oversee their implementation by the administration. His first day in office he sacked the entire administrative team of his predecessor, and began to appoint academics and individuals successful in small enterprises to the city administration. Of his ten chairmen of city administration committees, for example, only one could be identified as a bona fide member of the former *nomenklatura*.[42] Shoikhet quickly launched an agenda that pushed for an international business center, a foreign-currency hotel and bank, an international airport, and capital expenditures for developing the local infrastructure for local business (especially direct telephones and fax services).[43] In February, Shoikhet and his administration held an open meeting for all local enterprises, establishing contact and open communications with the business community. He knew his constituency: in less than ten months the number of small enterprises and cooperatives had mushroomed from 1,000 to just less than 4,200 (1,178 cooperatives, and more than 3,000 small enterprises and associations)—with earned income of more than 600 million rubles.[44]

The city soviet represented a much wider variety of interests. Elections in 1990 had returned only 20 percent of incumbents, and the deputy corps was comprised of roughly 40 percent "conservatives," 40 percent reformers (although both groups were very loose coalitions), with the remaining 20 percent independents in the true sense of the word—individuals without commitment to one side or the other.[45] Vladimir Varnavskii, who served also as first secretary of the gorkom, had been reelected chairman of the soviet, winning 92 of 164 votes. But Varnavskii accepted pressure from reformers to appoint the runner-up, Ryzhenko, as deputy chair, and soon won support from many reformers for his fair play and effective leadership.[46]

The new administration led by Shoikhet was supported by a significant minority of city deputies, but less so by the soviet leadership and apparatus.

For the most part, both executive and legislative branches stayed within the parameters of their authority as defined by the Russian Law on Local Self-Government. But among the ranks of the city soviet apparatus, Shoikhet's name most often evoked derisive comments. The mayor was criticized for his style of leadership, for an overly probusiness agenda, and for overstepping his authority. His success as a businessman and his personal wealth were noted frequently by a critical press, who often turned against him with the claim that having him in charge of municipal administration was like having a wolf guard the sheep—the mayor stood to gain the most by the "commercialization of government."[47] While all sources recognized him as a dynamo of action and a strong advocate of change, he remained much more the businessman than the politician, used to calling his own shots, and guilty of a sometimes abrasive personality. In his defense, some local newspapers supported the mayor, pointing to an alleged alliance between the city soviet and oblast administration directed against Shoikhet.[48]

For their part, the leadership of the city soviet did line up closer to the oblast administration on the political spectrum. While the city soviet represented the vast array of interests that could be found in the city, the soviet leadership maintained a middle-of-the-road approach to government, supporting reform, but trying to cushion the blows of change. Its main priorities included rationalizing its authority, and establishing and developing local resources in an "orderly" manner. A new law on municipal taxes, for example, attempted to establish a firm base for revenue without contributing to economic decline. At the second reading of the law in the small soviet, opposition was directed against the law from those representing business, who felt a payroll tax and commercial licensing fees were undue attacks on local enterprises. In contrast, other deputies claimed the law did not tax local business enough, and proposed a tax on the use of computers (since any firm with computers must have excess money!). In defense of the law, officials pointed out that the law did not aim to "maximize" revenue as much as it aimed to strengthen revenue with a minimum of fiscal pain. Of the eighteen sources available to municipal governments for tax revenue, this new law used only six. Why, deputies were asked, should the soviet endorse taxing the private sector into further poverty?[49]

New Institutions, Elites, and Political Conflict

The emergence, all within two years, of four "new" organs of government and administration (one might even include a fifth: Minzhurenko's office of presidential representative or *namestnik*)—each with its own position on the political spectrum, and each struggling to establish independence, political authority, and power—has been at the center of local politics in Omsk. Each of the four institutions represent distinct constituencies: the oblast soviet strongly represents rural and agricultural interests; the oblast administration has close ties to large industry in Omsk; the city administration advances a small business agenda; while the city soviet represents varied and disparate urban constituencies. In 1992, a number of local issues reflected the clash of local interests and personalities, and conflict among government organs. In this last section, I draw from dominant issues of local politics in 1992 in Omsk to portray the different dimensions and various dynamics of local politics.

Privatization

Privatization opened up the question of current property ownership. Decades of public ownership bequeathed a legacy of confusion when the unitary system of soviets was finally vanquished in 1991. Which properties were owned by the oblast and which belonged to municipal authorities? Federal legislation decreed that municipalities would receive the following properties within their territory: residential properties; establishments dealing with city infrastructure; enterprises of retail trade, public catering, and domestic services; and wholesale and industrial complexes required for those services.[50] Oblast property was not identified by law, since the oblast remained a territorial division of state power (in contrast, municipalities are now, in theory, self-governing, separate jurisdictions). Yet there are many gray areas concerning the issue of property and privatization, and many property titles that must now, in accordance with law, be transferred to the proper owner. This transfer of property to municipalities is a crucial component in the development of municipal power. The ownership and control of property is directly linked with political authority, and revenues from privatization are important additions to municipal budgets. In 1992, for example, municipal privatization added more than two billion rubles to the city budget.[51]

An example of the problems involved in the process of privatization is found in the privatization of housing. The city administration rejected the December 1991 oblast proposal to privatize housing, which would have merely turned over residences to their occupants without any compensation. In late January 1992, the city alternatively proposed to transfer title of domestic dwellings to their respective inhabitants—free of charge for apartments and homes where there was less than 18 square meters per resident, and for compensation when living space exceeded that measure. Various other factors were to be considered, such as the floor on which the apartment was situated, the age of the building, and the location. The rationale behind the city's proposal was twofold. First, it would target some of the privileged elites that had secured access to superior housing during the previous regime. Second, and more important, the city hoped to augment its limited sources of independent revenue and strengthen its financial autonomy. A.P. Potapova, head specialist for the municipal committee for privatization of housing, stated that the city's hopes were "that the resources obtained through privatization of apartments would find their way into the extremely tight local budgets."[52] The oblast responded by ridiculing the city's proposal, and pointed out that according to Russian law, municipal authority had no jurisdiction over the privatization of housing.[53] The city administration, however, based its claim on the law concerning the transfer of property cited above. It refused to concede its case, in spite of support for the oblast position from the city prosecutor's office and the oblast court. Through 1992, the case lay before a Federal court, delaying the privatization of housing in Omsk until the matter could be resolved.

A further example of city vs. oblast conflict was the battle over the Torgovyi Tsentr (TTs), which operates a large retail "mall" in the middle of the city. The TTs is a member of the OTD conglomerate. During the spring of 1992, worker collectives from TTs submitted their application for the transformation of TTs to a closed shareholders' company to the office of Aleksandr Saraev, chairman of the city municipal property committee. Saraev's committee normally requires at least three weeks to process applications, and then requires the agreement of the city soviet before the process can continue. In this instance, the city administration had some doubts concerning the formation of a closed shareholders' company, which often served as a front for the privatization of profitable firms to former members of the nomenklatura.

As the city administration considered the application, the oblast administration began to create waves, claiming that TTs was really oblast property. At issue was the vested interest of the TTs directorship, coupled with the fact that the lion's share of any privatization revenue went to the institution that held title. Once the oblast administration began meddling in what even the oblast soviet agreed was municipal property, Saraev and Shoikhet went on the attack. Rather than allow TTs to become a closed shareholders' company, it approved only the creation of an open-type shareholders' company, a move that the city administration believed would limit control of TTs by large corporate interests in the city (i.e., OTD). Called to explain the decision before a meeting of the workers' collective, Saraev failed to attend. He later appeared at a subsequent meeting accompanied by Shoikhet, where the latter made a spirited defense of his subordinate's decision. As a prime investment opportunity, he declared, TTs should be available to all citizens of Omsk, rather than to the allegedly manipulated labor collective of TTs.[54] The whole incident was a public relations disaster for the city administration, but it was successful in preventing (at least in the short term) any buyout by OTD interests. At the end of 1992, TTs had only temporary status as a shareholders' company, while the issue awaited permanent resolution.[55]

Another example concerns a private consumer service corporation known as Omskservis. The formation of this company is a prime example of "piratization" (prikhvatizatsiia) of state property by members of the nomenklatura that was rampant in 1990 and 1991. By late 1990, the directors of the state consumer service industry in Omsk Oblast moved to maintain their positions of privilege and authority, and forced the rapid creation of AO Omskservis. The "new" closed shareholders' company assumed the functions of managing state-run domestic services, ranging from film developing to hair salons to television and radio repair. At the founding meeting of the company, which was attended by workers' delegates and controlled by the existing directorship, the vast majority of delegates reportedly spoke out against the formation of Omskservis. Yet the vote for privatization "mysteriously" showed two-thirds support. The oblispolkom supported the move, and even contributed a sizable donation to the "new" enterprise. They transferred some sixty-five million rubles of what would shortly have become municipal property to Omskservis free of charge. And so, as one local reporter observed, the leadership of the oblast consumer service administration resettled into the easy chairs of the board of directors of AO Omskservis. Since then, Omskservis has been putting the squeeze on its competition and uncooperative labor collectives, buying up its own stock, and maintaining a commanding monopoly over local services.[56] According to oblast administration documents, Omskservis held a 60 percent market share of local consumer services, an annual 588-million-ruble industry in Omsk Oblast.[57]

The existence of Omskservis contradicted Russian law. But since Omskservis ducked in under the wire of legislation intended to prevent the formation of such privately owned monopolies, the company continued to exist while political and legal battles were waged over its status.[58] The city administration responded by issuing a decree in February 1992 with three basic demands: the reorganization, by March, of Omskservis and its constituent enterprises independent of any official (state or municipal) property; the return of municipal property transferred earlier to Omskservis by the oblast ispolkom; and then the liquidation of Omskservis and recreation of municipal commercial enterprises. Directors would then be appointed by city and (outside the city) rural raion administrations.[59] The motivation for city soviet and administration opposition to Omskservis is multifaceted. On one hand, the pro–small business platform of the city administration has been noted.

But two other factors are also significant. The first of these is the issue of property. Property valued at sixty-five million rubles prior to the rampant inflation of 1992 is a valuable collection of real estate. That it was essentially pilfered from city authorities prior to the emergence of effective municipal power is a loud call to arms for municipal officials, led by Iurii Shoikhet. The mayor's stated purpose in the struggle was to strengthen the power and authority of the city administration against that of the oblast.[60]

The second factor is that Omskservis is also part of the grand conglomerate (OTD), the nemesis of small business in Omsk. Shoikhet's opposition to OTD is based not only on his concern for small independent enterprises, but, more importantly, may be a result of concern for his own trust, AO Omsk, which made inroads into the consumer service industry. Placed in trust during Shoikhet's tenure as mayor, it is nevertheless run by Pavel Borisov, his close assistant. Polezhaev did reverse the decision that transferred property to Omskservis, but the company continued to operate and hold on to the property with impunity. The oblast administration appealed to the oblast soviet and rural constituencies for support in a losing cause to defend Omskservis, claiming that if the corporation fell into municipal hands, the service sector in rural areas would be decimated. Shoikhet, they claimed, was only interested in maximizing profit, and would quickly close any unprofitable shops. As with other examples, the issue of Omskservis was tied up in the courts.

Anti-Monopoly Politics

The Omsk Anti-Monopoly Committee (AMC) was formed in January 1992 by the State Anti-Monopoly Committee in Moscow. Local AMC officials, self-described "comissars of the market," are agents of the state committee, and answer directly to the center. The AMC has no direct horizontal accountability. The Omsk AMC is led by Sergei Sumenkov, a former engineer from "Polyet," a large aerospace company in Omsk. He was recommended for the position by Aleksandr Minzhurenko. Leonid Polezhaev had recommended someone else for the post, and so there was a significant amount of administrative opposition to Sumenkov's appointment. According to Malykhin, chairman of the oblast administration's economic committee, Sumenkov and his assistants were "unprofessional," had no understanding of economics, and did not comprehend the common language of administration.[61]

The AMC has seventy comprehensive and complicated criteria through which they define a monopoly. When their equations and formulas identify an enterprise as such, the AMC attempts to force the enterprise to reduce either the price of a given product or the market share. If these endeavors should fail, the AMC slaps the enterprise with a fine. Problems emerge once enterprises are "listed" as monopolies.[62] When enterprises fail to comply with price- or market-share reduction, the AMC can act unilaterally and impose a fine, which is transferred directly out of the enterprise's accounts. Appeals are directed not toward resisting payment, but for the return of monies already confiscated. This transfer of money from an account to the AMC, however, requires the approval of the chairman of the oblast administration's economic committee. The oblast administration's ties to the large enterprises in the territory has already been noted, and Vyacheslav Malykhin had no qualms about defending the interests of these firms. For example, when the AMC determined that "Omskshina," a large tire manufacturer, possessed a complete monopoly over the sales of tires throughout Omsk and applied a fine of 1 million rubles, Malykhin refused to approve the confiscation of monies. He argued that Omskshina really produced for the national market, and that its market share throughout Russia was the only criterion upon which such judgment should be made.

A more revealing example of the oblast administration's defense of large firms is the case of "Khozstroimebel'torg," a domestic furniture maker and wholesaler that controls 96 percent of the oblast domestic furniture market. All thirty-eight retail furniture stores in the oblast are compelled by contract to purchase their goods from this firm.[63] When Khozstroimebel'torg was listed by the AMC, its director quickly appealed to Malykhin, who gathered alternative data and information and was influential in preventing the firm from being fined. Sumenkov pressed his case, enlisting the help of Aleksandr Saraev, the chairman of the municipal property committee of the city administration, and state agent for privatization. Saraev's stated interest in breaking the monopoly of Khozstroimebel'torg was to help out the smaller retailers in the city (part of the platform of the city administration), but he also had a personal feud going with Malykhin, his former boss.[64] While Malykhin was initially successful in defending Khozstroimebel'torg, the issue soon transcended mere economic concerns and developed as a battle between rival institutions and personalities. Encouraged by the support of the city administration, the AMC continued to press its case, and eventually succeeded in penalizing Khozstroimebel'torg.

Conclusion

Politics in Omsk is dominated by conflict among the various institutions of local government. The question that then arises concerns an explanation for the conflict. Two alternative answers appear most plausible. The first suggests that some measure of institutional interests is at work. New institutions of government and administration have not yet established fully functional working relationships. In addition, all the institutions of local government are engaged in the pursuit of resources (especially such independent revenues as those from privatization) necessary to fulfill their allotted functions and increase their political power. Oblast and municipal governments continue to lack the necessary revenues to provide even basic services. If we ask how clearly the jurisdictions and authority of local organs are defined, how effectively the accountability of executives has been established, how independent institutions of local government are from particular local interests, and how capable local institutions are of implementing policy, then we go a long way toward understanding current problems of local government and administration. Analysis of the situation in Omsk leads to the conclusion that the breakdown of the old Soviet administrative system has not yet been replaced by a fully functional system of government in the provinces. Immature organs of local government possess sometimes ill-defined authority, lack the resources for real political power, and yet are called upon to implement far-reaching and often unpopular reforms. Until such problems as property ownership and adequate tax revenues, as well as those involving the lack of clarity in defining and dividing local powers and authority, are fully addressed, local politics will undoubtedly be marked more by conflict than cooperation.[65]

Notwithstanding this institutional confusion, or perhaps even because of it, local elites are the dominant actors in local politics in Omsk. In each of the examples described here, particular interests, such as the agricultural lobby and big and small business, were represented by various institutions of government. In some instances, the distinction between an institution and a particular interest was sufficiently blurred to cause one to wonder when a political leader was acting as a leader of an institution, and when he was acting as a member of a particular elite. The relationship between the oblast administration and OTD, for example, goes well beyond what would be acceptable in a mature political system. The fact that these local leaders are working with poorly defined authority, weak institutions, and limited official resources forces them to rely more heavily on local elites. As one group of authors has pointed out:

older networks continue
conflicts of local elites
lack of funds

Leaders are, of course, more keenly aware of governing arrangements than are ordinary members [of coalitions]. And they may regard themselves not only as leaders of particular groups, but also as members of the governing group. If so, they have a stake in these governing arrangements, perpetuating what they are a part of and perhaps bending these arrangements in a way that corresponds with their understanding of what is appropriate.[66]

In summary, current politics in Omsk appears to come closest to Stone's construct of systemic power. While the public interest is a factor in local politics, resources remain hierarchically distributed, and local leaders seem to be actively guided by economic elites—even to the point of interfering in federal government policy. This is especially so at the oblast level, and particularly relevant in the oblast administration. In municipal government, the distinction between elites and municipal institutions seems at least marginally less blurred. But this may be primarily a consequence of the result of less powerful elites aligned with the municipal administration.

An important distinction from Stone's systemic power, however, is the existence of distinct and rival elites. The conflict among these different elites has revolved around the distribution of resources, and suggests that as the conflict continues, resources may become less concentrated with any one group, or, alternatively, more concentrated with a newer group. In this sense, Omsk may compare with the early history of Robert Dahl's New Haven, where in the nineteenth century, old elites were displaced by a rising class of entrepreneurs who, in turn, were later displaced by a wider group of middle-class residents.[67]

The distribution of various resources may thus become more diffuse over time—perhaps not to the extent that elites cease to exist, but at least to the extent that their role in local politics will more closely resemble what Jones and Bachelor label a "sustaining" hand.

At present, scarce resources remain concentrated in the hands of local elites. Institutions of local government lack required resources and hence, lack sufficient amounts of political power. Politicians are thus required to rely on narrow coalitions of elite interests, and a "workable power-sharing arrangement" among these elites is extremely tenuous. This suggests that one problem presently plaguing Russia is not so much that of an excess of autonomy of local governments, but an excess of power of local elites.

Notes

Research in Omsk was conducted with the support of the Centre for Russian and East European Studies (University of Toronto), which included an exchange with the Economic Committee of the Omsk Oblast Economic Committee in May–July, 1992. Some

ill defined authority

of the more nuanced observations included here were made during interviews with municipal and oblast officials, and attendance at meetings of the local councils. Further support was received from a Social Science and Humanities Research Council of Canada Doctoral Fellowship. An earlier version of this paper was presented at the annual meeting of the Canadian Association of Slavists, Ottawa, June 3–5, 1993.

1. Local elites and conflicting societal interests in local politics in Russia have already received some focused attention from Western analysts. See, for example, Mary McAuley, "Politics, Economics and Elite Realignment in Russia: A Regional Perspective," *Soviet Economy* 8:1 (January–March 1992): 46–88; Joel C. Moses, "Soviet Provincial Politics in an Era of Transition and Revolution, 1989–91," *Soviet Studies* 44:3 (1992): 479–509; Jeffrey W. Hahn, "Local Politics and Political Power in Russia: The Case of Yaroslavl'," *Soviet Economy* 7:4 (October–December 1991): 322–41; and Gavin Helf and Jeffrey W. Hahn, "Old Dogs and New Tricks: Party Elites in the Russian Regional Elections of 1990," *Slavic Review* 51:3 (fall 1992): 511–30.

2. At least 60 percent of industrial production in Omsk was under the umbrella of the military-industrial complex—from tires to T–80 tanks, communication equipment, aerospace technology, and petrochemicals (Omsk is connected by pipeline to Tiumen). The city also services a productive regional agricultural industry.

3. A brief list would include Floyd Hunter, *Community Power Structure* (Chapel Hill: University of North Carolina Press, 1953); Robert Dahl, *Who Governs? Democracy and Power in an American City* (New Haven, CT: Yale University Press, 1961); Nelson W. Polsby, *Community Power and Political Theory* (New Haven, CT: Yale University Press, 1963); G. William Domhoff, *Who Really Rules? New Haven and Community Power Reconsidered* (Santa Monica: Goodyear, 1978); Bryan Jones and Lynn W. Bachelor, *The Sustaining Hand: Community Leadership and Corporate Power* (Lawrence, KS: University of Kansas Press, 1986).

4. By "resources," most scholars of local government refer to such elements as money and revenues, property, knowledge, political experience and know-how, access to media, and public support or contingent consent.

5. See Thomas J. Anton, "Power, Pluralism and Local Politics," *Administrative Science Quarterly* 7:4 (March 1963): 425–57, for an early discussion of this question, as well as Peter Bachrach and Morton S. Baratz, "Two Faces of Power," *American Political Science Review* 56:4 (December 1962) 947–52.

6. Clarence N. Stone, "Systemic Power in Community Decision Making: A Restatement of Stratification Theory," *American Political Science Review* 74:4 (December 1980): 978–90.

7. Jones and Bachelor, *Sustaining Hand*. See also Brian Jones, "Causation, Constraint and Political Leadership," in Bryan Jones, ed., *Leadership and Politics: New Perspectives in Political Science* (Lawrence, KS: University of Kansas Press, 1989) 3–16.

8. Margaret Levi, "A Logic of Institutional Change," in Karen Schweers Cook and Margaret Levi, eds., *The Limits of Rationality* (Chicago, IL: University of Chicago Press, 1990) 406.

9. Ibid., 407.

10. By "local" I include here the oblast level, although this earlier Soviet usage of the term "mestnyi" is no longer in currency. The current Russian usage of the term applies to levels of government below that of oblast/krai.

11. See the Union law on local government "Ob obshchikh nachalakh mestnogo samoupravleniia i mestnogo khoziaistva v SSSR," *Vedomosti s"ezda narodnykh deputatov SSSR i Verkhovnogo Soveta SSSR*, no. 16 (April 18, 1990). This law encountered stiff resistance from central ministries, particularly the Ministry of Finance. In the interim between Union and RSFSR laws on local government, most oblasts drafted their

own legislation, some of which bordered on the bizarre. In Gorkii (Nizhnii Novgorod), for example, the oblast designed a system of local government that included nine different levels (four rural and five urban), primarily based on a naively expected convergence of interests. See *Gorkovskaia pravda,* March 30, 1990.

12. See "O mestnom samoupravlenii v RSFSR" *Vedomosti s'ezda narodnykh deputatov RSFSR i Verkhovnogo Soveta RSFSR,* no. 29 (July 18, 1991) (hereafter *Vedomosti RSFSR*) and "O kraevom, oblastnom sovete narodnykh deputatov, i kraevoi, oblastnoi administratsii," *Vedomosti RSFSR,* no. 10 (March 5, 1992). The latter has yet to be signed by President Yeltsin, because of his objections to the legislative control over executive appointments.

13. See "O poriadke naznacheniia glav administratsii," *Vedomosti RSFSR,* no. 48 (November 28, 1991). Yeltsin reserved the right to appoint the heads of administration (mayors) of cities that functioned as oblast centers.

14. *Vechernii Omsk,* November 14, 1991.

15. Polezhaev stood for election to the Russian Congress but failed to win his urban constituency, in which eight other communists and one noncommunist contested. *Omskaia pravda,* March 8, 1991.

16. The joint meeting was held on August 20. See *Omskii vestnik,* September 3, 1991 for a stenographic report.

17. *Omskaia pravda,* August 22, 1991.

18. *Omskii vestnik,* no. 46 (November 29–December 5, 1991). It seems Polezhaev had promised Minzhurenko that, if appointed head of administration, personnel changes in the oblast administration would be a given. See *Vechernii Omsk,* November 14, 1991. A brief note on the main local newspapers: *Omskaia pravda* was the newspaper of the oblast Communist Party and the oblast soviet until late 1990, when *Omskii vestnik* was launched as a voice of the oblast soviet. *Vechernii Omsk* was a joint newspaper of the city Communist Party and city soviet until after the coup, when it became sole possession of the city soviet. After the coup, *Omskaia pravda* continued as a "popular" newspaper, although it resurfaced only in October 1991.

19. *Omskii vestnik,* no. 46 (November 29–December 5, 1991).

20. Ibid.

21. *Vechernii Omsk,* November 14, 1991.

22. *Omskaia pravda,* January 17, 1991. Polezhaev's political position thus resembled more the platform of the Civic Union in the federal arena, and had more in common with Aleksandr Rutskoi and Arkadii Volskii than with President Yeltsin. Still, as an astute politician, Polezhaev directed his criticisms against then acting Prime Minister Gaidar rather than against Yeltsin.

23. *Vechernii Omsk,* June 9, 1992.

24. *Omskaia pravda,* April 29, 1992.

25. See the RSFSR law "O nekotorykh voprosakh pravogo regulirovaniia deiatel'nosti kraevykh, oblastnykh Sovetov narodnykh deputatov," *Vedomosti RSFSR,* no. 51 (December 19, 1991). The oblast soviet had 250 deputies, and met two to four times a year. The small soviet became a more permanent legislative chamber. Although the law specified that the small legislatures were to be organized at the oblast level, most city soviets, having authority to form their own organs, followed suit.

26. Personal interview with V.M. Shipilov, chairman of the obsovet standing committee for soviet affairs, and *Omskaia pravda,* April 9, 1992. The committees have between 9 and 30 deputies each. For more information on the oblast small soviet, see "O raspredelenii obiazannostei mezhdu chlenami malogo soveta i oblastnogo soveta narodnykh deputatov" *Reshenie malogo soveta omskogo oblastnogo soveta,* no. 15 (January 16, 1992).

27. Leont'ev and his close assistants owed the bulk of their political support to rural constituencies. Leont'ev's own seat was in the small city of Tara (pop. 100,000), which historically had been the home of obkom first secretaries and chairmen of the obsovet executive committee for the Omsk Oblast. Leont'ev's close assistants in the soviet are all from outside the city of Omsk. Leont'ev had been elected chairman of the soviet in April 1990, before run-off elections had been finished, and when 43 vacancies remained (36 from the city of Omsk). Support for his candidacy was connected to the proposal to allow the combination of party and soviet leadership. This proposal was supported by 115 deputies, 95 of them from rural seats. Eighty-two deputies were opposed, 65 from the city. A full complement of deputies would have made Leont'ev's leadership less secure. In all, one-third of the oblast deputies were "reformers." See *Demokraticheskii Omsk*, no. 7, 1990.

28. *Omskaia pravda*, January 17, 1991.

29. *Omskaia pravda*, April 25, 1992.

30. *Omskii vestnik*, January 21, 1992.

31. *Vechernii Omsk*, June 9, 1992.

32. Leont'ev's decision to push for price increases was credited to the obsovet's ties to the agricultural lobby, dominated by directors from collective farms.

33. *Omskaia pravda*, September 12, 1992.

34. *Omskaia pravda*, September 8, 1992, personal interviews with V.V. Malykhin, and A.A. Mikhailov, Malykhin's assistant.

35. *Omskaia pravda*, September 12, 1992.

36. L. Polezhaev, "Pravitel'stvo oblegchit sebe golovnuiu bol', esli dast bol'she prav regionam," *Narodnyi deputat*, no. 10, 1992.

37. From a transcript of Polezhaev's speech "K deviatoi sessii oblastnogo soveta narodnykh deputatov," *Material v Doklad Polezhaeva, L.K.*, in the Library of the Economic Committee of the Omsk Oblast Administration.

38. In between these two posts, Glebov had worked as Polezhaev's assistant in the oblast executive committee. After the August coup, OTD became the main employment opportunity for out-of-work party and government officials. OTD has been the recipient of central media coverage. See, for example, *Izvestiia*, April 27, 1991. For local media, an article in *Omskaia pravda*, May 21, 1992 is quite detailed.

39. *Vechernii Omsk*, November 22, 1991. Glebov had faced pressure to resign his post in municipal administration when he received only 7 percent support for his candidacy to the Russian Congress in 1990.

40. Ibid., and interviews with various deputies and officials in the city soviet and administration. For his part, Shoikhet personally claimed that his nomination had been entirely proper, and that he had been appointed on the strength of his abilities (from an interview with Shoikhet).

41. Personal interview with Shoikhet, and *Omskii vestnik*, no. 46 (November 29– December 5, 1991).

42. Personal interview with Shoikhet, and "Mer i ego komanda: press-biulleten' administratsii goroda" no. 1 (Omsk 1992). Shoikhet conceded that at least one individual with experience was helpful in establishing an efficient administration.

43. *Omskaia pravda*, January 3, 1992.

44. *Omskii vestnik*, February 6, 1992.

45. This classification was made by Sergei Bogdanovskii, editor of a succession of prodemocratic newspapers. The same figures were given by prominent officials in the city soviet. See *Demokraticheskii Omsk*, no. 7, 1990. Unfortunately it is easier to identify a "reformer" than describe what the term represents. In the shifting sands of Russian politics, the term has been applied to those who support legislative power against the

executive, and vice versa. Much depends on the particular issue at hand, and the time frame within which the issue presents itself. Thus, a "reformer" tended to support legislative power from 1990–91, but recognized the need for strengthening executive power in 1991–92. Through all this, economic reforms, such as privatization, have been strongly supported by "reformers." In contrast, many "conservatives" have shifted from opposition to market reforms and legislative power toward defending legislative power and grudgingly accepting the need for economic reform, but advocating a slower, controlled pace.

46. Ibid.

47. "Razmyshleniia nad programmoi razvitiia predprinimatel'stva i grustnye mysli eiu naveiannye" (no author, no date, but, during private conversation, attributed to an official in the oblast administration). See also *Omskaia pravda,* May 21, 1992, which hinted at well-circulated local rumors that Shoikhet was buying up local enterprises for his wife.

48. *Oreol,* no. 27 (July 1992). Both organs of municipal government held the oblast soviet in contempt, although officials from the city soviet blamed Shoikhet's loud and obnoxious style for poor relations with the oblast. It seems, however, that Shoikhet's concern for small business is not unconstrained—he later launched attacks against unlicensed street kiosks. See *Izvestiia,* February 23, 1993.

49. "Polozhenie 'O mestnykh nalogakh i sborakh na territorii g. Omska' (proekt)"; meeting of the Omsk city little soviet, July 7, 1992; interviews with A.N. Kostiukov, who wrote the law and, in addition to his responsibilities as docent at Omsk State University, worked for the city soviet.

50. Decree of the Supreme Soviet of the Russian Federation, "O razgranichenii gosudarstvennoi sobstvennosti v rossiiskoi federatsii na federal'nuiu sobstvennost', gosudarstvennuiu sobstvennost' respublik v sostave rossiiskoi federatsii, kraev, oblastei, avtonomnoi oblasti, avtonomnykh okrugov, gorodov Moskvy i Sankt-Peterburga, i munitsipal'nuiu sobstvennost'," *Ekonomika i zhizn',* no. 3 (January 1992).

51. *Izvestiia,* January 28, 1993.

52. *Omskii vestnik,* February 20, 1992.

53. "O privatizatsii zhilishchnogo fonda v RSFSR" *Vedomosti RSFSR,* no. 28 (July 11, 1991). See, in particular, article 12. This law seems to contradict directly the decree of December 27, 1992 cited in footnote 51 above.

54. Rumormongers quickly claimed that Shoikhet, whose personal wealth was well known throughout Omsk, was interested in buying controlling interest in TTs for his wife.

55. On TTs see *Omskaia pravda,* June 4, 16, 1992; *Omskii vestnik,* June 1, 1992; *Biznes Omsk,* no. 12 (June 15–22, 1992). Also from personal interviews with Shoikhet, Saraev, and Malykhin.

56. *Novoe obozrenie,* October 18, 1991.

57. Document no. 314 of the Economic Committee of the Omsk Oblast Administration, dated April 9, 1992.

58. See "O konkurentsii i ogranichenii monopolisticheskoi deiatel'nosti na tovarnykh rynkakh," *Vedomosti RSFSR,* no. 16 (April 18, 1991); plus the presidential ukaz, "O kommertsializatsii deiatel'nosti predpriiatii bytovogo obsluzhivaniia v RSFSR," *Vedomosti RSFSR,* no. 48 (November 28, 1991). See also *Novoe obozrenie,* June 4, 1992. While the political battles raged, the directorship of Omskservis continued to milk the profits of affiliate enterprises. See *Vechernii Omsk,* June 5, 1992.

59. "O kommertsializatsii predpriiatii bytovogo obsluzhivaniia," Decree of the Head of Administration of the City of Omsk, February 20, 1992, no. 91-P.

60. Personal interview with Shoikhet; *Omskaia pravda,* March 5, 1992; *Vechernii Omsk,* January 22, 1992.

61. Personal interviews with Malykhin and with V.A. Sharov, Sumenkov's assistant.

62. *Omskii vestnik* published the AMC's initial list of some seventy-two monopolies in Omsk on February 19, 1992.

63. *Omskii vestnik,* May 12, 1992.

64. *Biznes Omsk,* no. 12 (June 15–22, 1992); and personal interviews with Malykhin and Saraev. Both Malykhin, the chair of the oblast administration economic committee, and Saraev have candidates' degrees in economics. The former was a protégé of Aganbegyan at Novosibirsk, the latter a student of Gaidar in Moscow. In addition to rival approaches to economics, it was apparent that Malykhin had held back the able and more gregarious Saraev from promotion and academic opportunity while Saraev was employed in the economic committee of Omsk Oblast. Both are young—Saraev is 38, Malykhin 41. [Malykhin was tragically killed in late 1992, and Saraev was then appointed by Polezhaev to head the oblast economic committee.]

65. A new law on local budgets was in the works throughout late 1991 and 1992, and was finally passed in April 1993. Experts on local government in Moscow in late 1992 entertained little hope that the new law would resolve the problems of local budgets. The law reflected the conflict between those who recognized the need for local budgets to be based on independent revenues, and those who advocated the need for higher organs to create norms and control the budgets of lower levels. See "Ob osnovakh biudzhetnykh prav i prav po formirovaniiu i ispol'zovaniiu vnebiudzhetnykh fondov predstavitel'nykh i ispolnitel'nykh organov gosudarstvennoi vlasti respublik v sostave Rossiiskoi Federatsii, avtonomnoi oblasti, avtonomnykh okrugov, kraev, oblastei, gorodov Moskvy i Sankt-Peterburga, organov mestnogo samoupravleniia," *Rossiiskaia gazeta,* April 30, 1993.

66. Clarence N. Stone, Robert K. Whelan, and William J. Murin, *Urban Policy and Politics in a Bureaucratic Age,* 2d ed., (Englewood Cliffs, NJ: Prentice-Hall, 1986) p. 200.

67. Dahl, *Who Governs?*

6

Perestroika in the Provinces
The Politics of Transition in Donetsk

Theodore H. Friedgut

The Historical and Social Background of Donetsk

Donetsk is a comparatively young city for the Old World. It began as the settlement of Iuzovka in 1870, founded by John Hughes, a Welsh industrialist who had been invited by the Russian government to develop a metallurgical complex that would provide iron, steel, and above all, rails for Russia's developing railway system. Throughout its 125-year history, as it grew from 164 souls in 1874 to well over 1 million in 1989, the city of Donetsk and indeed the entire surrounding region have remained centered on the coal mines and steel mills that made them the hub of Russia's late industrial revolution.[1]

The result is that Donetsk remains to this day a workers' city, however much the working class may have changed from its origins in the nineteenth century and its reconstruction after the two world wars. While the city has diversified over the years, there still remains a powerful proletarian core of more than 100,000 miners and steelworkers, deeply imbued with the sense of status with which the Soviet regime endowed them from the earliest days of the revolution, through the Stakhanov period and World War II.

But the unchanging basis of the economy also means that Donetsk and its entire region face the same problems of obsolescence and pollution that plague the smokestack industries in so many other parts of the world. In the Donetsk region these difficulties are particularly felt. Although the reserves of coal around the city are said to be sufficient for another 500 years, their extraction is expensive. The mines have been intensively worked over the past century and a growing number of them are running deep, some more than a kilometer underground. Almost half are more than 700 meters in depth. This complicates the technologies of pumping, ventilating, transporting workers, and removing coal. The economic problems have been rendered all the more difficult because the last 20 years of Soviet history and economics have seen a relative neglect of investment in the coal industry in favor of the development of nuclear energy and the gas and oil industries.

While remaining primarily a producer of coal and steel, the city has diversified broadly. It now boasts 2,000 productive enterprises, half of them in heavy industry, but a growing number provide for consumer demand, and are moving toward hi-tech, science-based enterprises. Diversification of the city has not been exclusively industrial—there has been a broad cultural growth as well. Donetsk boasts an internationally known ballet troupe, with a world-class soloist, Vadim Pisarev. The city was the tennis center of the USSR, hosting Davis Cup matches. Sergei Bubka, the world-record holder in the pole vault, hails from Donetsk. Donetsk has a large university, medical and technical institutes, and a variety of smaller institutions of higher learning affiliated with the coal, chemical, and metallurgical industries. It thus is home to a broad spectrum of cultural and technical intelligentsia, who have become deeply involved in the political affairs of the city. In addition, the economic incentives offered to coal miners have drawn many university graduates into the labor force, providing an important stratum of worker-intelligentsia.

Like much industry in the Donets Basin (Donbass), Donetsk was founded and developed by foreign capital, while the labor force was provided by displaced Russian peasants seeking additional income to supplement the pittance they earned from agriculture. This meant the introduction of essentially foreign populations to the Ukrainian steppe. These foreigners came to dominate this sparsely settled region, first economically and then demographically. Donetsk matured as a city of many nationalities, and has remained as such, with Greeks, Germans, Tatars, and other minorities in addition to its larger ethnic groups. Nevertheless, the city has been predominantly Russian throughout its existence. The first significant influx of Ukrainians came only with the industrialization of the late 1920s. Even when an additional wave of Ukrainian workers was mobilized after World War II, the town has remained Russian in ambience, and the Ukrainians there live a largely Russified life, although their numbers today are equal to those of the Russian inhabitants. Although Ukrainian was taught in schools in Donetsk, it was as a second language; the first fully Ukrainian school was established only in late 1989. To the extent that Ukrainian culture was maintained in the city, it was as folklore rather than as the living heritage of the second largest ethnic group living in what was nominally its own national republic.

Jews were once prominent in Donetsk, drawn to the settlement by economic opportunity in its early days. First the rapid growth of the city diluted their relative prominence, then the Nazi occupation decimated them. In the 1980s the Jewish population of some 20,000 was further diminished by a steadily growing stream of emigration. Those Jews who remain are very much intermarried and integrated. It should be noted here that the Russian population of the city, many of whom trace their ancestry to the early immigrants, feel perfectly at home, having long ago shed any sensation of foreignness. Unlike Russians in the Baltic republics or in parts of Central Asia, they neither feel foreign nor are they today regarded as such by the great majority of their Ukrainian neighbors.

The stage for a drastic realignment of politics in Donetsk was set by one outstanding event of the era of *perestroika*. This was the July 1989 coal miners' strike that rocked the entire USSR. Though it did not begin in the Donbass, it took on full development there, totally paralyzing the economy for its duration.[2] The aftershocks were felt through to 1991 when a renewed two-month strike—this time political and antigovernment—played an important part in changing the balance of politics away from Gorbachev's then-conservative course. More immediately (and locally), the miners' strikes and organizing initiatives produced a sense of citizen competence and empowerment among all sectors of the population. The miners organized their strike and the internal life of their work collectives independently, examining and electing their leaders and representatives without the "guiding hand" of the party or the trade unions that had previously controlled all such matters. With perestroika, other groups in society that witnessed the strike became more confident of their own ability to run their collective lives. As other political and social groups organized, the miners concentrated more and more on their own professional affairs, but in moments of crisis, the city strike committee repeatedly stepped in, bringing the weight and prestige of the miners to bear on the political battles that were taking place.

No less important in this respect was the delegitimation of the incumbent political elites of Donetsk. The local Communist Party leadership and the trade unions had opposed the strike, and had done everything they could to prevent it, and then to sabotage it once it started. In this they badly misgauged the mood and determination of the miners, and of their own rank and file. The old trade-union organization was ignored by the strike activists, who formed an independent coal miners' union that held its founding conference in Donetsk. Within the party there was a growing split, as indeed was the case all over the Soviet Union. Increasing numbers of Communist Party members began to leave the ranks. During the year following the strike nearly 13,000 members left the Donetsk City Communist Party Organization, a drop of 14 percent. In the coal industry with its 100,000 workers and employees, only 1 in 8 held party membership at the end of the year.[3] Thus, when elections were scheduled for the beginning of March 1990, there was no longer a recognized monopoly of force to block the nomination of independent candidates.

The 1990 Elections to the Donetsk City Soviet—The Campaign

Although the Communist Party was no longer the all-powerful ruler that it once had been, its functionaries were still well entrenched in strategic positions, and could influence all stages of the election campaign. Moreover, the *nomenklatura* understood that they were engaged in a life-and-death battle for power and status, indeed, that their whole way of life was on the line. The former cochair of the city strike committee, B.A. Grebeniuk, now head of a cooperative (and thus doubly detested by the party bosses), was nominated for the city soviet in a fourth-round runoff by the workers' collective of the cooperative, but was refused registration by the party-dominated election commission.[4] The party elite was determined to freeze out all possible interlopers from the ranks of rebel miners. In a separate instance, nine candidates for local soviets in Donetsk wrote a letter noting that in the Kuibyshev District Soviet, one-third of the 150 seats were uncontested, and while allowing that this might be due to a lack of consciousness on the part of the public, they noted that it might also be "what our fellow-citizen K.G. Fesenko, speaking at the February plenum of the CC CPSU called 'idiotic *apparat* games.' "[5] The citizens of Donetsk may have been relatively unorganized, but there was a growing civic awareness and activism among them that held immense potential.

The civic innovation that accompanied the nomination campaign was the Donetsk Municipal Voters' Association. The association was headed by Professor G.A. Atanov, and its platform, composed by Professors Ia.N. Granovskii and G.K. Gubernaia, candidates for the Supreme Soviet of Ukraine, reflected the views of the Democratic Platform of the CPSU of that time. It called for a Soviet Union of free and voluntarily associated republics on the basis of a new Union Treaty, separation of powers of the three branches of government, and the abolition of Article 6 of the USSR Constitution—a step that Gorbachev had by this time already pushed through the Central Committee. In addition, the Voters' Association called for broad civil rights on the basis of the United Nations' Universal Declaration of Human Rights, a mixed economy with various forms of property-holding, and abolition of all privileges of the Communist Party leadership.[6] Alongside the declaration of the association's platform, there appeared the appeal of fifteen candidates to the Ukrainian Supreme Soviet, who, while not agreeing to all the details of the platform, rallied around it to unite all the "constructive, democratic forces" in Donetsk who saw the elections as a watershed between the past and the future. Among the fifteen signatories were V.V. Ladygin, chairman of the Donetsk Territory Committee of the Coal Miners' Union, and Aleksandr Charodeev, the secretary of the Communist Party Group at the "Glubokaia" coal mine. Both of these were supporters of radical reform, though they professed support for Gorbachev and for work within the Communist Party as the sole unifying institution of Soviet society, and expressed doubts as to the haste and extremism voiced by some of their more radical comrades.[7]

The election campaign took an unexpected turn on February 7, when an indignant meeting of 5,000 citizens, spontaneously called to protest the reported under-the-counter sale of a consignment of imported shoes, demanded the resignation of almost all the high party and administrative officials of the city on charges of corruption and incompetence, and the appointment of a citizens' committee to run the city and supervise the imminent elections for a new municipal administration. The Donetsk City Strike Committee had assumed responsibility for running the meeting. As was later explained, officials of the strike committee undertook this role by default, for fear that an uncontrolled meeting might turn violent.

The party authorities replied by having a counterdemonstration organized by their supposedly well-controlled veterans' and women's committees. This turned into a debacle when some of the appointed speakers departed from the texts and resolutions supplied them by *raikom* (district committee) secretaries, and voiced support for the February 7 resolutions.[8]

Another sign of the new times was evident when four veterans of Afghanistan, elected in the second round of voting, published a statement supporting another *afganets* who was candidate for a third-round runoff. "A former warrior, he fulfilled his civic duty, bearing arms in an unjustified war that brought bitterness and shame to the Soviet people. Today he takes an active civic role, speaking out for the swiftest resolution of our city's problems." Despite this organized and passionate support, the candidate lost, placing fifth of eight contestants, perhaps because he was a Komsomol secretary.[9]

The election campaign was a confused hybrid of old and new. Of great importance was the fact that the only organized group contending was the

CPSU. Weakened as it was, it still commanded the strategically placed manpower, the resources, and the organizing experience to mount a strong campaign. The constitutional amendment legitimizing the existence of other parties came only in March 1990, too late for any other party to build a base, adopt a clear platform, nominate candidates, and run a successful campaign. Indeed, the law setting forth the conditions for registration of new parties was passed only in October 1990. Even in the subsequent rounds of elections to the city soviet no parties appeared, and it is only for a by-election in October 1990 that we find notice of the "Democratic Platform" nominating a candidate to the soviet.[10] Yet individual candidates were plentiful. Almost every one of the 150 election districts was contested and on election day, March 4, more than two-thirds of the voters turned out.

Election Results

The voting took place under an amended election law, prepared by the Supreme Soviet of Ukraine to accommodate the changes that Mikhail Gorbachev was introducing in the electoral system of the USSR.[11] In Donetsk, all constituencies were drawn as single-member districts, but the number of candidates running was unlimited. Although there had been complaints by the more radical supporters of perestroika that "many" party and soviet leaders had prevented free competition by allowing themselves to run unopposed, the results do not show that such tactics were effective.[12] There were originally 150 seats to be determined, only fifteen of which were settled in the March 4 first round. This was evidently a mass rejection of the apparat, including the first secretary of the *gorkom* (city committee) and former chairman of the executive committee of the *gorsovet* (city soviet), G.I. Onishchuk, who afterward bluntly stated that he would not participate in any further balloting for a place in the soviet, resigned as first secretary of the gorkom, and later left the city. In 129 other constituencies where more than two candidates had run, there were runoff elections between the top two contenders, and in six constituencies in which there had been either one or two candidates but none had gathered the necessary 50 percent plus one needed for election, nominations were reopened.

In these latter six constituencies we can discern two clear phenomena. First of all, the Donetsk electorate, or at least the politically active part of it, was very much interested in this first general, free, and competitive local election since August 1917. A total of sixty-seven candidates registered for these six seats, and in no constituency were there less than eight competitors. The second phenomenon emerging here is that the Communist Party no longer controlled its members. There was no "chosen Party candidate."

In all six of these districts more than half of those running were members of the CPSU or the Komsomol.

The elections for the 129 runoffs took place on March 18, with the participation of two-thirds of the eligible voters. The results confirmed the near-total rejection of the party apparat, though as we shall see, numerous members of the administrative and industrial nomenklatura retained places in the soviet. The reformers were not to have an easy time of it. Although 90 of the deputies elected were party members, only two held paid party positions, and one of these was Alexander Charodeev, head of the Communist Party group at one of the coal mines, and, as noted above, an outspoken supporter of perestroika.[13] Charodeev was later elected to the Supreme Soviet of Ukraine as well. Only one trade union official gained a seat in the soviet.

The voting results showed trends similar to those throughout the USSR.[14] Ninety of the new deputies were members of the CPSU, though it was already clear that this identification was losing its significance.[15] The communist deputies themselves rejected Onishchuk's suggestion that they form a party faction in the soviet. At the meeting of communist deputies where this hitherto routine proposal was discussed, a number of the participants, including the person whom Onishchuk had proposed to chair the party group, stated that deputies should represent their constituents and their own principles—not some external sociopolitical organization. Onishchuk's proposal was defeated by a 25–20 vote.[16] Two points are worth noting here. First, judging by the vote against forming a Communist Party group, only half of the ninety party members who were elected to the city soviet saw fit to attend the meeting called by the gorkom first secretary. Perhaps more important than the long prospect of political development, the deputies present expressed a distinctly negative view of party organizations, regarding themselves as constituency representatives or as personal delegates of the public. Later in the year, a Communist Party group of deputies was nonetheless formed, headed by G.T. Fedorenko, the director of a clothing factory, though it is not clear how many deputies participated in this group. The legacy of Communist Party domination would not be easily left behind.

Only ten women were elected among the 150 deputies. Fifty-one workers (of whom half were said to have higher education) and fourteen executives of economic institutions were elected.[17] Twenty-four deputies were from the scientific and educational intelligentsia of Donetsk. Nine others were executives of the city's district soviets. Though these latter deputies were certainly part of the nomenklatura, they were evidently better able to present themselves to the public than were the Communist Party officials. Among those missing from the deputy corps along with Onishchuk were the city prosecutor, Litvin, as well as three activists of the July strike, all of whom were defeated in their electoral campaigns.

Restructuring the Donetsk Gorsovet

The new soviet began work eagerly, inaugurating a period later characterized by its chairman as one of enthusiastic creativity. A working group prepared the first session of the soviet, drawing up proposals for its new structure, which included sixteen standing committees of deputies, some reflecting the changing agenda of Donetsk society. The standing committee on industry, for instance, included in its mandate new forms of economic activity and development of the economy. There was a committee on ecology and rational use of natural resources; a committee on *glasnost;* and a committee on interethnic and intercommunity relations. Two ad hoc committees were to investigate the existence of unwarranted privileges and the rational use of administrative buildings owned by the soviet. Quite clearly, these two groups reflected the antiparty mood of the public and the soviet.

As chairman the soviet chose Aleksandr Gafurovich Makhmudov, the 41-year-old acting chairman of the Department of Computer Applications in Economics and Engineering at the local technical institute. Makhmudov, a moderate reformist, was evidently a compromise choice. It took four rounds of voting in which 13 candidates rose and fell before he defeated his rival, gaining the required 76 votes against 55 for L.S. Lavrov, the former chairman of the executive committee of the Kuibyshev District Soviet in Donetsk. The fragmentation of the soviet was revealed when it took two rounds of voting to elect a deputy chair of the soviet's presidium, a solidly establishment figure, Viktor G. Bychkov, director of the Political Department of the Higher Military-Political School for Engineering and Communications, whose position brands him as one of the Communist Party conservatives, while the attempt to elect a second deputy was abandoned, stalled between reformers and conservatives with no candidate able to muster the necessary support.[18]

Though a party member with a long record of activism, Makhmudov immediately stated his support for reform. His first test was in transforming the soviet's executive committee into a salaried administrative body, separate from and subordinate to the elected soviet, in keeping with the political reforms instituted by Gorbachev. The presidium of the soviet published an advertisement calling for candidates for the post of chair of the city executive committee. In the revolutionary spirit of the times the advertisement was headed: "To All! To All! To All!"[19]

The old *ispolkom,* or executive committee, headed by E.G. Orlov, who had been elected to the soviet in a runoff election, but demanded the right to retain his post as chair of the ispolkom, staged a collective resignation. The soviet refused his demand, electing Viktor I. Migel, an architect and former head of the capital construction department of the municipal executive committee as the new chair.[20] At the same time, the soviet also refused to accept the collective resignation of the other department heads, calling it "an attempt at political sabotage" and ordered them to return to their duties.[21] Only gradually were they replaced by new appointees, maintaining at least a minimal continuity of administration. The soviet passed this first test of authority with flying colors, and this strengthened its standing with the public, raising anticipations as to its further ability to solve Donetsk's economic and social problems. However, it rapidly became clear that there was no accepted program and no common approach to improving municipal services and the living standards of Donetsk citizens.

The Donetsk City Soviet at Work

The newly elected deputies, 80 percent of whom were serving their first term in public office, came into power in a city torn by economic, political, and social tensions. This was the fifth year of perestroika, and though much of the old command-administrative system had been dismantled, no new structure had yet been put in place. Previously, various enterprises had been allocated tasks of snow removal, street cleaning, and so forth, within "their" districts, and plan fulfillment had been overseen by the party network. Under the new conditions of *khozrashchet* (cost-accounting), every ruble was counted, and the party secretaries no longer mattered. But the city did not as yet have the manpower, equipment, and budgets to do all of this work, and parts of the city were lapsing into an unsanitary state that reminded people of Old Iuzovka—particularly when a diphtheria epidemic threatened.[22] No less serious was the enterprises' refusal to participate in maintenance work on water pipes and sewers for which they had previously taken responsibility. As a result, during the summer of 1990 only 2.7 kilometers of water pipe were replaced instead of the planned 26 kilometers. Some of this opposition was based on economic grounds, with the enterprises hoarding their scarce resources for direct production needs, but in the presidium and executive committee of the soviet there was a sense that some of it was calculated opposition bent on discrediting the new city administration.[23] Altogether the city had to untangle a knotted skein of jurisdictions in which Donetskugol', the coal conglomerate that operated the city's twenty-one coal mines, was owner of half the city's water and steam pipes, and various other enterprises funded, operated, and controlled enrollment in kindergartens and preschools. These and many other difficulties were the heritage of the Soviet culture of company towns in which enterprises ran these and a host of other municipal services.

The political tensions focused on relations among the Communist Party nomenklatura, the reformers who formed the majority of the soviet, and the various other political groups that were springing up in Donetsk. The political struggle took on three different forms. The soviet tried to maintain the age of perestroika's spirit of political freedom, but met with difficulties from two different directions. On the one hand, a small group of Anarchists, and a splinter group of the Ukrainian Popular Front called "Democratic Rukh," held frequent unauthorized street meetings that often led to violence. Their laying of a wreath at Lenin's statue with an inscription to "Seventy Years of Red Terror" caused a weeks-long furor with letters to the press and mass demonstrations "in defense of Lenin." Within the soviet, a hard-core group of communists attacked Makhmudov at every opportunity, raising repeated votes of no confidence and obstructing debate.[24] Yet when a resolution was proposed to have the Donetsk City Soviet join the Association of Democratic Soviets of Ukraine and of Democratic Blocs in Soviets of Ukraine, only 2 deputies voted against and 13 abstained.[25]

The first session of the soviet had produced a jubilantly ringing programmatic statement. "We regard as our programmatic tasks: liberation from the power monopoly of the command-administrative party and state nomenklatura; the restoration of morality and affirmation of legality; the developing of a multifaceted city economy based on multiple forms of property; establishment of conditions for improving the well-being of the population; development of all national languages and cultures. We are ready for constructive dialogue with all political forces and public organizations in the city."[26] But translating these desires into programs of action was quite another matter. The lack of institutionalized parties that might have served as a forum to prepare proposals for the soviet's consideration and the lack of any stable bloc of deputies committed to support Makhmudov, further weakened the soviet's potential. Nevertheless, the period opened with its face toward a new politics in Donetsk.

The first phase of organizational creativity, establishing the authority of the soviet and drawing up its program, was brief. Though much of the summer and autumn of 1990 was characterized by Makhmudov as a period of productive work—drawing up an inventory of city-owned land and housing, and making plans for their future use or disposal to the public—little was actually accomplished. A great deal of thought and effort was invested in drafting legislation on local self-government for the consideration of the

Supreme Soviet of Ukraine, yet the law eventually adopted by that body was a distinct retreat from the basis on which the soviet had been elected.[27] In particular, by reinstating the chairman of the soviet as chairman of the executive committee and allowing executive committee members to serve as elected deputies, it abolished the separation of powers and the checks that had been created between legislative and executive. This returned the soviet to its pre-Gorbachev principles, reunifying government and administration. While this development may well have suited the hard-pressed leaders of the soviet who were faced with immediate and acute problems of everyday life, it set back the development of a competent, effective, and interested body of elected deputies who would act as legislators in the soviet's plenum and as auditors of the executive in its standing committees. In addition, it meant that much of the organizational work that had been accomplished to establish the competence and responsibilities of the various organs of the soviet now had to be redone. Whether it was this change or the deputies' general inexperience that affected their performance, recurrent complaints appeared in the press regarding nonattendance and general ineffective performance of the legislators.[28] As a result, the number of standing committees was cut back. As so often happens, wielding power has been found to be a far more complex task than the attainment of power. This is particularly the case in which city deputies are essentially amateurs drawn into what was intended to be serious political reconstruction. They may have good intentions and ideas, but few appear to have the experience, education, and time needed for such an undertaking.

Typical of the dilemmas in which the soviet finds itself is its position between the district soviets of the city (*raiony v gorode*) and the Donetsk Oblast Soviet. Under the new spirit of democratic government, the districts of Donetsk claim that they are the basic links of government, and that planning and budgets should proceed from below. In fact, the new law on local government stipulated that the city was the basic structure of local government and that the urban districts were to be its subunits. As might have been anticipated, administrative procedure lags behind the formalities of legislation, and while the districts and the city are in reasonable harmony concerning putting together a proposed schedule of expenditures, the oblast soviet, which is of a distinctly more conservative cast, is, as we shall soon see in some detail, dragging its feet about giving up its right to determine both allocations and expenditures for the lower level. This was so not only regarding the district budgets, but in other matters as well. Allocation of meat to the city comes through the oblast administration. The oblast authorities decided to subsidize meat sales, protecting Donetsk's citizens from the April price increases, but deducted the subsidy from sums payable to the city for its various needs. When the city government objected to these arbitrary deductions, they were told: "If you don't like it, then raise the price of meat." The result of these disagreements in 1991 was a budget that raised the prospect of municipal bankruptcy by autumn.[29]

In its program statement the soviet expressed its intention to create a mixed economy in Donetsk, but as far as private and cooperative businesses are concerned, there appears to have been little done from the city's side. There has been some reorganization of municipal maintenance and repair services into "small enterprises," but these are still operating fully within the control of the various executive committee departments. Beginning with the 1991 budget year, many service functions were to be tendered out on a contractual basis with payment on the basis of the amount of work actually done. The expectation of the executive committee was that leased equipment and cooperatives would be motivated to maximize their efforts, and that this would lead to effective sanitation work in the city.[30] In addition, the municipal authorities maintained their control over all the principal distribution outlets for foodstuffs and other consumer goods. As food shortages through 1990 and 1991 became acute, the soviet sought to establish control over the buying and allocation of foodstuffs, contracting with various firms to supply their products to the city. These firms, however, were still under Union or republic subordination and were obliged to fill government orders before supplying Donetsk's needs.[31] The city soviet was caught in the web of contradictory and ambiguous legislation that characterized the transition period. At the very outset of the election campaign B.V. Boiko, an economist later elected a deputy, pointed out that these difficulties would remain unsolved until legislation defining property rights and institutional responsibilities was completed, clarified, and tested in practice.[32]

The city soviet initially recognized the urban districts as the fundamental level of government, but in the first flush of creativity passed a law regarding municipalization of all land within the city limits. There were two basic aims to this law: the first was to create a tax base, with all enterprises and institutions paying property taxes to the city; the second was to rationalize the use of urban land, building up unused areas and providing more jobs within the city limits. Additional benefits accruing from this law would be the ability to control tax benefits for the purpose of attracting new industries to the city, and the opportunity to write ecological measures into the new land-lease contracts in an attempt to overcome one of the city's major problems.[33] Another consequence of this law was the appropriation to the city soviet of lands and tax resources that had hitherto been under the

control of the Donetsk Oblast Soviet. This was part of an ongoing contention for power between the two very differently inclined bodies.

Following the city soviet's failure to have its concept of local government written into the republic law, this was probably the most important
step that it had taken. The law, however, had been passed without consultation with the nine district soviets, which voiced a common protest and
reasserted their interest in these resources, creating a coordinating council
between city and districts that meets weekly to discuss common problems
and prevent the city from taking such unilateral steps in the future.[34] This
forum has shown itself to be useful particularly in the coordinating of
budgets at the various levels.

Throughout 1990 there was no agreement as to whether the city should
have the principal powers of taxation, and dole out money to the districts on
a "precedent and fair share" basis, or whether the districts should retain tax
powers, turning only their surplus income over to the city. The Law on
Local Government solved this problem, naming the city as the basic unit. In
fact this was probably healthy for two reasons: with the economic crisis that
was hitting Donetsk (and given the backlog of need and the natural propen-
sity of any government to spend whatever it has) there could be very little
expectation of surplus. In addition, there were great differences among the
various urban districts. The Proletarian District is almost purely residential.
It includes no large industrial enterprises and therefore has no income from
profits, turnover, or high-priced industrial lands. For 1991 its estimated
income was 12 million rubles, while its needs for services were put at 30
million.[35] Not so the Kuibyshev District, which included two large coal
mines and several other industrial plants.

In the three central districts of Donetsk a small beginning was made on
selling housing to the populace, with two-room apartments selling for
10,000–12,000 rubles, and three-room apartments for up to 30,000. About
350 flats were sold at these prices, to two main categories of buyers. Pensioners were buying their flats to leave to their children, and Jews emigrat-
ing to Israel were buying their flats for resale, to cover the costs of
emigration.[36] In addition, Donetskugol' sold 200 apartments and received 2
million rubles.[37] When it appeared that the market value of flats was on the
order of twice the price charged by the soviet, sales were discontinued. As
of October 1992, the price was set at close to 1,000 rubles per square
meter.[38] The spiraling inflation of 1992 and the start of 1993 has disrupted
all such plans. Though sympathetic both to the economics and the social
principle of individual home ownership, the soviet executives are caught up
in a web of conflicting pressures that they have not yet found a way to
resolve.

The presidium of the soviet, led by Makhmudov, tried earnestly to change the economic structure of the city. On the one hand, the soviet had encouraged the formation of "small enterprises" on a leasing or cooperative basis, contracting with them to perform part of the service work of the municipality. On the other, there was the effort toward creating a clear division of labor between the city and its enterprises. The presidium initiated invitations to the directors of all the major enterprises to form an industrial coordinating council that would cooperate in meeting the city's needs and advancing the aims of creating a mixed economy. The contribution of the new first secretary of the Donetsk City Party Committee, Aleksandr Bolotov, was a stern warning against a market economy. Despite his strictures, fifteen enterprise directors joined the council, which was chaired by the head of the soviet's Standing Committee on Industry, Economic Reform, and New Economic Initiatives.[39] When the council held its first full meeting, Makhmudov proposed that it was the city's job to fund services such as kindergartens, sewers, and sanitation, while the enterprises should concentrate on producing goods and paying taxes to fund the municipal budget.[40] At the same time, the Declarations of Municipal Self-Rule and of Municipal Economic Autonomy, drafted by the presidium and passed by the soviet, remained primarily declarative for lack of an appropriate legal and financial framework within which to implement them.

Other early efforts of the Donetsk City Soviet were characterized more by enthusiasm and good will than any administrative skill. Seven new trolleybuses were to be ordered from a factory in Engels in Saratov Oblast. Paying for them involved getting a local firm to provide the factory in Engels with insulating material that was in short supply, while the remaining cash payment was solicited from the factories and district soviets whose population would be served by the new equipment.[41] The trolleys were duly delivered and celebrated.

The test of the soviet was, of course, its budget. Here all the difficulties of the period came to bear. The new soviet had been elected and had begun its work under the budgetary framework that it inherited from the past, the great bulk of which was passed down and earmarked by higher soviets. When the new law on local self-government was promulgated in December 1990 there were many ambiguities and unclear provisions to be discussed and tested. The head of the Finance Committee of the Gorsovet estimated expenditures of 716 million rubles during 1991, a sum far beyond what the city might expect to receive by any calculation.[42] The Donetsk Oblast Soviet, meanwhile, had been drawing up estimates of income and expenditure for the city soviets. In a joint letter to the oblast authorities, the mayors of the cities pointed out that the expenditure estimates did not take into account the inflation that was ravaging their economies, and protested the fact that shunting the cost of subsidized food onto the municipal authorities was illegal. The mayors informed the oblast executive that their budgets would be drawn up on the principles of: (1) income determined solely from sources under municipal control; (2) a balanced budget; (3) noninclusion of disputed food subsidies.[43]

Working on the basis of the previous system, the oblast Finance Department notified the city authorities that it was allocating to them a total of 559 million rubles, calculated on certain percentages of turnover tax, profits tax, and sales tax. Of this sum, 279 million would be earmarked to cover the disputed subsidy for meat and milk prices. The municipal authorities estimated that the income side would add up to only 451 million rubles, while expenditure would balloon with inflation. In the end, however, it was on the principle of municipal economic autonomy that the soviet, rejecting a motion of the conservative bloc to accept the oblast offer, voted for a budget based on the city's own resources. The budget totaled 338 million rubles, of which the largest single item, 80 million rubles, was slated for education, with the municipality taking over all educational institutions.[44]

Despite the difficulties they were experiencing, the citizens of Donetsk did not lose their civic vision. In the March 17, 1991, referendum, three-quarters of the voters turned out, with 79 percent supporting the continued existence of the Soviet Union, and 82 percent affirming their desire for the sovereignty of Ukraine within that Union.[45] Apparently there was neither apathy nor overwhelming alienation in the public at that time. Indeed, there was a growing politicization, for in March and April the coal miners were striking, demanding the resignation of Gorbachev and the government and the transfer of the Donbass coal industry to the republic. Battle lines were drawn between conservatives and reformers. In this matter the city soviet was clearly acting for reform. In mid-January a large group of deputies from the soviet passed a resolution and organized a demonstration condemning the killing of Lithuanian civilians by Soviet troops in Vilnius.[46] When the mine strike entered its second month, the soviet passed a resolution funding free school meals for all the children of Donetsk, and called for a half-hour general work stoppage in the city to demand radical economic and political reform.[47]

The Soviet and the August Coup

The real test of politics in Donetsk in 1991 came, as elsewhere in the USSR, during the days of the attempted coup of August 19–21. Here the city's three protagonists—the coal miners in the person of their city strike committee, the Communist Party, and the Donetsk City Soviet—as though in the dénouement of a Greek tragedy, came together to meet their respective fates. Activities began in Donetsk early on the morning of August 19. By 8 A.M. deputies were beginning to gather at the city soviet, and by 10 A.M. a meeting conducted by deputy chairman V. Bychkov, a hard-core conservative, was calling for a full session of the soviet to express its view on the coup and the State Emergency Committee (GKChP).[48] At the same time, telephone communications were being established with other cities, with the Moscow Soviet, with the Supreme Soviet of Ukraine in Kiev, and with local political and social groups in Donetsk, including the city strike committee. By 2 P.M., this network had received, copied, and begun distribution throughout the city of Boris Yeltsin's declaration against the State Emergency Committee. It should be noted here that the soviet was the vortex of all this activity, indicating that it enjoyed both legitimacy and authority, despite its shortcomings. The Donetsk gorkom called a conference of party members who were deputies of the gorsovet or who were executives of the city's district soviets only at 2 P.M. Following this consultation, some of the communists proposed an appeal to the citizens of Donetsk that called upon them "to receive with understanding the decrees of the State Emergency Committee which has assumed full power." Bychkov drafted this appeal, and deputies were solicited for their signatures. The city prosecutor, Litvin, lent his authority to this stand, stating that he could not give a definitive legal assessment of the events in Moscow, but did not view them as anticonstitutional. Other communists demanded that the soviet "leave off its involvement in high politics, and concentrate on solving the city's problems," and one deputy, E. Garshin, heckled any deputy who tried to speak against the GKChP. The Donetsk gorkom first secretary, Bolotov, denied reports emanating from the city strike committee that tanks had entered Moscow and were preparing to storm the buildings of the Russian Supreme Soviet, stating that he had quite different information from Central Committee sources in Moscow.

Communist Party authority was not what it had once been. The tactics of the communists were rejected or ignored, and two other appeals, very different in tone, were drawn up, one to the people of Donetsk, and one to the Supreme Soviet of Ukraine. The first denounced the State Emergency Committee and all its actions as unconstitutional; the second stated that the Donetsk City Soviet would not follow the orders of the Emergency Committee and considered itself bound only by the laws of Ukraine and by its constitution. The communist resolution was withdrawn without being brought to a vote.

At the same time, the oblast ispolkom convened a meeting of leading soviet and administrative officials in which no resolutions whatsoever were taken, but the statement of the first deputy director of the oblast Administration of Internal Affairs regarding the impermissibility of any unsanctioned actions, meetings, or strikes, was recorded. The first secretary of the obkom, E.V. Mironov, "announced the position of the Donetsk Oblast Communist Party Organization regarding the given situation." No details were added to this terse announcement. The participants agreed that it was necessary to maintain the usual work routine in all enterprises and branches of the economy. The conservatives were waiting, holding their collective breath.[49]

The next day, August 20, at 7 A.M. the gorsovet's appeal to the Supreme Soviet of Ukraine was flown to Kiev by three deputies. Both appeals were published in *Vechernii Donetsk,* alongside the proclamation of the State Emergency Committee and the carefully noncommittal statement of the chairman of Ukraine's Supreme Soviet, Leonid Kravchuk.

The Donbass miners, unlike many of their colleagues in Kuznetsk Basin and Vorkuta, did not strike in response to Boris Yeltsin's call. Formally, they were not obliged to, for as president of the Russian Republic, his call was directed to the workers of Russia. In addition, Ukraine, as Kravchuk had carefully pointed out, was not among those areas declared under emergency by the State Committee, and therefore life could proceed normally. Despite these facts, the USSR minister of the coal industry, Mikhail Shchadov, sent official telegrams to all coal-producing enterprises, calling upon them to obey the State Emergency Committee. Two days later, after the collapse of the coup, the Donbass Regional Strike Committee demanded the immediate dismissal of Shchadov for his support of the plotters.[50]

On August 20, the city soviet reached out to the Donetsk public, and convened a meeting of various social and cultural groups, including the Ukrainian Language Foundation, Prosvita; Ednannia, the coordinating umbrella of all Donetsk public groups; Memorial; and Rukh. The participants agreed on the sending of a telegram of good wishes to the Supreme Soviet of Ukraine requesting that it not recognize the State Emergency Committee, since the latter was an unconstitutional body.[51]

On August 21, Makhmudov, the chairman of the Donetsk City Soviet, published his resignation from the CPSU, declaring that he could not associate himself with a party that had taken a shameful and unprincipled position in the face of violation of law and the constitution. It may be assumed that he was not the only party member to take this course. This step, however, proved insufficient. Makhmudov was accused in the soviet of having been slow off the mark in condemning the coup and was forced to resign. It will be remembered that the conservative vice chair, Bychkov, conducted the session of the soviet on the first morning of the coup. For over a year the city was administered by an acting mayor until in November 1992 the soviet elected E.L. Zviagil'skii to head the municipal administration.[52] He came to power with the help of a curious coalition of conservative elements —who see in him a member of the old elite—together with a substantial part of the reform-minded representatives in the soviet—who see in him a man with a proven administrative track record and one capable of putting some order into the city's floundering administration and communal economy. This election may prove to be a turning point, for Zviagil'skii is broadly, though not unanimously, accepted in Donetsk as a person of international caliber.[53] A deputy to both the city and the republic soviets, he brings to his new post a proven record of remarkable initiatives.[54]

Zviagil'skii began his incumbency by attacking the housing shortage, one of Donetsk's most acute problems. At municipal initiative, more housing was completed in the first quarter of 1993 than in the whole of 1992. He turned this to the advantage of the sorely depleted municipal treasury by holding two public-housing auctions in which seventeen apartments were sold, bringing in substantial sums. At the same time he has contracted with various state farms in the vicinity, promising to sell them fuel supplies from the city's allotments in return for the marketing of their produce in Donetsk.

The soviet, apart from its executive organs, barely functions. The deputies have little influence and have not coalesced into effective parties, despite the beginnings in 1990 and 1991 of a number of political parties within the city. The standing committees that began their activities with considerable fervor have declined, and barely function today. Social differentiation and spreading poverty have drained much of the idealism that characterized the miners' movement and the emergent civic society of Donetsk in the latter years of perestroika.[55]

Conclusion

The stand of the Donetsk City Soviet, its chairman, and the most influential of its many social and political groups must have brought satisfaction to the city's citizens—particularly in light of the ultimate failure of the coup attempt. Yet the city still faces a mountain of unsolved problems.

The problem of political leadership is perhaps the key to solving many of the others. The former communists tightly coordinated with higher echelons through to Kiev and Moscow have been ousted from control of the municipality, though many of their supporters still manage the key administrations and enterprises that are the heart of the city's economy. Institutionalization of alternative groups and the growth of a clear and stable set of political parties appears to be as yet far off, despite the development of numerous social and political bodies in the city.

The economic difficulties that have inundated Ukraine as a whole have not spared Donetsk, and in the absence of reform at the higher levels, the local authorities have difficulty extricating themselves from a faltering economy. Meanwhile, as part of the deteriorating economic situation, 15 clubs and libraries in the oblast had been closed and 426 amateur cultural groups had been dissolved because they could not cover their own costs and no money was available to subsidize them—nor, in a time of galloping inflation, were there funds to raise the pay of 10,000 employees of cultural institutions.[56]

The coal industry has not found a way out of its long-standing economic dilemmas, and the two-month strike in 1991 only made the problems of the mines more acute. Even where strict management has made a goal of eliminating the deficits caused by the strike, the solution is too often a reduction in maintenance and investment, further diminishing the ability of the mines to compete.[57] The closing of one of Donetsk's coal mines due to its inability to earn and pay wages made these problems clear and immediate. The successes of a local shoe factory and a furniture factory in exporting and modernizing could not disguise the weakness of the coal and steel foundations of the city's economy. Unemployment is growing rapidly.

The new city soviet also inherited a badly neglected infrastructure. While central areas of the city boast of broad streets, green belts, and modern buildings, other areas have been "swallowed up" by Donetsk and have remained unchanged throughout the century. They have no running water, no sewers, no paved streets, and no street lighting. The fact that city transit is chronically overloaded explains why the soviet went through such acrobatics to obtain its seven new buses. Of the 200 kilometers of water pipes under the city streets, half are in urgent need of replacement. There are also 1,230 kilometers of steam and hot water piping, of which "dozens of kilometers" are said to be in "dangerous condition."[58] Bringing these facilities up to standard would be a daunting task for any administration, even under far more propitious conditions.

In addition, longstanding problems of health, housing, and pollution have plagued the area for the past decades. Thirty of the city's enterprises have been categorized as "ecologically dangerous," and environmental conditions in all nine of the urban districts are substandard.[59] During the past generation, the incidence of heart disease in the Donbass has grown by a factor of eleven, and diabetes between six and nine times. There is a steady growth in the number of babies with congenital defects. Monitoring and stemming the growth of pollution requires large and continuing investments, and these are becoming harder and harder to find.

Housing has been one of the city's chronic shortages since its founding, with 86,000 families currently on waiting lists. One million square meters of new housing is needed each year if the deficit is to be overcome, but actual plans are for only three and a half million by the end of the decade.[60] The overcrowding of homes creates numerous social problems. During 1989, Donetsk hospitals terminated the pregnancies of 700 girls aged 12–15.[61] The expansion of the public communications system in Donetsk has put all these problems on the social agenda at once. Leading the public through this threatening wilderness of transition will be a prolonged and formidable task, far beyond the capacities of the city's present political system.

Notes

1. For the early history of the founding and development of Iuzovka (later Stalino and then Donetsk), see T.H. Friedgut, *Iuzovka and Revolution: Vol. I, Life and Work in Russia's Donbass, 1869–1924* (Princeton, NJ: Princeton University Press, 1989, and *Vol. II, Politics and Revolution in Russia's Donbass, 1869–1924* (Princeton, NJ: Princeton University Press, 1994). A fine film treatment of the entire history of the city is Colin Thomas, producer, and Professor Gwyn A. Williams, script and narration, "Hughesovka and the New Russia: Hughesovka, Stalino, Donetsk," Cardiff: Teliesyn Productions, 1991.

2. A detailed account and analysis of the strike will be found in Theodore H. Friedgut and Lewis H. Siegelbaum, "The Soviet Miners' Strike, July 1989: Perestroika From Below" (Pittsburgh: University of Pittsburgh Center for Russian and East European Studies, the Carl Beck Papers, no. 804, 1990). For a film depiction of the miners' democracy see Barbara Abrash and Daniel J. Walkowitz, producers, "Perestroika From Below" (New York: Past Time Productions, 1990).

3. See the report by party first secretary G.I. Onishchuk, *Vechernii Donetsk,* May 15, 1990.

4. See *Vechernii Donetsk,* May 25, 1990.

5. *Vechernii Donetsk,* February 13, 1990.

6. The principles of the Donetsk Municipal Voters' Association were published in *Vechernii Donetsk,* February 13, 1990, p. 4.

7. See their speeches and comments at the stormy and frank session of the Donetsk Obkom in *Vechernii Donetsk,* February 12–13, 1990.

8. The February 7 meeting was not reported in the local newspaper, but was occasionally referred to as the "unsanctioned meeting." For an account of the February 11 fiasco see *Vechernii Donetsk,* February 12, 1990. A comprehensive picture of the February 7 meeting may be constructed from the heated debate as to its significance at the Donetsk Obkom meeting. See the stenographic record in *Vechernii Donetsk,* February 12 and 13, 1990.

9. See *Vechernii Donetsk,* April 12, 1990.

10. See *Vechernii Donetsk,* October 11, 1990.

11. The text of the Law on Elections to Local Soviets of the Ukrainian SSR was published by *Vechernii Donetsk* on November 3, 1989.

12. For such complaints, see the debate at the stormy Obkom plenary session reported in *Vechernii Donetsk,* February 12, 1990.

13. See his speech in the stenographic report of the Donetsk Obkom plenum, *Vechernii Donetsk,* February 13, 1990.

14. The names and brief details identifying party affiliation and work of the 126 deputies elected in the first round appear in *Vechernii Donetsk,* March 20, 1990.

15. This, too, was a general feature of the 1990 elections to the local soviets. See V.M. Bebik, "Deputatskaia deiatel'nost' glazami izbiratelei: otsenki, motivy, ustanovki, ozhidaniia," *Filosofskaia i sotsiologicheskaia mysl'* (Kiev), no. 1, 1991, p. 21.

16. See the report in *Vechernii Donetsk,* May 7, 1990.

17. *Vechernii Donetsk* of May 5, 1990, mentions forty-three workers, perhaps using a different definition of "worker".

18. See the report of these elections in *Vechernii Donetsk,* April 10, 1990.

19. See *Vechernii Donetsk,* April 9, 1990. When all the candidates who applied were judged unsuitable, the ad was repeated on April 20.

20. See Migel's biography and notice of his election by the soviet in *Vechernii Donetsk,* May 7, 1990.

21. See the resolution of the presidium of the soviet in *Vechernii Donetsk,* May 3, 1990, and Orlov's report to the meeting of communist deputies of the soviet, *Vechernii Donetsk,* May 7, 1990.

22. See *Vechernii Donetsk,* August 10, 1990, and September 25, 1990. This is a general phenomenon throughout Russia and Ukraine. In the first seven months of 1993, 1,462 cases of diphtheria, 41 of them fatal, were reported in the republic. See *World Health Organization,* Press Release WHO/70, September 10, 1993.

23. See the discussion in *Vechernii Donetsk,* October 13, 1990.

24. See A.A. Mokliuk's attack on Makhmudov and on the soviet in *Vechernii Donetsk,* September 27, 1990, p. 2. Also his speech resigning from the presidium of the soviet, *Vechernii Donetsk,* May 30, 1990. See the debate at the opening of the second session of the soviet in *Vechernii Donetsk,* September 25, 1990.

25. At that time the association numbered twenty-nine soviets, seventeen of them in cities of Ukraine, including Kiev, Kharkov, Dneprodzherzhinsk, Odessa, Tarnopol, and L'vov.

26. *Vechernii Donetsk,* April 13, 1990.

27. See the text of the law as published in *Vechernii Donetsk,* December 15, 1990.

28. See the complaints of E. Svetlichnyi in *Vechernii Donbass,* June 28, 1991. Svetlichnyi, a teacher at the medical institute, was defeated in the 1990 elections. See also *Vechernii Donetsk,* June 12, 1991.

29. The budget material and many of the other current plans and problems of the soviet are from a personal interview by the author with one of Aleksandr Makhmudov's assistants in July 1991.

30. See the discussion in *Vechernii Donetsk,* August 27, 1990.

31. See discussions, first militantly hopeful, then despairingly frustrated, in *Vechernii Donetsk,* July 4, 1990, and June 28, 1991.

32. *Vechernii Donetsk,* February 28, 1990.

33. See the discussion of the law's provisions in *Vechernii Donetsk,* October 1, 1990.

34. See the interview with Adamov, chair of the Voroshilov District Soviet in *Sotsialisticheskii Donbass,* December 31, 1991.

35. *Vechernii Donetsk,* November 2, 1990.

36. *Vechernii Donetsk,* December 22, 1990.

37. *Vechernii Donetsk,* December 8, 1990.

38. Private communication from Donetsk, October 1991.

39. *Vechernii Donetsk,* December 5, 1990.

40. *Vechernii Donetsk,* December 14, 1990.

41. *Vechernii Donetsk,* January 11, 1991.

42. *Vechernii Donetsk,* January 15, 1991.

43. *Vechernii Donetsk,* January 23, 1991.

44. The budget debate in the soviet continued intermittently over a period of nearly a month, as various parts of the law were discussed and clarified with higher authorities and local legal advisors. The report of the budget's adoption is in *Vechernii Donetsk,* March 14, 1991.

45. The results of the voting are in *Vechernii Donetsk,* March 18, 1991.

46. *Vechernii Donetsk,* January 21, 1991.

47. *Vechernii Donetsk,* April 24, 1991.

48. The following account is based on I. Zaria, "Khronika protesta i malodushiia," *Vechernii Donetsk,* August 30, 1991. Zaria was the secretary of the Donetsk City Soviet.

49. *Vechernii Donetsk,* August 20, 1991.

50. *Nezavisimaia gazeta,* August 24, 1991.

51. *Vechernii Donetsk,* August 21, 1991.

52. See *Izvestiia,* November 26, 1992. Zviagil'skii was later appointed Deputy Prime Minister of Ukraine and in this capacity was reelected to the Ukrainian Parliament in March 1994.

53. One of the activists of the Donetsk strike committee, Valerii Samofalov of the Kuibyshev mine, criticized the new head of the municipality for having "bought himself the position." Personal communication from Lewis H. Siegelbaum, April 1993.

54. For a description of how he built the Zasiadko mine into a self-sufficient empire that controlled its own *sovkhoz* with slaughterhouse, meat processing plant, dairy, and bakery, bought a freighter to export the mine's coal, and invested part of the profits in video recorders and tape decks to be sold cheaply to his workers, see *Vechernii Donetsk,* April 17, 1991. The Zasiadko miners took no part in the 1991 political strike, but passed resolutions of solidarity and contributed generously to the strike fund.

55. The foregoing paragraphs are based on an interview with a deputy to the Donetsk Soviet, M.M. Girshman, Jerusalem, May 1993.

56. *Vechernii Donetsk,* June 26, 1991.

57. See the plan discussed by a mine director in *Vechernii Donetsk,* June 6, 1991.

58. *Vechernii Donetsk,* October 9, 1990, and December 8, 1990.

59. *Vechernii Donetsk,* February 18, 1991.

60. *Vechernii Donetsk,* December 5, 1990.

61. *Vechernii Donetsk,* October 19, 1989. One of the points made in the article was the growth in the percentage of abortions performed outside the hospitals.

II

Systemic Studies

7

Main Currents in the Development of Russian Local Self-Government

The First Post-Soviet Year

Georgii V. Barabashev

General Summary

The salient characteristic of the period surveyed is that the problems entailed in the implementation of the Law on Local Self-Government in the Russian Federation, adopted in June 1991, have not been readily resolved. On the whole, the process of creating a system of local government that measures up to accepted standards of the Western democracies is far from complete. The difficulties in developing such institutions were created by general economic and political instability on the one hand, and on the other by the persistence in the localities of the stereotypical thinking inherited from the "administrative-command system."

The federal authorities did not evince sufficient firmness and political will in dealing with the following questions, each of which has vital significance for local self-government.

(1) The statute on Budgetary Rights of Local Authorities that received a first reading in the Supreme Soviet of the Russian Federation was never signed into law. Thus, there is no guarantee of financial independence for each local government body. Instead, there is a continuing and near-total dependence of local budgets on annual allocations set by the republics and by the krai and oblast authorities, who are in turn financed out of the federal government's tax income.

(2) In accordance with a law that was passed, there were to have been popular elections for the office of head of local administration. These elections were not held. Throughout this entire period the heads of administra-

tion were appointed by the president or by the heads of administration of krais and oblasts. Moreover, the federal authorities intensified their efforts to subordinate the heads of local government bodies to the executives above them. This was in the tradition of democratic centralism, which had been the organizational principle of the system of local soviets in the Soviet period. For instance, an order promulgated by Boris Yeltsin, president of the Russian Federation, on August 7, 1992, confirmed the "Regulation on Disciplinary Responsibility of Heads of Administrations." This regulation gives the president, or head of administration of a krai or oblast, the right to apply disciplinary measures to the heads of local governments within his territory. These measures may be in the form of a warning, a reprimand, or even dismissal from one's post.

As part of the concept of "a strong and unitary executive power," there are attempts to enhance the role and status of presidential representatives in the various regions. One of the most fervent supporters of this approach is President Yeltsin himself. A presidential decree of July 15, 1992, confirmed the regulations "On Representatives of the President of the Russian Federation in Krais, Oblasts, Autonomous Oblasts, Autonomous Okrugs, and in the Cities of Moscow and St. Petersburg." Under the terms of this regulation, the presidential representative has the right to review the actions of local organs of administration and self-government. In practice there is a noticeable tendency for presidential representatives to intervene in the work of local administrations.

(3) The legislative and organizational measures necessary for implementation of the laws regarding land, local self-government, and the division of real property among the federal authorities, krais and oblasts, and municipalities, were not set in motion. What is more, the draft of the principles of land legislation for the Russian Federation, which passed its first reading in the Supreme Soviet, attempts to reserve the rights of property in land solely to the federation, republics, krais, and oblasts, omitting municipalities. It is heartening that this attempt was met with fierce criticism by a number of deputies, and most probably will not pass its second reading.

(4) The creation of the concept of municipal property should be considered this period's most positive innovation toward realizing the concept of local self-government. A decree of the Supreme Soviet of the Russian Federation defined the inventory of objects belonging to municipalities, districts, krais, and oblasts. It also set forth the procedures by which property was to be turned over to any unit of local self-government. This included granting the local soviets representation in the higher soviets, or more precisely, in the committees for property management of the higher territorial administrative units. When it came to parcelling out properties to the vari-

ous governments, there was a noticeable tendency on the part of the krai and oblast authorities to keep control of items that should, by law, have been turned over to the districts and municipalities.

On the other hand, the localities witnessed considerable development in the privatization of municipal property by sale or by conversion into share-holding companies. The institutions of local government adopt their own local plans of privatization. These generally include as a first stage the food industry, service enterprises, and trade outlets.

(5) The legislation on local self-government contains almost nothing regarding the development of public organs of self-government. There is a great lag in providing for public committees for blocks, urban micro-districts, and small rural settlements. It appears that such institutions will develop only after the village, district, and municipal institutions of self-government begin to function regularly.*

Institutional Problems

Problems regarding the establishment of legislative foundations for local self-government arise first and foremost from the need to begin implementation of the norms set forth in the federative agreements included in the text of the constitution drafted by the sixth session of the Congress of People's Deputies of the Russian Federation. According to this draft constitution, the jurisdiction of the federation in organizing local self-government is limited to adopting legislative principles that set out general guidelines for the activity of the representative and executive organs of the local authorities. As for detailed regulations of such activity, they will be set forth in the laws of the republics of the Russian Federation and in the decisions of the krais and oblasts, on the basis of federally legislated principles. Thus the Russian Federation's "Law on Local Self-Government" will be superseded by a new network of legislation based on federal fundamental legislation, regional acts regarding local government, and the regulations on urban and district self-government (municipal charters) already being drafted in numerous localities.

The transition to the new system of regulating local government has to its credit several achievements, but has led to certain difficulties as well.

---

* The federal treaty signed in the summer of 1993 was intended to be an integral part of the constitution but was not included in the constitution adopted by referendum on December 12. Chapter 8 of this constitution (articles 130–133) deals with local self-government and its rights to deal with local matters. Article 12 of the constitution places local self-government on an independent basis outside the structure of organs of state power. Each local government is free to determine its own structure. (Art. 131)

Among its merits, the transition period can count the possibility of a polymorphous system of organization of municipal and district government that borrows from differing systems of Western, and in particular, European, local government. The present law on local self-government sets out a single model for the entire country, something akin to the American council –strong mayor system." Experience has shown that in many regions this model has exacerbated the conflict between the representative and executive branches, between the councils and the heads of administration. The first draft of the fundamentals of legislation on local self-government prepared by the Russian Federation's Supreme Soviet Committee on the Work of Soviets and on the Development of Local Self-Government proposed that each republic, krai, and oblast should decide its own form of local government, taking into account the wishes of its populace. Some might favor a council and a strong mayor elected by the public, while others would prefer a mayor elected by the council, or a mayor who is a popularly elected member of the council and chosen by council members as chairman.

A potential negative aspect of the new regulatory system is that, when we take into account the general tendency for krai and oblast authorities to retain their control over the districts and cities, there is a danger that in the process of establishing the administration at the regional level, local powers will be whittled away, giving rise to the creation or restoration of a system of rigorous control of local authorities' activities by regional administrators. For this reason, the fundamental laws on local government must contain limitations on excessive krai and oblast intervention in local affairs.

Additional Miscellaneous Questions

Among the remaining miscellaneous questions, two are of particular urgency. The first is the weakening of any real possibility of the public's exercising an influence on the activity of the local bureaucracies and enjoying any measure of protection against arbitrary decisions. The proposed legislation regarding judicial protection of citizens' rights in disputes with local administrative bodies is woefully ineffective. The courts have neither the experience nor the desire to occupy themselves with the complaints of citizens against incumbent bureaucrats. Local deputies as well generally give little attention to investigating their constituents' complaints.

The second urgent matter is the total lack of an appropriate system for appointing local administrative officials. The former system of Communist Party control of appointment to executive positions has ceased to exist, but no appropriate system has as yet been instituted for forming a municipal civil service that will meet the needs of a democratic society.

The problem of popular elections to the local councils and to the leadership of local administrations remains unresolved. President Yeltsin hopes to defer the election of heads of administration until the end of the term of office of the current soviets. It is highly probable that the parliament will concede this to the president, not least of all since public interest in elections is at an extreme low, as is the popularity of the local authorities.

Moscow, November 1992
(Translated from Russian by
Theodore H. Friedgut)

8

Local Support for Market Reform
Implications of a Consumption Bias

Daniel Berkowitz

In January 1992, the president of the Russian Federation, Boris Yeltsin, attempted to eliminate one of the main vestiges of the command economy: price controls. By presidential decree approximately 90 percent of retail and 80 percent of wholesale prices were released from administrative control (Bush 1991: 27; Decree 1991). The reasoning behind this radical policy was that broad price controls place a major drain on the federal and subnational budgets. More importantly, a flexible price system that provides information about relative scarcities of goods and services is critical for successful transition to a market economy.

Despite the advantages of a flexible price system, many local governments[1] ordered their retail enterprises and organizations to maintain prices below market-clearing levels. When price liberalization began, the Russian federal government established regulated prices for fourteen basic food products, including salt, sugar, bread, and dairy products. Funds were allocated to local governments to subsidize state retail enterprises selling these basic commodities. While most local governments did not receive sufficient funding to support these low prices, "in many regions the mandatory list was expanded at the initiative of the local administration" (Demchenko 1992a: 29). During the first half of 1992, prices of some twenty-seven food groups were controlled by local authorities. In the second quarter of 1992, the Russian federal government gradually began to lift these price restrictions and phased out its financing of subsidies. Most local governments, however, continued the subsidies with funds from local budgets (Demchenko 1992a: 29).

The objective of this chapter is to develop a simple framework for understanding the economic reasons for local resistance to or support for a price liberalization in state retail stores. A local government supports price liberalization when it allows the prices of goods sold in its state stores to rise to a level at which demand is no greater than supply, and resists liberalization when it sets a price in its state stores at which demand exceeds supply.

The model incorporates several important features of the contemporary Russian local environment. First, there is both state and private provision in the local consumer market. The local government regulates the state-sector price and entrepreneurs freely set the private-sector price.[2] Second, because of the increased importance of voting and grassroots interest groups, local governments may use state provision of consumer goods to win the loyalty of their constituents. Specifically, this chapter argues that in general local governments are driven by a "consumption bias," and at the margin are willing to forgo a unit of locally generated state firm profit in order to gain an additional unit of local consumer welfare.

The existence of a consumption bias implies that the level of private-sector development is an important factor in determining whether a local government will support or resist a state-sector price liberalization in the consumer market. When the private sector is poorly developed and most of the productive capacity is under the jurisdiction of the local government, enforcement of low state-sector prices effectively promotes consumer welfare. In this case, a local government would tend to resist liberalization, and rationing in the state sector would persist. When the private sector is sufficiently developed, however, local administrators will tend to favor liberalization. An effective liberalization would induce the private sector to cut prices and increase output and would eliminate rationing in the state sector.

The model in this chapter is related to two bodies of literature. Papers by Rees (1984, Section 7.1), Bos (1986), Hagen (1979), Harris and Wiens (1980), and Beato and Mas-Colell (1984) analyze how a public (state) firm in competition with a private firm can improve efficiency in an imperfectly competitive market. These contributions analyze the extent to which a public firm should optimally deviate from marginal cost pricing under different assumptions regarding the timing of the public/private interaction. In all of these studies, prices are set so that supply equals demand. The current study extends these works by incorporating disequilibrium pricing.

The model presented here also uses the literature on price competition under capacity constraints that began with Edgeworth (1897) and continues with Levitan and Shubik (1972), Kreps and Scheinkman (1983), and Brock and Scheinkman (1985) in the context of a supergame. In these papers, all firms maximize profits. In our study, although a private firm maximizes profit, the state firm sets a vote-maximizing price.

This chapter is organized in the following manner: Section I summarizes current regional developments in Russia and argues in favor of a consumption bias. Section II sets up a simple model for understanding how a local government that is driven by a consumption bias determines the state-sector price. Section III analyzes the implications of private provision in the consumer market, and Section IV concludes.

I. Local Government Incentives

During the Soviet period, local governments (local soviets) had jurisdiction over enterprises and organizations that directly influenced the local standard of living. Between 1976 and 1989, 77–89 percent of local budgetary expenditures were allocated to the social consumption fund, which includes financing for restaurants, retail shops, light (consumer goods) industries, housing, education, and public health (see Berkowitz and Mitchneck 1992: 4–6; and Wallich 1992). Thus, local governments were responsible for overseeing pricing, sales, payments, and tax collections in those state enterprises and organizations that provided consumer goods and services to their constituents.

Even though local governments managed much of the state provision of consumer goods and services, evidence suggests that they were not under strong pressure to advance the local standard of living during the pre-perestroika period. During this time, popular voting was a pro forma exercise that often legitimized candidates chosen by local party officials. Under the system of dual subordination, local executives, who were nominally accountable to the deputies of the soviet that had elected them, were responsible for fulfilling the commands issued by higher-level ministerial officials. In principle, deputies to the local soviets were responsible to their constituents. Nevertheless, since spending and hiring decisions in the local soviets were controlled largely by higher-level organizations (Hahn 1991: 93), the deputies often approved and worked to fulfill projects and planned quotas that were detrimental to their constituents (see Kolomiichenko and Parotikov 1989; Pabat 1985).

Throughout the perestroika period and since the demise of the Soviet Union, local soviets in Russia have retained jurisdiction over the state enterprises and organizations that provide basic consumer goods and services.

Under the current system, oblasts have received more responsibility for managing small businesses, light industries, and consumer enterprises. The lower-level cities and raions now have the responsibility both to regulate prices in their consumer enterprises and organizations and to finance consumer price subsidies (Wallich 1992). In March 1990, for the first time, deputies to the local soviet gained office on the basis of competitive elections. The extent to which voting has forced local governments to represent their constituents' interests is a matter of debate. As Jeffrey Hahn points out, the elections to local offices in March 1990

> were held at a time when local control still rested largely with the local Party organization and those dependent on it. It was also held in the absence of multi-party competition leaving voters with little to guide their choices among a large number of candidates competing in a large number of districts often over the course of several elections (Hahn 1992: 4–5).

Hahn further argues (in this volume, p. 213) that local government resistance to market reforms does not imply that local governments do not represent their constituents.

> Many critics of the soviets contend that the 1990 elections were not a true reflection of voters' preferences because the results were manipulated by the existing authorities. This view may have some merit, but there was little evidence of widespread cheating; it also ignores the possibility that many people . . . may have had reservations about what the democratic movement would mean for them. Arguments that the soviets are "ineffective" because they resist policies made at the center obscure the fact that many voters are unhappy with these policies.

While deputies were elected for five-year terms, starting in 1992 there were many calls for early elections. The threat of early elections, which became a reality in October 1993, and the emergence of local political parties implies that the traditional system of dual subordination no longer exists.

II. Local Price Regulation in the Absence of Private Provision

There are three sets of actors in local government who can regulate state-sector prices: local deputies, the executive committee, and local department heads and administrators.[3] Of these, local deputies are, in principle, most sensitive to constituent opinions since they are elected. Members of the local executive committee—the hired managers of the region's branches— are largely insulated from voter pressure since they are no longer elected in many regions. Finally, local department heads and administrators are unelected officials. Each of these groups has different objectives. Even though local deputies are formally sovereign, the mayor and members of the local administration can thwart the decisions made by the deputies.

In what follows, it is assumed that local administrators implement the regulations passed by local deputies.[4] Local deputies choose a price-regulation policy that maximizes the number of votes they might receive from their constituents in the next election.[5]

To capture this situation, first consider a local market in which there is only state-sector provision in the consumer market.[6] In particular, the state enterprise is regulated by the local government and can sell up to k_s units of a homogeneous consumer good that has a constant unit cost, c_s. For simplicity, market demand for the consumer good is described by the linear function $P(q_s) = p_s = a - q_s$, where q_s denotes market demand and p_s denotes the marginal consumer's willingness to pay for a unit of the consumer good.

This local market is illustrated in Figure 8.1. The financial variables— price (p_s) and state-sector unit cost (c_s)—are on the vertical axis and the physical variables—state-sector capacity (k_s), market demand (q_s), and sales (Z_s)—are on the horizontal axis. Segment EBGD represents the market inverse demand curve, $P(q_s)$, and the segment $HIGk_s$ represents the state firm's supply curve. The fixed-supply curve implies that the analysis is limited to the short run. To ensure that the state firm is viable, it is assumed that the state firm can earn a profit when it sells all of its capacity:

$$P(k_s) = a - k_s > c_s \qquad (A1)$$

The price chosen by a local regulator determines state-sector sales in the following fashion. First, any state-sector price, p_s, induces market demand for state good, q_s:

$$q_s = a - p_s \qquad (2.1)$$

Thus, sales, z_s, is the minimum of capacity and market demand:

$$z_s = \min \{k_s, a - p_s\} \qquad (2.2)$$

By inspection of equation (2.2) there are three kinds of prices that the state firm can charge. When $p_s > a - k_s$, market demand is less than supply and the state enterprise charges an *excess capacity price*. Any price above point F in Figure 8.1 is an excess capacity price. When $p_s = a - k_s$, supply equals demand and the state enterprise charges the *competitive price* (point F in Figure 8.1). Finally, when $p_s < a - k_s$, market demand exceeds supply and the state enterprise charges a *ration price*. Any price below point F in Figure 8.1 induces rationing.

To determine the vote-maximizing state-sector price, consider point B in Figure 8.1. Point B lies on the market-demand curve and corresponds to the excess-capacity price and quantity pair $\{p_s{}^b, q_s{}^b\}$. By setting this excess

Figure 8.1. **State Market**

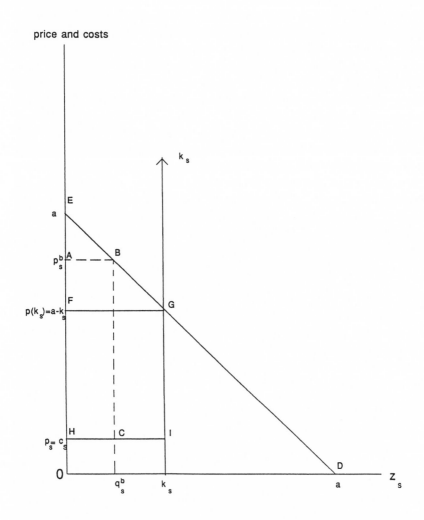

capacity price, p_s^b, local regulators effect both consumer welfare and state enterprise profits. Consumer surplus is the area of triangle ABE:

$$\text{Consumer surplus} = .5(a - p_s^b)^2 \qquad (2.3)$$

By inspection of equation (2.3), consumer surplus increases for any small cut in the state price. This holds for two reasons. First, all consumers who buy the good at the initial price p_s^b, now get a discount. Second, a lower price means that additional consumers are willing to buy the state good. Thus, if a local government represented consumer interests only, it would always cut an excess capacity price.

When the state firm charges excess-capacity price p_s^b, profit is the differential between price and cost times sales:

$$\text{state profit} = (p_s^b - c_s)(a - p_s^b). \tag{2.4}$$

The area of rectangle HCBA in Figure 8.1 represents state profit. Increased state profit serves the interests of the managers and shareholders in the state firm. Furthermore, the share of state enterprise profits that flow into the local budget could be used to finance local projects.

A vote-maximizing price takes into account the interests of consumers as well as state-sector managers, shareholders, and the local budget. For these reasons, the vote function is written as:

$$V = V \text{ (Consumer surplus, state profit)}. \tag{2.5}$$

V denotes votes in the next election. Clearly, V is increasing in both consumer surplus and state profit.

When the local government has a consumption bias, it believes that an increase in consumer surplus attracts more votes than an increase in state profit. The assumption of a consumption bias captures two important features of the current local environment. First, voting has become more important. Thus, local deputies must be more responsive to their constituents, most of whom are simple consumers. This would hold if incumbents ran for reelection, voters were well informed, and the local government was held responsible for consumer welfare. Second, local enterprises have become a much weaker tax base. Local governments in Russia are having an increasingly difficult time collecting taxes from their enterprises because of the rise in interenterprise arrears (see Ickes and Ryterman 1992) and because much of the collection is controlled by nonlocal administrators.[7]

A vote function that operationalizes a consumption bias is:

$$V = V \left[(1 - \lambda) \text{ Consumer surplus} + \lambda \text{ state profit} \right]$$

where $\qquad\qquad\qquad\qquad 0 < \lambda < 0.5,$ \hfill (2.6)

V is a monotonically increasing function.

The existence of a consumption bias has several implications for price regulation in a local market. These implications are summarized in the following two propositions.

Proposition 1. *Suppose there is no private provision. If a local government has a consumption bias, then it never sets an excess-capacity price.*

Proposition 2. *Suppose there is no private provision. If a local government has a consumption bias and has a break-even constraint, then the vote-maximizing price is* $p_s = c_s$.[8]

The arguments for these results are as follows. If the state sets an excess-capacity price, then a small cut in the state price would always increase consumer welfare. The existence of a consumption bias implies that the potential loss in state profits is more than offset by a gain in consumer welfare. Therefore, the local government gains votes by cutting any excess-capacity price down to the competitive price, $P(k_s)$, at which supply equals demand. The competitive price–quantity pair is point G in Figure 8.1.

By proposition 2, the local government sets the ration price $p_s = c_s$. If the local government set the competitive price, then supply would equal demand and there would be no rationing in the consumer market. In this case, consumer surplus is the area of triangle FEG and state profit is the area of rectangle FGHI. Any cut in the state price, however, induces a one-to-one transfer of social surplus from state-firm profit to consumer surplus. Thus, a local government driven by a consumption bias would discount its price to the minimal level and thus transfer all of its potential profit, rectangle FGHI, to consumers.[9] A plausible minimal level under the current conditions of self-financing in enterprises is the price that just covers costs.[10]

In this section we have argued, in the context of a simple model, that a local government resists market reform and sets a ration price when it is driven by a consumption bias and when there is no private provision. The next section incorporates private provision into the analysis.

III. Local Price Regulation with Private Provision

Local governments in Russia have always depended upon private provision in the consumer market. Private producers are significant suppliers of food, clothing, housing construction, handicrafts, small electronics, and repair services. In this section we argue that the capacity of the local private sector to provide goods may induce a local government to abandon rationing and thus support a state-sector price liberalization.

To capture the impact of private provision, consider a local market with a capacity profile, $k = \{k_s, k_p\}$, in which k_s and k_p are components controlled by the local government and a private entrepreneur. The state and private firms can sell up to k_s and k_p units of a consumer good at a constant per unit cost and market inverse demand remains $P(q_s + q_p)$. The state enterprise has no cost advantage: $c_s \geq c_p$. Finally, to ensure viability, it is assumed that both firms can earn a profit when all capacity is sold:

$$P(k_s + k_p) = a - k_s - k_p > c_s \geq c_p = 0. \tag{A.2}$$

where $P(k_s + k_p)$ denotes the competitive price.

To draw a sharp distinction between the state and private firms, it is assumed that the local government cannot regulate the private firm.[11] Thus, while vote-maximizing politicians supply price regulation for the state firm, the private firm maximizes its profits. The next proposition limits the range of private-sector pricing policy.

Proposition 3. *The private firm sets* $p_p \geq P(k_s + k_p)$.

PROOF (see Kreps and Scheinkman, 1983, lemma 2). By naming $p_p < P(k_s + k_p)$, private profits are, at most, $(p_p - c_p) k_p$. By setting $p_p = P(k_s + k_p)$, private profits are, at least, $[P(k_s + k_p) - c_p]k_p$.

Proposition 3 makes the simple point that if a profit-maximizing private firm set a price lower than the competitive price, $P(k_p + k_s)$, it would forgo potential profit. Thus, the private firm sets a price no lower than $P(k_p + k_s)$.

Suppose that the state firm charges the ration price $p_s = c_s$. Then, by proposition 3, the private firm sets a higher price, since

$$p_p \geq P(k_s + k_p) > c_s = p_s \tag{3.1}$$

Assuming the highest valuation consumers buy the state good, demand for the private good is

$$q_p = \max \{a - k_s - p_p, 0\} \tag{3.2}$$

Private sales, z_p, are the minimum of capacity and market demand:

$$z_p = \min [k_p, \max \{a - k_s - p_p, 0\}] \tag{3.3}$$

The private market is illustrated in Figures 8.2a and 8.2b for the case in which the state firm charges the ration price $p_s = c_s$. In both cases MN is the residual market demand, that is, the demand for the private good net of the

Figure 8.2a. **Low-Capacity Private Market**

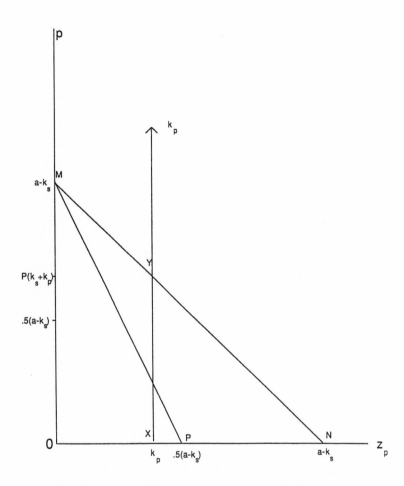

consumers who buy from the state enterprise. Segment MP represents the marginal private revenue for an additional unit of sales[12], and marginal costs, c_p, are normalized to zero for simplicity.

A profit-maximizing private firm with market power sets a price at which marginal revenue equals marginal cost. In the absence of private-capacity constraints, the profit-maximizing price is

$$p_p = 0.5(a - k_s), \qquad (3.4)$$

Figure 8.2b. **High-Capacity Private Market**

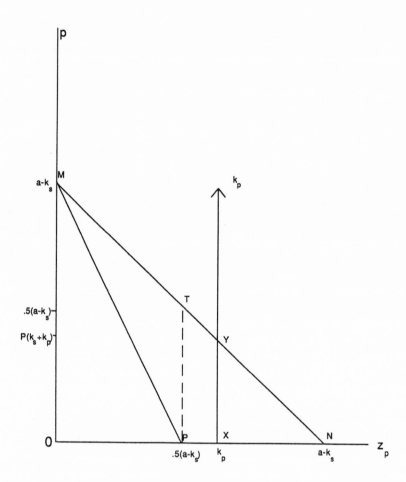

which corresponds to private sales, z_p, and profits π_p:

$$z_p = 0.5(a - k_s) \qquad\qquad (3.5)$$

$$\pi_p = 0.25(a - k_s)^2 \qquad\qquad (3.6)$$

In Figure 8.2a private capacity is low: $k_p < 0.5(a - k_s)$. Thus, the private firm is capacity constrained and its profit-maximizing strategy is to choose the competitive price: $p_p = P(k_p + k_s)$. Point Y in Figure 8.2a is the optimal private price–sales pair. Because the private firm sets the competitive price and sells all of its capacity, it is efficient.

In Figure 8.2b the private sector is more developed: $k_p > 0.5(a - k_s)$. In this case the private firm's profit-maximizing strategy is to choose the excess capacity price: $p_p = 0.5(a - k_s)$. Because there is excess private capacity, the private market is inefficient and generates a deadweight loss:

$$= 0.5(k_p - 0.5(a - k_s))(1.5a - 1.5k_s - k_p). \tag{3.7}$$

$$\text{Private deadweight loss} = \text{area quadrilateral TYXP.} \tag{3.8}$$

Suppose that the local government knows the level of private development and understands that the private entrepreneur maximizes profits.[13] The next proposition shows that local support or resistance to a state-sector price liberalization depends upon the size of private capacity.

Proposition 4. *Suppose private capacity is small:* $k_p \leq 0.5(a - k_s)$. *If the local government has a consumption bias and a break-even constraint, then it maintains a ration price:* $p_s = c_s$. *If the private sector is sufficiently developed:* $k_p > 0.5(a - k_s)$, *then the local government might set a state-sector price that eliminates rationing.*[14]

The idea behind proposition 4 is as follows. When private capacity is sufficiently small: $k_p \leq 0.5(a - ks)$ and $p_s = c_s$, the private market is efficient. In this case the local government maximizes votes by maintaining a ration price and resisting price liberalization. When private capacity is larger: $k_p > 0.5(a - k_s)$, rationing in the state sector induces private market inefficiency. The private firm charges an exorbitant excess capacity price and therefore wastes available capacity.

A local government might consider abandoning rationing in the state sector if this would eliminate private-sector inefficiency. Specifically, an increase in the state-sector price might increase votes for the local deputies *if* it induces the private sector to cut its price and sell at full capacity.[15] A sufficient condition for local government support of a price liberalization is that state-sector profits do not decrease and consumer surplus increases once rationing is eliminated. Proposition 5 summarizes two conditions under which a local government is more likely to support a price liberalization.

Proposition 5. *Suppose that the private sector is highly developed:* $k_p > 0.5$ $(a - k_s)$. *If the local government has a consumption bias and a break-even constraint, then it is more likely to support a price liberalization when:*

> *(a) there is an increase in private capacity;*
> *(b) the state firm's costs, c_s, increase.* [16]

Suppose that there is rationing in the state sector: $p_s = c_s$. When private capacity, k_p, increases, private excess capacity holdings increase and rationing becomes no longer desirable from the local government's perspective. A state-sector price liberalization, however, becomes more desirable, since the private sector will provide even more goods at a cheaper price.

An increase in the state firm's costs, c_s, has no impact on prices and sales and, therefore, no impact on welfare in the liberalization regime. An increase in c_s in the resistance regime, however, means that the state firm sells the same amount of goods at a higher price while the private firm's price and sales level remain constant. This induces a decrease in consumer welfare and implies that the local government is more likely to support liberalization.

IV. Conclusions

A basic tenet driving the Russian price liberalization in January 1992 is that liberalization of state-sector prices is critical for a successful transition to a market economy. This chapter presents no arguments against the benefits of free-market pricing, but it does offer an explanation as to why local governments have resisted raising the prices of many consumer goods and services.

We have argued that state-sector prices are regulated by vote-maximizing politicians who are driven by a consumption bias. These regulators are willing to forgo an increment of locally generated profits in order to increase consumer welfare. The existence of a consumption bias explains why local governments continue to hold prices down when private capacity holdings are sufficiently low. It also predicts that once private capacity holdings reach a sufficiently high level, a local government will increase both consumer welfare and local budgetary revenues by supporting a price liberalization.

The basic model used for arguing this point is a local market in which a government-regulated state firm competes with an unregulated profit-maximizing private firm. This implies that one entrepreneur controls all of the private pricing decisions within a region, but the basic argument can be generalized to analyze a local market in which the private sector consists of more than one firm.

Suppose that the private sector contains two equal-sized firms that maximize profits. In Berkowitz (1993, section IV) it is shown that when the local government supports a ration price in the state sector, this local anti-monopoly policy has two effects. First, it makes the private sector more competitive. Thus, it is less likely that any private firm will charge an inefficient excess-capacity price. If the private sector is inefficient, however, then there will be price volatility in the private sector as the private firms engage in price wars. Thus, if the private sector is inefficient, a state-sector price liberalization both induces private-sector efficiency and eliminates private price volatility.

Notes

I am indebted to Martha Banwell, Michael Conlin, Raymond Deneckere, Theodore Friedgut, Jeffrey Hahn, and Jan Svejnar for their thoughtful comments. This research was supported by the National Council for Soviet and East European Research under contract 807–09.

1. In this chapter, local governments include the deputies and administrators overseeing the oblasts and cities in the Russian Federation.

2. Thus, the model ignores local capacity controlled by non-local state organs. This is reasonable, since in the former Soviet Union most state provision of consumer goods and services was and still is under the control of local governments. See Berkowitz and Mitchneck (1992) and Wallich (1992).

3. I thank Theodore Friedgut for both raising and carefully explaining the significance of this point.

4. Thus, in the language of modern economics, this paper ignores *principal-agent* problems, in which unelected officials, whose interests are different from those of the deputies, implement legislation in a way that misrepresents the spirit of the law.

5. The objective function of a vote-maximizing politician was introduced by Peltzman (1976).

6. The model that is set forth in this and the next section is rigorously developed in Berkowitz (1993).

7. I thank members of the Yaroslavl' city and oblast government, especially V.V. Istomina, for emphasizing this point to me during interviews conducted in the summer of 1992.

8. Formal proofs of both of these propositions are available upon request.

9. This result follows from the efficient rationing assumption, which states that when there are no income effects, the highest valuation consumers obtain the state good when there is rationing. This rationing rule allows for resale among consumers (see Levitan and Shubik (1972) and Kreps and Scheinkman (1983)). For the sake of simplicity, however, it ignores the social costs of rationing, such as queuing and hoarding. If the consumption bias was sufficiently strong, that is, λ was sufficiently lower than 0.5, then the results of this analysis would generalize to the case in which there were social costs associated with rationing.

10. This result could be generalized to include subsidies.

11. In reality, local governments can sometimes regulate private firms through tax and credit-policy, as well as by imposing price restraints. Nevertheless, the local government's ability to regulate private pricing is limited.

12. Since demand is linear, the marginal revenue curve is linear. It intersects the vertical axis at the demand curve and intersects the horizontal axis at half the distance of the demand curve.

13. In the language of modern economics, the local government is the leader and the private firm is the follower in a Stackleberg game. The local government first sets the state enterprise price in anticipation of the best reaction of the private firm. The order of moves reflects a situation in which the private firm is more flexible in its pricing policy than the state enterprise. The state enterprise may have significant "menu costs" since pricing decisions are subject to the approval of government officials who do not work in the enterprise. An unregulated private firm, however, can simply change its price without bureaucratic interference.

14. A detailed proof of proposition 4 is in Berkowitz (1993).

15. Any state-sector price that induces this private sector to sell at full capacity must generate private profits no less than the private profits when the state good is rationed, $0.25(a - k_s)^2$. This implies that the state-sector price in a liberalization is no less than $0.25(a - k_s)^2/k_p$.

16. A proof of this proposition is in Berkowitz (1993).

References

Beato, P., and Mas-Colell, A. (1984). "The Marginal Cost Pricing as a Regulation Mechanism in Mixed Markets." In M. Marchand, P. Pestieau, and H. Tulkens, eds., *The Performance of Public Enterprises.* Amsterdam: North Holland.

Berkowitz, D. (1993). "Price Liberalization and Local Resistance." Working Paper #285. University of Pittsburgh.

Berkowitz, D., and Mitchneck, B. (1992). "Fiscal Decentralization in the Soviet Economy." *Comparative Economic Studies,* 34(2), 1–18.

Bos, D. (1986). *Public Enterprise Economics.* Amsterdam: North Holland.

Brock, William, and Scheinkman, Jose (1985). "Price Setting Supergames with Capacity Constraints." *Review of Economic Studies,* 52, 371–82.

Bush, Keith (1991). "Russia: Gaidar's Guidelines." *RFE/RL Research Report,* 1(15) 220–25.

Decree of the President of the Russian Soviet Federated Socialist Republic (1991). "On Measures for the Freeing up of Prices." *Rossiiskaia gazeta,* December 25, 1991, p. 1. Translated in the *Current Digest of the Soviet Press,* XLIII (52), p. 6.

Demchenko, Irina. "Prices Take Revenge for Their Former Restraint." *Izvestiia,* September 7, 1992, p. 2. Translated in the *Current Digest of the Soviet Press,* XLIV (36), p. 29, 1992a.

Demchenko, Irina. "The Provinces are Trying to Help Keep Prices in Check. But This is No Longer Helping." *Izvestiia,* November 25, p. 2. Translated in the *Current Digest of the Soviet Press,* XLIV (47), p. 30, 1992b.

Edgeworth, F.Y. "La Teoria Pura del Monopolio." *Giornale degli Economisti,* 40, 130–31, 1897. Reprinted in English as "The Pure Theory of Monopoly." In F.Y. Edgeworth, *Papers Relating to Political Economy,* I. London: Macmillan, 1925, 111–42.

Hagen, K.P. (1979). "Optimal Pricing in Public Firms in an Imperfect Market Economy." *Scandinavian Journal of Economics,* 81: 475–93.

Hahn, Jeffrey W. (1991). "Developments in Local Soviet Politics." In Alfred J. Rieber and Alvin Z. Rubinstein, eds., *Perestroika at the Crossroads*. Armonk, NY: M.E. Sharpe, 3–30.

Hahn, Jeffrey W. (1992). "Counter-Reformation in the Provinces: How Monolithic?" Manuscript presented at the annual meeting of the American Association for the Advancement of Slavic Studies, Phoenix, AZ, November.

Harris, R.G., and Wiens, E.G. (1980). "Government Enterprise: An Instrument for the Internal Regulation of Industry." *Canadian Journal of Economics*, 13: 125–32.

Ickes, Barry, and Ryterman, Randi (1992). "The Inter-Enterprise Arrears Crisis in Russia." *Post-Soviet Affairs: Formerly Soviet Economy*, 8 (Oct.–Dec.): 331–61.

Kolomiichenko, O.V., and Parotikov, V.I. (1989). "Mestnye sovety i predpriiatiia." *Finansy SSSR*, 12: 18–21.

Kreps, David, and Scheinkman, Jose (1983). "Quantity Precommitment and Bertrand Competition Yield Cournot Outcomes." *Bell Journal of Economics*, 14: 326–38.

Levitan, Richard, and Shubik, Martin (1972). "Price Duopoly and Capacity Constraints." *International Economic Review*, 13(1).

Pabat, M.G. (1985). "Rol' byudzhetnoi sistemy v razvitii ekonomiki regiona." *Finansy SSSR*, 9: 41–45.

Peltzman, Samuel (1976). "Towards a More General Theory of Regulation." *Journal of Law and Economics*, 19: 211–40, August.

Rees, R. (1984). *Public Enterprise Economics*. London: Weinfield and Nicholson, 2d edition.

Wallich, Christine (1992). *Fiscal Decentralization: Intergovernmental Relations in Russia*. Studies in Economies in Transition #6, the World Bank, Washington, DC.

9

Reforming Post-Soviet Russia

The Attitudes of Local Politicians

Jeffrey W. Hahn

political culture
Regional Politics

The Problem

Perhaps the dominant fact of political life in Russia since the failure of the August 19, 1991, putsch has been the continued struggle for power between those who held it under the old regime and those who would take it away from them; between the members of the old Communist Party leadership and their *nomenklatura* allies, and the "reformists" led by President Boris Yeltsin. It is a conflict whose roots can be traced to the policies of the former president of the USSR, Mikhail Gorbachev, especially those policies aimed at economic modernization within the old Soviet system. In pursuing policies of economic change, Gorbachev generated widespread opposition among members of the party apparatus and government bureaucracy, who had a vested interest in preserving the status quo; Gorbachev's proposals to reform it directly threatened their powers and privileges.

While the protagonists in this struggle remain much the same, the venue has changed. In postcommunist Russia, the institutional base of the opposition to the reformists is no longer the Communist Party but the soviets, and it is no longer in the center but at the periphery. It is here that the old opposition regrouped; it is in the provinces that the forces of counterreformation appear the strongest. At least this is the way Yeltsin and his allies see it. The metamorphosis of the old elites was described early on by, among others, Yeltsin's state secretary, Gennadii Burbulis. In an interview published in *Literaturnaia gazeta* of November 13, 1991, he asserted: "It is well known where the party nomenklatura at the krai, oblast, city, and district (raion) levels have gone. Within a month, the vast majority of these people have emerged in the bodies of state executive power; many have remained in the soviets and where no positions were available for them, they had to be created."

What is even more alarming to the self-proclaimed forces for change, however, is that since the attempted coup the momentum seems to have shifted to their adversaries. Yeltsin's meeting in Cheboksary, the capital of the Chuvash Republic, on September 11, 1992, with the leaders of oblasts and krais in the Russian Federation was almost certainly a recognition of this fact. In his speech the president charged that regional bodies of power "violate the laws of the Russian Federation and fail to fulfill presidential decrees and government decisions." While ruling out "coercive" means in settling federal-regional differences, he demanded an end to what he referred to as "legal separatism" in the provinces.[1] He then announced that he would postpone new elections to the local soviets, which had been tentatively rescheduled for December 1992, and allow those elected to office in March 1990 to finish their five-year terms. In fact, it was a realization that those supporting Yeltsin and the reformists would probably lose locally. It was a sign of retreat.

Given the apparent strength of local opposition, the prospects that Yeltsin and his government can succeed in implementing reformist policies from above, especially those aimed at the creation of a market economy, would appear diminished (Reddaway). But are all local authorities necessarily or equally opposed to the reformist policies of the center? Based on an analysis of changes in the elite from 1985–91 in twenty-five Russian and Ukrainian provinces, Joel Moses developed a political topology divided into those he labeled establishment, antiestablishment, and transitional (Moses). Even Yeltsin claimed in his speech in Cheboksary that problems with the local authorities were acute in only about half of the oblasts of Russia. Moreover, his remarks were directed to leaders at the oblast level. There is reason to believe that greater support for reformist policies may exist among officials elected to the soviets at the city level, especially in the oblast capitals (Hahn 1991a; Slider 1991; Moses). Finally, as Mary McAuley has argued, what is at stake may not be reform as such, but the issue of who will control local economic resources. According to McAuley, "It was not surprising that an elite, losing control of political resources, sought another basis for its power and privilege" (McAuley, p. 76). By adapting to the new economic system instead of fighting it, some older elites may be better able to position themselves to become the new property owners.

The question, then, to which this chapter is addressed, is: What is the nature of opposition to reforms at the local level and how solid is it? Any assessment of Yeltsin's ability to pursue his reformist agenda, especially on economic issues, must take this point into account. This chapter offers a preliminary analysis of this question based on survey interviews with 1,280 deputies in five Russian oblast and city soviets. In particular, we will try to answer the following: What are the attitudes of locally elected deputies to matters of political and economic reform? Are there significant differences between deputies of city and oblast soviets in their attitudes and orientations toward reform? If there are, are they consistent across different parts of central Russia? We begin by outlining the development of the struggle for power as it has unfolded in the period since the attempted coup and delineating what appear to be the major points of contention.

The Nature of Local Opposition

The reasons for the political dynamics just described are not hard to find— they are rooted in the elections to local offices and to the RSFSR parliament held in March 1990. While relatively democratic by previous Soviet standards, the elections were held at a time when local control still rested largely with the local party organization and those dependent on it.[2] They were also held in the absence of multiparty competition, leaving voters with little to guide their choices among a large number of candidates competing in a large number of districts, often over the course of several elections (Hahn 1994). As a result, while many voters took their revenge on the local political establishment by "throwing the bums out," the old *apparat* managed to gain a foothold in the new soviets by finding safe seats (often in rural areas) or by mobilizing constituencies in districts open to their influence. In coalition with members of the managerial elite and other nomenklatura-controlled appointments, they were often able to form working majorities in the soviets, especially at the oblast level, where a majority of seats came from rural constituencies (Helf and Hahn; Moses).

The "conservative" political coloration of many of the deputies elected to these soviets become readily apparent to the central leadership during their first year in office.[3] Even before the coup attempt, Boris Yeltsin, who had been elected president of Russia in June 1991, was determined to undermine the influence of these deputies and to end their opposition to the reform programs instituted by the Russian government. On August 14, 1991, he appointed Valerii Makharadze from Volgograd, one of the few reformist oblast soviet chairs, to the position of chief state inspector in charge of overseeing the implementation of federal legislation at the oblast level.[4] In the wake of the coup, the support shown by a number of provincial leaders for the attempted overthrow of the Soviet government served to confirm Yeltsin's suspicions about their motives, and several were removed from office. He took even firmer measures to consolidate his authority locally by appointing "presidential representatives" and by moving to control the appointment of the new "heads of administration" (Teague and Hanson, p. 10; Slider, pp. 10–11). Since both moves were central to his strategy for overcoming local opposition, they deserve brief discussion.

The *presidential representative* was to be a temporary position held by a presidential appointee who reported directly to Yeltsin on whether local authorities were carrying out the will of the federal government. They were not to interfere directly in local administration and were to be removed after an undefined transitional period.[5] The *head of administration* was a new position and represented a permanent change in the structure of local government. In conception, the incumbent would be the sole chief executive at the local level, replacing the chair of the executive committee (*ispolkom*) that existed under the old system. At the city level, the head of administration was also referred to as "mayor" (*mer*); at the oblast level, as "governor" (*gubernator*). Instead of being elected by the soviets (and accountable to them), heads of administration would be elected directly by the voters. Thus, the existing structure of local government according to which there were two heads (a chair of the soviet and a chair of the ispolkom) would be replaced by one in which a single person was responsible for governing (known as *edinonachalie*). The heads of administration could veto decisions of the soviet, which would need a two-thirds majority to override.[6]

Prior to the August 19, 1991, coup attempt, elections for the new heads of administration had been scheduled for December 8, 1991. Sensing, however, that the likely winners of such a contest, especially at the oblast level, would be the incumbent chairs of the soviets, Yeltsin requested and (after initially being refused by the Russian Federation Supreme Soviet) obtained, in October 1991, a postponement of elections. At the same time, he received the authority to appoint the heads of administration.[7] In principle Yeltsin made such appointments only after receiving nominations from the local soviet, but in practice he could disregard their choice and act independently, usually on the advice of his presidential representative. It may be helpful to use the example of what happened in Yaroslavl to illustrate the process and the politics behind it.

In Yaroslavl in the winter of 1991 there were meetings of both the city and oblast soviets to nominate candidates for Yeltsin's consideration. In the case of the city, the incumbent chair of the ispolkom, Viktor Volunchunas, received the most votes and was appointed mayor by Yeltsin. At the oblast level, the incumbent head of the oblispolkom (the oblast executive committee) and a deputy of the Russian parliament, Vladimir Kovalev, also received the most votes from the soviet, but was rejected by Yeltsin on the recommendation of the presidential representative, Vladimir Varukhin, in favor of Anatolii Lisitsyn, a former ispolkom chair from Rybinsk, who had gotten only a few votes at the meeting of the oblast soviet. The likely reasons for Yeltsin's rejection of Kovalev were the latter's ties to the old apparat and his apparent support for the coup attempt. For his part, Lisitsyn promptly purged the old ispolkom of those with links to the former elite and named a new team loyal to himself and, not coincidentally, to the president.[8]

In short, the thrust of Yeltsin's strategy was to outflank the soviets wherever he perceived that his opponents were stronger. He did so by strengthening executive authority and by ensuring that the executives would be answerable to him.[9] The reaction was predictable. As the soviets dug in against what they perceived as an encroachment on their authority, they were increasingly characterized as the chief bastion of nomenklatura resistance to reform. The battle was joined in the spring of 1992 in anticipation of the Sixth Congress of People's Deputies to be held in April. In an editorial published on February 28, *Izvestiia* charged that "The current alignment of forces in the oblast- and district-level soviets, where there is an established and growing conservative majority, threatens to undo the reforms, the fate of which is always decided at the local level." In a press conference reported in *Rossiiskaia gazeta* on March 4, 1992, two political analysts associated with the government claimed that more than 80 percent of oblast-level soviet chairmen and administrators were former party secretaries or held nomenklatura positions. The solution favored by these critics was to oust the incumbents elected in 1990 by adopting a new constitution, effectively abolishing the existing soviets, and by holding new elections.[10]

The soviets were not without their supporters, however. Matters came to a head shortly before the Congress convened when Yeltsin refused to sign the "Law on Krai and Oblast Soviets and on Krai and Oblast Administration," which was passed by parliament on March 5, 1992. He sent it back to parliament with a number of proposed changes, all of which would have given the head of administration greater power, especially in matters of personnel. All were rejected by the Supreme Soviet (whose chair, Ruslan Khasbulatov, gradually became the chief defender of legislative prerogatives) as granting the executive branch excessive control. According to Khasbulatov, the law did a good job of defining the respective rights and obligations of the legislative and executive branches. The problem, he said, was that "some heads of administration don't want to be bound by any sort of law. They would like, according to their own wishes, to distribute such things as resorts and factories."[11]

In response to the parliament's rejection of his proposals, Yeltsin suggested to the Congress that he would impose a moratorium on the implementation of the law. He made his remarks in the context of emphasizing a theme that he would repeat often: the inadmissibility of legislative interference in the work of the executive branch.[12] Sergei Shakhrai, the president's chief legal advisor, later informed Georgii Zhukov, the chair of the Supreme Soviet's Committee on the Work of the Soviets, that the law could not be introduced until after new elections, thus effectively, if temporarily, blocking the assertion of greater legislative power locally. Not coincidentally, Yeltsin's announcement of September 12, 1992, postponing all elections until 1995, suggests that he intended a further delay in implementing the law on oblast soviets.[13] Regardless of his intentions, however, the law is considered to have been in force since March 5, 1992.

Those making the case *for* the soviets rest their more favorable assessment on the fact that incumbent deputies were elected. The deputies, they argue, have a popular mandate, which administrators currently do not; the latter were appointed by Yeltsin, not popularly elected as stipulated in the law on oblasts.[14] Many critics of the soviets contend that the 1990 elections were not a true reflection of voters' preferences because the results were manipulated by the existing authorities. This view may have some merit, but there was little evidence of widespread cheating; it also ignores the possibility that many people, especially in rural areas, and among the elderly and unskilled, may have had reservations about what the democratic movement would mean for them. Arguments that the soviets are "ineffective" because they resist policies made at the center obscure the fact that many voters are unhappy with these policies. As one angry deputy put it: "Representative bodies of power are called that precisely because they are called upon to represent the interests of their constituents, interests which are far from always the same as those of the executive branch" (Nemkov, p. 43).

The irony is that those calling themselves democrats now favor stronger central authority in the face of resistance from below. Noting this irony, the legal scholar and chair of the committee on the soviets, Georgii Zhukov, in the interview noted earlier, included Burbulis, Shakhrai, Popov, Sobchak, Makharadze, and Yeltsin in this category and forcefully argued: "The persecution of the soviets is a dangerous path. It in no way justifies the deliberate effort to give full control to the executive bodies. To do so would be unlawful; it would eliminate democratic oversight of their activities. It would be an irreversible step in the direction of dictatorship" (pp. 34–35). Whatever political reasons Zhukov may have had for making this argument, it may well resonate in a population increasingly restive with Yeltsin's reforms.

The Ninth Congress of People's Deputies held in March 1993 provided further evidence of the continuing struggle between parliament and the president over who controls local government. On March 30, the Congress passed a resolution abolishing the institution of presidential representatives (*Rossiiskaia gazeta,* April 1, 1993, p. 3). The effect of this resolution was unclear, however. Since the representatives were not appointed by parliament, they did not feel obliged to obey this decision. Despite the nonbinding referendum on Yeltsin's popularity held in April 1993, the conflict over the issue of executive rule has continued and it is far from clear that the reformists will carry the day as they were able to do in the autumn of 1991 and again in the spring of 1992.

Deputies' Attitudes Toward Reform

It seems clear from the review presented so far that the horizontal struggle between executive and legislative authority is interwoven with a vertical conflict between central and local power (Hahn 1991). The center has ascribed to itself the mantle of reform and cast its opponents in the role of defenders of the old order using the soviets as cover. For their part, local deputies and their allies in the parliament warn of impending return to dictatorship if executive authority is not limited. Behind this maneuvering, however, remains Harold Lasswell's famous definition of politics as the process of deciding "who gets what, when and how" (Lasswell). In the context of today's Russian politics, will it be the old elite reincarnate or their "democratic" opposition who decide?

What is *not* clear from the foregoing is precisely what the attitudes toward reform of locally elected representatives really are. If we accept the characterization of the "reformists," deputies to the local soviets are, at best, ineffective meddlers in the affairs of proreform administrators, and, at worst, nomenklatura-dominated opponents of reform who would secretly like to return to the "good old days." Yet at face value such a characterization is hard to accept, if only because of the homogeneity of views it ascribes to the deputies. To test this view, we now return to the questions posed at the outset: What are the attitudes of local deputies toward reform and are there any significant differences in their views? The answers may tell us something not only about the political dynamics of Russian politics today, but help define some parameters for the future as well.

Hypotheses

Based on previous research, some of which has been cited above, and in light of the analysis offered above, the principal thesis of this chapter is that the portrayal of local soviet deputies as the center of resistance to reform needs to be reconsidered. In particular, we would expect that:

(1) there is support among soviet deputies in general for reforms aimed at the development of a market economy and a more democratic political system;

(2) support for such reforms will be greater among younger, better-educated, professionally employed, and male deputies holding office for the first time;

(3) support for such reforms will be greater among deputies to city soviets than among those in the oblasts;

(4) support for such reforms will vary among different regions of central Russia, depending on whether leadership changes took place in the wake of the failed coup.

Data

The data on which the following analysis is based come from a survey conducted of 1,280 oblast and city (oblast capital) deputies in five provinces in central Russia during the period of March–June, 1992.[15] Since the total possible number of deputies in the areas surveyed is 2,119, the average response rate was just over 60 percent. Breakdowns for each area are included in the descriptive information on each region that follows. The choice of regions to be surveyed was dictated partly by the availability of qualified personnel to collect the data. Within that constraint, however, it was decided to concentrate on deputies from regions contiguous to Yaroslavl, where the author has been conducting field research since February 1990. At the same time, in an effort to determine how much variation would be found in other parts of central Russia, two other oblasts were added—one predominantly industrial in the southern Volga region (Saratov), and one mostly agricultural oblast located in the black-earth region on the border with Ukraine (Belgorod).

The survey was conducted in the field by the Center for the Study of Public Opinion at Moscow State University using a questionnaire designed by the author in cooperation with Aleksandr Gasparishvili, the director for research at the Center. It was self-administered by the deputies under the guidance of trained local specialists affiliated with the Center. The questionnaire contained 171 items intended to elicit information about the activities of the deputies and the sources of influence on their decisions, including relations with constituents, with others holding office, and with the media. In addition, thirty agree/disagree questions measuring political attitudes were included, which replicated some of the items used in the "Values in Politics" study, the results of which were published in 1971, and which are part of a current study called "New Democracy and Local Governance."[16] Data were coded and processed by the Center in the summer of

1992 and made available to the author on diskette using an SPSS system file. What follows is a brief description of each region (in alphabetical order) used in the survey.[17]

The Regions

Belgorod

Belgorod Oblast is a comparatively small region (27,100 sq. km.) in the central black-earth zone on the border with Ukraine. The oblast capital is 695 kilometers. south of Moscow. Belgorod is primarily known for agriculture and food processing, but its population of 1,377,000 (40 percent rural) is also engaged in machine building, mining, and metal working. The population of the oblast capital is 286,000. The city soviet has 191 deputies, of whom 146 were surveyed in April 1992. The oblast soviet has 148 deputies, of whom 119 were surveyed. Belgorod has long held the reputation of being a bastion of "conservatism"; the province was represented by Egor Ligachev at the last USSR Congress of People's Deputies. Politics in the oblast continues to be dominated by the old elites. After the failed coup there were no major personnel shake-ups. The oblast administration has been headed since December by Viktor Berestovoi, the former chairman of the oblast soviet, and the immediate past second secretary of the obkom, the oblast committee of the Communist Party. Yeltsin did appoint a presidential representative to Belgorod, Nikolai Melent'ev, a former member of the CPSU who had joined the local democratic movement. However, reflecting the continuing conflict over presidential representatives being played out in the Kremlin in 1992–93, Melent'ev was declared persona non grata by the oblast soviet in February 1993. This fact and Berestovoi's continued tenure suggest that Yeltsin has been unable to undermine the local political establishment. It is worth noting, however, that despite continued "conservative" opposition to free market policies, 71 of the *city's* 183 commercial enterprises have been privatized.

Ivanovo

Ivanovo Oblast is also relatively small (23,900 sq. km.) and is located adjacent to Moscow Oblast in the forested Volga basin to the northeast. Its capital is 318 kilometers from Moscow. The oblast population of 1,318,000 (18 percent rural and 97 percent Russian) is engaged primarily in light industry (especially in textiles) and forestry, although some military-related industry is reported as well. More than 476,000 people live in the oblast capital. There are 190 deputies in the city soviet and 192 at the oblast level.

Of these, 70 and 52, respectively, were surveyed in May 1992. Politically, as in Belgorod, the coup did not precipitate any major personnel changes. The chair of the oblast soviet, Vladimir Tikhomirov, who had also been a member of the obkom, retained his post as chair after calling for a vote of confidence in the wake of the coup attempt. The vote apparently included Adol'f Laptev, chair of the oblast executive committee. At the city level, the chair of the soviet, S. Kruglov, was appointed head of administration by Yeltsin. There is also a presidential representative, V.I. Tolmachev, and it is unlikely that Kruglov would have been appointed without his support. Ivanovo, because of its dependence on Uzbek cotton, faces tough economic times. Thirty percent of the region was without heat in October 1992. As elsewhere, the introduction of free markets is seen as beneficial primarily to the local "mafia" and popular support is decidedly lukewarm, with 10 percent using these markets, and 65 percent supporting the government's efforts to control street trade.

Kostroma

Kostroma's profile is similar to Ivanovo's. It is larger in size, however (60,000 sq. kilometers), but smaller in population (797,000), of which 32 percent is rural. The oblast capital numbers 273,000 and is located on the Volga River 372 kilometers northeast of Moscow. Economically, Kostroma differs little from Ivanovo: light industry, textiles, and timber. There are 175 city soviet deputies (126 surveyed in May) and 164 at the oblast level (125 surveyed in April). The politics of Kostroma is less clear. Prior to the coup attempt the chair of the oblast soviet was Vladimir Toropov, formerly obkom first secretary. The chair of the oblispolkom was Valerii Arbuzov, also a member of the obkom. In the wake of the coup failure, however, Arbuzov has become oblast head of administration despite active opposition from a group of deputies known as "Narodnoe soglasie" (Civic Consensus) but, presumably, with the approval of Yeltsin's presidential representative, one Iurii Litvinov. The head of the city soviet remains V.I. Maklakov, Kostroma Oblast's KGB chief until his election in 1990. Despite the apparent continuity of control by old elites, there is some evidence of an active reformist minority favoring privatization in both soviets; of 170 commercial city properties, 32 were privatized in the first half of 1992.

Saratov

Saratov Oblast is the largest of those chosen for this study in both size (100,200 sq. km.) and population (2,628,000, of which 25 percent is rural).

Ninety percent of these are Russian, and proposals to repatriate Volga-German residents to the lands in Saratov from which they were evacuated in World War II are highly controversial. The oblast is located on the southern Russian steppe, and its capital city of nearly 1 million inhabitants is a major port on the Volga River located 858 kilometers from Moscow. It is an economically diverse region with food processing, gas and oil refining, and machine building among the leading industries. It is also home to a large aviation plant producing military aircraft since 1938. The oblast soviet has 295 deputies (106 surveyed in April); the city has 193 (146 were surveyed).

The political situation in Saratov is marked by conflict. There were some important leadership changes after the coup attempt. Most notably, Konstantin Murenin, the incumbent chair of the oblast soviet and previous obkom first secretary was forced to resign. N.S. Makarevich was elected in his place. However, Nikolai Grishin, incumbent chair of the oblispolkom, managed to avoid a similar fate and retained his position through the coup. Yeltsin moved quickly to appoint a presidential representative (V.G. Golovachev) and, within a few months, a new head of administration (Iurii Belykh). A classic division along the lines discussed earlier appears to have developed between a strongly reformist executive and a relatively "conservative" oblast soviet.[18] A recent survey published in *Saratovskie vesti* on September 5, 1992 (p. 2), showed scant support (17 percent) among the deputies for private ownership.

Yaroslavl

Yaroslavl Oblast is in the middle range in both size (36,400 sq. km.) and population (1,453,000; 19 percent rural). It is located north of Moscow Oblast and shares common borders with it and with Kostroma, Ivanovo, and Vologda. Yaroslavl is primarily industrial, with some food processing and timber. In the oblast capital set overlooking the Volga River, most of the 630,000 inhabitants are employed in factories producing engines, ships, petrochemicals, and synthetic rubber for tires. It, too, is overwhelmingly Russian (96 percent). There are 185 deputies in the city soviet, of whom 127 were surveyed in April and 192 at the oblast level (52 surveyed in May).

The politics of Yaroslavl is discussed earlier in this chapter and elsewhere in greater detail by the author.[19] In short, however, prior to August 19, 1991, the conflict between a city soviet in which reformists predominated and an oblast soviet controlled by the former party–state elites was evident. In the wake of the coup failure, Yeltsin moved to consolidate his hold over the executive branch by appointing a head of administration,

Anatolii Lisitsyn, to replace the discredited former chief of the ispolkom, Vladimir Kovalev. The rest of the leadership remained in place, including the oblast chair, Anatolii Veselov, despite his apparat credentials as former first secretary of the Pereslavl-Zalesski gorkom, or city committee. Some tension remains, however, between the soviets and the executive, but mostly on the oblast level. The presidential representative, Vladimir Varukhin, does not appear to play a major role except, perhaps, on appointments.

Methodology

To test the hypotheses stated earlier, variables were chosen from the survey data that would indicate the attitudes of deputies on matters related to political and economic reform. The basic approach was to create scales that would provide a summary measure of how respondents felt about a market economy and about democratic values. These summary measures could then be cross-tabulated by level of soviet (oblast vs. city) for all deputies to see if there were significant differences. The results would then be broken down separately for each of the five regions to see if any differences found for the deputies as a whole held up consistently in different parts of central Russia. In addition, individual items on each respondent's age, education, occupation, gender, and on whether the respondent had previously served as a deputy, would also be used to determine if there was significant variation that could be explained by demographic or other factors. The first step was to obtain a frequency distribution for all variables. Not only was this essential for creating scales, but it would show whether there was much variation among the deputies in support of free-market principles and democratic values.

To create the scales, factor analysis of thirty attitudinal variables was used to see if some variables clustered more than others. Those that did were then combined in a simple additive scale and tested for reliability using mean inter-item correlations and Cronbach's alpha. Scales used had to exceed a mean coefficient of inter-item correlation of 0.088, which is considered the minimum level acceptable at a significance level of 0.01 for a sample of 900 or more (Kuder and Richardson 1937). Some items that did not scale, but that seemed potentially revealing, were used independently.

In this way, five scales were developed to measure deputies' attitudes: two economic and three political. Of the two economic scales, one measured how the respondent felt about the accumulation of wealth. An "agree" response was unfavorable (e.g., "the scythe always cuts down the tallest blade first" mentality). The other economic scale tapped deputies' feelings about a free-market economy, only in this case an agree response indicated a positive evaluation.[20] The scales measuring political attitudes dealt with the deputies' feelings about popular participation in decision making, their support for the principle of a strong leader, and their assessment of the work of the Russian Federation's Supreme Soviet. All variables used in the analysis are listed in the Appendix to this chapter with a notation indicating which were used to construct scales.

Findings

Hypothesis 1: *There is support among soviet deputies in general for reforms aimed at the development of a market economy and a more democratic political system.*

The evidence presented in Table 9.1 does not sustain the view that the deputies to oblast and city soviets are broadly opposed to free-market reforms and democratic values. On the contrary, there is more support for them than one would expect, especially if one accepted at face value the portrayal of the soviets as the bastion of counterreformation. On economic issues, the deputies do not appear to share strongly the view often ascribed to Russian folk culture that no one should do better than their neighbors. Only one-third responded favorably to the statement that becoming wealthy was a bad idea. A similar pattern shows up also in their answers to individual item 2 (var. 134): 38 percent agreed that "if some are poor, the government should see to it that none should be rich." On the other economic attitude measured, support for a free-market economy is clearly apparent. Only 25 percent of the scaled response was unfavorable. Moreover, 79 percent of the deputies agreed that the private sector should be expanded (see item 3, var. 148).

On political issues the picture is less clear, but there is little in the data to sustain the view that the deputies would like to return to their authoritarian past. The balance of responses to our popular-participation scale was more favorable than not (40 percent–28 percent) and 71 percent of the deputies agreed on the importance of all citizens having an equal chance to influence their government (item 4, var. 128). There was also strong support for the emergence of a multiparty electoral system (item 1, var. 172). Another central democratic value is a preference for dispersed rather than concentrated power.

An argument often heard among Russian intellectuals, as well as from Moscow cabbies, is that what the Russian people want and need is an "iron hand" (Migranian). As noted earlier, even many observers sympathetic to

Table 9.1

Political and Economic Attitudes of Deputies to Oblast and City Soviets in Five Regions of Russia, 1992 (in percent; s = 1,280)

		Value	Percent (%)
A. Scales			
1. Accumulation of wealth	Unfavorable	1.	33
		2.	28
	Favorable	3.	39
	$\bar{X}$ = 2.056		
	Valid *n* = 1199		
2. Market economy	Favorable	1.	36
		2.	38
	Unfavorable	3.	25
	$\bar{X}$ = 1.916		
	Valid *n* = 1150		
3. Popular participation	Favorable	1.	28
		2.	32
	Unfavorable	3.	40
	$\bar{X}$ = 2.123		
	Valid *n* = 1165		
4. Strong leader	Favorable	1.	28
		2.	37
	Unfavorable	3.	35
	$\bar{X}$ = 2.067		
	Valid *n* = 1198		
5. Russian Supreme Soviet	Favorable	1.	35
		2.	22
	Unfavorable	3.	43
	$\bar{X}$ = 2.082		
	Valid *n* = 1155		
B. Selected Individual Variables			
1. (V. 172) Support for a multiparty system	Definitely	1.	39
	More Yes than No	2.	30
	More No than Yes	3.	22
	Difficult to Answer	4.	8
	Valid *n* = 1241		
2. (V. 134) If some are poor, none should be rich	Strongly Agree	1.	23
	Agree	2.	15
	Disagree	3.	27
	Strongly Disagree	4.	35
	$\bar{X}$ = 2.735		
	Valid *n* = 1213		

Table 9.1 *(continued)*		Value	Percent (%)
3. (V. 148) Increase private sector in business and industry	Strongly Agree	1.	44
	Agree	2.	35
	Disagree	3.	13
	Strongly Disagree	4.	7
	$\bar{X}$ = 1.987		
	Valid *n* = 1213		
4. (V. 128) Equal opportunity to influence government for all people	Strongly Agree	1.	44
	Agree	2.	27
	Disagree	3.	17
	Strongly Disagree	4.	12
	$\bar{X}$ = 1.987		
	Valid *n* = 1223		
5. (V. 132) Strong leaders able to do more for country than laws and debates	Strongly Agree	1.	19
	Agree	2.	26
	Disagree	3.	31
	Strongly Disagree	4.	24
	$\bar{X}$ = 2.602		
	Valid *n* = 1227		

Note: The full information for all items cited here, and that were used in forming the scales, may be found in the appendix.

the democratic movement are often in the forefront of those arguing for stronger central authority. This view does not appear to be widely shared by the deputies. Our scale measuring support for a strong leader shows more opposed than in favor, and when asked to agree that strong leaders are preferable to strong laws, 55 percent declined (item 5, var. 132). These findings may be interpreted to mean that deputies perceive strong authority as strengthening the center (read: Yeltsin and the reformists) and that they are opposed to that idea. However, the data do not permit us to rule out a genuine preference on their part for a greater dispersion or, if you will, balance of power.

Hypothesis 2: *Support for reforms will be greater among younger, better-educated, professionally employed, and male deputies holding office for the first time.*

Age.[21] There is evidence to suggest that there may be generational differences at work in explaining levels of support for reforms among the public, with younger people being more supportive than their elders (Bahry; Hahn 1991b). Is this also true of younger deputies? Analysis of the data from this survey suggests that there are clear differences on economic issues, but less so on issues related to democratic values. Younger deputies were far more likely to view the accumulation of wealth favorably (0.25); and were significantly more supportive of free-market values (0.12)[22]. For the scales on popular participation and assessments of the Russian parliament, no significant differences were found. This was also true for the item measuring support for a multiparty system. The one political issue on which there was a modest, but significant, difference was on support for a strong leader. The younger the deputy, the less favorably disposed.

Education.[23] Education is generally regarded as a strong predictor of differences in political attitudes and behavior in general (Milbrath and Goel) and in the former USSR (Bahry; Hahn 1991). Those with higher levels of education are expected to hold democratic values more strongly (Almond and Verba). For our sample of deputies, there is some evidence that education indeed has this effect. The differences between those with higher education and those without were modest but significant; higher education correlated with higher levels of support for popular participation (0.12) and for a free market (0.13). On other scaled issues no significant variation was found, but some individual items were revealing. Those with higher education strongly rejected the view that profit brings out the worst in people (–0.21) and supported the effectiveness of private enterprise (0.13). On political items, they clearly rejected the view that popular participation leads to unwanted conflict (–0.18) and that strong leaders can do more for the country than strong laws (–0.15). As with age, however, there was little difference in support for a multiparty system or in their assessment of the Russian parliament.

Gender. It can be hypothesized that, compared to Americans, Russian women are more likely to exhibit the political values and behavior of traditional cultures and that the gender gap is wider in Russian politics. The data from this survey suggest that this is indeed the case: the attitudes of women deputies *are* relatively more "conservative" on some questions related to economic and political liberalism. Although there were no significant differences on scales dealing with the accumulation of wealth, free-market values, or popular participation, women deputies were significantly more supportive of the idea of a strong leader (0.14). On individual items they were far less likely to support a multiparty system (0.20) and much less likely to look favorably on the need for a strong leader (0.21). Finally, on individual economic items they were significantly more willing to support limits on income (0.18) and to favor the idea that if some are poor, none should be wealthy.

Occupation.[24] Occupation is generally considered an important predictor of political attitudes (Milbrath and Goel). There may be additional reasons in the Russian context to expect that deputies with a professional occupational profile will hold views more supportive of reform. Leaders in other occupations, especially in government and management, were part of the nomenklatura and therefore subject to approval by the corresponding party secretary. One would expect them to hold more "conservative" views. As indicated in note 23, we have operationalized this variable to test for differences along these lines. The findings with respect to occupation are generally consistent with the findings for the other variables specified in this hypothesis, except gender. Those deputies coming from professionally related occupations score significantly lower on the "economic envy" scale (0.16) and are much more supportive of free-market values (0.19). They are much less likely to look favorably on the need for a strong leader (0.18) and are somewhat more favorably predisposed toward popular participation, though not significantly (0.07). There were no surprises among the individual items except one: those whom we labeled "officials" were more likely to agree that "all citizens should have an equal opportunity to influence government policies."

Incumbency. One of the questions asked in the survey was whether the deputies had held such office previously. As it turns out, having been an elected deputy before is a strong predictor of attitudes on reform. Correlation of incumbency with our scales showed incumbents to be far more opposed to the accumulation of wealth (–0.27), and to free-market principles (–0.25), and more in favor of a strong leader (0.15) than freshmen deputies (who, incidentally, make up 60 percent of those surveyed). On other political variables (do they favor popular participation or a multiparty system?) there was little difference, however. In retrospect, the findings presented here that incumbent deputies hold more "conservative" views make intuitive sense. Elections under the system that existed prior to 1990 were designed to ensure control by the local apparat over the formation of government. There was only one candidate for each seat, and nomination had been foreordained by the party organization (Friedgut). Freshmen deputies, on the other hand, had been the first elected in a competitive environment, one that was not wholly dependent on the party organization's good graces, and whose views they did not necessarily have to share.

Hypothesis 3: *Support for reforms will be greater among deputies to city soviets than among those in the oblasts.*

The basis for this hypothesis comes from a growing body of literature suggesting that deputies to city soviets are more open to reform than those at the oblast level. Joel Moses found this pattern to be characteristic in at least two of what he labeled "transitional provinces," Odessa and Kaliningrad (Moses, pp. 490–91). The implication, at least, was that such a relationship would be found elsewhere. Darrell Slider has referred to "the common pattern in the local elections [of 1990] of a conservative oblast soviet and a radical city soviet" (Slider 1991, p. 8). This author contrasted the reformist-dominated city soviet of Yaroslavl with that of the oblast soviet, where nomenklatura candidates hold a working majority with members of the old apparat. He suggested that a vertical struggle for power would result, and that what was true for Yaroslavl might be true elsewhere (Hahn 1991).

But, if there are such differences, why should they exist? The major difference between city and oblast soviets is that oblast soviets draw on constituencies outside the regional capital. Many of these seats are rural. In cities, and especially in provincial capitals, one might reasonably expect a better-educated, urbanized population to elect to the city soviet deputies more favorably inclined toward reform. If there is a pattern of the sort hypothesized here, it may indicate that there is an urban–rural cleavage in Russian politics that is a permanent feature of the Russian political landscape (Helf and Hahn).

Does the evidence from our survey offer support for this view? There are significant differences between deputies to oblast and city (oblast capital) soviets, many of which, but not all, are anticipated by our hypothesis. Using four of the variables discussed in hypothesis #3, it can be shown that there are some clear differences in the composition of the deputies: those elected to oblast soviets are considerably older, much more likely to have a higher education, and far more likely to have been deputies previously. Gender, however, does not vary significantly with the level of the soviet. Predictably, deputies to each level have strongly conflicting views (–0.44) on whether the oblast soviet has too much influence over the city soviet or not (see var. 166).

On issues of economic and political values, the differences on economic issues were the clearest, and they tend to support the hypothesis: city deputies are much more favorably disposed toward the accumulation of wealth (0.26) and toward a free market (0.16). Differences in political attitudes, however, were not significant, with one exception. On the one hand, deputies from oblast and city soviets showed little difference on the issue of a strong leader and on the question of a multiparty system. On the question of popular participation, however, oblast deputies were significantly *more* favorable than city deputies (0.13). A similar anomaly, it may be remembered, was found among those professionally employed, who liked the idea of a capitalist economy, but who were *less* favorably oriented toward popular participation. In short, what these data seem to suggest is that while city deputies may be more "free market" in their attitudes on the economy, they do not necessarily hold more democratic values. Yet are these findings consistent across different regions of central Russia? That is the question addressed by our fourth and final hypothesis.

Hypothesis 4: *Support for reforms will vary among different regions of central Russia, depending on whether leadership changes took place in the wake of the failed coup.*

There are two ways to examine the question of whether there is variation in the political and economic attitudes of deputies to the soviets across different regions of central Russia. The first is to use data from all deputies in each of the five regions and look at their mean scores on the various measures employed. These results are reported in Table 9.2. The second way is to see if there are consistent differences in attitude between oblast and city deputies *within* each region. We will follow this order in our presentation here.

In the first case, there *is* evidence of considerable regional variation for some of our variables. While the regions differ little in education and age, Belgorod clearly has a higher rate of incumbency; Yaroslavl has the lowest. Yaroslavl deputies are significantly more supportive of a multiparty system than those of Ivanovo or Belgorod. They also score lowest on the "economic envy" scale, and are second only to Saratov in supporting the idea of a free market. On democratic values, they rate highest in support for popular participation and lowest in their admiration for a strong leader, although generally speaking the variation on political attitudes is not as significant as it is for the economic ones.

If Yaroslavl deputies emerge as the most supportive overall of "reformist" values in our sample of regions, those in neighboring Ivanovo appear the most "conservative." Deputies there are not only the most opposed to a multiparty system, but also to the idea of people getting richer than their neighbors. In their relatively unfavorable view, they are second only to Kostroma, although they are closer to Yaroslavl in their discomfort with a strong leader. Kostroma, another neighbor of Yaroslavl, is antithetical in

Table 9.2

Reformist Economic and Political Attitudes of Deputies in Five Regions of Central Russia, 1992 (mean scores with ranks in parentheses)

Variable	Belgorod	Ivanovo	Kostroma	Saratov	Yaroslavl
1. Education (1.000 is high)	1.259	1.230	1.207	1.184	1.240
2. Age (1.000 is low)	2.507	2.828	2.637	2.751	2.635
3. Incumbency (1.000 = incumbent)	1.491	1.681	1.578	1.573	1.683
4. Multiparty system (1.000 = favorable)	2.624(4)	3.306(5)	2.263(2)	2.287(3)	1.806(1)
5. Accumulation of wealth (1.000 = unfavorable)	1.922(4)	1.820(5)	2.088(3)	2.085(2)	2.120(1)
6. Free market (1.000 = favorable)	2.049(5)	1.947(4)	1.932(3)	1.832(1)	1.918(2)
7. Popular participation (1.000 = favorable)	2.157(2)	2.119(4)	2.088(5)	2.125(3)	2.331(1)
8. Strong leader (1.000 = favorable)	2.066(3)	2.067(2)	2.013(5)	2.060(4)	2.095(1)
9. View of Russian Parliament (1.000 = positive)	2.091	2.120	2.058	1.960	2.187
Summary Score of Reformism (Based on ranking of each variable 4–8)	18	20	18	13	6

views on popular participation and on the desirability of a strong leader. To provide a summary score of the differences, points were assigned on the basis of rank for variables 4–8 used in Table 9.2. Yaroslavl was easily the most "reformist," followed by Saratov, with Kostroma, Belgorod, and Ivanovo bunched at the relatively more conservative end of the spectrum. Next we turn to differences *within* the regions between oblast and city deputies.

Belgorod. The findings for the Belgorod city and oblast deputies tend to follow the same pattern that was found for the deputies as a whole. Oblast deputies were significantly better educated (0.43) and were far more likely to have held office previously (0.48). There was little or no difference in composition with respect to age or gender. Oblast and city deputies clearly disagree in predictable ways on whether the oblast soviet has too much control over the city (–0.48). There are clearly conflicting views on economic issues with oblast deputies being much more critical of inequality of wealth (0.49) and much less supportive of free-market values (–0.44). As with the deputies as a whole, there was much less difference on political matters. They were more agreed than not on the popular participation scale and on the question of a multiparty system. The only area of modest disagreement (0.14) was on the question of a strong leader, with oblast deputies more apt to accept the idea that such leadership might be good for the country. Their evaluation of the Russian parliament was also somewhat more favorable with oblast deputies more likely to agree that the press and the public undervalued the work of that body.

Ivanovo. In some respects, the findings for Ivanovo are similar. Oblast deputies are much more likely to be better educated, older, and incumbents. Women, however, are proportionately better represented in the city soviet. City deputies are far more apt to feel that the oblast soviet has too much influence on what they do. Beyond this the findings are less clear, and even contradictory. We do not find the kind of strong differences on economic issues that is found for the deputies as a whole. There do appear to be differences on political values, however, with city deputies more favorably oriented toward popular participation as a scaled item (0.25) and on the question of a multiparty system. At the same time, city deputies also showed more support for the strong leader idea (0.14), though this may be a statistical quirk.[25] There also seems to be something of a populist sentiment among oblast deputies, who were much more favorable to the idea that all citizens should have an equal right to participate (var. 128, g = 0.35), and that leaders are obligated to fulfill the will of the community even if they disagree (var. 139, g = 0.30). On other political values, however, they were more "conservative" than city deputies.

Kostroma. In Kostroma we see a pattern similar to that of Ivanovo in terms of the composition of the soviets. Deputies at the oblast level are much more likely to have a higher education, to be incumbents, and to be male. They are also somewhat older than those in the city soviet and, as we have come to expect, they feel that the influence of the oblast soviet on the city is just fine. On political and economic views, there are not the clear divisions that are characteristic of Belgorod and of the deputies as a whole. At least on economic issues, there is a consistency of response, even if it is not strong. We found higher support for egalitarian economics and less for free-market values among oblast than among city deputies. Politically, there were no striking differences, but those that did exist were contradictory. Oblast deputies seemed a bit more comfortable with multiparty elections, but less so with popular participation. There was also a weak correlation favoring strong rulers.

Saratov. In Saratov, the differences between oblast and city deputies appear to be weaker than in the other regions that we have discussed so far, but what differences there are seem to follow the same pattern with minor exceptions. Oblast deputies are more likely to be older, male incumbents, but unlike in other regions, they are not better educated. On economic issues there is a weak correlation (0.15) between oblast deputies and egalitarianism, but there are no differences with city deputies on the question of a free market (Table 9.2 indicates greater support for a free market in Saratov than in the other regions). On politics, there are no apparent differences on the issues of a multiparty system or popular participation, but oblast deputies are more comfortable with the idea of an "iron hand" (0.23).

Yaroslavl. There are some powerful cleavages between city and oblast deputies in Yaroslavl on certain issues, but not on all, and in the case of politics, the directions appear contradictory. Oblast deputies are a bit better educated, but there are no significant differences in gender or age. They are, however, less likely to be incumbents, a reversal of the pattern found in the other regions. The deputies from the two soviets are widely divided over the question of whether the oblast soviet has too much influence (0.75), a confirmation of the vertical struggle for power noted in Yaroslavl by the author earlier. Economic differences of opinion are modest, though they are in the direction hypothesized, with city deputies more willing to allow inequalities in wealth and more in favor of a free market. Politically, however, there is an apparent contradiction: oblast deputies are much more in favor of a multiparty system, but at the same time are less well disposed toward public participation than are city deputies.

In summary, the findings presented here suggest that while there are significant differences in the attitudes of local deputies toward reform *among* the regions of central Russia examined here, the differences in deputy attitudes *within* each region do tend be fairly consistent. Taking the second of these findings first, similar differences between the attitudes of city and oblast deputies were found across each region: in general, city deputies were significantly more favorably oriented toward market reforms than oblast deputies, but not toward democratic values. There were also similarities in the different composition of the city and oblast soviets and in their views of the fairness of the jurisdictional balance of power between them.

In speculating on how to account for the differences *among* regions, it seems appropriate to recall former U.S. House Speaker "Tip" O'Neill's aphorism that "All politics is local." Some of the differences are probably due to economic conditions particular to the region. Ivanovo, for example, has been hard hit by the cotton shortage since Uzbekistan's independence; the defense industry played an important role in Saratov, so conversion is a major issue there. Belgorod, with its agricultural base, probably suffers less from food shortages and high food costs. One common thread that does seem to emerge, however, is political. The regions with the greatest support for reform, Yaroslavl and Saratov, are also those in which there had been some major personnel changes in the city or oblast leadership following the failed coup and in which there appears to be greater conflict between city and oblast deputies. Belgorod and Ivanovo, by contrast, exhibited more political continuity than change and were also least supportive of the reforms.

Conclusions

The central question that this chapter set out to explore was: What are the views of locally elected deputies in the Russian Federation on issues of economic and political reform? What makes the question salient is the portrayal, by the leadership of the Russian government, of local officials as the main source of opposition to the introduction of democracy in Russia, including the adoption of a market economy. It was argued in the first part of this chapter that the struggle for power between legislative and executive authority was, in reality, a vertical struggle for power between old elites and new ones. To bolster their case for stronger executive authority, Yeltsin and his allies have characterized those elected to the soviets as the forces of counterreformation. If this portrayal is accurate, then the growing success of national and local legislatures in asserting their authority would lead one to a pessimistic assessment of the chances for reform.

The findings presented in this chapter, however, offer little support for the view that deputies to city and oblast soviets in the central regions of Russia are broadly opposed to free-market reforms and to democratic values. On the contrary, there seems to be more support for them among the deputies than not. Beyond this general conclusion, there do appear to be some significant variations among the deputies in their *levels* of support, especially on issues of economic reform. Demographically, we found consistently higher support for free-market values among younger, better-educated, professionally employed deputies holding office for the first time. Education and gender proved to be the only significant predictors of deputies' political attitudes with the better-educated respondents favoring democratic values. Women deputies, however, were found to have significantly more "conservative" values on both issues.

In comparing the attitudes of deputies to the city (oblast capital) soviets with those at the oblast level, consistent differences on economic issues were also found, with city deputies more favorably disposed toward a free-market economy. Patterns for political questions were much less apparent, and sometimes contradictory. On the question of whether the oblast soviet had too strong an influence on the city, the difference was consistent and strong. In terms of composition, oblast deputies were more often older incumbents with a higher education, but gender distribution was not significantly different. Broadly speaking, these findings held up across the five regions studied, despite the fact that there was considerable variation *among* regions in their support for "reformist" views. One tentative conclusion that emerges from the analysis is that while city deputies may be more pro-market in their attitudes than those in the oblast soviets, they do not necessarily hold stronger democratic values.

In short, if there does appear to be a vertical struggle for power between the center and the periphery, the findings presented in this chapter suggest that the struggle is not over reform *per se* so much as it is over who will get to decide who gets what, when, and how. Why should older elites be opposed to democratic and free-market reforms if they can control their implementation for their own benefit? The differences we found between deputies at the city and oblast level on economic issues may reflect the fact that more of those at the oblast level are drawn from the ranks of the former managerial nomenklatura and see their control over the regional economy threatened. The differences may also be generational, with younger deputies hoping to use their leverage to replace the local managerial elite. All in all, there is some support here for the view that what is at stake is control over local resources (McAuley). Having abandoned (or lost) their base of power in the obkoms, the old elites are seeking a new one in the economy.[26] While that may be true, however, it does not make them forces of counter-reformation.

Appendix

Attitudinal Variables and Scales Used in This Analysis

A. *Variables* (survey question number)

1. (112) On the average, how many hours of contact do you have each month with enterprise leaders? (1) None; (2) 1 hour; (3) 2–5 hours; (4) 6–10 hours; (5) More than 10 hours.

2. (118) The Russian Supreme Soviet is gradually learning to operate more effectively. (1) Agree; (2) Disagree; (3) Difficult to answer.

3 .(119) The Russian Supreme Soviet's authority over the population has fallen during the past 12 months. (1) Agree; (2) Disagree; (3) Difficult to answer.

4 .(120) In most cases, the Russian Supreme Soviet makes correct decisions. (1) Agree; (2) Disagree; (3) Difficult to answer.

5 .(122) The press underestimates the positive role of the Russian Supreme Soviet. (1) Agree; (2) Disagree; (3) Difficult to answer.

6 .(123) The population underestimates the positive role of the Russian Supreme Soviet. (1) Agree; (2) Disagree; (3) Difficult to answer.

7. (124) The complexity of today's problems allows only the simplest questions to be exposed to the public's scrutiny. (1) Definitely agree; (2) Agree more than disagree; (3) Disagree more than agree; (4) Absolutely disagree.

8. (125) A high level of public participation in making decisions often leads to unwanted conflicts. (1) Definitely agree; (2) Agree more than disagree; (3) Disagree more than agree; (4) Absolutely disagree.

9. (128) All citizens should have equal opportunity to influence government policies. (1) Definitely agree; (2) Agree more than disagree; (3) Disagree more than agree; (4) Absolutely disagree.

10. (129) Talented and strong-willed leaders always achieve success in any undertaking. (1) Definitely agree; (2) Agree more than disagree; (3) Disagree more than agree; (4) Absolutely disagree.

11. (132) A few strong leaders might have been able to do more for their country than all laws and discussions. (1) Definitely agree; (2) Agree more than disagree; (3) Disagree more than agree; (4) Absolutely disagree.

12. (133) An upper limit should exist on earnings, so that no one accumulates more than anyone else. (1) Definitely agree; (2) Agree more than disagree; (3) Disagree more than agree; (4) Absolutely disagree.

13. (134) If others live in poverty, the government should react and make it so that no one can become wealthy. (1) Definitely agree; (2) Agree more than disagree; (3) Disagree more than agree; (4) Absolutely disagree.

14. (135) Wealthy people should pay more for societal needs than the poor should. (1) Definitely agree; (2) Agree more than disagree; (3) Disagree more than agree; (4) Absolutely disagree.

15. (137) There are situations when a leader should not divulge certain facts. (1) Definitely agree; (2) Agree more than disagree; (3) Disagree more than agree; (4) Absolutely disagree.

16. (139) A leader is obligated to execute the will of the community, even when he feels the people are mistaken. (1) Definitely agree; (2) Agree more than disagree; (3) Disagree more than agree; (4) Absolutely disagree.

17. (141) When resolving important problems, a leader should not pay attention to how the community feels about his position. (1) Definitely agree; (2) Agree more than disagree; (3) Disagree more than agree; (4) Absolutely disagree.

18. (145) A system based on profit brings out the worst in human nature. (1) Definitely agree; (2) Agree more than disagree; (3) Disagree more than agree; (4) Absolutely disagree.

19. (146) A system of private enterprise is effective enough. (1) Definitely agree; (2) Agree more than disagree; (3) Disagree more than agree; (4) Absolutely disagree.

20. (147) State regulation of business usually brings more damage than good. (1) Definitely agree; (2) Agree more than disagree; (3) Disagree more than agree; (4) Absolutely disagree.

21. (148) The share of the private sector in business and industry today should be increased. (1) Definitely agree; (2) Agree more than disagree; (3) Disagree more than agree; (4) Absolutely disagree.

22. (149) People accumulate wealth only at the expense of others. (1) Definitely agree; (2) Agree more than disagree; (3) Disagree more than agree; (4) Absolutely disagree.

23. (151) It is the government's responsibility to ensure that the rights of minorities are observed. (1) Definitely agree; (2) Agree more than disagree; (3) Disagree more than agree; (4) Absolutely disagree.

24. (166) On the city soviet the oblast soviet has, in your opinion: (1) Too strong an influence; (2) Such influence as is necessary; (3) Too weak an influence; (4) Too difficult to describe the influence.

25. (167) Were you previously an elected deputy? (1) Yes; (2) No.

26. (172) Do you support the institution of a multiparty electoral system, in which candidates participate in elections as representatives of parties and movements? (1) Yes, definitely; (2) More yes than no; (3) More no than yes; (4) Difficult to answer.

B. *Scales*

Mean Inter-Item Correlation (Cronbach's Alpha)

	Inter-Item correlation	Reliability coefficients
1. Accumulation of wealth vars. 133, 134, 135	0.321	0.61
2. Support for free market vars. 145(R), 146, 147, 148, 149(R)	0.272	0.65
3. Popular participation vars. 124, 125, 128(R)	0.205	0.44
4. Strong leader vars. 129, 132, 137, 141	0.114	0.33
5. Support for Supreme Soviet vars. 118, 119, 120, 122, 123	0.231	0.60

Note: Minimum acceptable correlation is 0.088 for 0.01 significance level for 900 or more cases (Kuder and Richardson 1937). Wherever an "R" is indicated, the direction of the variable was reversed.

Notes

The author would like to thank the Carnegie Corporation of New York for the financial support to conduct the field research on which this chapter is based, and the National Council for Soviet and East European Research for a grant that enabled him to take time from teaching to analyze the results of the research. Thanks also to Joel Moses, Gavin Helf, and Henry Hale for their help in providing information on the five regions used for analysis in this chapter and to my research assistant, Mya Anderson, for tracking down articles for me. Finally, my gratitude goes to Nurit Freedman of the Human Organization Sciences Institute at Villanova for her extraordinary efforts in providing the statistical tables I needed when I needed them. An abbreviated version of this chapter appeared in the journal *Post–Soviet Affairs* vol. 9, no. 2 (1993).

1. For more on the meeting in Cheboksary see *The Current Digest of the Post-Soviet Press* (hereafter *CDPSP*), vol. 44, no. 37, pp. 6–8. The reference to "legal separatism" is from the original speech.

2. There is a considerable body of literature on these important elections. See Hahn (1991a), Mann, Embree, Colton, and Kiernan, among others.

3. There are obvious problems with using terms like "conservative" and "liberal" in the context of contemporary Russian politics and they can be misleading especially if the point of reference is Western ideology. (Are deputies favoring a radical free market and a strong executive branch of "democrats"? In Russia, they are.) Moreover, it is not clear that the old elites oppose market reform, for example, as long as they can control it

for their own benefit. In defense of using the term, it must be said that Russians themselves regularly do so and seem to know exactly about whom they are talking.

In this chapter, the term "conservative," when used, will be narrowly construed to refer to those among the old elite who want to hold on to their power. Whether they are for or against market reform *per se* is one of the main questions that the present chapter seeks to explore.

4. *Izvestiia,* September 13, 1991, p. 3. Darrell Slider also makes this point (Slider 1992, p. 10).

5. The role of the presidential representatives is described by Valerii Makharadze in an interview with *Izvestiia* on September 13, 1991. He stated that they "have no right to interfere in administrative affairs," but could report violations of federal law and presidential decrees—actions that, however, could presumably result in efforts to remove offenders from office. The decree establishing the position was called "On Questions of the Activity of Executive Power in Russia" and was issued on August 24, 1991. *Izvestiia,* August 26, 1991, p. 3. Other articles dealing with this position appeared in *Izvestiia* of August 27 and 28 and suggested a more active role was being undertaken in some areas of the country.

Interestingly, the assertion of strong executive authority has had the general support of many intellectuals in varying degrees associated with pro-democratic sentiment. See, for example, the interview with Andranik Migranian in *Moskovskie novosti,* October 6, 1991, p. 9, and the opinions of former Moscow Mayor Gavriil Popov and of St. Petersburg Mayor Anatolii Sobchak (Thorsen 1992; Orttung 1992).

6. On legislation pertaining to city soviets (which come under the heading of *mestnoe samoupravlenie*), see "O mestnom samoupravlenii v RSFSR," adopted by the Russian parliament on July 6, 1991. The oblast soviets are to be governed according to the law of the Russian Federation "O kraevom, oblastnom Sovete narodnykh deputatov i kraevoi, oblastnoi administratsii," which was passed on March 5, 1992, but has yet to be implemented by President Yeltsin. The latter was published in *Rossiiskaia gazeta,* March 20, 1992. Articles 35–40 of this law are relevant to our discussion.

7. Initially, Yeltsin had requested the Russian parliament on October 16, 1991, to postpone elections for heads of administration on the grounds that they were expensive at a time when Russia was in crisis, and that they would result in friction between administrators and the elected soviets. His request was denied, prompting his chief legal advisor, Sergei Shakhrai, to threaten resignation as chair of the Joint Committee on Legislation. *Izvestiia,* October 19, 1991, p. 2. He renewed his request for postponement on October 29, 1991, at the same time asking for the right to form executive power at the local level (e.g., to control appointments of heads of administration) in order to exclude the "blocking of central decisions by local administrative organs." *Izvestiia,* October 30, 1991, p. 2. These powers were granted after four days of debate. As could be expected, they were met with resentment in many areas. See, for example, Viacheslav Shchepotkin's article in *Izvestiia,* November 5, 1991, p. 2.

8. The information on the personnel changes in the Yaroslavl oblast and city soviets comes from the minutes of meetings, which were made available to the author during his visits, and from interviews conducted with those involved and with other deputies in January and April 1992.

9. For a case study of the conflict between a reformist governor and a soviet dominated by former leaders of the local CPSU in Voronezh, see V. Novichikhina, "Bolsheviki namereny vernut'sia," *Narodnyi deputat,* no. 6 (1992), p. 32.

10. The *Izvestiia* article was published February 28, 1992, p. 7; the one in *Rossiiskaia gazeta* on March 4, 1992, p. 2. See also *Nezavisimaia gazeta,* February 22, 1992, p. 2. A description of continued nomenklatura control within the government of

Taganrog can be found in the account of a city deputy there, A. Nikolaenko, *"Vivat, nomenklatura?" Narodnyi deputat,* no. 5 (1992), pp. 42–44.

11. See the interview with Khasbulatov in *Narodnyi deputat,* no. 5 (1992), p. 12. See also the *New York Times,* October 25, 1992, p. 18. A good description of the battle over the law on the oblast soviets can be found in an interview with Georgii Zhukov, "Goneniia na sovety—put' k diktature," *Narodnyi deputat,* no. 9 (1992), pp. 33–39.

12. Yeltsin's speech to the Sixth Congress of the Russian Federation People's Deputies was reported in the *CDPSP,* vol. 44, no. 16. His comment on the moratorium can be found on p. 3.

13. See the interview with Zhukov in *Narodnyi deputat,* no. 9 (1992), p. 36.

14. The claim that presidential representatives and administrators are appointed and not elected is technically true, but overlooks the fact that many of the administrators hold elective office elsewhere, usually in the Russian parliament. Thus out of six krais, four of the presidential representatives and two heads of administration had been elected to the Russian or USSR Congress of People's Deputies. In the forty-nine oblasts, twenty-nine of the representatives and eighteen of the administrators had won such an election. (The data are from Gregory Embree in a communication to the author of January 4, 1993.)

15. In addition to the five sets of data for city and oblast deputies from Belgorod, Ivanovo, Kostroma, Saratov, and Yaroslavl, there are interviews with 179 deputies from the Vologda city soviet, which had originally been chosen for this study. The *oblast* deputies, however, refused to be surveyed due to political divisions among their ranks and a survey from Ivanovo was done instead. The data from the Vologda city deputies remain part of the base for analyzing the deputies as a whole, but not for the regions individually.

16. The original study was: The International Studies of Values in Politics, *Values and the Active Community* (New York: The Free Press, 1971), and was edited by an international team of specialists. The value scales appear in the appendix. Findings from the "New Democracy and Local Governance" project were reported at a conference held at the Kennan Institute for Advanced Russian Studies in Washington, DC, on November 5–7, 1992.

17. I am greatly indebted to Professor Joel Moses (Iowa State University) and to graduate students Henry Hale (Harvard) and Gavin Helf (Berkeley) for providing the information on which these profiles are based. The information comes from various sources, but primarily from the local press and from RFE/RL archives in Munich. I also made use of the *RSFSR Administrativno-territorial'noe delenie* for 1986, published by the Presidium of the RSFSR Supreme Soviet. The discussion of local politics in these regions represents my best guess as to what is going on locally, based on these collective sources, but are offered with the warning that I may be very wrong.

18. According to a report to me from Henry Hale, a graduate student from Harvard who is currently in Moscow, Belykh, head of administration, wrote an article in the oblast newspaper accusing Makarevich of instigating popular pressure against the administration to resist the Yeltsin–Gaidar reforms. *Saratovskie vesti,* September 19, 1992, p. 1.

19. The author has been conducting research on local government reforms in Russia, using Yaroslavl as a case study, since early 1990. Among other publications, see Jeffrey W. Hahn, "Local Politics and Political Power in Russia: The Case of Yaroslavl'," *Soviet Economy,* vol. 7, no. 4 (1991), pp. 322–41.

20. One would expect that those who scored high on what I came to call the "envy" scale (no one should have more than his neighbor) would also be less supportive of a free market. And, indeed, the correlation coefficient for the two scales was 0.44 (p < 0.000).

21. On the basis of a frequency distribution, our population was divided into four roughly equal age groups: 24–39 (25 percent); 40–44 (24 percent); 45–50 (21 percent); over 50 (31 percent). (Note: all percents are rounded off.) Although this division was based primarily on statistical considerations rather than an attempt to identify possible generational or cohort effects, those in the first two groups obviously had been born after World War II and were no older than seven when Stalin died.

22. The correlation coefficients reported here are gamma statistics and unless otherwise noted, they are statistically significant at a level of .01 or better.

23. Because most of our respondents reported having completed higher education (76 percent), the education variable was dichotomized into those who had it, and those who did not. This obviously is not the most desirable distribution, but there was little choice in the matter. Since a question that better discriminated for *type* of education might have produced sharper attitudinal differences, the results reported here may understate the importance of education as an explanatory variable.

24. The variable used here for profession is dichotomous (professional; official) and was created by regrouping the fourteen occupational variables originally employed into four categories: professional (including scientific, legal, medical, clergy, and educational personnel), working class, specialists in industry, and officials (including workers in the government, the trade unions, and other social organizations; enterprise directors; military, and police).

Unfortunately, the category "industrial specialist" was not broken down further and neither that variable nor "working class" lent itself to the kind of monotonic measurement of the sort that normally appears in Western sociology and that would facilitate cross-tabulation. Consequently, those two groups (about half the population) were left out of the analysis in the interest of trying to secure some basis for assessing whether professionals held distinct views.

25. The cells in the table seem to suggest that the correlation effect is due more to a noticeable lack of support among oblast deputies than widespread support among city deputies.

26. See Gavriil Popov on "nomenklatura privatization." Tat´iana Boikova, "Gavriil Popov—I Refuse to Play Cards," *Megapolis-Express*, July 8, 1992, p. 3. (*CDPSP*): vol. 44, no. 27, p. 29).

References

Almond, Gabriel, and Verba, Sidney (1963). *The Civic Culture.* Princeton, NJ: Princeton University Press.

Bahry, Donna (1987). "Politics, Generations, and Change in the USSR," in James R. Millar, ed., *Politics, Work and Daily Life in the USSR.* Cambridge: Cambridge University Press.

Colton, Timothy J. (1990). "The Politics of Democratization: The Moscow Election of 1990," *Soviet Economy,* vol. 6, no. 4 (October–December).

Embree, Gregory J. (1991). "RSFSR Election Results and Roll Call Votes," *Soviet Studies,* vol. 43.

Hahn, Jeffrey W. (1991a). "Local Politics and Political Power in Russia: The Case of Yaroslavl," *Soviet Economy,* vol. 7, no. 4 (October–December).

Hahn, Jeffrey W. (1991b). "Continuity and Change in Russian Political Culture," *British Journal of Political Science,* vol. 21, no. 4 (November).

Hahn, Jeffrey W. (1994). "How Democratic Are Local Russian Deputies?" In Carol Saivetz and Anthony Jones, eds., *In Search of Pluralism: Soviet and Post-Soviet Politics.* Boulder, CO: Westview Press.

Helf, Gavin, and Hahn, Jeffrey W. (1992). "Old Dogs and New Tricks: Party Elites in the Russian Regional Elections of 1990," *Slavic Review,* vol. 51, no. 3 (fall).

Kiernan, Brendan (1993). *The End of Soviet Politics.* Boulder, CO: Westview Press.

Kuder, G.F., and Richardson, M.W. (1937). "The Theory of Estimation of Test Reliability," *Psychometrics,* vol. 2.

Lasswell, Harold D. (1951). *Politics: Who Gets What, When, How.* New York: The Free Press.

McAuley, Mary (1992). "Politics, Economics, and Elite Realignment in Russia: A Regional Perspective," *Soviet Economy,* vol. 8, no. 1 (January–March).

Mann, Dawn (1990). "RSFSR Elections: The Congress of People's Deputies," *RFE/RL Report on the USSR,* April 13.

Migranian, Andranik (1989). "Dolgii put´ k evropeiskomu domu," *Novyi mir,* no. 7.

Milbrath, Lester W., and Goel, M.L. (1977). *Political Participation.* 2d ed., Latham, MD: University Press of America.

Moses, Joel (1992). "Soviet Provincial Politics in an Era of Transition and Revolution, 1989–91," *Soviet Studies,* vol. 44, no. 3.

Nemkov, M. (1992). "Mavr dolzhen uiti?" *Narodnyi deputat,* no. 7.

Reddaway, Peter (1992). Cited in the October "Seminar Report" from the Center for Naval Analysis, Alexandria, Virginia.

Slider, Darrell (1991). "Political Reform and Republic/Local Government," paper presented to the Annual Meeting of the American Association for the Advancement of Slavic Studies, Miami, Florida, on November 24.

Slider, Darrell (1992). "The CIS: Republican Leaders Confront Local Opposition," *RFE/RL Research Reports,* March 6.

Teague, Elizabeth, and Hanson, Philip (1992). "Nikolai Travkin Attempts Painless Economic Reform," *RFE/RL Research Reports,* vol. 1, no. 38 (September 25).

10

Federalism, Discord, and Accommodation

Intergovernmental Relations
in Post-Soviet Russia

Darrell Slider

The purpose of this chapter is to examine the changing relationship between the Russian national government and provincial authorities. One of the legacies of the communist period was a complicated patchwork of administrative units within the union republics that became independent states with the collapse of the Soviet Union. Nowhere was the assortment of administrative entities as varied as in Russia. There existed a total of 86 administrative units higher than the city and district level, including 16 autonomous republics (autonomous soviet socialist republics, or ASSRs, based on ethnic groups), 6 krais (mostly large, sparsely populated territories), 49 oblasts (the most widespread unit), 5 autonomous oblasts (ethnic units within krais), and 10 autonomous okrugs (lower-level ethnic units within oblasts and krais). In addition, Moscow and St. Petersburg had a special status virtually equal to that of oblasts. Thus, by early 1993, with the breakup of the Chechen-Ingush ASSR into the separate Chechen and Ingush republics, there were 89 administrative units in the Russian Federation.

Often there was no good reason for the different status given different types of regions or autonomous areas in the Soviet period. Many were larger and had more people than some of the fifteen union republics, which had the highest status within the Soviet Union. It was also the case that, as with union republics, the boundaries of these administrative units were often drawn capriciously (if not maliciously) and contained within themselves the seeds of future conflict.

Relationships among this array of administrative entities in the communist period could best be characterized as one of unitary subordination to the

Soviet national government. The Russian Republic was formally designated a federation (the RSFSR, or Russian Soviet Federated Socialist Republic) but the Russian government, at least until after the 1990 elections, was mostly a hollow shell. Real policy in Russia's provinces was determined by government and party officials at the national level who interacted directly with provincial and city officials. Russia did not even have its own republic-level Communist Party until 1990, and while there were Russian government institutions and an RSFSR Supreme Soviet in the communist period, they were even less significant than the limited communist-era parliaments in the other fourteen union republics.

Elections to provincial parliaments or soviets took place in 1990. Many of the newly elected soviets of autonomous republics within Russia followed the example of the Baltic republics and began to pursue greater independence from Russian authorities, including at a minimum the right to control their own economic resources. In the late summer and fall of 1990, a succession of provinces within the Russian Federation began to adopt declarations of sovereignty or independence. Among the first, in August 1990, was the parliament of the Karelian Autonomous Republic, which declared sovereignty while acknowledging that it would agree to delegate some of its rights to Russia and the USSR.[1] Komi followed suit that same month with a declaration of sovereignty, and it claimed a status equal to that of Russia itself—the Komi Soviet Socialist Republic.[2] The Mari Autonomous Republic adopted a draft law on sovereignty in August that was formally adopted in October. At the same time, the name of the republic was changed to Mari El.[3] Tatarstan also adopted a declaration of sovereignty at the end of August, without any mention of membership in the Russian Federation.[4] In September 1990 the Udmurt Autonomous Republic declared itself the sovereign Udmurt Republic within a "renewed" Russian Federation.[5] In October 1990 the Buriat Supreme Soviet changed the status of the republic from an autonomous republic to the Buriat Soviet Socialist Republic, while acknowledging that it was still part of the RSFSR.[6] At the end of November 1990 the Chechen-Ingush Republic was proclaimed, taking the place of the autonomous republic.[7] In January 1991 Kabardino-Balkaria also declared itself a soviet socialist republic and asserted that it would decide all questions of state policy "excluding those which it voluntarily, on the basis of agreements, cedes to the USSR and the RSFSR."[8]

At the time of these declarations, of course, the Soviet Union still existed, and Gorbachev and other leaders sought the support of the so-called "autonomies" in their effort to preserve the powers of the central Soviet leadership and prevent the breakup of the Union. Meanwhile, Yeltsin and other republic leaders, were adopting the same types of resolutions against the central Soviet leadership. The Soviet leadership's implicit threat was that the autonomous units would be admitted to a newly formed union as full members, not as part of the union republics, which could result in the breakup of Russia and other multiethnic republics.

The conflicts over power during the Soviet period and afterward were intensified by divisions along ideological lines. Most parliaments in the autonomous republics were heavily dominated by communists who looked with disfavor on Yeltsin's confrontational approach toward central Soviet authority and the Communist Party of the Soviet Union. In part this reflected the more conservative political atmosphere in the autonomous republics, which were far removed from glasnost and other political reforms introduced by Gorbachev.

In some cases there was also an ethnic dimension to the conflicts that emerged between republic and provincial authorities, though less than one would expect. Autonomous republics were initially set up on the basis of traditional homelands for non-Russian ethnic groups. The results of years of Soviet development and in-migration, however, often changed substantially the ethnic mix of these homelands. Of the sixteen autonomous republics in the Russian Federation, only in seven did the titular nationality make up the largest ethnic group of the population in 1989. (Dagestan, with the lowest percentage of Russians, is the only one of the autonomous republics not designated for a specific ethnic group or groups.) Russians were the most numerous ethnic group in eight of the autonomous republics (see Table 10.1).

The Russian government recognized the special nature of most ethnic-based units within Russia and gave autonomous soviet socialist republics the status of "republics within the Russian federation." By January 1993, 21 entities had achieved this status; there remained 6 krais, 49 oblasts, 1 autonomous oblast, and 10 autonomous okrugs. Of the 21 republics within the federation, 17 (separate Chechen and Ingush republics were formed on the basis of Chechen-Ingushetia) had previously been autonomous republics. Of the four republics that were elevated in status, all had been autonomous oblasts (Gornyi Altai from Altai Krai, Karachai-Cherkess from Stavropol Krai, Khakassia from Krasnoiarsk Krai, and Adygei from Krasnodar Krai). In November 1990 an assembly of deputies from soviets at various levels in the Karachai Autonomous Oblast—which lies within Stavropol Krai—declared the region a "soviet socialist republic" within the RSFSR.[9] Khakassia, an autonomous oblast within Krasnoiarsk Krai became a sovereign republic in July 1991.

There were numerous attempts by autonomous okrugs, which are ethnically based administrative units located within larger entities, to declare

Table 10.1

The Ethnic Mix of the Russian Autonomous Republics, as a Percentage of Each Republic's Population, 1989

Republics	Titular Groups	Russians
Dagestan ASSR	na	9
Avarts	27	
Dargints	16	
Komiks	13	
Lezgin	11	
Chuvash ASSR	68	27
Chechen-Ingush ASSR	67	22
incl:		
Chechen	55	
Ingush	12	
Tuva ASSR	64	32
Kabardino-Balkar ASSR	57	32
incl:		
Kabards	48	
Balkars	9	
North Ossetian ASSR	53	30
Tatar ASSR	48	43
Kalmyk ASSR	45	38
Mari ASSR	43	48
Mordovian ASSR	33	61
Yakut ASSR	33	50
Udmurt ASSR	31	59
Buriat ASSR	24	70
Komi ASSR	23	58
Bashkir ASSR	22	39
Karelian ASSR	10	74

Source: 1989 USSR census data.

themselves republics within the federation. .In none of the following cases was the declaration of republic status ratified by the Russian parliament. In September 1990 the Chukotka Autonomous Okrug (within Magadan Oblast) appealed to the USSR Supreme Soviet for recognition as a sovereign republic.[10] In October 1990 the soviet of the Koriak Autonomous Okrug (within Kamchatka Oblast) declared itself an autonomous soviet republic within the RSFSR. This decision was in part a response to a resolution adopted by the Kamchatka Oblast Soviet to shift to a market economy, which ignored the existence of the Koriak region as an entity, even though it contained half the industry and two-thirds of the territory of the Kamchatka Peninsula.[11] In November 1990 the Nenetsk Autonomous Okrug Soviet (within Arkhangelsk Oblast) declared itself a sovereign republic.[12] Similarly, the Yamalo-Nenets Okrug, administratively subordinate to Tiumen Oblast, declared itself a sovereign republic within Russia. As with the others, this decision was protested by the oblast soviet.[13]

Unlike earlier distinctions in administrative nomenclature, the status of republic within the Russian Federation was clearly separate from the status of other units. As is shown below, substantially greater autonomy was granted to these units by Yeltsin and the Russian parliament. In the period before the breakup of the Soviet Union, Yeltsin advocated an approach toward Russia's component parts that differed completely with Gorbachev's attacks on "separatists." In a speech in Kazan, capital of Tatarstan, in September 1990 Yeltsin challenged autonomous regions to take "as much independence as you can handle," a statement he reaffirmed in March 1991.[14]

Breakaway Republics

This pledge by Yeltsin and subsequent policies failed to satisfy many republic leaders. Various regions within the Russian Federation attempted to leave and become completely independent. The two cases that were of the greatest importance were Chechnia and Tatarstan, which were sometimes joined by Bashkortostan (formerly the Bashkir ASSR), and Sakha (formerly Yakutia). When a new Federation Treaty was signed in March 1992 (see below), the leaders of Chechnia and Tatarstan refused to give their approval. Tatarstan, Bashkortostan, and Sakha sought to coordinate their strategy in dealing with Moscow. In August 1992, for example, leaders of the three republics issued a joint statement that threatened "further steps to increase our sovereignty" in a dispute with the federal government over budgets and taxation.[15] Together with the Republic of Bashkortostan, Tatarstan and Sakha sought to establish their relations with Moscow on the basis of separate bilateral treaties. Of the four republics, only Chechnia is located on Russia's borders; both Tatarstan and Bashkortostan are entirely surrounded by Russian territory, a fact that serves as a natural limit to complete autonomy. Sakha's border also does not give it direct access to the outside world except through Russian territory.

The autonomous republic of Chechen-Ingushetia in the North Caucasus presented the first and most serious challenge to the territorial integrity of the Russian Federation. At the time of the August 1991 coup, the local government—like others, still mostly communist—supported the coup leaders. The Chechen national movement, which had been staging round-the-clock demonstrations on the main square of the capital, Grozny, took advantage of the defeat of the Moscow coup to stage its own coup against the local government. Military units under control of the nationalists seized the local radio and television stations and blocked access to government buildings. Jokhar Dudaev, a former Soviet air force officer who had been chairman of the Chechen All-National Congress since its formation in November 1990, became the de facto ruler of the republic, and its Supreme Soviet agreed to disband. Soon thereafter, political figures from the center, including the chairman of the Russian parliament, Ruslan Khasbulatov (himself an ethnic Chechen) and Vice President Aleksandr Rutskoi, came to Grozny, met with Dudaev and the former Communist leadership, and sought to put in power a thirty-two-man Provisional Higher Council with over half of its members coming from the old soviet. This effort failed, and in October 1991 the Chechen All-National Congress organized new parliamentary and presidential elections.[16] As expected, Dudaev was elected president, although Russian and Ingush voters largely boycotted the election. The Russian Supreme Soviet then declared the election invalid. The new republic parliament soon declared the region independent and proclaimed the creation of the Republic of Chechnia.

In November 1991, at Rutskoi's urging, Yeltsin imposed a state of emergency in the region and authorized the sending of troops to restore central control. The first attempt by Russian authorities to use the military to bring order to a breakaway region ended badly. Dudaev's forces surrounded the Russian expeditionary force on their arrival at the airport and quickly disarmed them.

As a result of these developments, Russia lost effective control over Chechnia. Dudaev formally created his own army, subordinate to him rather than to parliament.[17] Chechen deputies to the Russian parliament were ordered to return home in early 1992. Dudaev rejected Moscow's choice to head the local successor to the KGB. Dudaev also attempted to conduct his own independent foreign policy, though he had no success in overcoming the reluctance of foreign governments to recognize Chechen independence. The Chechen government maintained subsidies for basic consumer needs and fuel out of its own funds, with the result that, at the end of 1992, Chechnia had the lowest prices for bread and gasoline in the former RSFSR (Chechnia produces and refines its own oil). Russian economic and financial authorities in 1992 attempted to establish a "blockade" of Chechnia, which included cutting off air transportation to the republic, but Dudaev was able to reach separate trade agreements with several Russian provinces, including Stavropol, Krasnodar, Rostov, Volgograd, and Astrakhan. The Chechen Republic's budget for 1993 was worked out completely independently of Russia and on the basis of zero allocations from the central budget. Naturally, Chechnia did not intend to collect Russian taxes or contribute to the budget of the Russian Federation.[18] Russian authorities set up customs posts on the border between Stravopol Krai and Chechnia in January 1993.[19]

In early 1993, negotiations between representatives of the Russian government and parliament and Chechen parliamentary authorities resulted in agreements on economic ties and other issues of mutual concern. The Russian side hoped to reach an accommodation that would keep Chechnia within the federation. The approach of the Chechen delegation, which did not have Dudaev's full support, was to seek a treaty that would recognize Chechnia as an equal of Russia. The Chechen delegation also raised the possibility of separate membership of Chechnia in the Commonwealth of Independent States.[20] In a conciliatory step, Russia announced in March 1993 that it would resume paying pensions to citizens of Chechnia.[21] During the constitutional deliberations during the summer of 1993, however, participants commonly referred to the "eighty-eight subjects of the federation," all but formally acknowledging the secession of Chechnia.

Events in Tatarstan also threatened to end that republic's affiliation with the Russian Federation. The Tatars, who claim to be descendants of the Mongols who invaded and ruled Russia in the thirteenth and fourteenth centuries, had a long history of competing with Russians for influence in the Middle Volga region.[22] Ethnically, Tatars comprised 48 percent, and Russians 43 percent, of the population of Tatarstan in 1989. The republic is economically important, producing 26 percent of Russia's oil and enjoying a well-developed industrial base. In the Soviet system, however, oil production and most industrial enterprises were under direct central control. Several times under Soviet rule the Tatars unsuccessfully sought union republic status in an effort to gain greater autonomy.[23]

Mintimer Shaimiev, who was the first secretary of Tatarstan's Communist Party until 1990, became chairman of the parliament and in June 1991 was elected president with 74 percent of the vote. He adopted an increasingly nationalist position, particularly on the rights of Tatarstan to control its natural resources and industry. In March 1992, Shaimiev pushed for a referendum that would determine voters' attitudes toward Tatar sovereignty and relations with the Russian Federation "on the basis of a treaty between equals." On March 13, 1992 the Russian Constitutional Court declared the wording of the referendum unconstitutional since it amounted to a unilateral secession from the Federation. Nevertheless, on March 21 the referendum took place, at a time when in Moscow the new federation treaty was being finalized. Of those voting (the turnout rate was 81.6 percent), 61.4 percent voted for sovereignty, while 37.2 percent voted against. The negative vote was highest in the republic's major cities, where a majority opposed the measure.[24] In November 1992, the Tatarstan parliament adopted a new constitution that described the republic's relation to Russia as an "associa-tion." However, it retained dual Russian and Tatar citizenship for all citi-zens and gave equal status to the Russian and Tatar languages.[25]

Having learned the limits of military force in Chechnia, the Russian authorities did not seek a confrontation, but entered into negotiations with the Tatar leadership. Yeltsin held several rounds of face-to-face talks with Shaimiev in order to prepare a treaty governing relations. Shaimiev insisted that Russia treat Tatarstan as an equal, though he indicated that the republic was willing to delegate some responsibilities to the federation. Tatarstan continued to use the ruble as its currency, and in practice it still depended on Russia economically and for most of its contacts with the outside world. Defense factories in Tatarstan continued to receive supplies and credits from Moscow.[26] The Russian government also allowed Tatarstan to keep the proceeds of its oil sales. In addition to winning these concessions, Tatarstan established its own policies in many areas—it retained rationing and price subsidies for basic consumer goods, continued to pay agricultural subsidies, continued to play a major role in enterprise decision making, and established its own procedures for privatizing state enterprises.[27]

Tatarstan's achievements stimulated other republics to seek similar con-cessions from Moscow, though they did not go so far as to declare them-selves independent. Bashkortostan, another oil-rich republic that borders Tatarstan, stressed control over its economic resources. Led by the chair-man of the Supreme Soviet, Murtaza Rakhimov (formerly director of an oil refinery), Bashkortostan sought special economic status that would equal that of Tatarstan.[28] At the time of the Russian referendum of April 25, 1993 the Bashkortostan Supreme Soviet added an extra question on whether the republic should have economic independence and a separate treaty with Russia "on the basis of the Federation Treaty." Thanks to this ambiguous formulation, the question was passed overwhelmingly and was used by local authorities to justify ignoring decrees from Moscow.[29]

The far-eastern republic of Yakutia, renamed Sakha in 1990, was also rich in natural resources. The great geographical distance from Moscow made it easier for Yakutia and other provinces in Siberia to exercise their autonomy from the center, both in the Soviet and the post-Soviet period. Nevertheless, Yakutia considered itself exploited by past relationships with Moscow. Yakutia was the source of most of the Soviet Union's diamonds and much of its gold, but central agencies had effective control over mining operations, while Yakutia received almost none of the profits. Mikhail Nikolaev, an ethnic Yakut who was previously chairman of the Yakut Su-preme Soviet, was elected president in December 1991. Negotiations with Russia led to agreements by the end of 1992 on dividing federal property and tax receipts. Yakutia also won the right to sell 20 percent of its diamond output on its own. Partly as a result, average wages were three times higher (and social benefits four times higher) than in the rest of Russia, and the Yakut president indicated at the time that virtually all of the republic's complaints had been resolved.[30] By mid-1993 Yakutia was threatening to introduce its own gold-backed currency if disputes over federal budget subsidies were not resolved.[31]

The Federation Treaty

Efforts to negotiate a new federation treaty for Russia began well before the breakup of the Soviet Union. It was only after Russia became independent, however, that these efforts came to fruition. In the negotiations, the most intransigent parties were the republics within the federation. The central authorities, fearing a breakup of the country, gave in to their demands for special concessions—they were described as "sovereign republics within the Russian Federation." The government was not willing to make the same concessions to krais, oblasts, or autonomous okrugs. As a result, the Federation Treaty that emerged was actually a set of three agreements, with the republics within the federation receiving the greatest independence. Separate agreements offering more limited powers were negotiated with the krais and oblasts and with the autonomous oblasts and okrugs.[32] On March 13, 1992, delegates from nineteen of the twenty-one "republics within the federation" initialed the draft of their part of the new treaty. The formal signing ceremony took place on March 31, 1992, and leaders of the republics within the federation were joined by more than sixty representatives of Russian oblasts and krais and the cities of Moscow and St. Petersburg.[33] The Russian Congress of People's Deputies overwhelmingly approved the new treaty at its sixth session in April 1992.

Not all republics were ready to accept the Federation Treaty in its final form. Chechnia boycotted the talks entirely. The Tatar delegation participated in the process only as observers and refused to initial the document. Unexpectedly, the delegations from Bashkortostan, Karelia, and Yakutia (Sakha) signed the treaty. It turned out that all three republics had successfully insisted on separate negotiations that required Yeltsin and Khasbulatov to sign bilateral addenda to the treaty that gave them rights beyond those given in the Federation Treaty. In the case of Bashkortostan, for example, the addendum ceded full rights to the republic over its natural resources, independence in international and foreign economic ties, tax policy, legal matters, and other areas. According to the text of this document, any role for the Russian Federation in those fields would have to be approved explicitly by Bashkortostan.[34] The special status attained by these republics was later used by other republics as well as krais and oblasts to justify additional demands on the center.

The Federation Treaty set out to distinguish between the functions of the national ("federal") government and those of the republics and other units comprising the Russian Federation. One of the ways that the treaty elevated the status of republics within the federation was to give them the right, along with the Russian parliament at the national level, to pass legislation (*zakonodatel'stvo*). Krais and oblasts could adopt binding resolutions (*resheniia* or *postanovleniia*), but not laws. While republics within the federation could write their own constitutions, krais and oblasts could adopt only charters (*ustavy*).[35] In several oblasts and krais, for example in Tomsk and Arkhangelsk, leaders of local soviets used the process of adopting charters in an attempt to expand their autonomy—essentially to bring their provinces the same status enjoyed by republics.[36] This effort was aided by the fact that drafts of a new Russian constitution were still being debated at the national level as provinces acted to define their own role.[37] Clearly, some of the provisions of local constitutions and charters would not be in accord with any new Russian constitution. Perhaps the most glaring example of this was the constitution of the Republic of Tuva, which included an explicit provision allowing the republic to secede from the Russian Federation.[38]

One key provision of the treaty with republics within the federation was that the republics were to be consulted in advance on legislation and other government policies. This greatly complicated the process of policy making in Moscow, and provisions of the agreement requiring consultation were frequently ignored in practice. After repeated protests from the republics, then-Prime Minister Yegor Gaidar issued instructions in November 1992 that all central government agencies send to the republics for comments and suggestions all draft laws not exclusively within the competence of federal authorities.[39] In May 1993 the Council of Ministers adopted a resolution ordering ten major ministries and state committees to form advisory councils made up of top ministry officials and representatives of executive authorities from subjects of the federation. Another resolution put forward "proposals" on the activities of territorial organs of the federal ministries, which set out general principles for cooperation and for gaining the consent of regional officials.[40] One week later Yeltsin issued a directive requiring the Council of Ministers to implement the Federation Treaty by making their normative acts consistent with its provisions.[41] As for the Congress of People's Deputies and the Supreme Soviet, in the first year of operation of the Federation Treaty not one piece of legislation followed its dictate to specify the relative competence of federal and republic-level authorities.[42]

In areas where Moscow-based ministries claimed primary jurisdiction, there were a number of conflicts with provincial—particularly republic—officials. Ministries, of course, were reluctant to share or delegate power, and in many areas the treaty provided for joint responsibility without defining roles more precisely. The Ministry of the Economy, for example, sought to control developments in the provinces without taking into account decisions by local leaders and soviets. In March 1993 complaints from the provinces led Yeltsin to remove the head of this ministry, Andrei Nechaev.[43] In the area of diplomacy, primary responsibility lay clearly with Moscow and the Ministry of Foreign Affairs. Yet there were also cases when republic leaders, attempting to advance the interests of their regions, contradicted Russian policies in direct dealings with foreign leaders.[44] Many republic leaders sought at least a consultative role with the Ministry of Foreign Affairs in determining Russian policy.[45]

In the area of tax and budgetary policy, the Federation Treaty increased the proportion of locally raised taxes and local budgets in financing many activities. Given the vast economic differences that characterize the regions of Russia, tax and budgetary policy is a potentially significant tool for redistributing wealth. At the same time, excessive centralization in the past led local governments to demand control over their own budgets and taxation policy. In the late 1980s as much as 90 percent of a region's tax receipts had been turned over to higher authorities, mostly the central Soviet government.[46]

Bashkortostan, Tatarstan, and Sakha advocated the elimination of federal taxes, to be replaced instead by a voluntary sharing of locally raised taxes—a "one-channel system" of taxation. Meanwhile, in 1992 all three of these republics (along with Chechnia and Ingushetia) virtually stopped paying taxes to federal authorities. Political leverage appeared to be the major factor determining how much of locally collected taxes a region turned over to the center. For the remaining republics, krais, oblasts, and okrugs the share of taxes collected that went to the federal budget ranged from 29 percent to 72 percent.[47] The effect of these policies was to limit the ability of the central Russian government to reduce economic inequalities in the regions. Reinforcing this inequality were the new local taxes levied by regional authorities to supplement funds allocated from the center.[48]

The question of how monies turned over to the center were reallocated to the provinces was also politically charged. In a November 1992 budget document, the target for the share of federal tax receipts to be turned over to the regions was set at 40 percent. Yeltsin, in a speech to heads of administration, indicated the percentage should be increased to fifty.[49] Central finance authorities repeatedly sought to reduce the provinces' share of these receipts, however. Republic, krai, and oblast leaders complained in early 1993, for example, that the announced ratio of expenditures between the federal budget and the budgets of members of the federation was unfairly set at 67.2 percent to 32.8 percent; they asked that the ratio for each be changed to 50 percent.[50]

Actual budgetary allocations from the Russian federal government and parliament to particular regions were heavily influenced by lobbying from the regions. Most successful in this effort in 1992 was the Republic of Komi, which reportedly received the equivalent of almost 91,000 rubles per capita; Bashkortostan, at the other extreme, got only 320 rubles per capita from central funds (but, as indicated above, Bakhkortostan had virtually stopped paying taxes to the center).[51] As a rule, autonomous oblasts and okrugs were most successful in obtaining federal funds, and republics within the federation did significantly better than krais and oblasts.[52] Table 10.2 (see pages 252–3) provides data on the relative share of taxes paid and budget allocations received by each republic, krai, and oblast. ("Budget allocations" includes various subsidies, credits, and other benefits.) All republics, with the exception of Udmurtia, Chuvashia, and Mordovia received net subsidies, while oblasts, with the exception of Irkutsk and Kamchatka, contributed more in taxes than they received in benefits.

At the same time, local leaders and soviets adopted their own sets of priorities in the use of budgetary resources. In Ulianovsk, for example, the oblast head of administration Iurii Goriachev, devoted a large share of the oblast's funds to subsidize food prices and to continue the use of ration coupons for the distribution of basic consumer goods. As a result, Ulianovsk had the lowest food prices in Russia at the beginning of 1993.[53] Goriachev achieved a degree of popularity that was virtually unmatched among provincial leaders. Other heads of administration used their resources to provide subsidies to public transportation—including the total elimination of fares in some regions. As the foregoing indicates, price deregulation also varied considerably from region to region in 1992, the first year of Yeltsin's reforms. In the middle of the year local governments of about two-thirds of Russia's provinces continued to regulate prices; by the last quarter it was reported that thirty of eighty-nine Russian regions maintained price controls.[54]

In the area of banking and money supply, the deepening economic crisis in Moscow forced republics and oblasts to adopt their own policies in this area. Republics within the federation created their own national banks and set their own policies on issuing credits. The shortage—particularly in Siberia

—of cash needed to pay wages led the Republic of Yakutia (Sakha) to issue its own legal tender worth millions of rubles. Officials in Kemerovo Oblast resorted to the use of lottery tickets as a cash substitute. Krasnoiarsk Krai printed its own "internal accounting unit" that resembled the U.S. dollar and would circulate alongside the ruble.[55]

Regional leaders sometimes sought to adopt restrictions on trade, particularly on the shipment of goods outside their provinces. In Voronezh, for example, A. Kovalev, the popular local governor, issued a series of directives that required enterprises and entrepreneurs to obtain local governmental approval for the export of thirty-five goods. This was in violation of Yeltsin's directives prohibiting restraints on free trade and free enterprise. Kovalev argued that his measures were necessary to prevent the avoidance of taxes and to reduce "speculation."[56]

The Federation Treaty was ambiguous on the relative rights of provinces to engage in foreign-trade operations on their own.[57] Moscow-based trade officials threatened to remove provincial representatives from future Russian trade missions abroad, after some had negotiated separate deals for their regions.[58] Many republics and subregions sought special foreign trade advantages, including the designation of a free-trade zone. Among those most active in seeking this status were the Komi Republic, Karelia (on the Finnish border), Sakhalin Island, Kaliningrad, and St. Petersburg. Several regions convinced Yeltsin to grant them beneficial terms in keeping foreign currency earned by enterprises on their territory. Karelia was allowed to keep 75 percent, for example.[59] Tiumen Oblast, the site of three-fourths of Russia's oil and natural gas reserves, won the right to sell freely 20 percent of its total output.[60]

Presidential Representatives

Yeltsin set out to create a hierarchical structure of executive authority that would extend from himself, the president, to leaders at the provincial and local level. To this end, Yeltsin made two major changes in the administrative system in late 1991. First, he created a system of presidential representatives to the provinces. The second change was to create a system of executive authority in the oblasts and krais, heads of administration, also having direct links to the center.

Presidential representatives were introduced in August 1991, just before the failed coup attempt that month. The chief purpose of these officials was to monitor implementation of presidential decrees and instructions. Since the president's powers in this sphere were limited to "the period of economic reform," a permanent legal basis for the institution was lacking.[61] In

Table 10.2

Payment of Federal Taxes and Receipt of Federal Budget Allocations per Capita for Russian Regions (thousands of rubles per person; data for 1992)

	Taxes Paid Per Capita	Budget Allocations Per Capita	Net Subsidy/ Contribution
Tiumen Krai	74.8	9.8	65.0
Samara Oblast	28.8	2.8	26.0
Yaroslavl Oblast	24.0	3.2	20.8
Moscow (city)	25.8	5.4	20.4
Nizhnii Novgorod Oblast	22.0	3.9	18.1
Perm Oblast	20.8	2.9	17.9
Magadan Oblast	29.1	12.5	16.6
Belgorod Oblast	18.9	2.4	16.5
Ulianovsk Oblast	18.8	3.9	14.9
Kursk Oblast	17.0	2.2	14.8
St. Petersburg (city)	17.7	3.1	14.6
Vladimir Oblast	17.3	2.8	14.5
Sverdlovsk Oblast	20.2	6.3	13.9
Smolensk Oblast	15.6	1.9	13.7
Riazan Oblast	15.5	2.0	13.5
Khabarovsk Krai	18.2	5.1	13.1
Murmansk Oblast	26.9	14.2	12.7
Ivanovo Oblast	15.1	2.6	12.5
Tambov Oblast	14.6	2.1	12.5
Moscow Oblast	15.5	3.4	12.1
Kaliningrad Oblast	13.8	1.9	11.9
Primor'e Krai	16.8	5.2	11.6
Tomsk Oblast	16.3	4.9	11.4
Volgograd Oblast	15.9	5.0	10.9
Tula Oblast	14.5	3.9	10.6
Vologda Oblast	14.6	4.0	10.6
Rostov Oblast	12.5	2.1	10.4
Lipetsk Oblast	16.5	6.1	10.4
Krasnodar Krai	12.6	2.4	10.2
Voronezh Oblast	12.9	2.8	10.1
Orel Oblast	13.8	3.8	10.0
Tver Oblast	13.4	3.5	9.9
Saratov Oblast	12.3	2.7	9.6
Kirov Oblast	12.3	2.8	9.5
Arkhangelsk Oblast	13.2	3.7	9.5
Novosibirsk Oblast	12.1	2.8	9.3
Krasnoiarsk Krai	20.3	11.0	9.3

Table 10.2 *(Continued)*

	Taxes Paid Per Capita	Budget Allocations Per Capita	Net Subsidy/ Contribution
Orenburg Oblast	15.1	6.0	9.1
Omsk Oblast	13.7	4.6	9.1
Udmurtia Rep.	12.1	3.8	8.3
Briansk Oblast	11.6	3.2	8.4
Stavropol Krai	10.3	2.2	8.1
Kostroma Oblast	13.6	5.8	7.8
Sakhalin Oblast	16.9	9.3	7.6
Cheliabinsk Oblast	23.7	16.6	7.1
Kaluga Oblast	10.4	3.5	6.9
Novgorod Oblast	12.7	6.0	6.7
Penza Oblast	9.7	3.4	6.3
Kurgan Oblast	10.9	5.1	5.8
Kemerovo Oblast	21.1	15.4	5.7
Altai Krai	9.6	4.7	4.9
Chuvash Republic	9.8	5.3	4.5
Astrakhan Oblast	8.3	4.9	3.4
Pskov Oblast	9.5	6.3	3.2
Leningrad Oblast	11.0	8.1	2.9
Amur Oblast	10.8	9.7	1.1
Mordovia Republic	8.7	7.8	0.9
Chita Oblast	7.0	6.7	0.3
Bashkortostan Republic	0.03	0.3	−0.3
Chechen/Ingush Republic	0.04	0.7	−0.7
Kabardino-Balkar Republic	4.7	5.4	−0.7
Mari El Republic	7.3	8.3	−1.0
Sakha (Yakutia) Republic	1.0	3.0	−2.0
Kamchatka Oblast	13.8	16.2	−2.4
Buriat Republic	7.7	10.9	−3.2
Karelia Republic	10.8	15.6	−4.8
Kalmykia Republic	5.4	12.2	−6.8
Irkutsk Oblast	17.3	26.4	−9.1
Dagestan Republic	2.0	12.1	−10.1
Tatarstan Republic	0.03	10.3	−10.3
Tuva Republic	2.7	16.1	−13.4
North Ossetia Republic	5.5	63.2	−57.7
Komi Republic	31.3	90.2	−58.9

Source: Calculated from data presented by Leonid Smirniagin in *Segodnia,* June 25, 1993.

the words of the decree creating the institution, the representatives were named in order to "coordinate the activities of organs of executive authority of the RSFSR, krais, and oblasts." By November 1991 Yeltsin had appointed sixty-two representatives.

The presidential representatives were placed under the supervision of another presidential appointee, Valerii Makharadze, who had recently been named the Russian Chief State Inspector and who had been the reformist chairman of the Volgograd Oblast Soviet.[62] In March 1992 Makharadze was promoted to the post of deputy chairman of the Russian government, where he continued to oversee regional issues. Another highly visible radical deputy, Iurii Boldyrev, replaced Makharadze as Head of the Control Administration.[63] (Makharadze was removed as vice premier in December 1992, with the change in leadership of the government from Gaidar to Chernomyrdin.) After September 1993 the head of the presidential office overseeing the regions was Nikolai Medvedev. Medvedev had previously headed a similar department in the apparatus of the Supreme Soviet.[64]

Of 68 presidential representatives named by the end of 1991, 42 were either deputies to the Russian Congress of People's Deputies or former USSR people's deputies, and about 15 were deputies in oblast or city soviets. Almost all were from the Democratic Russia reform faction.[65] Despite the clear democratic-reformist character of most of the appointments, presidential representatives were prohibited from retaining membership in any party or political movement. This paralleled Yeltsin's decision to remain outside of party politics after he resigned his membership in the Communist Party. Nevertheless, the common political orientation of the presidential representatives was designed to facilitate Yeltsin's goal of introducing political and economic reforms.

Conflicts between governors and presidential representatives took place in many regions. In the case on Voronezh discussed above, for example, restraints on trade introduced by the head of administration, A. Kovalev, led to constant disputes with the president's representative in the oblast. Yeltsin's representative convinced the Russian chief state inspector to annul Kovalev's orders.[66] In Vologda, the president's representative uncovered officials illegally holding positions in commercial structures, which set him on a collision course with the oblast's head of administration.[67]

Conflicts often arose between presidential representatives and regional soviets. In February 1993, for example, the Belgorod Oblast Soviet became so incensed at investigations of its financial operations by the presidential representative that it declared him persona non grata in the oblast, attempted to cut his funding, and ordered the local police to block access to his office.[68]

Further controversy over the role of the personal representatives was caused by changes in the institution introduced by Yeltsin in early 1993. In February 1993 Yeltsin reorganized his personal staff and executive agencies. One decree expanded the authority of his representatives in the regions, giving them in particular the right to "coordinate the activity of territorial services of federal bodies of executive authority" in their region, to take part in the work of these agencies, and also the right "to appoint and relieve of [their] duties the leaders of territorial services of federal bodies of executive authority."[69] According to the newly appointed deputy head of Yeltsin's administration, Viacheslav Volkov, who was assigned to monitor the president's representatives, their new task was to shift from monitoring performance to a more activist role—the representatives were to help implement Yeltsin's decrees and directives.[70] Volkov was previously coordinator of the Democratic Russia faction within the Russian parliament and a leading "radical."[71]

Yeltsin signed a decree in March 1993 abolishing the post of chief state inspector and removing Boldyrev from the post.[72] Boldyrev complained that he had been the victim of a purge of the president's staff organized by "radical-democrats" who were unsatisfied with his "depoliticized" approach toward investigations of provincial leaders. Boldyrev stated, for example, that of the four heads of administration removed under his tenure, three had been supporters of Yeltsin.[73]

Even before the February–March 1993 changes, the post of presidential representative in the krais and oblasts was resented by the local soviets and provincial leaders. These groups were heavily represented in the body of deputies to the Russian Congress of People's Deputies, and the Congress and Supreme Soviet repeatedly attempted to curtail the powers of presidential representatives.[74] In February 1993, parliamentary chairman Ruslan Khasbulatov urged local soviets to drive out the president's representatives by cutting off their salaries and by depriving them of official vehicles and office space.[75] In March 1993, in the midst of a confrontation between Yeltsin and the parliament, the Congress passed a resolution that abolished presidential representatives as an institution. The parliament contended that Yeltsin had violated the principle of separation of powers by claiming supervisory and administrative functions for his representatives in the provinces.[76] Yeltsin's response was to ignore the parliament's actions, as he had in the past.

To reflect the difference in status between republics and other administrative entities within the federation, Yeltsin created a dual system of "permanent representatives" of the president in the republics and representatives of the republics to the president. It was clear that the status and power of presidential representatives in the republics within the federation were sub-stantially reduced from that enjoyed by presidential representatives at the krai or oblast level. According to the September 1991 presidential directives on the respective institutions, the republic representatives could participate in the work of republic supreme soviets or councils of ministers only with the permission of these bodies. If republic soviets or governments adopted provisions in conflict with Russian law, the representatives in the republics could only make "proposals" to correct the problem; in oblasts, krais, and other provinces, presidential representatives could force the local organs of state administration to reconsider their actions. Unlike representatives in the provinces, republic representatives were not assigned explicitly to monitor compliance with central governmental policy.[77]

Heads of Administration and Republic Leaders

The second major administrative change made by Yeltsin was the creation of a new executive post, "head of administration" (*glava administratsii*), at the krai and oblast level—a post that was soon informally called "governor" (*gubernator*). In cities the head of administration was usually referred to as the mayor (*mer*). These officials replaced the communist-era *ispolkomy,* or executive committees, of the corresponding soviets. The post of head of administration was introduced in a new law on local government adopted in July 1991. These officials were supposed to be popularly elected, and elec-tions were initially scheduled for December 1991.[78] In November, however, in light of Russia's deepening economic crisis, Yeltsin proposed that the elections be postponed for one year, and he was given the right to name local leaders.[79] On November 25, 1991 Yeltsin signed a decree "On the Appointment of Heads of Administration." The precise rights of the heads of administration were left unclear, just as the rights of the president of the Russian Federation were ambiguous.

In the wake of the August 1991 coup, Yeltsin initially sought to use nominations to the post of head of administration to make fundamental changes in the political map of Russia's regions, including that of the re-publics within the federation. He followed this approach in several oblasts and krais, initially removing conservatives in Nizhnii Novgorod, Ulianovsk, Cheliabinsk, Khabarovsk, and Krasnodar. In each of these cases the oblast soviet sought to have Yeltsin's choice removed and replaced by the current head of the oblast soviet.[80] In the face of this opposition and impending paralysis of local government, Yeltsin backed down on several of his early appointments and agreed that new appointments would be subject to ap-proval by the oblast soviets and by members of the RSFSR parliament from that territory.[81] Thereafter, most of the appointments simply redesignated the current chairmen of soviets as heads of administration.

As a result, the background of heads of administration contrasted greatly with that of representatives of the president in the regions, who were often drawn from the ranks of the "democrats." Most of those appointed heads of administration had been *nomenklatura* officials—managers of factories or farms and former top officials of the Communist Party at the regional level. These differences in background and outlook were behind a number of the conflicts that arose between holders of the two posts. Heads of administration complained vociferously about Yeltsin's February 1993 decree giving presidential representatives in the regions the right to oversee and coordinate the work of federal agencies at the regional level. In general, they argued, the institution of presidential representatives in the provinces was unnecessary.[82]

Despite the fact that heads of administration were approved by oblast or krai soviets, conflicts frequently emerged between these two branches of power. Oblast soviets in Orel and Lipetsk passed votes of "no confidence" in their heads of administration in January 1993. In Lipetsk, there was a bitter struggle between head of administration Gennadii Kuptsov, formerly a professor at the local technical institute, and the oblast soviet. Kuptsov accused the soviet of being controlled by the "underground CPSU oblast committee," while the soviet accused Kuptsov of ignoring its decisions. Each party ultimately filed lawsuits against the other in the local courts.[83]

Elections, held at the initiative of oblast soviets, were first held for a number of heads of administration in April 1993 in Smolensk, Cheliabinsk, Amur, Penza, Orel, and Briansk oblasts and in Krasnoiarsk Krai. Specialists on elections from the Yeltsin camp alleged extensive fraud in Briansk, Amur, and Orel.[84] In most cases, elections resulted in victories by former communists. In Cheliabinsk Oblast, elections were held in an attempt by the oblast soviet to replace Yeltsin's appointee as head of administration, Vadim Solov'ev, with the head of the oblast soviet, Petr Sumin. Sumin won, but his victory was not recognized by Yeltsin (who had ordered the elections canceled) nor by the oblast courts. For months, both "governors" claimed the office and tried to exercise its powers.[85] In Orel Oblast, Nikolai Iudin, the candidate favored by Yeltsin, was also defeated in elections by former Communist Party Central Committee Secretary Egor Stroev. Yeltsin responded by appointing Iudin his presidential representative in Orel.[86]

Heads of administration were not created in the republics within the federation, in deference to their special status as recognized in the Federation Treaty. Instead, republic leaders held either the post of president (several of whom were elected through popular elections in December 1991) or were chairmen of republic supreme soviets.

The non-implementation of central directives by local authorities was an issue that was at the heart of federal–local relations. In August 1992 Yeltsin issued a decree establishing a "Statute on Disciplinary Responsibility of Heads of Administration."[87] This directive extended to all levels of administration and gave Yeltsin broad powers to issue warnings and to fire administrators for not fulfilling his directives or the laws passed by the Russian parliament. A major role in this process was to be played by the president's representatives in the localities, who were to monitor the activities of local senior officials and make recommendations to the president on their dismissal. While on the one hand, this directive represented a threat to regional leaders, it also gave them greater control over heads of administration in subordinate administrative units down to the level of the rural district. An important limitation on this power, however, was that Yeltsin reserved to himself the right to go over the heads of oblast governors and control the mayors of the oblast capitals. Mayors, in turn, were given the power to remove heads of administration in urban districts (or boroughs) within their city. Given the political differences that frequently arose between city and oblast chief executives, this marked an important line of defense for reformers at the city level. One month later, in September 1992, Yeltsin relented on the issue of subordination of mayors of oblast capitals and gave power of control to heads of krais and oblasts.[88] After a delay of two months, in mid-November 1992, the Statute on Disciplinary Responsibility was changed to give oblast and krai leaders the right to fire heads of administration in the capitals, while it left the president's local representative with the power to recommend such dismissals.[89] In March 1993 Yeltsin issued another decree "On the Responsibility of Officials of Executive Authority in the Russian Federation," which assigned the prime minister, the head of the presidential administration, heads of the republics, and other provincial authorities to conduct an immediate review of the implementation of government policy. Yeltsin warned all executive officials that they would be held personally accountable for the nonimplementation of his policies.[90]

In practice, however, Yeltsin was surprisingly tolerant of governors who undermined his policies. Of forty heads of administration whose work was audited by Iurii Boldyrev, the Chief state inspector until March 1993, only four were removed from office. According to Boldyrev, a number of investigations, including one of the mayor of Moscow, were halted at Yeltsin's behest.[91] Yeltsin used his power to fire regional leaders sparingly, to the dismay of some supporters of reform at the local level.[92] Newly appointed oblast governors were removed in Voronezh and Pskov, not because they resisted reforms but because they were caught misusing their powers. In Voronezh, V. Kalashnikov and his deputy were accused of improperly allocating automobiles that had been sent to the region to sell to farmers who sold their output to the state. Kalashnikov was removed at Yeltsin's orders in March 1992.[93] In May 1992 Yeltsin removed A. Dobrikov as chief of the Pskov Oblast for corruption in allowing uncontrolled exports of fuel and other items to the Baltic republics.[94] In Krasnodar Krai, the head of administration, V. Diakonov, a reformer, was removed in November 1992 after it was discovered that he had employed his relatives in key posts in a fund for supporting entrepreneurship in the region. This followed months of impasse between Diakonov and the conservative krai soviet.[95] In January 1993 Yeltsin approved the "voluntary" resignation of Arkadii Veprev, a well-known director of a model state farm, from the post of head of administration for Krasnoiarsk Krai. Veprev had lost the support of the krai soviet, the democratic movement, and local elites for failing to devise an economic program for the region and for inadequate lobbying efforts on the krai's behalf in Moscow.[96]

Provincial Leaders and National Politics

In the old communist system, national leaders in the Communist Party built and expanded their power base by solidifying relations with provincial party leaders. Obviously the political system had gone through enormous changes in the period from 1989 to 1992: legislatures replaced the Communist Party as the most important policy-making bodies, the Soviet Union ceased to exist, and the CPSU was abolished. Nevertheless, the mutual dependence of national and local leaders remained an important characteristic of the political system. In a move that paralleled past practices, Yeltsin and other national leaders courted regional leaders and got involved in local power struggles in an effort to build a base of support. At meetings with regional chiefs (see below) Yeltsin most often adopted a conciliatory approach toward local leaders. Yeltsin attempted to balance the need to implement his policies at the local level with the effort to gain their support against the Congress of People's Deputies at the national level. Given his lack of influence over the Congress, Yeltsin could not afford to alienate provincial leaders. At the same time, Yeltsin found natural allies among those leaders of republics and heads of administration who were engaged in a struggle with the chairmen of the oblast soviet that paralleled Yeltsin's fight with Ruslan Khasbulatov, chairman of the Russian Supreme Soviet.

Often the conflicts between province executive and legislative branches arose over the issue of implementing Yeltsin's reforms. In Cheliabinsk, in preface to the elections mentioned above, there was open warfare between the head of administration, Vadim Solov'ev (former first secretary of the city Communist Party), and the chairman of the oblast soviet, Petr Sumin (former second secretary of the oblast Communist Party committee). Solov'ev began introducing rapid market-based reforms, including privatization, freeing prices, and conversion of military factories. Sumin sought to retain social guarantees, price subsidies, and credits for military industrial enterprises. In June 1992 the oblast soviet unilaterally declared that it would retain a larger share of taxes collected in the oblast. Solov'ev countered by announcing that the local government would "not implement any populist decisions, no matter who adopted them, if they are illegal." In response, Sumin appealed for support directly to local enterprises and the trade unions.[97] Meanwhile, Yeltsin continued to recognize Solov'ev as the legitimate head of administration.

Mordovia was the only republic within the Russian federation to elect an openly reformist president, Vasilii Gusliannikov, of the Democratic Russia movement. The conservative Supreme Soviet was headed by Gusliannikov's former opponent in the elections, Nikolai Biriukov. Over half the deputies were former party officials or enterprise/farm managers. After a protracted struggle to control policy making, the republic soviet voted in April 1993 to abolish the post of president entirely.[98] Yeltsin protested the decision as unconstitutional and considered Gusliannikov to be the legal president of Mordovia.

Both Yeltsin and his rivals understood that policy goals would be implemented only with the support or cooperation of regional officials. At the same time, regional leaders used this dependence in their attempts to extract greater autonomy in their decision making at the local level. It is clear that many actually sought some form of confederation rather than a federal relationship with Moscow, and they hoped to incorporate this into the new Russian constitution. All parties in these maneuvers set about to create new types of institutions that would give them an added advantage in the struggle for power.

During 1992 and early 1993, institutional structures arose that provided a setting for interactions between provincial leaders and central authorities. Meetings between virtually the entire complement of local government and soviet leaders and Russian national authorities were at first organized by the Supreme Soviet. The first of these meetings was held in mid-December 1991, and later sessions took place in Krasnodar in May 1992 and in Cheboksary (capital of the Chuvash Republic) in September 1992. Assemblies of regional leaders were also held at which national leaders spoke.[99] By mid-1992, conflicts between the president and the speaker of the parliament, Ruslan Khasbulatov, came to dominate these proceedings. Yeltsin had considerable support among heads of administration. Khasbulatov naturally found allies in the leaders of the soviets at the republic, oblast, and local level, and sought to place himself at the top of a hierarchy of soviets that would dominate the executive or government at each level.[100] Khasbulatov organized several conferences with leaders of local soviets in an attempt to coordinate their activities, and he created a Department for Federative and Interethnic Relations within the Supreme Soviet apparatus for the same purpose.[101]

Yeltsin was even more active than Khasbulatov in strengthening his relations with provincial elites. The first group of provincial heads of administrations was apparently formed at the initiative of the local leaders themselves, during a recess of a session of the Congress of People's Deputies in April 1992. It was created as an advisory body and called an Assembly (*Sobranie*). Elected as chairman was Moscow oblast head administrator Anatolii Tiazhlov. Chief executives from Yaroslavl, Nizhnii Novgorod, Leningrad, and Sverdlovsk oblasts formed the board of the group.[102] In August 1992 another effort was made to form a "union of leaders of territorial organs of executive power" for the purpose of coordinating economic reforms and "to thwart any attempts to restore the administrative-command system."[103] In November 1992 the group was given new status with the formation and legal registration of the Russian Union of Governors (*Soiuz gubernatorov Rossii*). With Yeltsin's aide Valerii Makharadze presiding, Tiazhlov was again selected chairman, and Valerii Fadeev, governor of Smolensk Oblast, became deputy chairman. The union included heads of administration of fifty-three oblasts and krais. Among the powers granted the new union was the right of legislative initiative.[104] In subsequent months, however, little information was publicized about the union's activities.

In October 1992 Yeltsin initiated the creation of a Council of Heads of Republics (*Sovet glav respublik*) as a consultative body directly under his administration. The political importance of this group to Yeltsin quickly gave it a status beyond that of "consultation." Yeltsin designated himself chairman of the council, and Iurii Skokov, then secretary of the Security Council, was named to head the council's staff. The stated purpose of this organ was to work out a mechanism for implementing the Federation Treaty. In fact, Yeltsin indicated at the first meeting that it was his desire "to give the republics greater independence and rights than they have today or are provided in the Federation Treaty."[105]

In March 1993 another new structure was created under the Russian president to provide input from the remaining regional leaders. Called the Council of Heads of Administration (*Sovet glav administratsii*), the new body was composed of heads of administration at the level of krais, oblasts, autonomous oblasts, autonomous okrugs, and the mayors of Moscow and St. Petersburg. The new body was meant to parallel the Council of Heads of Republics. Designated as members of the Council of Heads of Administration were the prime minister, the secretary of the Security Council, and the chairman of the State Committee on Nationality Policy. The Council, which was to meet no less than once every two months, was, like the Council of Heads of Republics, chaired by the president and was supposed to facilitate the incorporation of regional perspectives in policy making. Heads of administration were, in effect, brought directly into national government. When the Council of Ministers met in February 1993, there were places in the hall for heads of administration from the oblasts and krais.[106]

Regional leaders, including heads of both soviets and executive authority, sought even greater status in national political life. At the Congress of People's Deputies in March 1993 they circulated a proposal to create a new institution, the Federation Council (*Sovet Federatsii*), to break the deadlock in national-level politics. Local leaders from the government and soviet of Nizhnii Novgorod, a notably innovative region, were the initiators of the proposal, and it was endorsed by representatives of seventy-three regions (of a possible total of eighty-nine). The draft was also supported by Yeltsin, Khasbulatov, and Valerii Zorkin, chairman of the Constitutional Court. In essence, the Federation Council, to be made up of leaders of local governments and soviets, would act as the upper chamber of a new parliament. The council would have to approve constitutional amendments, border changes, referendum proposals, and pre-term elections for president or parliament, and would meet once each month.[107] The Congress voted to reject the proposal, but it subsequently was included in the various drafts of the new Russian constitution. Significant opposition to the proposal came from republics within the federation; ten out of seventeen refused to endorse it. Republics feared that they would lose the special status that they enjoyed under the current constitution and the Federation Treaty.[108]

The drafting and discussion of a new constitution also served to increase the role of regional authorities in national politics. In June 1993 Yeltsin invited each subject of the federation to send four representatives to the Constitutional Assembly he created—two specialists and the leaders of the legislative and executive branches. One of the major working groups of the assembly, chaired by Sergei Shakhrai, head of the State Committee on

Federation Affairs (see below), was made up entirely of representatives of the regions. Debates and arguments at the conference demonstrated clearly the differing perspectives of republics, on the one hand, and oblasts and krais on the other.[109]

It was in this context that the idea of the Federation Council surfaced again in August 1993. Boris Yeltsin proposed this new "organ of power" at a meeting of heads of republics and regions in an effort to increase his leverage over the Supreme Soviet and to break the deadlock over the new constitution. The proposal was adopted in principle, but the regional leaders added the condition that it would act only as a "consultative-advisory organ." As the proposal was later fleshed out, the Federation Council would meet at least once every three months and would be chaired by the president.[110] In the constitution approved by popular referendum in December 1993, the Federation Council became an elected "Senate" with two representatives from each region.

Yeltsin sought to increase his impact on regional politics by making a number of changes in his personal staff. As part of the administrative reorganization of February 1993, a new office was created within the presidency to deal with both regional policies and relations with the Russian Supreme Soviet. The head of this agency and three deputies would deal with relations between the president and the administrations of the regions and would also coordinate the work of the president's representatives in the regions.[111] Yeltsin initially appointed Gennadii Vereteinikov to head this office. Vereteinikov was soon replaced by Nikolai Medvedev.[112]

Another already-existing governmental body that had a major role in policy toward the provinces was the State Committee on Nationality Policy (*Goskomnats,* for short). The importance attached to this office was underlined by the appointment of one of Yeltsin's most influential advisors, Sergei Shakhrai, to the post of chairman of the committee. In November 1992 he took over the post previously held by Valerii Tishkov, director of the Institute for Ethnography.[113] In February 1993 the State Committee on Nationalities was reorganized into the State Committee on Federation Affairs and Nationalities. Shakhrai remained its chair, and announced that the new body would open five regional centers and have two new subunits—on ethnic conflicts and on regional economics. The main function of the new body would be to oversee the implementation of the Federation Treaty, though it was not clear how the various elements of Yeltsin's administration were to coordinate their activities to pursue a consistent regional policy.[114] Shakhrai remained the top government official for nationality policy until May 1994.

Summary and Conclusions

The development of institutions that involved provincial leaders in national politics represented steps in a process that could, if allowed to develop, reduce the threat of a breakup of the federation. On the other hand, the power struggle between legislative and executive authority at the center of Russian politics seemed guaranteed to further weaken power at the center of the federation. This process was accelerated by the slow development of national political parties, the continuing economic crisis, and the resistance to reform by many entrenched local elites. Regional economic and cultural differences—sometimes as significant as those that existed between the former Soviet republics—also acted to push components of the federation in different directions. Republics and territories rich in natural resources and with the greatest foreign-trade potential were the most insistent on gaining additional control over their resources, while poorer provinces depended on the center for continued subsidies.

The process of fragmentation was intensified by a lack of consensus on the "boundary problem"—how to define the limits of local and federal authority. Central Russian government ministries continued to act as if their dictates were to be followed at all levels without consultation. For their part, regions often decided unilaterally which directives they would implement and which they would ignore or supplant with their own decisions.

The demonstration effect of such republics as Tatarstan, Chechnia, Bashkortostan, and Yakutia (Sakha) encouraged provincial leaders and soviets, for internal political reasons, to push for greater decentralization or confederation. In Vologda and Sverdlovsk oblasts, soviets added a question to the April 25, 1993 referendum that asked whether oblasts and krais should have equal rights with republics such as Tatarstan and Yakutia in the Russian Federation. In both oblasts over 80 percent of the voters answered yes.[115] The first oblast to attempt to change its status was Vologda, which proclaimed itself a republic on May 14.[116] On July 1, the Sverdlovsk Oblast Soviet formally declared itself the Urals Republic and invited neighboring oblasts to join it.[117] On July 8, the Primor'e Krai Soviet proclaimed the region a republic and called for a referendum for final approval. Similar efforts were begun by the oblast soviet in Voronezh in August, though it sought some status between republic and oblast.[118] In addition to the above list, a number of oblast or krai soviets adopted decisions in the summer of 1993, following the example of some republics, to withhold all or a portion of federal taxes collected in their regions. These regions included Magadan, Rostov, Belgorod, Yaroslavl, and Vladimir oblasts and Krasnoiarsk and Altai krais.[119]

Yeltsin's use of force in October 1993 to resolve the crisis between himself and the Supreme Soviet had the effect of halting, at least temporarily, these challenges to central authority. The new constitution, adopted in December 1993, formally established the principle of equality for all regions. In practice, however, the political "clout" of the republics and oblasts varied dramatically. Elections to regional legislatures and executive posts during 1994 were likely to set the stage for new conflicts over the nature of the Russian Federation.

Notes

1. *Sovetskaia Rossiia,* August 11, 1990.

2. *Izvestiia,* August 31, 1990.

3. Charles Carlson, "Cheremis Jump on Sovereignty Bandwagon," *Report on the USSR* (November 9, 1990), pp. 21–23; *Izvestiia,* August 25, 1990; *Sovetskaia Rossiia,* October 23, 1990.

4. The *New York Times,* September 3, 1990, and Ann Sheehy, "Tatarstan Asserts Its Sovereignty," *RRE/RL Research Report,* no. 14 (1992).

5. *Izvestiia,* September 22, 1990.

6. *Sovetskaia Rossiia,* October 9, 1990.

7. *Sovetskaia Rossiia,* November 28, 1990.

8. *Izvestiia,* February 1, 1991.

9. *Izvestiia,* November 18, 1990.

10. *Trud,* September 29, 1990. In June 1992, Yeltsin signed a law admitting Chukotka Autonomous Okrug into the Russian Federation directly. *Rossiiskaia gazeta,* July 8, 1992.

11. *Trud,* October 10, 1990.

12. *Izvestiia,* November 15, 1990.

13. *Trud,* November 14, 1990.

14. The *New York Times,* September 3, 1990, and interview in *Komsomol'skaia pravda,* March 14, 1991.

15. *Rossiiskie vesti,* August 18, 1992, and *Nezavisimaia gazeta,* December 19, 1992.

16. *Izvestiia,* October 28, 1991 and November 1. An interview with Dudaev appeared in *Moscow News,* No. 14 (April 5–12, 1992), p. 4.

17. See *Rossiiskaia gazeta,* July 1, 1992.

18. *Rossiia,* December 16, 1992, and *Nezavisimaia gazeta,* January 5 and January 13, 1993.

19. *Rossiiskie vesti,* January 26, 1993.

20. *Nezavisimaia gazeta,* January 27 and January 30, 1993.

21. Report on Russian evening television news, March 17, 1993.

22. On the history and ethnography of the Tatar-Russian relationship, see Ron Wixman, "The Middle Volga: Ethnic Archipelago in a Russian Sea," in Ian Bremmer and Ray Taras, *Nations and Politics in the Soviet Successor States* (Cambridge: Cambridge University Press, 1993), pp. 421–47.

23. Sheehy, "Tatarstan Asserts Its Sovereignty," *RRE/RL Research Report,* no. 14 (1992).

24. Ibid.

25. *Rossiiskie vesti,* November 21, 1992, and *Nezavisimaia gazeta,* December 1, 1992.

26. Interfax interview with Shamiev in *FBIS: Daily Report,* no. 28 (February 12, 1993), pp. 38–40.

27. *Izvestiia,* March 26, 1993.

28. For an explicit statement of this, see the Interfax report in *FBIS: Daily Report,* no. 32 (February 19, 1993), p. 44.

29. *Nezavisimaia gazeta,* April 6, 1993. For an analysis of politics in Bashkortostan, see the article by Khamid Gizatullin in *Rossiiskie vesti,* November 11, 1992.

30. *Federatsiia,* January 14, 1993; *Nezavisimaia gazeta,* December 30, 1992; *Rossiiskie vesti,* June 2, 1992, December 29, 1992, and January 5, 1993.

31. *Delovoi mir,* July 31, 1993.

32. See the discussion of the treaty by the head of the Tomsk Oblast Soviet, Grigorii Shamin, in *Nezavisimaia gazeta,* March 20, 1993.

33. *Nezavisimaia gazeta,* April 1, 1992; the text of the agreement with the republics within the federation was published in *Rossiiskaia gazeta,* March 18, 1992.

34. *Nezavisimaia gazeta,* April 4, 1992.

35. For an analysis by the legal scholar Iurii Tikhomirov, see *Rossiiskie vesti,* February 11, 1993.

36. *Nezavisimaia gazeta,* March 20, 1993, on Tomsk, and *Izvestiia,* January 27, 1993, on Arkhangelsk.

37. See, for example, the commentary on provincial charters in *Rossiiskie vesti,* September 12, 1992.

38. See the article by the political observer D. Ol'shanskii in *Rossiia,* no. 14 (March 31–April 6, 1993).

39. *Rossiiskie vesti,* November 19, 1992.

40. The two documents, both issued on May 27, appeared in *Rossiiskaia gazeta,* June 17, 1993, and *Rossiiskie vesti,* June 8, 1993.

41. *Rossiiskie vesti,* June 8, 1993. The decree was dated June 4.

42. Article by Fedor Shelov-Kovediaev, chairman of the Subcommittee of the Russian Supreme Soviet on Humanitarian Problems in *Nezavisimaia gazeta,* March 25, 1993.

43. *Rossiiskie vesti,* February 17, 1993 and March 27, 1993.

44. *Nezavisimaia gazeta,* November 18, 1992.

45. *Nezavisimaia gazeta,* February 9, 1993.

46. On budgets in the Soviet period, though the main units of analysis are union republics, see Donna Bahry, *Outside Moscow: Power, Politics, and Budgetary Policy in the Soviet Republics* (New York: Columbia University Press, 1987).

47. Figures on the 1992 tax payments to the center for regions within Russia were presented by Leonid Smirniagin in an article in *Rossiiskie vesti,* June 26, 1993.

48. A comprehensive list of local taxes and fees assessed by each region was published in *Ekonomika i zhizn',* no. 37 (September 1992), p. 19.

49. *Rossiiskie vesti,* November 18, 1992.

50. See the report on the statement of the chairmen of eight provincial soviets in *Rossiiskaia gazeta,* February 2, 1993.

51. From vice premier Shumeiko's report to the government, in *Rossiiskie vesti,* February 16, 1993.

52. See the article on budgetary relations in Russia by Oleg Rumiantsev, secretary of the Congress of People's Deputies Constitutional Commission, in *Rossiiskii monitor,* issue 2 (Moscow: Indem, 1993), pp. 45–58. Rumiantsev has been sharply critical of the demands of republics for sovereignty.

53. A lengthy analysis of Ulianovsk price policies appeared in *Rossiiskie vesti*, January 4, 1993, and a report on the "Ulianovsk miracle" by Russian government analysts appeared in the same newspaper on September 8, 1993.

54. Report by Aleksandr Surinov of the Center for Economic Conditions and Forecasting of the Russian Ministry of Economics. *Izvestiia*, February 13, 1993.

55. *Moscow News*, no. 26 (June 28–July 5, 1992), p. 9; *Izvestiia*, June 10, 1992.

56. *Izvestiia*, February 23, 1993.

57. See the article by Aleksei Gumilevskii in *Rossiiskie vesti*, December 23, 1992.

58. *Kommersant-Daily*, February 23, 1993.

59. See the report by Andrei Neshchadin in *Moscow News*, no. 26 (June 28–July 5, 1992), p. 9; also *Rossiiskie vesti*, October 28, 1992.

60. *Rossiiskaia gazeta*, February 15, 1992.

61. See the discussion by a sector head in the Control Administration, Safarali Dzhafarov, in *Rossiiskie vesti*, November 12, 1992.

62. See the interview with Makharadze in *Izvestiia*, November 1, 1991.

63. *Rossiiskaia gazeta*, March 5, 1992.

64. *Rossiiskie vesti*, September 17, 1993.

65. Gennadii Vladimirov, "Rossiiskii tsentr i mestnaia vlast': opyt instituta predstavitelei prezidenta," *Politicheskii monitoring*, no. 4 (April 1993), pp. 5–22. See also the analysis of presidential representatives done by Boris Bogatov in *Nezavisimaia gazeta*, November 6, 1991.

66. *Izvestiia*, February 23, 1993.

67. *Rossiiskaia gazeta*, June 6, 1992.

68. *Rossiiskie vesti*, February 19, 1993, and *Izvestiia*, March 4, 1993.

69. ITAR-TASS report translated in *FBIS Daily Report*, no. 25 (February 9, 1993), p. 15.

70. *Izvestiia*, February 18, 1993.

71. *Nezavisimaia gazeta*, March 6, 1993.

72. *Rossiiskie vesti*, March 6, 1993.

73. *Nezavisimaia gazeta*, March 10 and 11, 1993.

74. See, for example, the commentary by Vol'demar Koreshkov in *Rossiiskaia gazeta*, July 29, 1992.

75. Khasbulatov's speech was given in Novosibirsk. *Izvestiia*, February 23, 1993.

76. The *New York Times*, March 28 and 30, 1993, and *Rossiiskaia gazeta*, April 1, 1993.

77. *Rossiiskie vesti*, no. 17 (September 1991), p. 5; regulations on the missions of the president in the republics and on presidential representatives appeared in *Rossiiskaia gazeta*, September 6, 1991. A translation appeared in *FBIS Republic Affairs*, no. 33 (September 24, 1991), pp. 65–67.

78. The law "On Elections for Heads of Administration" was adopted by the Russian Supreme Soviet on October 25, 1991 and appeared in *Rossiiskaia gazeta*, November 14, 1991.

79. See Eugene Huskey, "The Rebirth of the Russian State," in E. Huskey, ed., *Executive Power and Soviet Politics: The Rise and Decline of the Soviet State* (Armonk, NY: M.E. Sharpe, 1992), pp. 249–69.

80. In the case of Ulianovsk, Yeltsin reversed his decision and appointed the head of the oblast soviet. *Izvestiia*, November 5, 1991. The case of Krasnodar was mentioned in *Izvestiia*, August 26, 1991.

81. *Rossiiskaia gazeta*, November 5, 1991.

82. *Izvestiia*, February 18, 1993.

83. *Rossiiskaia gazeta*, June 25, 1992, and *Rossiiskie vesti*, August 29, 1992.

84. *Izvestiia,* April 22, 1993, and *Rossiiskie vesti,* August 26, 1993.

85. *Rossiiskaia gazeta,* August 11, 1993, and *Rossiiskie vesti,* April 13 and September 1, 1993.

86. *Rossiia,* no. 32 (August 4–10, 1993).

87. *Rossiiskaia gazeta,* August 19, 1992.

88. *Rossiiskaia gazeta,* September 15, 1992.

89. *Rossiiskie vesti,* November 28, 1992.

90. *Rossiiskie vesti,* March 24, 1993.

91. *Nezavisimaia gazeta,* March 11, 1993.

92. See the commentary by Vladimir Gel'man in *Rossiia,* no. 42 (October 14–20, 1992).

93. Details of the case supplied by the Control Administration were published in *Rossiiskie vesti,* March 26, 1992.

94. *Daidzhest-Kuranty,* no. 20 (June 1992), and report on Russian television, February 12, 1993.

95. *Rossiiskie vesti,* November 28, 1992, and *Rossiiskaia gazeta,* July 24, 1992.

96. *Rossiiskaia gazeta,* January 29, 1993, and *Izvestiia,* January 30, 1993.

97. *Rossiiskie vesti,* June 25, 1993, and *Rossiiskaia gazeta,* July 15, 1992.

98. *Izvestiia,* January 6, 1993, and Ostankino Russian evening news, April 4 and 5, 1993.

99. *Rossiiskaia gazeta,* December 17, 1991 and May 20, 1992, and *Nezavisimaia gazeta,* September 12, 1992. Delegates from Chechnia did not attend. Among the most important of the regional meetings were those held in February 1993 of twenty Volga and Urals provinces in Samara and the meeting of the group "Siberian Agreement" in Novosibirsk.

100. For an astute analysis of Khasbulatov's effort, see the article by Sergei Chugaev in *Izvestiia,* March 20, 1993. Communication with the provinces was facilitated by the fact that the Supreme Soviet building used to be the home of the Russian Council of Ministers, and direct links to provincial authorities were at the disposal of the presidium of the Supreme Soviet.

101. *Kommersant-Daily,* April 6, 1993.

102. *Nezavisimaia gazeta,* April 9, 1992.

103. *Nezavisimaia gazeta,* August 29, 1992.

104. *Nezavisimaia gazeta,* November 18, 1992, and *Rossiiskie vesti,* November 19, 1992.

105. *Izvestiia,* October 15, 1992, *Kommersant-Daily,* October 16, 1992; *Rossiiskie vesti,* February 10, 1993. The leader of Tatarstan, Mintimer Shaimiev, did not attend the first meeting, but he did attend a session of the council in February 1993. The leader of Sakha indicated that he was one of the initiators of the council. See *Nezavisimaia gazeta,* December 30, 1992.

106. *Rossiiskie vesti,* February 12, 1993.

107. The *New York Times,* March 30, 1993, and *Izvestiia,* March 26 and 27, 1993.

108. *Nezavisimaia gazeta,* March 31, 1993. This fear proved to be well-founded, as shown in the Yeltsin constitution adopted in December 1993.

109. *Rossiiskie vesti,* July 8, 1993.

110. *Izvestiia,* August 14, 1993. The draft of Yeltsin's proposal for the Federation Council was circulated to regional leaders for comments at the end of August 1993, and excerpts were published in *Segodnia,* September 3, 1993.

111. The decree establishing the new agency was published in *Rossiiskie vesti,* March 10, 1993. As indicated above, Iurii Boldyrev was removed as chief state inspector at this time.

112. *Rossiiskie vesti,* March 27, 1993, and *Nezavisimaia gazeta,* March 30, 1993.

113. *Rossiiskie vesti,* November 6, 1992.

114. *Rossiiskie vesti,* February 23, 1993, and *FBIS Daily Report,* no. 36 (February 25, 1993), p. 41.

115. *Rossiiskie vesti,* July 13, 1993, and September 8, 1993.

116. *Izvestiia,* May 15, 1993.

117. *Rossiiskie vesti,* July 3, 1993.

118. *Rossiia,* no. 30 (August 6–12, 1993).

119. *Rabochaia tribuna,* July 31, 1993; *Izvestiia,* July 16, 1993; *Rossiiskaia gazeta,* July 22, 1993; *Rossiiskie vesti,* August 31, 1993; and *Nezavisimaia gazeta,* September 1, 1993.

Conclusions
Common Features of Post-Soviet Local Politics

Jeffrey W. Hahn

Perhaps it is fitting that a volume that opened with Lenin's revolutionary slogan "All Power to the Soviets!" should conclude by taking note of their demise. On October 9, 1993, Boris Yeltsin abolished the local soviets at the city level and below, and "invited" the oblast and republican soviets to dissolve themselves. A few weeks later, on October 22, he decreed new elections to "dumas" at the oblast level and below, to be held in the spring of 1994.[1] For someone like the author, who was a specialist on the local soviets, this was disconcerting news. Indeed, the next day a visiting Russian colleague stopped by my office to inquire how I felt about my new profession as an historian.

Upon reflection, however, the timing of Yeltsin's decree could not have been better for the purposes of this book. If real reform of local government in the Soviet Union began with the local elections of March 1990, then the dissolution of the soviets in October 1993 marks a convenient benchmark for assessing the transition from the old system of local politics that existed until 1990. As I write (February 1994), we appear to be on the threshold of a new phase in the transformation of politics in the former Soviet Union. What then can we learn from the empirical studies of local politics in 1990–93 presented in this book that may be useful in analyzing the next period of transition in post-Soviet politics? This chapter attempts to generalize, on the basis of the evidence presented here and elsewhere, about features of local political life in the former Soviet Union, and especially in Russia. This may be a useful point of departure for understanding the new period of political transition now underway.

The first point to be made is that local politics in the former Soviet Union matters. This may seem to state the obvious, but as Theodore

Friedgut notes in his introductory chapter, before 1990 this simply was not so. Behind the elaborate façade of elected legislatures and constitutionally accountable executives that characterized local government in the Soviet period was the reality that all power belonged not to the soviets, but to the Communist Party, whose local representatives were strictly subordinated to the center by the workings of democratic centralism. According to the principle of dual subordination, local executives were accountable to the deputies who elected them, but in practice they functioned as administrators of decisions made at the center. The task of the elected deputies was to approve unanimously whatever the local executive committee put before them. The idea that local authorities could make decisions at variance with those of the center was inconceivable.

While in a structural sense much of the old hierarchy of state power continued to exist after 1990, the nature of the relations between levels of government, and between the center and the periphery, was altered, probably for good. One of the principal features of politics in the post-Soviet period was the emergence of subnational political entities as major players whose decisions not only diverged from those of the center, but were often openly defiant.[2] In part this independence came about because a growing paralysis of political power at the center created a vacuum that local leaders filled. Correctly sensing that the old political elites controlled many local soviets outside Moscow and Leningrad, particularly the oblast soviets, Russian President Boris Yeltsin sought to outflank his opposition by creating a strong local executive authority that would be loyal to him. This he did in 1991–92 by appointing presidential representatives and heads of administration. The ensuing struggle between legislative and executive authority extended throughout the state hierarchy, reaching a resolution only with the abolition of all the lower soviets, except in the republics, in the autumn of 1993. In the process of attempting to establish strong local executive authority, however, Yeltsin not only engendered a fruitless struggle for power with the Russian parliament, but in the process made himself dependent on the support of local executives, effectively increasing their room to maneuver.[3]

Equally important to the emergence of local political power were the elections of 1990. Because they were genuinely competitive to an unprecedented degree, these elections gave local leaders a legitimacy that they had previously lacked. This implied that constituent concerns could no longer be ignored with impunity and local politicians could point to these concerns to justify positions that were at odds with the center.[4] In at least one important way that appears to be consistent across all the studies presented in this volume, the growth of real political constituencies appears to have confounded the ability of the center to dictate terms to local authorities: in the sense of being more resistant to change, rural voters are more conservative than those in cities.

How does this rural-urban cleavage affect center–periphery relations? Since many of the seats to oblast legislatures, as well as to the new lower house of the Russian parliament, the State Duma, are elected from rural areas, the composition of these bodies includes a higher proportion of former Communist Party officials and their allies among the *nomenklatura,* especially among collective farm leaders. They have been particularly vociferous in their opposition to "shock therapy" approaches to economic reform. Conversely, political leadership in the cities in all our case studies has been notably more receptive to market-oriented economic reform. As a result, there has been a conflict vertically between the cities and the oblasts and between the oblasts and the center that seems likely to persist.

The horizontal conflict between legislative and executive authority noted earlier overlaps this vertical conflict and further complicates the calculus of local power because it has aligned the executive branch with a "reformist" president and positioned local legislatures as the locus of opposition, especially at the oblast level. All of this has produced a sort of institutional chaos at the subnational level of government. In the old days, all decisions were made by or mediated through a single leader, the obkom first secretary. Now, as John Young and Darrell Slider point out in their chapters, there are five local leaders contending for power. In addition to the chairs of the city and oblast soviets, there is the provincial governor, the city mayor, and the presidential representative, (a position permanently established by Article 83(j) of the Russian Constitution adopted on December 12, 1993). Much depends on the ability of these individuals to cooperate both among themselves and with the center, but this appears to be the exception, not the rule, contributing to what Peter Reddaway has called the "ungovernability" of Russia. For all the reasons given here, institutional competition also seems likely to continue after the new round of local elections in 1994, but with one important difference: Yeltsin will no longer be able to dismiss local legislatures as artifacts of the communist past.[5] In fact, they may well enjoy more popular legitimacy than the executive officials, all but nine of whom were appointed by Yeltsin and none of whom must run for popular election until 1995.

A second generalization that can be offered on the basis of the studies presented here, and that is also likely to be a continuing feature at least of Russian politics, is the fact that there is considerable variation in politics at the local and regional level. Politics in St. Petersburg or Moscow has features quite unlike those found in Omsk; Omsk politics is different from Saratov politics; and, as Joel Moses informs us, politics in Saratov is far less progressive than in neighboring Volgograd. The chapter by this author presented data that indicated substantial differences in attitudes toward political and economic reform across five regions of central Russia. This variation is noteworthy for two reasons. For one thing, it represents a break with past practice when all the activities of local government were said to be "unitary," with interests indivisible from the Union as a whole. Whatever informal competition may have taken place among local party chieftains, official Soviet political usage held that the structure and functioning of government maintain external uniformity across all regions. Now, regional competition is conducted openly and the outlines of a regional politics not unfamiliar to students of American political life can be discerned.

Another reason for taking note of the regional variation in political development in Russia is that it offers a natural laboratory for testing theories about why and how political systems change. In particular, it is clear that while the reforms of local government introduced in 1990 were structurally the same for all local governments, the outcomes have varied widely. Why?[6] The evidence presented in this volume was not explicitly organized to explore the relation between political institutions and political development, but some of the findings are suggestive. One of these is that *who* was in power during the reform period made a great difference. This conclusion emerges most clearly in the chapters by Friedgut, Moses, and Young. In Donetsk, the strikes that took place in the summer of 1989 had greatly discredited the old elites and undermined their ability to govern or, when elections came, to hold on to power. In the case of Volgograd and Saratov, the differences in outcome are attributed to the fact that in Volgograd, the old elite had been purged just prior to the 1990 elections, while those in Saratov were firmly entrenched. In Omsk, it was the continuity of old elites that mattered, not institutional reform, leading John Young to conclude that the main problem with local politics in Russia today is not excessive autonomy but "an excess of power of local elites."

It seems clear, however, from research presented here and elsewhere, that it is not only elites that matter in accounting for regional differentiation; there do appear to be broader contextual, or social and economic, factors at work as well. Elizabeth Teague notes that in the April 1993 referendum on his presidency, Yeltsin did especially well in the northern regions of the country, as well as in Western Siberia and the Far East, "regions richly endowed with raw materials and the infrastructure to exploit them."[7] Combining referendum results with those from Yeltsin's election as president in

1991, another study by Aleksandr Sobianin and his colleagues confirmed the idea of a broad "north–south" division, arguing that support for reform was strongest in the wealthier, more industrialized regions of the north, and weakest in the primarily agricultural regions of the south, a generalization consistent with the author's earlier observation about rural conservatism.[8] One other "contextual" factor of obvious importance in explaining regional differentiation in Russia is ethnicity. This point is most clearly made in the chapter by Darrell Slider, which, in part, deals with the differences between the ethnically diverse republics and the comparatively homogeneous provinces.

Another generalization that emerges from the research presented in this volume is that older elites have proven to be more successful at adapting to the new rules of the political game ushered in by reform than their "democratic" opposition.[9] The chapter by Jo Andrews and Alexandra Vacroux, among others, makes it clear that party membership per se did not indicate much about a candidate's political orientation in 1990. Being a member of the existing political establishment, however, did matter, and many of this group ran for office in the new competitive environment. Moreover, except for Moscow and Leningrad where the democratic opposition emerged with a decisive majority, the old elites did rather well, especially at the oblast level as noted earlier. In all the case studies offered here, members of the old elite held leadership positions in the new local soviets and continued to hold leadership positions even after the CPSU ceased to exist. In some cases, as in Saratov and Omsk, their influence has been paramount. In others, like Donetsk and Volgograd, leaders strongly associated with the democratic movement (Makhmudov and Makharadze respectively) have been replaced by those who held local power under the old system. Where the democratic movement did emerge victorious, as in St. Petersburg, the majority has proven incapable of governing effectively, as the chapter by Vladimir Gel'man and Mary McAuley demonstrates.

How are we to explain the success of the old elites in holding on to political power and the failure of the democratic movement to do so? The explanation offered in the introductory chapter of this book is worth emphasizing: the older political elites were professional politicians and their opponents were amateurs. As Theodore Friedgut points out, despite Lenin's disdain for the "professional politicians" of parliamentary democratic systems and his injunction that only part-timers be elected to government, Soviet politics at all levels came to be dominated by a class of professional politicians, virtually all of whom made their career in the CPSU. Success in this career went to those who were the shrewdest, the toughest, the most motivated, and those who developed the best contacts—characteristics associated with the survival of the politically fittest in any political system.

When the rules changed and it became increasingly clear that being a member of the party apparatus was no longer an asset but a liability, the most able looked elsewhere for a new power base. They often found it in legislative seats from districts where they could win, or in provincial administrations, or in enterprises where their knowledge and contacts ensured them of ready access to managerial positions.[10] If the February 1994 elections to the oblast duma in Penza noted earlier are any indication, the influence of the professionals seems more likely to increase than decrease after the next round of local elections.

Those associated with the democratic opposition movement were, by contrast, political amateurs. Many of them, particularly among the leadership, came from the scientific or cultural intelligentsia where their professional skills or talents offered relative insulation from politics, except for obligatory ritual appearances at meetings called by their local partkom and for voting. For many, politics in the Soviet Union, especially at the local level, was at best irrelevant and at worst corrupt; in both cases it invited their contempt. Unable to oppose or change the system, they stayed aloof from it to the extent that they were able. The elections of 1990 offered the opportunity and the incentive to get involved. The initial rush of enthusiasm produced clear antiestablishment majorities in Moscow and Leningrad (later renamed St. Petersburg) and more or less sizable minorities elsewhere. What united the democratic movement was at the same time the source of its major appeal to the electorate: it was opposed to those in power.

Success at the polls gave the adherents of the democratic movement a voice in the formation of local government. The work of governing, however, proved more arduous and less glamorous. As Theodore Friedgut writes in his chapter on Donetsk, "wielding power has been found to be a far more complex task than attaining it." In the first place, the democrats lacked experience. Nothing in their professional background could have prepared them for the intricacies of municipal governance, even in normal times. Those who did have that ability were to be found in the bureaucracy, many of them holdovers from the old order. As it turned out, during the period covered here, even before Yeltsin's decisions to strengthen the executive, real power at the local level had gravitated increasingly to the executive branch if only by default, because that is where administrative experience and expertise was to be found. Someone, after all, had to govern.

The other major reason for the failure of the democratic movement to wield local power successfully was its lack of coherence and discipline. Since candidates could not and did not run as representatives of a political party, they were elected on their individual merits. In the case of many in the democratic movement, this meant little more than the fact that they were running against establishment candidates. Once elected they had no allegiance to anyone but their constituents, or even more narrowly, to the workplace that nominated them. What had united the democrats was their opposition to the old order, and when it collapsed, there was little in the way of a common program to hold them together. The result was that in place of a cohesive legislative platform, there was cacophony. Where the democrats held a majority, as in St. Petersburg, the additional consequence was ineffective government.

In all fairness, the failures of the local soviets in Russia in the period 1990–93 can hardly be laid entirely at the door of the democratic movement, although the poor performance of parties associated with this movement in elections to the State Duma may indicate a public willingness to do so. In fact, the problems of local government go beyond partisan conflict; they were also structural, inherent in the institutions themselves. As more than one of our authors notes, the old system of local politics was slow to break up; the new was even slower in taking hold. The problem was that reforming the old soviets was like pouring new wine into old bottles. The reforms introduced in 1990 introduced elements of parliamentary democracy into a system that was not designed to be democratic. As conceptualized, the soviets were, in accordance with the prescription of Karl Marx, "working, not parliamentary bodies" in which there was no separation of powers and in which those elected continued to work. As a result, the soviets in the old system were very large bodies composed mostly of people who knew nothing about governing and who were replaced after two and one half years in office. Their function was not to make policy, but to insure that policy decisions were carried out, particularly at the workplace.

As long as the soviets remained a rubber stamp for decisions made elsewhere, notably by the party hierarchy, their inherent difficulties as institutions of local government were not apparent or even particularly relevant. The reforms introduced in 1990 changed matters. They gave the soviets a real role in policy-making and they made it possible for what Robert Dahl calls "public contestation" to take place. The consequences of these changes became apparent during the period under review. To a large extent, competitive elections effectively ended the dominance of the party over local politics even before the failed coup of 1991. The soviets, to which local administrators were now accountable for their positions, suddenly found themselves carrying primary responsibility for making policy. Yet because of the legacy of the past, there were too many deputies with too little experience to excel as civic representatives. In addition, almost all of them were employed full-time elsewhere. Moreover, because the elections of

1990 were held with no provision for multiparty competition, there was little basis for building group consensus within these bodies about what was to be done. These flaws, inherited from the old system, were compounded by the sheer magnitude of the problems being faced by local governments all over the former Soviet Union at this time. Weak institutionalization in the face of hard policy choices doomed the soviets to endless and ineffectual debates that produced little, regardless of whether those from the democratic movement held a majority or not.[11] In part because of the institutional weakness, power at the local level is wielded by elites, as argued above. In the absence of established process, local Russian politics remains highly personalistic.

In retrospect, it is easy to see why the local soviets did not work very well and to see attempts at reform from 1990 to 1993 as a temporary bridge between the old system of local politics and a new one that is only beginning to take form. But it is also easy to overlook the accomplishments of this period. Among the more notable of these were: the introduction of competitive elections; the accountability of executives before the people's elected representatives; the emergence of locally elected deputies as real policy-makers who set agendas, debated alternative positions, and oversaw implementation; an end to the control of all local politics by the Communist Party; and the introduction in theory (and sometimes in practice) of the principle of the separation of powers. Nevertheless, in the end, reforming the old soviets didn't work; it remains to be seen if their abolition will improve things.

The foregoing suggests yet another feature of local politics in 1990–93 that is likely to persist: the importance of economics. Even governments run by experienced and dedicated local officials would have had trouble coping with the problems engendered by the transformation of the Russian economy. Several of the chapters in this volume, and especially the introduction, have drawn attention to the enormous difficulties inherent in trying to transform the economic and political systems of the former Soviet Union at the same time.[12] The introduction of a market economy based on private ownership has meant that local governments have had to take on many of the social services formerly provided by state enterprises that frequently dominated their locales, making them into company towns. Yet simultaneously they are supposed to divest themselves of many of the economic functions they previously performed, especially in retail sales and housing. Predictably, acquiring new obligations has proven much easier than shedding old ones. One of the results is what Daniel Berkowitz has called "consumption bias" on the part of local politicians. Those who must face reelection try to cushion the social costs of the transition by subsidizing the welfare of their constituents. At the same time, local governments lack the resources to underwrite the transition. Beth Mitchneck's chapter demonstrates the degree to which budgetary policy has become a focal point for conflict among different levels of government. It is also for this reason that Georgii Barabashev saw the lack of clear legislation giving local authorities greater budgetary control as one of the main deficiencies of Russian local self-government in 1992.

The chapters in this volume also suggest, however, that increasing local resources and local autonomy in implementing economic reform may actually make matters worse. Implicit in the idea of "consumption bias" is the view that local officials who are primarily concerned with using available resources in order to ease the pain of reform for their constituents may, as a result, retard the implementation of those reforms. In addition, there is the question of whether local officials are competent at managing the resources available to them. Gel'man and McAuley's sad conclusion about St. Petersburg, where "political freedom became a reality," is that while politics changed greatly in 1990–93, there was no change in the way the economy was managed. While new, more "democratic" elites replaced old ones, they had no coherent strategy for preventing the economic situation in the city from deteriorating. Added to the problem of incompetence in the misuse of local resources. John Young's description of politics in Omsk suggests that greater autonomy for local authorities may only benefit the power holders. A similar cautionary tale is offered by Joel Moses's description of the influence wielded by the provincial "godfather," Ivan Kuznetsov, over local officials in Saratov. One may well ask: Is greater local control over decision making as it relates to the economic life of Saratov really in the best interests of its inhabitants if Kuznetsov is one of the main beneficiaries?

In this concluding chapter, we seek to generalize from a wide range of empirical studies about local politics in the former Soviet Union, and particularly in Russia. What can we learn from this exercise that may be useful in understanding the context in which local politics will develop during the period of transition that will begin with the election of new local legislatures in the spring of 1994? It seems reasonable to expect that conflict between local and national authorities will continue to be an important fact of political life. Local defiance of the center was unthinkable under the old order, but local independence, like a genie released from its bottle, cannot be denied or reversed, short of reimposing a totalitarian regime. An important reason for the persistence of greater subnational autonomy is that the authority of local elites is derived from their various constituencies. As Theodore Friedgut notes in his introduction, politics is now "real." Contenders for political power derive their positions by successfully claiming to represent the interests of one or another social group. One cleavage that seems likely to continue to define Russian politics is urban-rural, but there are others: ethnicity, age, and economic status among them.

At the same time, it is also clear that local politics varies widely depending on where you are. Other than in their common assertion of autonomy from the center, there seems little homogeneity among the different regions of Russia. Not only does the voice of local politics modulate itself according to region, but the impact of local politics at the national level is also diluted because local politicians are themselves so divided. Older elites, more likely to be found in oblasts, conflict with reformers, more often found in cities; legislative leaders often compete with executives. Both are often uncomfortable with the local presidential prefect. Compounding this chaos, local bodies of power remain weakly institutionalized. For those hoping that the political reforms would mark a real break from the past, this may be a discouraging conclusion, since it is also clear from the studies presented here that many of those holding power today are the same people that held power before. Regardless of which elites are in charge, however, the nature of local politics in the former Soviet Union remains highly personalized; it seems likely to continue that way as we move further into the post-Soviet period.

Notes

1. *Rossiiskaia gazeta* October 12, 1993, p. 1. See also Elizabeth Teague, "Yeltsin Disbands the Soviets," *RFE/RL Research Reports,* vol. 2, no. 43 (October 1993).

2. The chapter by Beth Mitchneck demonstrates how local authorities have exercised increasing discretion with regard to raising and spending public monies. Examples of local defiance of central authority are numerous. Among them are the refusal of the Khabarovsk Krai and Irkutsk governors to pay their federal tax shares. See *RFE/RL Daily Reports,* February 7, 1994. Many rejected Yeltsin's decree abolishing parliament. See Elizabeth Teague, "North–South Divide: Yeltsin and Russia's Provincial Leaders," *RFE/RL Research Reports,* vol. 2, no. 26, November 26, 1993.

3. The new importance of local officials has been institutionalized in the upper house of the newly elected Russian parliament, the Council of the Federation. The council is composed of two representatives, one from the executive and one from the legislative branch, from each of the eighty-nine members of the Russian Federation. The creation of the council can be regarded as a concession by Yeltsin to local leaders and a recognition that he cannot govern effectively without their support.

4. In his chapter, Daniel Berkowitz notes how the presence of a "consumption bias" on the part of local deputies who must now appear responsive to local needs has retarded the center's efforts to privatize the economy.

5. The results of the first oblast election in Penza strongly support the view that many of these elections are going to produce legislatures dominated by "conservatives." In elections to the Penza Oblast legislature held on February 2, 1994, 40 of the 45 deputies chosen were former party nomenklatura despite competition from democratic

movement parties. This outcome was attributed to the fact that old pensioners and agricultural workers voted in force while the urban electorate did not. *RFE/RL Daily Report,* no. 23, February 3, 1994.

6. Students of Russian politics are in a position to test theories of institutional development similar to those tested by Robert Putnam in his ground-breaking study of Italian regional development. In 1970 the Italian government introduced governmental reforms that were essentially the same for all its regions. The effects of these reforms, however, varied greatly producing effective, democratic governance in some (generally in the North), but not in others. Robert D. Putnam, *Making Democracy Work* (Princeton, NJ: Princeton University Press, 1993).

7. Elizabeth Teague, "North–South Divide," p. 8.

8. Aleksandr Sobianin, Edward Gel'man, and Oleg Kaiunov, "The Political Climate in Russia in 1991–1993," *Mirovaia ekonomika i mezhdunarodnye otnosheniia,* no. 9, 1993.

9. By "older elites," we mean those who wielded local power prior to 1990, namely professional members of the oblast and city party committees (apparatchiks), ranking state officials, and their nomenklatura appointments outside of the party–state apparatus.

10. While the argument has been made that old elites used their privileged position to manipulate the elections of 1990, other evidence suggests that they won not because they cheated, but because they were more able politicians. See Gavin Helf and Jeffrey Hahn, "Old Dogs and New Tricks: Party Elites in the Russian Regional Elections of 1990," *Slavic Review,* vol. 51, no. 3 (fall 1992), pp. 511–30.

11. For an elaboration of this point based on the author's observations of sessions of the Yaroslavl city and oblast soviets, see Jeffrey W. Hahn, "How Democratic Are Local Russian Deputies?" in Carol R. Saivetz and Anthony Jones, eds., *In Search of Pluralism: Soviet and Post-Soviet Politics* (Boulder, CO: Westview Press, 1994), pp. 74–79.

12. Sarah Meiklejohn Terry refers to this problem of simultaneity as the "dual track nature of the present transitions" going on in all the formerly communist countries, including those of Eastern Europe. She considers it one of the main ways in which postcommunist transitions differ from postauthoritarian ones. See her commentary, "Thinking About Post-Communist Transitions: How Different Are They?" *Slavic Review,* vol. 52, no. 2 (summer 1993), p. 334.

Index